Date Due

NOV 1 1985			
FEB 1 4 1986			
NOV 27 1981			
FEB 1 6 1991			
MAR 02 1990			
APR 0 9 1994			
APR 2 9 1994			

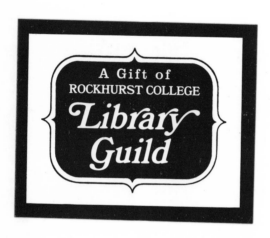

INTERNATIONAL BUSINESS

FOURTH EDITION

INTERNATIONAL BUSINESS

FOURTH EDITION

Richard N. Farmer
*Professor of
International Business Administration
Indiana University*

Barry M. Richman
*Late Professor of
Management and Industrial Organization
University of California, Los Angeles*

CEDARWOOD PRESS

Bloomington, Indiana

Copyright assigned to Richard N. Farmer and Barry M. Richman in
June, 1971 by Richard D. Irwin, Inc.

Second printing (a revised edition) August, 1971

Second printing by METROPOLITAN PRINTING SERVICE,
Bloomington, Indiana, United States of America.

A publication of Cedarwood Press, Bloomington, Indiana, United
States of America.

© 1974 by Cedarwood Press

Second edition (revised)

Second edition printing by METROPOLITAN PRINTING SER-
VICE, INC.

© 1980 by Cedarwood Press

Third edition (Revised)

Third edition printing by METROPOLITAN PRINTING SERVICE,
INC.

© 1984 by Cedarwood Press

PRINTED IN THE UNITED STATES OF AMERICA

IBSN 0-9304 17-01-1

To Christine and Viana
Two young ladies who already
have seen One World

Preface to the Fourth Edition

The major portion of this book grew out of our studies in comparative management, long ago. We initially were interested in the problems of why various business and industrial firms in different environments often were significantly more or less efficient than similar organizations in other nations. In our book COMPARATIVE MANAGEMENT AND ECONOMIC PROGRESS (Richard D. Irwin, 1965), we attempted to deal with this question.

Much of this earlier work dealt with environmental problems, since it was clear that firms necesarily must adjust their operations to mesh with whatever local environment they encountered. Hence the first edition of INTERNATIONAL BUSINESS, published in 1966, dealt extensively with environmental questions. But increasingly it become clear that managers can also affect their envrionments. Good management can overcome many local difficulties, as many multinational companies have demonstrated. In the Second and Third editions we included more materials on managerial strategies for multinational companies, and this material is expanded in this edition. Much environmental material is retained, since the environment still matters, but we have attempted to balance the presentation.

We have also included much material on the response of countries and international organizations to the challenges of multinational firms. Currently we are living in an era which is unique in human history, an age where global companies are spreading across traditional national boundaries without much regard for local sensibilities. These governments, sensing a loss of power and prestige, are trying to develop new and meaningful responses to this new threat. The older pattern of restricting foreign firms is attractive, but self-defeating, since the multinational corporation is the major wealth producing agent in the modern world. The country which bans the multinational firms tends to lag in the economic growth race. And, in the end, virtually all countries want and need economic wealth to accomplish their peoples' goals. In the next few decades the question of how to control unmanageable giants will be critical all over the globe.

We hypothesized in our comparative management book that management was at the very core of economic activity and economic progress. Without a clear understanding of how firms and their managers performed their critical functions, little progress could be made in terms of accelerating economic and growth. If this basic hypothesis is correct, then the international manager is indeed a catalyst for change. He or she typically knows how to manage better than capable persons in the host country, and he or she has much to teach. How this interaction between the local and international parts of a given country occurs is at the heart of this present study.

It seems clear now, as often is pointed out by many thinkers, that nationalism in its traditional form is already obsolescent, if not totally obsolete. Countries and peoples want more income NOW, and the cost of petty nationalism is often so high as to impede seriously progress toward this goal. This may explain in part why, in spite of innumerable obstacles to international investment, firms from many countries are able to enter other nations with relative ease. While there is a tendency to be suspicious of foreigners, the gains are too great to forgo by keeping these international operations away. One can visualize a sort of one world, where the entire productive system of the whole planet operates as an integrated, extraordinarily efficient unit, with perhaps a few die hard marxist and theologically oriented countries lurking in the poverty-stricken fringes, unable or unwilling to take part.

If this above sentence had been written 25 years ago, the authors would have been considered lunatic fringe extremists and visionaries, but while such a view may still prevail in some circles, the glimmer of possibility is there. Rapidly changing technology and managerial competence makes it as least possible to ponder economic and business integration on a scale undreamed of even a few years ago. Such integration will not be accepted enthusiastically by many, but the cost of not so integrating may well be high enough to preclude any other course. One cost is simply World War III, which would destroy everything. Those of us old enough to remember World War II, with all its hate, killing, and disasters, would far prefer to trade with anyone rather than shoot them, or worse, get shot at, with atomic weapons.

There is considerable irony here, since the mainstreams of intellectual thought in the present world often are marxist. The perfect country should be Albania, not Hong Kong. Yet the major change agents and wealth producers come out of Adam Smith, not Karl Marx. The multinational corporation, always profit oriented, somehow manages to create the wealth and change the world, for better or worse. Even the communist states these days move toward using such firms and philosophies to develop their economies. Many object philosophically, but none can present viable alternatives to the world order which would do the job half as well. Communists offer hate, violence, economic stagnation, and dispair...and little production. The improbable capitalists offer hope, growth, excitement, and rapidly growing production and incomes. Those interested in fast development these days study Japan, South Korea, Hong Kong, and Singapore, not Poland, Albania, Cuba, or Vietnam.

It is useful to study systematically the organizations which are changing things dramatically, which explains this book, in all its editions. We have attempted to draw a crude map of the world of international business, particularly of the parts dealing with management and technology. This map, or conceptual framework, shows some of the critical hazards, problems, and opportunities now to be found in this exciting business area. It also indicates the kinds of strategies which international firms may have to develop if they are to succeed in this demanding activity. The book is not a "cookbook" of formulae to use in given situations; rather, it is an analysis of the total problem of international business activity presented through a systematized conceptual framework. We have tried to show where the problems are, and how firms might either adjust to them or avoid them by adroit maneuvering. It is up to the various readers to judge how well we have succeeded.

Each edition of ths book has become more internationalized, in the sense that now many firms from many countries are now multinational companies, including those from such unexpected countries as India, Brazil, Argentina, Mexico, Taiwan, and Hong Kong, among others. The Japanese in particular have exploded into the international area with their multinational firms in the past fifteen years. Hence much new material in this edition has much less an American orientation than previous editions had. Examples now cover the world and many countries. Moreover, countries that used to ban foreign firms totally, such as the People's Republic of China, now are beginning to admit them, albeit cautiously, so country examples now are more widespread than they used to be. As in other areas, a phenomena thought initially to be totally American turns out to be global. It was only that the Americans got there first. Now some of the world's best managed companies are Japanese, German, or Indian, and this point is recognized in this edition. Provincials always believe that their country and their people are better than others; the types of cosmopolitans who will read this book will recognize that countries, like people, vary enormously in competence and abilities, and that no one race, sex, religion, or nationality can possibly dominate everyone. When we finally really believe this, we are indeed well on our way to a peaceful and interesting world.

I would like to thank Skip McGoun, Bannerjee, and Dr. Tom Sharkey for taking the time and trouble to read the entire manuscript and make valuable and useful suggestions and corrections. Having brilliant young doctoral students around to keep me thinking (and honest) made this new edition possible. Thanks, gentlemen...you did a terrific job.

My co-author, Barry M. Richman, died on June 5, 1978, just a short time before the Third Edition of this work appeared. He was 42. He could not take part in the creation of this edition, but he will always be my co-author, since virtually nothing I ever wrote, before 1978 or since, was free from his creative influence. He was larger than life, one of our truly creative thinkers, and it was a pleasure to work with him throughout the years. Thanks one more time, Barry.

The dedication of this volume remains as it always has been...to our two eldest daughters, who have seen One World, and who, to my surprise, really grew up. The world they live in is hardly perfect, but it certainly is interesting, and the possibilities for these young ladies, as we both hoped back in 1966, are much greater than it was then. I once speculated in 1967 that they might someday visit the People's Republic of China, and the audience thought that I was a madman to consider such a crazy idea. Now, perhaps, they can visit the moon when they are grandmothers, or perhaps the Seventh Edition will have to carry the title, INTERGALACTIC BUSINESS ADMINISTRATION. I hope so. A friend of mine who read the First Edition did not carry life insurance, since he felt that the world would end by 1967. If nothing else, the internationalized world we live in is still around, still full of problems, and still interesting. If international business made some small contribution to that result, it is well worthwhile.

I received absolutely first rate assistance and advice from Mssrs. McGoun, Bannerjee, Sharkey, and Barry, along with a thousand other students, colleagues, and friends, but being a stubborn old fud, I insisted on doing it my way. Hence all errors, omissions, and other sins in this volume are my responsibility entirely.

Richard N. Farmer
July, 1984.

Table of Contents

PART I

THE FIELD OF

INTERNATIONAL BUSINESS

Chapter 1

Introduction

In 1942, Wendell L. Willkie took a 31,000 mile airplane trip around a war-torn world. His trip was largely political in nature, but, because he was an excellent businessman, his perception of what the world might be in the postwar years was strongly tinged with business insights.

Mr.Willkie had lost the 1940 presidential election to F.D. Roosevelt, but he was basically a manager and businessman. He also was one of the earliest internationalists in the United States, which for many decades had been strongly isolationist, content to work behind high tariff walls and trade barriers, and let the rest of the world stew in its own juices. Mr. Willkie felt very strongly, however, that isolationism was dead, and that an internationalist new age would soon be dawning.

His dream was one world, economically and polically united, progressive, productive, and efficient, with all of the world´s productive organizations cooperating in a grand effort designed to lay to rest once and for all the endless story of man´s misery and inhumanity to man.

1942 was not a favorable year for such missions. The entire world was in the midst of a war which would claim over 35 million lives, destroy several trillions of dollars worth of property, and lay waste not only whole countries but also entire social systems. Western civilization was fighting for survival, and dreams of future international cooperation and business adventures had to wait.

By 1950, the one world dream seemed more remote than ever. Willkie´s vision seemed even more unrealistic as war began again in Korea and as shattered economic and social systems appeared terribly slow to revive. The cold war, begun in 1946, seemed likely to flare into hot conflict at any moment, and business all over the world was strangled in nationalistic passions, exchange controls, inflations, and chaos. Newly independent nations denounced their ex-colonial masters and desired to be left alone, free forever from the white man´s grasp, while ancient Europe struggled desperately with intractable problems of war reconstruction, preparation for new war, and the seeming inability to release itself from petty passions built up over the centuries.

Looking back from 1950 was enough to make any reasonable man

2

pessimistic about the future of one world. In the present was the new nightmare of atomic warfare, threatened by two seemingly implacable camps. Since 1914, the world economy had been subject to the traumatic shock of the 1914-1918 war, which had pushed the tight, neatly organized world of the late 19th century into ancient history; to the fevered, overheated boom of the 1920´s, which had left a legacy of international debts unpaid, investments unrealized, and petty states unable to survive; to the Great Depression of the 1930´s, with its grinding mass unemployment, its payments repudiations, its collapse of international trade, its rise of fanatic nationalism, and its development of half mad dictators; to the 1939-45 war, which seemed to deal the final blow to any semblance of international cooperation for any time in the foreseable future; and finally, to the Korean War, with its implicit threat of open atomic conflict between the great powers. Prophets of doom and gloom could see only total disaster, and even optimists despaired for all humanity.

The author recalls taking an international trade course in the fall of 1949. The Korean war had not yet begun, but the first of a dismal series of postwar recessions was well under way. The professor, a man rich in years, learning, and experience, who had lived most of his productive life in Europe and the United States in the shadows of total catastrophe, reviewed the developments in the international economy since 1914, and despaired. There really was no hope for any economic integration or cooperation in the foreseeable future. Europe was too torn with ancient rivalries, the Communist countries were too beligerent, the new nations too hypernationalistic and jealous of their hard won sovereignty, and the older, underdeveloped nations too poor and suspicious ever to form any meaningful integrated international economy in the pre-1914 style. The old world was finished totally, and the only recourse was to wait with foreboding to see what the new order would be like. If there was a new order, that is. Perhaps the vast majority of knowledgable persons in 1950 expected World War III and the end of the world within five to ten years. It was a fun time to be a college student, knowing that you would undoubtedly never live to see thirty! Being drafted a few years later during the Korean war did not lead to any great feeling of optimism either.

From 1914 to 1950, the typical American businessman was totally American. Other countries were strangely exotic places with inadequate plumbing, late trains (or no trains at all), and sources of occasional export orders. A few manufacturing firms had branches abroad, most notably in England, Canada and continental Western Europe, and many mining and petroleum companies had exploitative enclaves, complete with American style villages for their senior executives scattered around the world. In Latin America, a few agriculturally oriented American firms operated in tropical environments, growing bananas, sugar cane, and rubber.

There were some peculiar exceptions, which were regarded as out of the American business mainstream. The Singer Corporation had invested abroad in the 1890´s, but then everyone knew that sewing machines served a need everywhere, and Singer sometimes had to manufacture locally to avoid onerous tariffs. Henry Ford built his first car abroad in Canada in 1906, again to avoid a tariff, and he had established assembly plants in over a dozen countries by 1920, mainly to reduce shipping costs. By 1930, Ford was manufacturing cars in Germany, Canada, and the United Kingdom, but everyone knew that Mr. Ford was eccentric. The fact that over ten percent of Ford's gross revenues came from abroad even during the troubled 1930's was seldom noted.

General Motors had established manufacturing plants in the United Kingdom and Germany in the 1920's, just in time to lose money in the 1930's. In 1940, GM wrote off its German operation in its entirety, which was logical, considering that Hitler controlled Germany, and GM had no control over the operation. Clearly, GM would never return to make Opels again.

Also overlooked or forgotten was the quite extensive German, Dutch and English investment in the U.S., which occurred even before the turn of the century. Lever Brothers (Anglo-Dutch), came and prospered, as did other British firms. Most went broke or withdrew, unable to understand the mysterious ways of those American continentals. The comings and goings before 1930 included Mercedes, Rolls Royce, and Fiat. A few German pharmeceutical and optical firms prospered, only to be taken over during World War II as enemy assets (the U.S. never did give them back, which was not calculated to increase confidence in Europe about U.S. investments). But Royal Dutch Shell (Anglo-Dutch) prospered, and still does.

But the usual American investment abroad during the 1920's was portfolio investment, which is the acquisition of securities of foreign governments and firms without any managerial involvement. The world economic collapse of the 1930's had soured these investments almost totally, as most fell into default (some still are). Exports offered some interest to the more efficient companies, but again the Great Depression had caused dramatic declines in value, from $6 billion to $3 billion in the three years from 1929 to 1932. Except for a few quick profits to be made in mining and petroleum exploitation, investments abroad by American firms virtually ceased during the 1930s.

The period 1939-1950 was hardly better. Wars and reconstruction meant uncertainty abroad, and booming demand at home diverted attention from distant and risky markets. The inability of most countries to restore full convertibility to their currency after 1945 seemingly indicated and emphasized the riskiness of such foreign investment ventures. Even if firms could somehow make a profit abroad, they rarely could remit the earnings home in dollars.

Some European nations, most notably Britain, the Netherlands, France, and Belguim, had made extensive direct investments in their colonies as early as the mid-Nineteenth Century. Indeed, the British East India Company dates back to the 18th century. Much of this investment was in public utilities and plantations, and the typical process involved exporting the home business environment to the colony. By 1950, these investments were rapidly disappearing through sale to ex-colonials, expropriations, and revolutionary difficulties. Europe after World War II was not in a strong position to reassert its earlier direct foreign investment advantage, and losses involved in the decolonization process were not encouraging to private or government investments.

The Soviet Union and the new centrally planned economies (CPEs) of Eastern Europe were involved in reconstruction, but they refused to cooperate much with the outside world, regarding foreign investment as a capitalist conspiracy. Then, as now, such CPEs did not make such direct foreign investments, except under very special conditions. The CPEs were, and are, fond of barter trade, which doesn't involve money, and they were not willing or able to consider direct foreign investments.

Thus by 1950, any sort of one world, in the business and economic sense, appeared an absurdity. It was clear the political, nationalistic, and economic pressures all pointed in the direction of autarky, statism, Marxism, and eventual collapse of what remained of the international economy of years ago.

As the world economy stumbled into the 1950's, some basic underlying changes were occurring that would ruin the doomsday scenario. Western Europe was rapidly repairing its war damage, expanding local investment, increasing exports and imports, and increasing incomes. The less developed countries (LDCs), though far behind the more industrialized nations, were making development plans and attempting to carry them out. In far off and unknown desert kingdoms such as Saudi Arabia and Kuwait, American oilmen, one unusual group of internationally oriented businessmen, were finding huge reserves. The Soviet Bloc continued to expand its income rapidly, though still remaining outside the international economy for the most part. Obscure Japanese businessmen were listening to esoteric lectures on quality control by the then unknown Professor Deming, and pondering how to change the dubious world image of Japanese goods. And in the United States, economic growth continued, though at a slower pace than abroad.

A few steps were being taken to press suspicious countries toward world cooperation. The United Nations had been established in 1945, and it was a going concern. The enormous economic and military power of the United States was slowly leaning toward international cooperation, and as the cold war increased in intensity, the American government became more interested in reviving the shattered economies of Italy, West Germany, and Japan. One obvious way to do this was to encourage their industries to grow and to export, even to the U.S.

One result of this new international interest was the Marshall Plan, started in 1948, which provided billions of dollars of support to Western European economies. The idea behind the plan was to build up Western Europe as a buffer against communist penetration, and to give European countries the chance to grow economically. It was a brilliant success, as Western Europe did recover economically quite rapidly. For small European countries, recovery meant expanded foreign trade, and international growth occurred.

Relatively slow American economic growth meant, among other things, rather rapid accumulations of capital by stronger firms which could not immediately be invested profitably in the United States. As wartime shortages and sellers' markets steadily diminished, many corporations found that, while profits could be earned on new investments, rates of return steadily tended to decline. At the same time, a few adventuresome managers noted the rapid growth and apparent new stability of Western Europe, and American direct investments in European countries increased. Those mavericks and odd balls that had arrived early in Europe, such as Ford, did very well indeed, and suggested to more timid managers that it could be done, and done profitably and well. Even before 1950, a few special situations had attracted a great deal of American capital, particularly in the international petroleum sector. Firms such as Texaco, Standard of New Jersy, Gulf, and Standard of California invested hundreds of millions of dollars in petroleum development in LDCs which by any standards would hardly be considered stable. But instead of disaster, the firms profited, as did the countries.

By 1956, intra-European trade had already reached 192 percent of the 1938 average, and growth continued. Total international trade continued to expand at better than 10 percent per year, and more American firms were able to restore long broken prewar contacts with importers in many countries. Persistent dollar shortages throughout the world continued to make exports difficult, and, in an increasing number of cases, American firms, rather than lose markets retreating behind tariff and exchange control walls, decided to invest abroad in plants for local markets.

The dollar shortage also encouraged foreigners to try their hand at selling in the United States. Volkswagen shipped two funny looking buglike cars to the U.S. in 1949, got ridiculed for being so presumptuous as to tackle such automotive giants as Packard, Nash, and Hudson, but sold the two and a few more in following years. The Japanese pushed cheap toys and poor quality textiles at attractive prices, and the British successfully encouraged some Americans to sip scotch whiskey and to buy a few Jaguars and Rolls Royces. Few young Americans now realize just how impoverished American consumers were, in regard to choices, in the 1950's. If Americans didn't make it, it wasn't available, or you could only buy some low quality junk from Europe or Japan. One result of these new trade efforts, rapidly increasing American imports AND exports, is still going on.

In 1958, formation of the European Common Market (EC) gave new impetus to American investments overseas. A combination of the threat of new tariff barriers in the EEC to American goods, plus the potential gains of the new mass market within the EEC led to rapid expansions of American direct investments in Europe. Ironically, at first it was American rather than European firms which provided the actual large scale economic integration made possible through the creation of the EC. Thus, total American direct investment abroad was perhaps $12 billion in 1950, but by 1972 it had risen to $94 billion. By the 1970s, 800 of the largest American manufacturing companies were directly involved in foreign countries in manufacturing and trade. About a thousand new plants were being built overseas each year by some six hundred different American firms. Between $10 and $15 billion were invested annually abroad by private American interests.

The rapid rise of the international economy was not a one way street. Before 1914, the U.S. actually was a net debtor to foreign countries. But in the postwar era, billions of dollars poured in from all over the world to American money markets. Some foreigners were bringing their money for reasons of security from shaky regimes at home; others invested for more commercial reasons. And as these international flows of capital continued, more traditional trade in exports and imports continued to increase, binding countries more closely than before. After 1960, and increasing rapidly in the 1970´s, foreign owned multinational firms followed the American pattern of direct investment abroad, and now well over 1,000 English, French, Dutch, Italian, German, Swiss, Swedish, Danish, and Japanese companies have also joined the multinational company group.

In the 1980´s, the more traditional investing countries were joined by other, less well known countries in making direct U.S. investments. Significant amounts of Indian, Hong Kongian, Taiwanese, Singaporian, and South Korean direct investments have been made in the U.S. and other countries, often in the form of very small investments by unknown firms and individuals. An Asian Indian buying a small motel in Wyoming for perhaps $200,000 escapes notice, but such investments now total many billions of dollars in the aggregate.

A major foreign investment in the United States is in portfolios of stocks and bonds. One great advantage the United States has is its extremely efficient, honest, and well organized money markets and banking system, and many foreigners invest in U.S. securities, confident that they will probably not be cheated. Foreigners often buy U.S. government bonds as well, anxious to earn interest and hold dollars, and governments, companies, and individuals are all involved in such investments. Indeed, one major thrust of direct foreign investment is the purchase of existing U.S. banks or the establishment of new ones, just as major American banks have long invested and established branches abroad.

The late 1950´s and 1960´s were not immune from problems. Crisis followed crisis in international affairs. The 1956 Suez crisis, the 1958 Lebanese crisis, the 1962 Cuban missle crisis, and the Vietnamese crisis, to name a few of the larger ones, continued to disturb the equanimity of nations.

But the 1960´s and early 1970´s were also the golden age of the multinational companies. The whole world economy was very bouyant, trade was rapidly increasing, and Western Europe and Canada in particular were willing to allow much foreign direct investment. This was the period when many major American firms first got involved in direct foreign investments, and when scholars began to study this new phenomena. Growing and revolutionary new world communications and transportation systems were being put in place, and Americans could see far off events on TV in their own living rooms, along with hundreds of millions of people in other countries. The Viet Nam war was the first to be seen live and in color on TV at home, and it sensitized many to the fact that other countries did exist out there.

The American space program started seriously planning its major programs in 1961, and by 1969, we could observe the spaceship earth from 150,000 miles out, a unified, living globe. It really WAS one world!

By the 1960's, the Europeans and Japanese were beginning to gain a deserved reputation for manufacturing high quality products, and gradually American prejudices against all things foreign declined, often to the point where the Japanese or German or Swiss product was perceived as superior. World trade kept exploding, gaining ten percent per year in real terms, and the Americans found new and lively markets for jet aircraft, computers, agricultural products, and heavy trucks and equipment abroad as well.

But the cold war continued with varying intensity, and much later Afghanistan was occupied by the Soviets. At this writing in 1984, cold war tensions are high, but they have been high before. They have also been relaxed from time to time. But to date the balance of terror in nuclear weapons has stalemated the ability of major powers to wage major wars. All the crises have proved temporary in their effects on the development of a truly international economy. The trend continues upward, interrupted only by the change of the rate of increase in most nations.

The emergence of Japan as the third largest industrial power (behind the U.S. and the U.S.S.R.) was one of the big surprises of the 1970's. This small island nation, with few natural resources, tried to dominate Asia militarily during the period 1920 - 1945, and failed. Its decline, then fantastic rennaisance, startled everyone. The Japanese were unable to extend their military power, but they sometimes seem able to sell everyone to death in all major markets. Japan is a totally new national phenomena, a very powerful country without military power, and this is the first time in world history that this has occurred. It is perhaps not surprising that few thinkers even know how to ask questions about Japan, let alone answer them. Its enormous success really stems from the type of internationally oriented, trading world that has developed after World War II. If the United States had the same import tariff against cars today that it had in 1930, the world would indeed be a different place than it now is.

Another surprise has been the very rapid economic development of the newly industrializing countries (NICs), mainly found around the rim of Asia, but also including Brazil and Mexico. There is, and was, an awful lot of coffee in Brazil, but there also are now major export industries in such products as autos and components, shoes, and even executive jet aircraft. Singapore and Hong Kong have grown so fast economically in the period 1960 - 1980 that they are hardly classifiable as poor countries any longer, and developing countries everywhere study their policies to find the secrets of their success. These NICs thrive on the freer trade environment established since the war, since their strength lies in exporting labor intensive products such as consumer electronics and textiles to rich countries, while importing capital goods in return. Without free trade, South Korea, Taiwan, and Hong Kong would be very poor indeed. So would consumers in richer countries, who can enjoy cheaper and better toys and textiles and stereos as a result.

The mid and late 1970's saw yet another isolated group of countries begin to join the world. The Soviet Union and the East European communist countries, long isolated economically from the world mainstream, began to trade more extensively with the West. While private foreign ownership of assets was still prohibited in these countries, a new form of business organization, the cooperation agreement, developed. In such an agreement the communist country contracted with a private Western firm to provide a plant, workers, and related domestic facilities, owned by the communist state. The private Western firm provided technical expertise, tooling, machinery, designs, and Western markets for the plant's output. Often the plant would be paid for by sales of product in the West.

While some cooperation agreements have worked well, the Eastern European countries have not successfully penetrated Western markets, and in the early 1980's, Poland and other CPEs got into extreme economic difficulties, including de facto default on foreign hard currency debt owed Western banks. The Russians, ever nervous about foreign penetration, have also withdrawm somewhat from their earlier efforts to join the world. The CPEs face a major dilemma, in that they can't live with the West, and they can't live without it. That is, the vast majority of rapid technological progress comes from the West (including Japan, that most Western of Eastern countries), and the CPEs have to obtain this new technology, if for no other reason than to avoid falling behind militarily. Yet joining the West involves far more economic and social reform than these countries can tolerate, so at this writing they are in a deep dilemma, with actual falling or stagnant economies, less trade with the West, and a real need to figure out new strategies for the 1980's and beyond. They often try to steal this new technology, sometimes with some success, but their problems point up the fact that this modern world of ours is so internationalized that autarkic policies of the past are simply impossible, unless a country really wants to stagnate, decline, and decay. We have come so far internationally that we cannot return to our old world, even if we wanted to.

In 1979, even the People's Republic of China (PRC), long the isolated sleeping giant, joined this trend to integrate economically with the rest of the world and obtain critical technology and managerial skills which did not exist in that country. When Hong Kong can move from per capita incomes of perhaps $100 in 1950 to $3,000 today, while the PRC in the same period moved from perhaps $100 to $250, it is not surprising that thoughtful leaders in the PRC begin to rethink their strategies. Many European, Japanese, and American multinational corporations (MNCs) are now involved in working out various cooperation agreements and other programs which will enable them to take advantage of this new, potentially huge market. The PRC also has established free trading zones that look suspiciously like Hong Kong, and foreigners can (and do) make direct investments on a selective basis in the PRC.

The 1970's also saw the beginning of the Organization of Petroleum Exporting Countries' (OPEC) efforts to control the price of oil. Energy crises became a fact of life for the industrialized nations after 1973. Oil prices quadrupled in 1975 and then tripled again in 1979-80. Suddenly the world of cheap energy was over, which is a major reason why so many industrialized countries have such difficult economic problems today, the United States not excepted. Oil rich states which few persons had ever heard of, such as Kuwait, the United Arab Emirates, and Saudi Arabia, suddenly were awash with dollars as their oil wealth was converted to cash.

A dramatic increase in private international banking was another feature of the 1970´s. Large private banks in the developed countries had long lent money to various countries, but now those huge petrodollar hoards of some oil states were being deposited in these banks and being recycled by relending to other countries. States as diverse as Turkey, Poland, Zaire, Mexico, and Brazil were able to borrow billions of dollars in this manner, and an occasional revolution, economic catastrophe, or local mismanagement often raised the spectre of defaults in the early 1980´s. But once again, the world ended up more internationalized than ever by such financial activities. When a major American bank is owed perhaps $6 billions by a dozen foreign countries, and they cannot repay, the bank is going to stay internationalized for many years to come.

By 1984, it was clear that the world was still far from Mr. Willkie´s dream of one world, but it was equally clear that we have come a long ways from the provincial, war torn world of 1943. Instead of being a dream of an idle romantic, a totally internationalized world appeared to be at least an obtainable reality, given another few decades of development along the lines of the 1960´s and 1970´s. The 1980´s have so far been an era of international retrenchment and more military tension, but such periods have occurred before, and they will again. We have found that we cannot live very well without our neighbors, and on this small planet, we are all neighbors. They in turn find that they cannot do very well without us. Those who yearn to return to the old nationalism gone mad days of the 1930´s face two cold, intractable facts: First, it is economically impossible, given the foreign trade and investment that is critical to all; and second, such a world breeds war. World War III, carried out by major powers with atomic weapons, simply destroys the human race, which is hardly a pleasant scenario for anyone. So, with a sigh, we go back to bickering with those necessary neighbors, simply because we cannot do anything else. And Mr. Willkie´s dream may yet be even more realistic than it now is.

In most countries, some influential men and women of vision have expanded their horizons beyond the historic frontiers of their own nations and have pondered the implications, problems, and promises of a truly integrated international economy. The new customs unions, while far from perfect, had the effect of expanding trade within the blocs in a dramatic fashion. One could begin to think, by 1984, of the integration of blocs into super-common markets instead of the integration of countries into smaller common markets. Why shouldn´t Japan, Australia, New Zealand, Canada, and the United States form a customs union along EEC lines? Such suggestions would lead to one being certified insane in 1950, but now at least scholars, politicians, and businesspersons can ponder the implications of such a bloc. Mr. Willkie might be pleased.

The effect on businessmen of events of the past 40 years has been to expand their horizons to an international rather than a purely national standpoint. Even provincials, determined to stay home, have to consider how to meet new import threats, and traditionally local producers, such as farmers, now find that a half to a third of their output of most crops is exported. The dietary habits of people once considered totally exotic are now carefully studied by farm cooperative marketing experts. Now books are written noting the emergence of the international corporation, whose home office may be in almost any country but whose complete orientation is worldwide. American business schools, instead of concentrating exclusively on national business problems, increasingly insert material and courses about the international business dimension. Companies which used to have export managers now have vice presidents in charge of international divisions. The world economy appears a bit less parrochial, less suspicious of things foreign, and more willing to expand its interests than seemed even remotely possible 20 years ago.

Perhaps because this internationalization, particularly in the 1970´s, came a bit too fast for most people and countries, the 1980´s have been a period of consolidation. International trends have stabilized, and the international trade growth of around ten percent per year compounded, which lasted from about 1950 to 1980, has stopped. Countries such as the United States, which fervently supported more internationalization, and practiced what it preached by eliminating many trade and investment barriers, now impose new controls and quotas on imported textiles and cars. The EEC countries seem terrified of the Japanese, and express their terror in more trade barriers. Many LDCs, despairing of their abilities to increase incomes rapidly, relapse into autarkic nationalism, typically of the Marxist sort, but occasionally of the religious, conservative pattern, as seen in Iran. CPEs, ever nervous of capitalist plots and philosophies, withdraw further behind their borders.

And yet, we have taken a bunch of eggs called countries and thoroughly scrambled them in the past 40 years. No Western country could fight a World War II again, simply because, given huge increases in world trade and specialization, no one makes an airplane anymore, not even the Americans. Belguim makes the tail assemblies, Canada the wings, the U.S. the jet engines and electronics, the British the landing gear, and the West Germans the hydraulic controls. Who can fight whom, when your potential enemy makes half the product needed to fight the war? We want to go back to where we were, to being happy provincials, only to discover that we can´t restore our own egg, or we can only do it at exhorbitant cost. If the U.S. behaved like it did in 1950, it could survive, but personal incomes would drop 40 to 70 percent in the process. Anyone who actually tried to survive in 1950 will happily stay internationalized and affluent.

It has reached the point where all thoughtful people know exactly what will happen to the country that returns to autarky. Its income will drop; its unemployment will increase; and perhaps most importantly, no one outside will much care what the country does. Who is the leader of North Korea? Of Albania? What interesting things have such countries done recently? Total isolation and autarky just don´t work well. If the East European countries go back, they too will stagnate and decay, as will the Soviet Union if it tries this policy. Unhappily, we have to live in this one world, like it or not. And this is the most significant event of the past 40 years. Somehow the world has managed to avoid World War III, more than double world population, and more than double per capita income. Not all countries or individuals did equally well, but the vast majority were winners. This period 1945 -1980 just happens to have been the most successful 36 years in human history. Those who correctly point to existing miseries and sufferings should study closer earlier periods, any period. They were all worse, and most were a lot worse.

One unanticipated legacy we have inherited from the period 1950 - 1980 is rising expectations everywhere. This incredibly successful period convinced many persons in all countries that next year would be better, that their children could look forward to wealth beyond the dreams of parents. If for any reason, the economy doesn't grow, it is obviously the politician's fault, and they should be deposed. The relative stagnation of the world economy since 1980 has led to many politicians in many countries losing the next election, or being deposed in coups. People want MORE, and they want it now. Younger people have grown up in an expanding world economy, and they cannot understand why it just doesn't keep on expanding. Political leaders who ignore this factor can get into deep trouble rather quickly.

Exploring One World

The book evolved from this author's and the late Barry M. Richman's work in comparative management. Initially, we were interested in the problem of why different countries had such very different levels of managerial effectiveness in their local business operations. But it also became clear that a purely local business environment was impossible to find in the modern world. Everywhere business firms are crossing national frontiers in a variety of ways, leading to business results which are not purely local. Such international activities have a flavor and a set of problems all their own, often quite unique from those encountered by purely local enterprises.

However, it appeared that the same general methodology developed for studies in comparative management could be used in analyzing international business problems. This book is an attempt to advance the study of international business by the use of our analysis of how external environmental factors (or constraints) operate on internal firm management to cause changes in the manner in which internal managerial decisions are made. If such changes occur, it is to be expected that the efficiency with which the firm operates will change, for better or for worse. To analyze this process effectively, it is necessary to consider both the external constraints the firm faces, and the way in which firms operate internally.

Chapters 2 and 3 develop the basic framework of this analysis. We will then turn to the problems of the multinational corporations (MNCs), examining how they operate in a complex multinational world, where their environments differ, often dramatically, from one country to another. Such firms do what all firms do. They market their products, finance activities, and plan production. But the way this is done in a global firm will depend partially on local environments, so special attention must be paid to environmental influences on these functions. Overall managerial strategy and style also are much different for a firm with dozens of countries to consider. Chapters 9 through 13 consider these firm managerial problems.

Chapters 4 through 8 explore the nature of international and local environmental constraints which firms operating in more than one country must necessarily consider if they are to be efficient. And finally, in Chapter 14, we take a quick look at the future. What is and has been may not be what young students will find in 1990 or 2000, since the world of multinational business is evolving rapidly.

While no particular effort is made here to swamp the reader with data and fact about the 150 plus countries of the world, or to present the 19 rules for marketing in Japan, or similar detailed material, it is hoped that this book will prove to be quite useful in an operational sense for any firm which has multinational operations. What is commonly lacking in any international business analysis is a frame of reference for the types of critical business problems which usually arise. One is aware that problems of a unique sort exist, but, lacking any consistent theory of international management, it is difficult to determine even what the relevant questions might be, let alone profitable answers.

Much international business material fails to come to grips with essential business questions in this field, although the past decade has seen an explosion of quite good analysis and study of the field. Much material is economically oriented, considering such problems as balance of payments, international trade theory, economic growth of nations, and similar matters. While quite useful in a number of ways, such studies do not typically consider in any detail the problem of foreign firms operating in local environments. Another large block of material deals with anecdotal situations about firms overseas. Thus, the trucking markets in Saudi Arabia for one firm is described in detail (this author is guilty of this particular sin), or the adventures of a single firm in Bolivia may be told. Such tales are often amusing, occasionally informative, and may yield considerable insight into analogous problems in other countries. But to note that because of a certain Arabian tax law a certain managerial decison was made does not yield much insight into the problems of a television manufacturing plant in France when an important customs duty is lowered.

Still other large amounts of material deal with such issues as international law, the anthropology of manners in Ruritania, the sociology of a Southwest Pacific island, and similar issues. Typically the writers are not particularly concerned with business problems, although the material and studies they present may have considerable relevance for business managers and firms. The difficulty is deciding in which way, since few businessmen are trained lawyers, sociologists, or anthropologists. One suspects that such material is important, but it may be difficult to determine how.

Another vast mass of material deals with facts, figures, data, laws, and other information which can be of critical importance in given situations but which tends to bury the user in large amounts of basically irrelevant materials. It may be useful to know that Ruritania has 8 steel mills with a capacity of 5.7 million tons, or that the religion of Saudi Arabia is Moslem, but for most managers any given fact is irrelevant. The important ones can be determined after the proper questions have been framed. To begin with data, hoping that somehow the

proper analysis of the problem at hand will emerge, is a wasteful method
of solving critical problems.

What is attempted here is to build a framework of analysis of
international business problems, focusing primarily on the fact that the
firm managers have to make critical business decisions constantly in
complex environmental situations, typically without enough information.
If the managers understand their own companies, as they ordinarily do,
and if they understand what the key impacts of their environment will be
on their internal business operations, it appears likely that
understanding of the environment will lead to more efficient and
profitable internal firm operations. What is needed is a framework of
analysis which will lead to better firm operations, and it is with this
goal in mind that this book has been organized the way it is.

Our attention will be directed mainly to problems of international
business involving management in a foreign country. As the following
chapter will indicate, there are many types of international business
which do not involve much direct management by a foreign firm, such as
export operations. Such cases are interesting and important, both to
firms and countries, but the international management dimension here is
relatively small. More complex and interesting is the problem where a
firm must actually practice management in a foreign country. Typically,
in the modern world, such direct investments involve either industrial
production; complicated extractive operations, such as found in
petroleum or iron ore industries; or the management of sophisticated
service activities such as auditing, engineering planning, or financial
services. One intuitively expects that the kind of management which
will work well in France, Saudi Arabia, Nigeria, or Denmark will differ
somewhat from that practiced in the United States, and our major
interest will be to see why this might be so and to suggest how firms in
one country can efficiently transfer their management activities from
one culture to another.

The author is an American (Barry was a Canadian, which really
helped), and the Americans are the biggest overseas investors, so much
of this book refers to American practice and companies. However, this
does not preclude the use of this methodology in any international
situation, since if it is a valid theory, it should work anywhere. What
would change would be the necessary facts about the countries being
considered. If Japanese companies wanted to use the analysis for their
American operations, the same conceptual constraints would be used, but
the facts would change.

Conclusion

This book is about the problems of international business and the
role which MNFs are playing, and will increasingly play, in the
international economy. From the vantage point of 1984, it appears that
this role will be large and increasing, but problems still exist, and
the author still recalls those dismal prophecies of 1949. Hopefully we
are well on our way to one world, but regression is always possible. A
major part of this study will be concerned with existing obstacles,
efforts to ameliorate them, and dangers yet to be faced in pursuing a
course never before taken in human history. This study could become

irrelevant rather quickly if nationalism, Marxism, or international warfare intrudes to turn us back to provincialism. The cost in such case would be great, since one virtue of properly conducted international business is that everyone is somewhat better off as a result of its taking place. But there is a good possibility that one world may yet be a reality, and as we continue toward this elusive goal, it is hoped that this analysis may prove useful.

Questions for Discussion

1. The world somtimes looks like it will move to a one world concept, and somtimes it appears that it will go back to hypernationalization and war. From your own general knowledge of what is now going on, list two major world developments which tend to push toward one world. Consider such events as peace treaties, new customs unions, United Nations events, trade agreements, political events, and similar items.

Now list two recent events which seem to be pushing the other way. Consider new wars or rumors of wars, energy crises, political breakdowns, famines, or whatever.

2. If possible, interview some one in their 60´s or older, who was young during World War II. Ask them about the way the world was then, and how this person saw his or her international opportunities, if any. Ask also about what important things have changed, in the view of this person. What new impacts of the trend to internationalization seem really significant? How do these views differ from your own? Is there a generation gap here?

Supplementary Readings

Cappock, Joseph D. INTERNATIONAL ECONOMIC INSTABILITY: THE EXPERINCE AFTER WORLD WAR II. New York: McGraw-Hill, 1962

Farmer, Richard N., and Richman, Barry M. COMPARATIVE MANAGEMENT AND ECONOMIC PROGRESS. Bloomington: Cedarwood Press, 1970.

Miller, Ronald E. REVITALIZING AMERICA. New York: Simon & Schuster, 1980.

Willkie, Wendell L. ONE WORLD. New York: Simon & Schuster, 1943.

Chapter 2

The Field of International Business

The Dimensions of International Business

International business generally is business operations of any sort by a firm which take place within or between two or more sovereign countries. This general study can be subdivided into various branches of study as follows:

1. THE OPERATION OF A DOMESTIC FIRM IN OVERSEAS BRANCHES

An American firm may have branches in other countries. Ford of England is one example. Such branches may be involved in marketing, manufacturing, or the sale of services (as with an accounting firm). This type of international business involves a managment dimension in a foreign environment, and as such is one of the most complex and interesting types of international business studies. Firms cannot assume that management problems will be identical to those faced at home.

Firms that operate in many countries are called multinational companies (MNCs). These days, many large privately owned firms from most industrialized nations are MNCs, and even some state controlled firms invest abroad.

2. EXPORT AND IMPORT TRADE

An American firm may buy products from other firms in foreign countries and sell them in the United States, or an American manufacturer may sell his domestically produced products abroad. This area of study has long been of interest to economists, since the flows of international trade have considerable impact on the development and operations of the local economy, and because in earlier days, the productive factors of land, labor and capital were considered to be relatively immobile. Writings on foreign trade actually predate the historic development of economics proper, going back at least to the 16th century. The mercantilists of 1600 - 1800 made studies of international trade one of their major topics of interest. For that matter, Joseph, in the biblical GENESIS, was a major international grain trader, and probably the first internationalist.

This type of study is also clearly of interest to businessmen for a variety of reasons. Importers must be concerned with operational problems of tariffs and other trade barriers, as well as with marketing problems within their country. Exporters must also worry about trade restrictions, currency conversion issues, marketing problems in foreign countries, and questions of trade financing.

Governments are also preoccupied with this type of activity because in the international economy countries are analogous to individuals in the financial sense. Since there is no truly international currency, countries must earn or borrow the funds to spend in other countries. It is possible for a country to go bankrupt in the sense that it cannot meet its international bills and obligations. Because no citizen or firm can be responsible for an entire nation's international financial standing, every government in the world has taken this responsibility, and considerable attention is paid to flows of funds in the international economy.

3. COMPARATIVE MANAGEMENT

Domestic firms owned and operated by nationals in different countries can be compared, analyzed and studied. Here one is interested in insights into differences in operations, efficiency, and management. Thus Toyota of Japan can be compared to Ford of the U.S. Studies of this sort can cast light on the relative efficiency of similar firms in different environments and the impact of critical environmental factors on managerial performance.

The auto manufacturing comparison noted thus suggests that Toyota is more efficient than Ford, for many reasons. Some are environmental, and Ford cannot do much about these. But others are managerial, and Ford can change. If Toyota managers are better than Ford's, perhaps existing managers can learn new tricks. This particular example is now a much debated point in the U.S., because it has long been assumed, without much justification, that ALL American managers are better than foreigners. To discover that this is not necessarily true is a sobering and thought provoking point, and it has led to much serious work in this comparative management field.

4. COMPARATIVE ECONOMIC SYSTEMS

Economists have long studied the various economic environments of firms in different countries. It seems reasonable to suppose that a firm in a country such as the U.S.S.R. has strikingly different economic and political-legal constraints on it than a firm in the United States. It is possible to analyze such differences to determine how they influence the ownership, management, efficiency, and operations of companies. More subtle differences, such as between the United States and Canada, might also suggest insight into economic system changes for the better.

Note how comparisons can lead back to number 3 above. In analyzing Ford and Toyota, it may turn out that a Japanese tax on inventories spurs Toyota's management to do efficient things, while a similar, but slightly different American tax law leads to inefficient inventory management at Ford. If you want Ford to be better, change the tax law.

That is, change its economic environment. Recognition of this point has led to much debate and discussion about many economic and legal questions in this comparative manner, and interesting changes in almost any country are widely reported in the business press and analyzed by economists and business scholars. Particular attention is paid to what successful (e.g., high growth, high income) countries are doing, and foreigners have long analyzed the U.S. with this point in mind. More recently, Japan has received much attention, given its outstanding economic performance since 1950.

5. FUNCTIONAL BUSINESS ANALYSIS

Studies of international marketing, finance and management are concerned with problems of these functional operations between different countries. This type of study may be interrelated with several of the above studies. Thus an American manufacturer with a branch plant in France may study marketing problems in France or the EC, or an exporter may be interested in studying marketing systems in West Germany.

Functional studies of research and development or production are less common, and most are quite recent. This stems from the fact that such activities, being largely scientifically oriented, are perceived to be similar in the normative sense between countries. The modern production processes for making glass in China, Tunisia, and the United States are quite similar, and changes in production organization largely revolve around the costs of the various factors of production and raw materials which enter into the final product. However, marketing involves, in addition to rationally analyzed statistical data and mathematical models, many cultural elements. Swedish tastes in consumer goods may be very different from Mexican tastes. Similarly, the laws governing French money markets may be quite different from laws in the United States or Great Britain, and as a result, financial activities in these countries will be different. Studies of French law, institutions, and organizations may be necessary before firms can perform the finance function efficiently.

The realization by many Americans that the Japanese may have production superiority in such major industries as autos has led to considerable interest in production and R & D studies in the U.S. It is perceived that the Japanese my be superior...why? Often it turns out that production is not quite so scientific as once thought, and various environmental elements influence productivity. If this is so, then these environmental factors get close attention, since, as noted earlier, a country can change the environment by passing new laws or altering old ones. It might also restructure education, and possibly even figure out how to exhort workers to try harder. Whatever is involved might be changed for the better. Figuring out what is better leads to careful studies of Japanese practice, both at the micro and macro levels.

Academic interest in foreign trade and comparative economic systems has existed for centuries, but interest in more managerial dimensions of international business is quite recent. The first texts in international management and business date from the late 1950's, and comparative management studies mainly date from 1961. Most studies of functional international business materials are even more recent. It was only after the MNCs began to grow rapidly in influence and importance after World War II that they attracted much scholarly attention. Scholars rarely anticipate events; rather, they wait to see what is important. And as the 1950's and 1960's moved on, the MNCs were increasingly seen as perhaps the most important international development in centuries, not only because literally hundreds of billions of dollars were being invested by private firms in foreign countries, but also because the MNCs represented a new kind of economic and political force. Never before in history had so much of any country's economic system been dominated by foreigners. The very rapid growth of MNCs suggested that perhaps within a few decades, private firms might dominate the world. Today, enormous scholarly and practical attention is paid to the MNCs and international business generally, and all major business magazines and newspapers devote very extensive space to these matters. It is hard to avoid hearing or reading about MNCs and the international business situation today. Developments here impact virtually every citizen in the world.

This book will largely be focussed on problems of MNCs operating with direct investments in many countries. The choice is in part arbitrary, based on the notion that this type of international business activity has shown the most growth and the most intriguing probems in recent years. International trade theorists long assumed, with considerable justification, that the factors of production were immobile in a country. Hence only goods and services could be traded. Much of the work in the international business area historically has been connected with exports and imports, plus necessary international marketing and finance problems associated with this trade. But in recent years, most major firms around the world have been willing to move their capital abroad, and over $500 billion has been invested in foreign countries. The kinds of political, legal, economic, business, social, and cultural problems created by this massive surge of investment funds will be the primary object of attention here.

Necessarily, some attention must be paid to the other aspects of international business because all of the divisions noted above are interrelated to some extent. The establishment of an auto assembly plant in a foreign country usually leads to increased export of components and less export of finished autos, and such effects directly influence the kinds of decisions made in connection with the foreign plant. Functional studies in marketing, personnel, production, finance, and management are clearly related to the operation of firms abroad.

The Impact of Direct Foreign Investment

An important reason for interest in direct foreign investment by business firms results from the nature of such expenditures. In the case of export or import trade, the foreign influence is indirect. We see the products, but we are not professionally or emotionally involved with the business problems of the producers. There must be Toyota plants someplace, with all of the business problems connected with the production of autos, but few Americans know or care much about this problem. American businessmen see such imports as opportunities to become distributors or competitive threats, but they have little to do with the business problems of the exporter.

Similarly, comparative studies are generally reserved for the scholar, while passive portfolio investments rarely involve an investor directly in foreign management problems. If a Canadian buys a few shares of IBM stock on the New York Stock Exchange, American management will not be directly affected. Exporters may be concerned with the development of foreign markets, but they seldom are in a position to influence the foreign economy very much.

Direct investment, however, is quite different. Here a foreign firm directly becomes involved in a given country's internal problems. Local labor is hired, and foreign managers may enter the country. Real estate is purchased, and equipment is placed in the foreign nation. Local residents who work for or trade with the foreign MNC now see management in action directly, not as some remote activities which somehow send products from distant lands. Instead of being able to regard a country dispassionately, managements are now directly involved in the country and its culture. The result is a type of involvement in foreign countries which no other international relationships present. Such involvement implies uncertainly and risks, since the firm must obey unfamiliar local laws and observe possibly strange local customs which may make efficient management very difficult. It involves opportunities for profit as well, because the firm pays local wage rates and operates within the tariff or quota wall instead of without. It also involves considerable emotional, cultural, and economic sophistication since, as a guest firm, the MNC must accept whatever the local customs and law are, regardless of how desirable or repugnant these may be.

The visible part of foreign investment is the plant and equipment set in place in a foreign land, but direct investment implications run deeper than that. A firm operating abroad has also exported, inadvertently, management philosophnies and technques along with its other assets. Foreigners have a chance to observe how another culture plans and undertakes its productive affairs. If the country is poorer than the capital investor, which is often the case, citizens can see how individual wealthy aliens live. The difference in living standards, personal philosophies, and incomes of foreign residents as compared to local citizens can be striking if the company is operating in a relatively primitive environment. American managers generally expect to live like Americans even if the MNC happens to be operating in jungle or desert, and local residents, who may be quite poor, have an opportunity to see modern living on a day to day basis. In their work with the foreign firm, they can see how management and working conditions are handled by foreigners. Such demonstration effects have powerful influences all over the world, and the political and social repercussions of them are far larger than mere business change.

Most firms which invest in foreign countries are efficiency conscious, which is one major reason why they see opportunities that local citizens and firms do not see. In some cases, as with an American firm building a machine tool plant in West Germany, the foreign investor is not so much better than local firms as to cause undue comment or concern, although his or her activities and actions will be closely observed. But in major investments in Third World countries, the tremendous differences between foreign MNCs and local enterprises in productive techniques and management know how has been revolutionary. The usual result of such investments, quite apart from their profitability, is to create a completely new set of local cultural and political pressures. Often for the first time local citizens see the potential of modern production techniques in such a situation. Americans, Japanese, or Europeans performing these productive wonders are not so different from local people--but observe the differences in performance, in economic potential, in living standards! Economists interested in economic development have noted the powerful consequences on primitive economies of demonstration effects and rises in expectation levels caused by this type of foreign investment. In many cases, the institution creating the most increase in expectations and demonstrating most powerfully that a better life can be had is an American firm operating in a less developed environment.

The often unintended result is that private enterprise American businessmen, who often think of themselves as quite conservative politically, become the persons most responsible for carrying revolutionary viruses. A modern oil refinery, with its rather dramatic appearance, its unique products, and its highly trained and high living personnel, can be more revolutionary in character in a foreign environment than thousands of revolutionary tracts passed around the country. Marxism normally tries to disrupt societies, but, once in power, emulates the West as best it can in this sense. The revolution caused by new productive techniques, transport systems, energy uses, and other scientific and managerial developments is apolitical, but its impact on non-Western cultures is extreme.

Types of International Business

Any business activity which can be performed within one country can be performed internationally if the firm chooses to work in more than one country. However, various forms of enterprise do have different management and organization characteristics, and it is useful to categorize the more common forms of international business which now take place. Of particular importance in such categorization is whether or not management within the foreign country is performed largely by foreigners or by local citizens. Management of productive activity carries with it significant economic and political power, and much of the praise and objections to international activities revolve around this point. Most societies are somewhat dubious about enterprises owned and managed by foreigners, and often countries are unwilling to allow extensive ownership of businesses by such persons or companies.

INTERNATIONAL BUSINESS ACTIVITIES WITHOUT FOREIGN MANAGEMENT

These enterprises may be categorized as follows:

1. Import. Here a local buyer merely buys from the foreign firm. Such imports are restricted to goods which can be moved. Services such as haircuts do not get sold abroad.

2. Export. A local firm sells goods abroad.

3. Portfolio investment. An investor may buy stocks in foreign corporations or bonds issued by public or private agencies of a foreign country. He or she might also deposit savings in commercial banks in another country, a savings and loan organization, or some other financial institution. Many such banks and S & Ls in the U.S., particularly those near the borders and in major money centers such as New York, have very significant foreign owned deposits.

It is common today to find foreigners buying American securities of all sorts in this manner, and Americans also invest in foreign firms, particularly in Japan and advanced countries of Western Europe. Mysterious persons of possibly dubious reputation may put money in Swiss, Panamanian, or Bahamas bank accounts. Historically, this type of foreign investment has long been important, going back a millenia or more.

4. Loans to Governments. Since 1950, organizations such as the World Bank have made portfolio loans to many countries, and these loans now total many billions of dollars per year. Governments of more affluent countries have often loaned other countries billions as well, and nations as diverse as Mexico, Canada, the U.S.S.R., Saudi Arabia, the U.S., and Kuwait have lent significant amounts. Such loans often have political price tags, but they are common.

Private bank loans to governments began to rise rapidly in the mid-1970's, and now total over $750 billion. Major banks in many industrial countries had huge sums to lend after the 1975 oil price increases, which added billions of dollars to oil states' reserves. These billions, deposited in major banks, had to be loaned out, and the obvious borrowers were governments. CPEs such as Poland; Third World countries such as Brazil, Mexico, and Peru; and industrialized countries such as Sweden and Denmark, have all borrowed huge sums in this manner. Many of these loans are tied to specific business ventures, in which the banks support the exports of domestic clients by loaning to the client's customers. The international credit standing of countries has become a critical factor in their economic planning, given the possibilities of obtaining large loans in this way.

A major difficulty here, particularly for private banks, is that in case of default by a government or foreign firm, there is no recourse in law. Nations can go to war to force payments, and gunboat diplomacy was a popular means of accomplishing this up to the early 1930's—but in today's world such behavior is both dangerous and unpopular. A foreigner finds it difficult to press his claims in unsypathetic local courts. This is not a theoretical point at present. A wide variety of countries are now having extreme difficulty in repaying their loans, and these loans are so large that if major defaults occurred, many of the West's largest private banks would be insolvent. The impact of such insolvency on the U.S. or Western European economies could be extreme. At this writing, many countries in trouble have managed to reschedule debts, pay interest charges, but not principle, and generally avoid the problems of default. But so many countries are in trouble that the whole world financial system is threatened. We will return to this point in more detail in Chapter 4.

5. Licensing. A firm may license a foreign company to utilize its trademarks, patents, processes, or other knowledge which may have proprietary value. The licensee pays a royalty for the privilege of such use. In such cases, the licensor may take very little part in the foreign operations beyond merely policing to make sure that the licensing agreements are being observed. In other cases, considerable interplay of managerial talent, including particularly technical talent, may be observed; but the typical role of the licensor is advisory and consultative, not direct and managerial.

As in the case of portfolio investment, the lack of control of foreign operations carries a certain risk to licensors. The licensee may fail to pay royalties or may dispute the amount, and the question might be decided in a legal system alien to the licensor. The licensor may be unable to be on hand at all times in the foreign country to determine that his standards of quality are met, and as a result his name or his product line may mean a poor reputation through inept management of the licensee. Such difficulties have been emphasized by some firms who have had bad experiences in this activity, while others, having more success with their licensees, argue that it is a useful and inexpensive method of entering overseas markets. Much depends on the time and place where the licensing takes place. In any event, some risk is present which is not present in a single country.

Like exporting and importing, licensing can be done easily by smaller firms. As one example, the second edition of this book was licensed to a Spanish publisher for translation and publication in Spanish, and Cedarwood Press is NOT one of the publishing giants! Many smaller high technology firms are in a position to license their technology and patents very profitably long before they grow large enough to consider direct foreign activities.

6. Contracting. It is common in the modern world for a country or an enterprise to contract large and small projects out to foreign firms. Most major industrialized countries have specialist contractors who can design and build dams, highways, power plants, subway systems, and pipelines, and countries as diverse as Italy, South Korea, Japan, Great Britain, and the U.S. have many companies in this field. Often the project is funded in hard currency by the World Bank or another government as a part of foreign aid or lending.

This activity is a halfway house between taking management abroad and remaining at home. During the life of the construction project, which can last years, or even a decade or more, the contractor is in charge, and such construction companies have large cadres of competent project managers and technicians whose experience would include having worked in most of the countries of the world. These managers may work abroad for extended periods, and they have many of the problems of more permanent resident managers. But when the construction is completed, the firms leave and the project is turned over to local managers. Contractors´ representatives may stay on for additional years as teachers, trainers, and advisors, but they normally do not remain in charge of the project in a direct sense.

This activity can be considered as the export of a complex mix of goods (including cement, steel, machines etc.) plus services (design, engineering, management talent, education etc.). The contractor's job is to put the product/service mix together in the most economical manner possible, both to satisfy the client and to make a proft on the job. Given the tremendous complexity of many large engineering projects, success in this activity involves an extremely high level of managerial competence.

7. Turnkey projects. These projects could possibly be considered a subset of the contracting category. A foreign firm may design and construct a factory or other system, carrying the project through its initial operations. At that point, the project is turned over to local personnel for continued operations. It is useful to examine turnkey factory projects separately, however, since contracting generally involves a project which results in service production (as highways, water power, electrical supply, flood control, etc.), while turnkey projects often involve future production of industrial products. Governments or private firms may purchase such turnkey plants from firms in other countries, since 'they lack the expertise to do the job efficiently themselves. Such projects may well involve licencing of processes, patents, or know how, and they often result in both future imports, in the form of spare parts and inputs, and exports, in the form of finished product.

As in the general foreign contracting case, such projects often involve educational work by the contractor with local managers and technicians. The contractor may be responsible for bringing the new plant up to given standards of production and product quality before leaving, but the factory is eventually turned over to local managers and technicians, and the contractor and his personnel leave.

8. Management contracts. Foreign corporations are sometimes asked to manage operations for firms in other countries. Sometimes such contracts may be for indefinite periods; more commonly, the firm is also asked to train local managers to take over the operation.

An airline might be hired to provide technical and managerial personnel for airline operation in an LDC which as yet has not acquired this expertise. For an agreed fee, the airline will manage operations, possibly train technical and managerial personnel, and in the end turn the operation over to local management.

Such contracts are common in countries where foreign ownership is viewed with suspicion. Even a Marxist country might rely on such a contract and stay pure politically, since the foreigners do not own anything, and they will all go home eventually. In effect, the country is buying management and technical expertise which it might otherwise be unable to obtain.

INTERNATIONAL BUSINESS ACTIVITIES INVOLVING DIRECT FOREIGN INVESTMENT AND MANAGEMENT

Some types of international business activities require that the owners of the enterprise also provide managerial effort within the foreign country. If an enterprise is owned by foreigners, they have the right to manage the firm as they see fit, subject to local laws and rules. Ownership and control go hand in hand, since asset owners have the right to determine how their assets should be manipulated. Thus the owner of a factory normally can decide what to produce, how to produce it, what kinds of inputs to use, and so on. He may be constrained in the sense of being unable to use child labor, having to pay taxes on certain kinds of inputs, or being required to use domestic coal instead of imported fuel oil for his energy requirements, among many other constraints; but, within rather wide ranges, the owner has options which are his alone. As long as the owners hold the assets, they have these rights, a situation which normally implies a long term management effort for them.

Local managers may be local citizens or foreigners, but in either case, the owner is exercising direct management control. If local law allows this type of foreign ownership of productive assets, the owners must actively or passively provide the necessary management for these assets. As indicated in Chapter 1, this type of international operation is the main focus of this book. In effect, a firm has exported management to other countries. The major kinds of activities involving exported management are as follows:

1. Sole direct foreign investment. A firm may completely own and operate a business in a foreign country. Local management must be carried on in the local environment, including existing legal-political, eductional, behavioral, and economic situations which may be unique within a given environment. This point will be examined in more detail in Chapter 3.

Extractive and agricultural productive enterprises are largely dependent on the types and quality of local resources throughout the world, and such firms are relatively common. Of particular historic importance are the petroleum companies in the Middle East, Africa, and South America. Such firms had to invest where the oil is found, and this often led to major international investments. In the past decade, virtually all of the major investments in crude oil extraction have been taken over by local governments, usually on a buy out basis, and more modern oil ventures often take the form of joint ventures with government companies or exploration contracts, with the local government holding title to the oilfields. The politics of oil leads to relatively little direct investment these days, although oil is by far the single largest internationally traded commodity.

Agricultural direct investment was once quite popular, particularly in tropical and subtropical agricultural products. The English and French both exploited such possibilities extensively in their colonial possessions, and large foreign owned estates in Africa, Asia, and Latin America supplied cocoa, rubber, tea, copra, bananas, and similar items to the home country. Many of these estates are still active. However, the post-1945 liquidation of colonial empires has meant considerable discouragement of such agricultural enterprises. Newly independent nations, pressured by their own land hungry peasants, have discouraged such ventures. Many estates have long been nationalized by governments, and rapid popuation increases in most Third World countries have made much of this type investment of historical interest only. The products are still produced, but more commonly on state or peasant owned land.

Besides the postwar boom in extractive international industries, another booming area is manufacturing. Many countries are willing to tolerate foreign firms wanting to invest in plant and equipment in the country, seeing in such investment a rapid potential increase in employment, incomes, and welfare, plus potentially rapid technology transfers. U.S. firms led in such investment into the 1970s, but increasingly West European and Japanese firms are moving abroad as well.

Local services, particularly in transporation and public utilities, have a long history of international ownership and operation. In the railroad era from 1850 to 1910, the British in particular invested heavily in railways in many parts of the world. Such ownership and operations have become increasingly difficult as previously colonial states have gained independence and insisted on local control of key social overhead capital projects. A similar pattern has taken place in other public utility sectors. Power and light companies are regarded as critical national industries, and this sector has a lengthy record of expropriation and purchase by local governments. In various parts of the world a few such firms still operate, but most of these ventures now belong to local governments.

A more active service sector is that of finance, market promotion (including advertising agencies), management consulting, insurance, and retailing. Here the foreign company sells a service which may be unobtainable in the home country, and the relative lack of visible capital investment dampens nationalistic ardor about foreign exploitation. What are being sold are techniques, ideas, and methodologies which assist local firms and individuals in performing their productive operations. If the service offered is clearly desirable, countries are willing to allow foreigners to operate them.

But as with agriculture, many local service firms have been expropriated. If locals can perform about as well as foreigners, then why pay outsiders to do the job? It is common to find specific prohibitions against foreign ownership of life insurance companies, retail operations, and similar activities which do not require enormously sophisticated managers. Firms offering highly sophisticated services such as management consulting or engineering design, are less vulnerable.

2. Joint ventures. These are activities of any type which are performed by at least two firms from different countries in some type of equity partnership arrangement. The local firm may hold majority control, or the foreign firm might be the dominant partner, or a 50-50 arrangement might result. Some countries, such as Mexico, require 50-50 ventures, although exceptions always can be found. Local partners can be privately held or government companies. It is also possible to have two firms from countries A and B operate jointly in country C, in which case the situation is similar to wholly owned foreign ventures working abroad. A foreign firm with a minority interest in a local company runs the risk that its interest will be compromised by its local

partners. Cases have occurred which amplify this point, although others suggest that the attitude with which firms approach such ventures may determine success or failure. Mutual trust and respect are critical in such situations.

Many larger firms will not engage in any joint ventures as a matter of policy, feeling that total control gives them the needed managerial muscle to get things done properly. A few such firms only work in joint ventures, feeling that the politics of foreign ownership are minimized. Still others have joint ventures only when they cannot hold total ownership. One can find every possible variant of this pattern around the world.

3. International services. A major modern example of services which cross national frontiers is the international air transport industry. Here firms from various countries, publicly and privately owned, operate aircraft between countries and are subject to laws and regulations of at least two nations. Like the more traditional maritime activities, airplanes as well as airlines must be domiciled in some single country, although all international airlines will own some assets in various countries in which they operate. Such owneship can range from a few minor items of office furniture to complete maintenance facilities and terminals.

A modern type of free international service agency is one operated in a foreign country by a country or a state, which offers free information to tourists or investors about the homeland. The intent is to encourage foreigners to visit or otherwise spend money in the given country. Thus many American states have offices abroad that perform this service, and Ireland has similar offices in other countries.

Other forms of international services are the sale of insurance, stocks and bonds, and similar items across national frontiers. Often foreign management goes with these investments. Unlike local services mentioned earlier, such international servies do have multiple country implications in the sense that any sale will involve activities in two or more countries.

Modern electronic communication blurs the lines between local and international activities. An American bank might be lending all over the world, but its offices will be at home. Or these offices might be scattered in many countries. Insurance is sold for many reasons by companies domiciled in one country, although these firms may well have branch offices also. When branches can communicate with each other or headquarters in fractions of a second via telephone, telex, or even two way television, then where a service seller is actually located may be unimportant. Revenues can be enormous. As one example, foreign borrowings by governments and their agencies now total over $750 billion, which means that around $75 billion annually is earned in interest by lenders. Some of these earnings come from branches in foreign countries; many stem from home office loans. In either case, there is a major international implication and involvement.

4. Cooperation agreements. CPEs do not normally allow direct private foreign investments, although these communist states are often

interested in Western firms' technology and hard currency earnings from exports to the West. In the past fifteen years a form of joint venture known as the cooperation agreement has developed to meet CPE needs. As noted in Chapter 1, these agreements have not worked out as well as Western firms or CPEs would have wished, and few new ones are being contemplated, but many cooperation agreements are working at present, a few with considerable success.

In the modern world, every conceivable variation of the forms of international business noted here can be found. The deep world recession of the early 1980's slowed international business down in most countries, but there is no slackening of interest in companies everywhere seeking out new opportunities. Often such opportunities lie abroad, and while a few firms disinvest abroad, more expand. The world of international business is a constantly dynamic and moving one, where a few firms are expanding rapidly in many countries; new firms are entering the field; and some older ones are liquidating or withdrawing. One major development in the 1980's in many countries, including the U.S., is that foreigners can often provide badly needed jobs and technology which local firms cannot. These days it is as likely to find countries trying to figure out how to attract foreigners as it is to find countries trying to take them over or keep them out.

The most popular forms of foreign investment, from the country point of view, are those which bring high technology, exports, and jobs. Everyone feels they need more good, high paying jobs, and high technology industries are synonymous with the best type of high prestige, modern economy. Often such industries are critical to defense industries as well. Firms in such areas find themselves subsidized, welcomed, and urged to do more. And everyone needs more hard currency, so firms which export are welcomed. Note that the high technology firms also are often the biggest exporters, so these requirements often go hand in hand. High technology genetics and electronics firms rarely lack for major foreign opportunities, if they wish to take them.

The Location of International Business Activity

International business activity does not just happen. It is the result of conscious decisions made by public and private businessmen in various countries whose usual major interest is in profiting from activities in various other countries.

While virtually any firm can take part in international activities in almost any country, it is typically true that certain basic pressures and economic and political characteristics, plus the desire for profitable operations, have led to most managerially oriented international business occurring under a rather narrow set of conditions.

The mere existence of these basic conditions does not automatically insure that international business firms will enter a given country. The actual entry decision will depend on more detailed analysis of specific possibilities.

An immediate first question is, why go abroad at all? A second question, where are the best possibilities, is also relevant, and to these matters we now turn.

WHICH FIRMS GO ABROAD?

It is typically true that doing business locally is much simpler than operating internationally. The local firm only has to worry about its own country´s law, economics, labor problems, financial constraints, and so on, while an international firm faces all of these complexities at home and in the host country, and in addition must struggle with complex international problems arising when one moves goods, money, or people across national frontiers. Unless compelling pressures arose at home, most firms would choose to remain local, confining their international business activities to import and export, and possibly to the relatively simple patterns such as licensing of patents and processes.

Most firms in fact do stay home. Of the some 13 million American firms, perhaps less than 50,000 have direct investments abroad. Over half of these 13 million are very small, having no employees (except family) at all. Millions more are too small to contemplate any foreign ventures. Still more millions are professional organizations, such as law offices, that are tied by professional certification requirements to the country or the state of residence of the owners. Hundreds of thousands of others are service organizations, such as electric companies, phone companies, trucking operations, and similar firms, who would find it impossible to go abroad without obtaining licenses or franchises in other countries. Tens of thousands of others might find foreign options, except that their owners or managers simply are not interested. Literally millions are so financially pressed that any expansion would be difficult or impossible. And finally, many very well managed and fast growing smaller firms find that they can continue to expand and prosper within the U.S. for many years to come. Such expansion takes all of the talent and expertise of their managers, so overseas ventures will wait. Every year, a few of these firms will ponder foreign options, thus adding to the pool of MNCs in the future, but for the moment, they stay local.

One major reason for considering international options might be that opportunities at home are getting thin. Profit rates may be declining, even though the firm is still extremely profitable. But marginal new investments are not likely to pay off as well as they have historically. Moreover, a mature firm organized around a cadre of professional managers may find that it has developed a surplus of competent men and women in both the technical and managerial sense. Junior people are getting restless, seeing advancement paths blocked by competent senior personnel. Most professionally managed firms have a built in dynamic of their own; and if local market rates of growth tend to slow down, management actively begins to seek new alternatives for the kinds of talent the firm possesses.

Local markets may not offer good markets for products, processes, or patents that the firm has developed. Indeed, it may well be that foreign companies or governments have approached the firm, anxious to obtain useful goods, services, or technology the firm offers. The firm may be aware of foreign options through its export and import business, or through various licensing deals it may have become involved in over the years. It may have aquired another company with a few overseas activities. There are many ways of becoming aware of foreign options, including a very common one of having the boss visit an interesting place on his or her vacation! Competitor watching is another way of seeing new possibilities; if one's key competitors are expanding abroad, managers get interested very quickly. The modern world of instantaneous communication and rapid transportation makes the obtaining of information about foreign options relatively easy.

The points made above fit modern, professionally managed industrial firms in the more advanced countries. Few companies of this type exist in the Third World, and only a handful of such companies have multinational operations. But Third World countries usually have more to do locally than has been done, and competent local firms can take advantage of local opportunities.

Family firms typically stay home, although there are many exceptions, typically tied into family connections. A capable cousin may be in another country and can expand there, or in countries with inconvertible currencies the family may wish to expand to a country where cash flow can be converted to dollars or other hard currencies. Thus quite a few Indian family firms have branches in Singapore or Hong Kong. But the usual pattern is for a family firm to have considerably less interest in foreign ventures than in companies in which executives are trained to consider endless expansion as a way of life.

State owned firms also typically stay home, usually because of political pressures. Few politicians favor giving jobs and incomes to foreigners, no matter what the long term benefits. The majority of Western public firms are in such businesses as railroading, electric power, or other public utilities, where foreign expansion is difficult. State owned airlines are a major exception, since they typically own at least some assets in countries to which they fly. A few manufacturing firms, such as the French Renault auto company, do have major overseas investments, but these are rare.

Communist countries rarely are interested in foreign investments, except in a few ocean shipping and airline cases. A few banks also are owned by communist governments in other countries to handle trade financing. But the typical pattern in CPEs is for local investment only.

The large professionally managed firms are also much more likely to accumulate cash surpluses or to be able to obtain more funds from money markets. Financial constraints, folklore to the contrary, tend to be much less compelling in modern industry than personpower problems, particularly supplies of highly skilled managerial and technical talent.

In such firms, some factor eventually sends the company overseas in a direct way. A very common case is when another country cuts off imports with quotas or tariffs, and the only way to maintain the firm's market is to build plants within the country. Ford and General Motors both built Canadian and West European auto plants, starting in the

1920´s, for this reason, and Japanese companies are now building plants in the U.S. and Western Europe for exactly the same reason. The firm either loses its market or goes multinational. It may be that for purely economic reasons connected with good management, local assembly operations are started. Transport costs on low volume, high weight components may be so much lower than transport costs on finished products that local assembly is a logical step. Or any of the reasons noted earlier might lead to consideration of direct foreign investment.

Whatever the reason for investing abroad, the company has to have a significant advantage over local firms in order to compete effectively. Professionally managed firms tend to develop special advantages through time, and they tend to look for situations where these special advantages can be utilized. We can taxonomize these advantages as follows:

1. Market oriented firms. These companies have their major strength in marketing, although they may produce goods efficiently and well. A classic example of this type of firm is Proctor & Gamble. This firm can market consumer products extremely well, having developed its expertise over a century in the U.S.

Such a firm will look for good markets where incomes are high and the economy is growing rapidly. For such companies, Western Europe, Australia, and Canada are the logical expansion points. If it is profitable to build production facilities in these countries, they will be built to serve the new, affluent markets.

Japan would be another logical choice, but under Japanese law, it is impossible or very difficult to make direct investments in consumption goods factories. Hence few American or European companies have managed to moved into this market. The affluent communist countries such as East Germany would be tempting markets, but no communist country would allow such investments. Note that here, as with all direct foreign investment, it requires the right company and the right country to make a deal. If either is unwilling or unable to make such investments, nothing happens.

Once markets are established in more affluent countries, such an MNC can continue to expand to Third Wolrd countries. Markets for low priced soap and toiletries often emerge early and get very large in such countries as Brazil, Mexico, and India. As always, the MNC has to be able to get in. Brazil and Mexico these days might allow such an investment, but India might not.

2. Raw materials oriented firms. A firm which needs raw materials, such as petroleum, ores, or a key agricultural product such as bananas has to go where the material is. The country involved has to agree, but no one looks for oil unless there is some high probability of finding it.

Here the firm will make investments virtually anywhere, and such countries as Angola, the United Arab Emirates, Liberia, Great Britain, Norway, and Iraq have received major American and European investments. In the past two decades, many of these investments have been nationalized, but many remain, and even now mining and petroleum companies negotiate new concessions. Countries willing to gain income as rentiers of their depleting assets may find such propositions attractive.

3. Cost reducers. Some firms, which may also belong in the marketing category, are also interested in getting production costs down. Americans sometimes think that Western Europe and Japan are low labor cost countries, but this is no longer true. In some industrial sectors, wage rates in these countries are even higher than in the U.S. But many Third World countries do have very low labor costs, and some will allow foreign firms to invest and produce in the country. If the economy is open, in the sense that key personnel, capital, and components can easily be imported, with the finished product being exported, then cost reducers can gain significant advantage by investing in such countries. Taiwan, Hong Kong, South Korea, Haiti, and special zones in Northern Mexico and the People's Republic of China (PRC), among others, now offer such advantages. These countries now produce large amounts of labor intensive products such as clothing, toys, and consumer electronic goods.

This development is only a few decades old. It requires firms looking for cost reductions, a wealthy consuming country willing to allow such imports, and an open Third World economy willing to allow such firms to operate. Only since the 1960's have all three conditions been common around the world. In the 1950's, Americans could only buy consumer goods made in the U.S., and many of these were expensive. Product choice was also quite limited. But one only has to visit a local department or discount store anywhere in the U.S. today and see where consumer goods come from to realize just how much world production patterns have changed.

Trade unions in rich countries are very nervous about this development, which does eliminate jobs in labor intensive industries. Firms are accused of running away from high wages, which they are doing. But in many industries with relatively simple production problems, firms often have no choice, given that local and foreign competitors are doing the same thing. Poorer countries with limited resources, except their own low paid, hard working people, often have no choice either. They can gain something by producing for foreign markets, or they can stay poor. Countries which have tried this strategy now rank among the fastest growing poorer countries in the world, and such giants as the PRC and India, which have long been dubious about foreign investment, are now experimenting with this new idea. If they get into world markets in this manner in a major way, we may see some profound changes in the way all business is done all over the world.

4. Brain renters. Some American, Japanese, and West European firms sell nothing but the services of their very talented staffs. In effect, they rent brains to their clients. Advertising agencies, management consultants, architects, accounting firms, insurance companies, banks, and other financial institutions are in this position.

Such firms may go to almost any country that can use their services, but the majority of them go to high income, sophisticated economies that need such services.

PROFITS AND MNCS

Firms almost always invest abroad to make a profit. Non-profit ventures typically are done at home, and by organizations that are rarely interested in international activities. To make a profit, the firm has to be highly competent, which is why so much foreign investment is done by professionally managed large corporations. MNCs have to be somewhat better than local firms, given the inevitable extra costs they incur in moving to alien environments. They also tend to be somewhat more closely watched and controlled than local firms by suspicious governments. This profit seeking inevitably puts all MNCs under suspicion in a modern world where many persons feel that profits are immoral. Yet many countries allow such MNCs to operate, since the gains they offer countries, such as more foreign currency earnings, jobs, tax revenues, and technology transfers, tend to be large.

In the early postwar period, most MNCs were American, and others received the investments. These days all wealthy industrial countries have their own MNCs, and even poorer countries sometimes have a few firms making overseas investments. The key is always managerial and firm competence. No matter where a company comes from, if it can compete successfully in other countries that allow such direct investments, one can find such firms in action.

As noted earlier, it takes a willing MNC and a willing country to make a deal. Western industrial countries typically have rather relaxed rules about foreign investment, and one finds much foreign investment in all such countries, including the United States. In these days of industrial and investment stagnation, one often finds that countries will not only welcome foreign MNCs, but often offer them subsidies, tax concessions, and other benefits if they do come. The gains are seen to far outweigh the losses. One major gain is that the MNCs often are the most technologically advanced firms in the world, which is a major reason why they are so good. Every country would prefer more new technology to less, and one way to get it is to invite the IBMs of this world to please build a plant in your country. Since the vast majority of workers will be local citizens, such investments offer a major new way to acquire such technology. Moreover, the products can often be exported, which means that your country will gain a reputation as one of the truly advanced countries of the world, as well as having rapidly increasing exports.

Communist countries, at the opposite extreme, rarely permit foreign investment, so few MNCs are actively creating wealth in these countries. Third World countries have widely varying policies about allowing foreign investment. Most of the larger Third World countries have fairly restrictive policies, and only selected firms can enter. Often joint ventures are preferred to wholly owned direct investments. Some smaller poor countries have become open economies as noted above, and they are studied with great care, as they are the most successful poorer countries in terms of economic growth.

A few Third World countries have grown very rich because they have key natural resources, usually oil. Saudi Arabia, Kuwait, and the United Arab Emirates are examples. Such countries may well have fairly relaxed direct investment policies, although they may not. It depends more on local politics than anything. Third World Marxist states, such as Ethiopia, North Korea, and Cuba, follow the usual communist pattern of not allowing direct foreign investment. Such countries tend not to do too well economically.

An MNC contemplating a foreign investment thus begins by pondering this expansion path, as compared to local options. It may find that local options are few and unattractive, so it examines its comparative advantages in marketing, production, or whatever and scans the world environment for intriguing prospects. Countries that allow at least some foreign investment may become possible options, and at this point the detailed analysis of what might be allowed or accomplished follows. Often long and tortuous negotiations with government officials may follow before investment permission is granted. Virtually any foreign investment is perceived by MNCs to be more risky than local investments, given that any foreigner might be expropriated or otherwise inconvenienced. History is full of such examples, so political risk becomes a critical part of the MNC's analysis. Stability and predictability of the country's government is seen as extremely important. Hence profits must be larger, to offset the extra risk, than might be accepted at home. And, if the deal is made, we see yet more international investment and yet more expansion of MNCs.

Wealthy countries with relaxed foreign investment rules, such as the United States, Canada, and Western Europe, offer the most interesting possibilities, and these areas receive the majority of foreign investment. They might receive even more, but one characteristic of all such economies is that their own local firms tend to be very good. The competition can be fierce! One can be upset by major American firms blundering around in very poor countries, but well over two thirds of all U.S. direct foreign investment is in other wealthy, sophisticated countries.

Countries can change their rules any time, and many have. Thus Iran a few years ago was a good place for foreign investment, but now, after most such investments have been expropriated, it is not, and new investments are also virtually banned. Ethiopia and Cuba once welcomed foreign investment, and now do not. They have also expropriated all existing foreign firms. But the PRC, which long banned foreign investments, is now cautiously welcoming a few, and India, which also severely restricts foreign investments, is rethinking its policy. At present (1984), given world recession and stagnation, the MNCs are not expanding very much, and some scholars are questioning whether they can ever expand again as they did from 1950 to 1980. But if the PRC and India, with 1.7 billion people, get seriously into the international direct investment game, we may yet see phenomenal expansion of the MNCs. Note that what happens depends more on government policies than on firms. The countries control the firms, and if they choose not to allow such expansion, it will not occur.

The 1980's have seen the growing realization by many governments, in rich and poor countries, in socialist and communist ones as well, that the future may well be won by the countries with the best technological base. The United States and Japan are seen as the two countries with the best and most advanced technology, and one result of this new perception is new interest in attracting MNCs from these countries which can bring such technology. Even communist states are trying to work out ways to do this, in addition to cooperation agreements and spying. Firms noted for their high technology achievements tend to be much more welcome in many more countries than more mundane firms, and those investment subsidies can more easily be obtained by such firms. It is possible that the future of the international economy will belong to such firms.

But then, it always did. We forget that the auto, television, canned food, machine tool, and many other MNCs once were at the cutting edge of world technology, and when they made their major foreign investments, they were welcomed because they brought such new technologies. The areas of rapid technological growth have changed, but the general patterns have not.

Conclusion

The general analysis of international business activity covered in this chapter is useful in indicating the general patterns of development in this field. However, the fact that firms will tend to move into international business because of the factors discussed does not indicate in any detail the kinds of key problems they will face in making actual decisions about foreign projects. To determine what these problems are, managers must consider carefully the factors, both domestic and foreign, which will directly influence the way in which the firm can operate. Proper analysis of the international management process must take into account what the management process is all about as well as the environment in which it operates. The following chapters will be concerned with these critical problems.

Questions for Discussion

1. Take any country that looks interesting to you and find out something about it. Consult such sources as encyclopedias, atlases, magazine articles, and books. What kinds of general information might be useful to a company interested in business opportunities in this country?

2. Now consider the various types of international business that a private foreign company might do in this country of yours. Which types of international business might prove difficult or impossible? Which types might be potentially feasible and profitable?

3. A small but very rapidly growing company in Illinois operates three restaurants in three cities in the central part of this state. The owner is a very clever manager/chef, who presently manages all three operations personally. He earns over 15 percent return on sales of $880,000 per year.

Recently one of his restaurants was visited by a Japanese gentleman who was very pleased with the service, food, and prices. This man suggested that the owner consider starting a similar venture in Tokyo. The Japanese felt that this quality of service in Japan, along with the exotic food, would provide the base for a very profitable operation. Since the Japanese was a wealthy businessman himself, he was even willing to consider a joint venture.

At the same time, the owner was considering expanding to Chicago. He felt that his style of restaurant would be a big success in that city. For this type of firm, which new investment seems most reasonable? Why?

4. A fast growing electronics components manufacturer with sales of around $85 million per year is also considering expansion. The company's marketing vice president points out that the firm has already gained 47 percent of the total market for the key components it produces in the United States. Expansion into related lines would bring the firm into direct competition with such giants as IBM. The major reason for this company's rapid expansion is a very solid technical base. The firm's scientists are very good and have innovated often and well in the company's basic product area. The company holds many patents on innovations and processes, along with products. Indeed, for three years a West German and a Japanese company have been licensed to use several key production processes. This licensing yields about $220,000 per year.

The company president recently took a trip to Great Britain. He feels that it may be useful to consider an investment in such an affluent country, but he is hesitant because the firm has never operated anything abroad before. He feels that the firm has the choice, given its limited capital and technical skills, betwen going abroad, probably in England or Scotland, and starting a new product line in the United States.

For this firm, which investment seems most reasonable? Why? Take your choice and suggest three possible problems the company might face if it starts to go the way you suggest.

Supplementary Readings

Blough, Roy. INTERNATIONAL BUSINESS: ENVIRONMENT AND ADOPTION. New York: McGraw-Hill, 1966.

Center for Strategic and International Trade Competition. WORLD TRADE COMPETITION. New York: Praeger, 1981.

Dean, James W., and Schwindt, Richard. INTERNATIONAL BUSINES. Durham, N.C.: Eno River Press, 1981.

Farmer, Richard N. and Lombardi, John V. (Eds.). READINGS IN INTERNATIONAL BUSINESS: THIRD EDITION. Bloomington, IN: Cedarwood Press, 1984.

Fayerweather, John. INTERNATIONAL BUSINESS MANAGMEMENT: A CONCEPTUAL FRAMEWORK. New York: McGraw-Hill, 1969.

Kindelberger, Charles P. AMERICAN BUSINESS ABROAD. New Haven: Yale University Press, 1969.

Kolde, Endel J. INTERNATIONAL BUSINESS ENTERPRISE. Englewood Cliffs, NJ: Prentice-Hall, 1968.

Robinson, Richard D. INTERNATIONAL BUSINESS POLICY. New York: Holt, Rinehart & Winston, 1964.

Robock, Stefan H. and Simmonds, Kenneth. INTERNATIONAL BUSINESS AND MULTINATIONAL ENTERPRISE. Homewood, IL: Richard D. Irwin, 1973.

Vernon, Raymond. MANAGER IN THE INTERNATIONAL ECONOMY. Englewood Cliffs, NJ: Prentice-Hall, 1972.

Chapter 3

Basic Methodology

Introduction

It is useful to have an analytical structure in exploring any problem, and this chapter presents one for international business. Since we are dealing with complex large firms in many countries, whose activities often flow across national frontiers, we need to structure three basic problems. The first deals with the internal management of the companies; the second deals with local environments in which the companies operate; and the third deals with international flows of money, men, and materials. If we can organize these three sets of variables correctly, and if we can interrelate them properly, we will have a complete framework for further analysis.

FIRM AND MANAGERIAL FUNCTIONS: In discussions of business and managerial activities, it is often assumed that all parties are aware of and in agreement with the implicit definitions of such activities. Rarely is this the case. More often, various persons, because of their education, experience, and insights, have quite different ideas of what a business function might be. Since we will be dealing with these firm and managerial functions throughout the book, it is necessary to indicate clearly the nature of these internal activities of firms and managers in any productive organization.

A firm function is a process which necessarily must be performed by the firm in any economy. The usual division of such functions is production and procurement, marketing, research and development, finance, and public and external relations. Note that every enterprise does not necessarily have to perform all of these functions, since it can contract out any one or several of them to specialist organizations. But these firm functions must be accomplished if the economy is to perform at all. It is also true that firms often perform them in an intuitive rather than planned manner. Thus a firm may have no formal public relations plans or policies, but regardless of its interest in the matter, outsiders do form opinions and images about the firm. Here, the lack of policy becomes policy.

A management function is a process which necessarily must be performed by managers in the course of carrying out firm functions. A common division of managerial functions is planning and innovation, control, staffing, direction, and leadership and motivation. These managerial functions do not occur in a vacuum. Managers plan marketing or production processes and functions; they staff finance departments; they direct men and women engaged in all enterprise functions; and so on. Actually the firm and managerial functions are closely interrelated in many ways. Marketing seldom occurs without reference to production; finance is related to marketing; and so on.

The Productive Job

The basic productive unit in any type of economic system is the firm. The firm takes inputs, comprising land, labor, capital, components and outputs from other firms, and management, and transforms them into outputs consisting of usable goods and services. Inputs cost something, and in private enterprise societies the usual primary goal of any firm is to sell the outputs at some price greater than the cost of the inputs. More precisely, the firm usually tries to maximize profits by adjusting costs and revenues to yield the maximum differential between them.

Figure 3-1 illustrates the general process. Land consists not only of real estate but also of such diverse factors as minerals (coal, oil, ores), weather conditions, and water supplies. Labor inputs are usually measured in labor hours, and capital inputs are measured in machine hours. In any complex society, firms form long chainlike links, with one firm selling its output to another firm as inputs. Thus a power company will buy coal to make electricity to sell to other firms, who use the electricity to make parts to sell to still other firms who eventually produce products for final consumption. The management factor is the one which coordinates and plans the entire process.

FIGURE 3-1

FIRM PRODUCTION PROCESS

The factor transformation is accomplished through the enterprise functions combined with the managerial functions by management, the fourth input factor.

This general productive process is accomplished by the performance of the various firm functions. The concept of a firm organized to perform this type of productive process is useful, since it focuses on the basic functions of the firm. In practice, firms range in size and complexity from one person retail shops to huge modern corporations with hundreds of thousands of employees and billions of dollars of invested capital. But in every case, the firms' basic functions are identical.

It is rare to find any firm which performs every possible productive process on all of its products, from basic raw materials to the final sale of the finished products. Firms usually buy some or all of their inputs in the form of semifinished products from other firms rather than produce everything. In any economy, regardless of political orientation, complex firms manufacture many diverse products and services to be sold to other firms and final consumers.

Productive enterprises are not necessarily privately owned, although this is typical in the Western world. Soviet or PRC firms also perform these basic functions, as do public firms in India and Egypt. In all kinds of systems, profits go to the owners of the firms' assets. In the West, the private shareholders receive them, and in Marxist countries the state takes receives profits by selling goods and services.

These productive functions are discussed below.

PRODUCTION

Goods and services must be produced before any further economic activity can take place. As a part of production, components and raw materials must be purchased, and procurement is a part of the production function.

In the process of producing goods and services, the firm (or its management) must decide which items are to be manufactured and which are to be purchased from vendors; and what types of inputs are to be used in production. This functional area is closely connected to technology, science,and engineering, since the feasibility of any production process will depend on the current state of the arts. The usual problem in production is that there are many ways to produce the needed item, and the manager's task is to select the process which does the job most efficiently. Trade offs may be made between capital and labor, or between one type of raw material or component and another. The basic production processes used will depend, in addition to available technical knowledge, on the costs of various inputs, levels of productivity, availability of skilled labor, and capital equipment on hand, among other factors.

In international operations, such production problems may become more complex, because in each country in which production takes place the prices of various inputs may differ. Thus the supplier of heavy electrical equipment may use aluminum wire in some of its American production, since this material is cheaper than copper. But in its West German plant, the copper will be used, because copper is cheaper. A diesel engine manufacturer in the United States might subcontract certain parts, because he can be confident that the subcontractors are able to produce to his specifications without difficulty. But in India, where quality control standards are much less developed, he might decide to produce some of the parts himself, even if costs are higher.

Production lines laid out with the implicit notion that certain kinds of skilled labor and management are available may have to be modified when the firm begins to operate in a country with different labor supply characteristics. A common error in production planning by international firms is that because much of production is highly technical and scientifically oriented, it can be the same in any country. But it is often true that production activities do have direct connection with the environment, and increasing complexity of this function almost always occurs as the firm moves from its home country to other nations.

MARKETING

Products must not only be produced, but also distributed and sold. Some managers and firms must necessarily be concerned with the way in which the firms´ outputs are to be distributed to consumers. Marketing generally is concerned with the creation of place and time utility, and included in this firm funciton are such problems as pricing and price policies pursued by firms and channels of distribution of products. This function interlocks closely with production, since the prduct line chosen by the firm for marketing reasons will have direct impact on the kinds of production plans and policies pursued. Marketing executives may prefer to change models often in order to expand sales, while production personnel may prefer the longest production runs possible in order to keep production costs down. A typical important function of top management is to balance such conflicting demands by submanagers.

Marketing activities also become more complicated when the firm sells in many cultures. Thus Europeans prefer smaller refrigerators than Americans, because they shop more often and frequently do not have as much space in their homes. Swedes buy space heaters, while Italians are interested in air conditioners. If an American company is to succeed in Europe, it must design and produce a new product line, which involves extensive engineering an production activity as well. Japanese and European firms that come to the United States often find special pollution and safety requirements, in addition to taste differences, which can also mean extensive product alterations.

Many cultural variables become relevant in this international marketing process. Often they involve problems of design, and even innocent local design features can cause trouble abroad. An Aemrican manufacturer which had a six pointed star as a part of its sales emblem on cleansing tissue had its entire first shipment to Saudi Arabia confiscated, because the star was interpreted to be pro-Israeli propaganda, and its entire marketing effort was aborted. Such problems rarely arise in one country, but they can become extremely complex when the firm engages in international marketing.

FINANCE

Every economy in the world uses one scare resource, money, to allocate resources, at least partially. Firms never have unlimited resources, and typically the most scarce resource is liquid funds. Managers must decide which types of financing to use, if more than one option is available; they must decide how these funds are to be allocated among conflicting claimants within the firm; they must decide how to protect the capital presently tied up in the company; and they must decide on how earnings are to be distributed between owners and new demands on the enterprise for more investments. Since money is typically so scarce, this is usually one area which receives major attention by managers at all times.

Firms in international business have enhanced financial options, as well as greater risks, than purely domestic companies. Toyota or Ford can tap money markets in Japan, Western Europe, or the United States, although the terms of lending may be very different in these three areas. This ability to select from additional markets means, among other things, that the firm has greater choices to consider in its financial operations. The MNCs may also have the additional option of bringing in scarce capital from another country. If the money market in India is very tight, local firms may suffer, but a Japanese based MNC can obtain its funds at home and move them to India. MNC risks are higher, but options are greater.

As we will discover in Chapter 4, each country creates its own currency, and the values of these currencies differ often. MNCs, exporters, and importers quickly discover that they have to watch currency values and fluctuations very carefully, since payment in a depreciating currency could lead to major losses. Moreover, some currencies are inconvertible, which means that they cannot be converted to other countries' money, and a firm may discover that it has much money which it cannot use. Any company involved in any way in international business has to know a great deal about the international monetary system, which is the subject of Chapter 4.

RESEARCH AND DEVELOPMENT

R & D work has been a relatively recent innovation for many firms. Only since 1920 have many companies seriously and systematically tried to develop new products and processes which might give them some competitive advantages. But in one sense, any search for information, plus the attempt to integrate new knowledge into managerial decisions, is a form of research and development. Obtaining knowledge of prices of raw materials, as one example, can be considered research. The informal changes often made by foremen and workers on production lines to improve performance or make work easier, can be considered development. In this sense, every firm performs this function to some degree, although they may not do it very efficiently.

The modern view of R & D is a systematic effort to improve performance, through the extended use of scientific methodology. Many firms all over the world do have such formal programs, although the majority of them are located in the advanced countries. A key constraint here is a supply of highly trained personpower to perform the job, and relatively few countries are in a position to supply enough qualified people to do this function properly.

An MNC may have significant advantages in this area. If Germany has a superior environment for conducting chemical research, the American firm with branches in Germany can focus its chemical reseach activities there. At the same time it might be conducting extensive microcomputer research in the United States, where superior research personnel are available. The company can increase its advantage over competitors by locating its research facilities in countries which are at the forefront of research.

Rapid technological changes in many industries in the 1970´s, most notably in genetics and electronics, have led to great interest in systematic R & D in many countries. The relative decline of traditional industries in advanced countries, such as steel and autos, has led many country leaders to the belief that only with very rapid technological advances in the industries of the future can a country maintain its industrial leadership. The United States and Japan are commonly regarded as the leaders in the new technologies, and other countries study their new industries with the idea of transferring such technology to their countries. Poorer countries have often transferred more traditional technology in steel, autos, consumer electronics, and other light industry with great success, leading them to ponder how to accelerate such transfers. This has led to great interest in technology transfer internationally, and many firms, countries, and institutions are intrigued with figuring out how to do this most efficiently.

Not to be forgotten is the enormous trade in armaments, and the observation that the winners in wars usually have superior technology. Countries like France, the United States, and the Soviet Union spend much time trying to develop superior weapons systems, utilizing the best technology, and every country that generates advanced technology has the problem of what to release to foreigners and what to keep to itself. Such countries also face the problem of industrial espionage and reverse engineering, which is the practice of figuring out how the product was designed and developed by observing the final product. Even more peacefully oriented firms, such as computer companies, have much difficulty with spies from abroad, who are very anxious to obtain scientific and industrial secrets.

In the 1980´s, this preoccupation with technology and technology transfer has accelerated. New industries have developed very rapidly, and the countries that have them do well internationally. If a country can somehow gain this technology, either with local work or by getting it from foreigners, it can forge ahead, or so it is widely believed. Older industries, hard hit by foreign competition, also study those foreigners to determine just why they are so good, and what technology might be obtained from them. As a result, there is very extensive discussion of this topic everywhere, and much debate on proper industrial policies for every country. But in a fast moving technological world, the countries and firms with the best ability to generate new technology seem to be the winners.

Technology is often perceived as hardware, in the form of machines and new designs for computers. But much of the superiority of fast moving firms lies not so much in the hardware they use, but the software. That is, they not only have superb machines, but they also know what to do with them. Such fields as marketing, finance, and accounting are not normally seen as generators of new technology, but a brilliant marketing or finance innovation, properly applied, can be as effective as any hardware development. Firms with defective accounting systems collapse as easily and regularly as those with defective technology. The growing realization that such things do matter has led, among other things, to the internationalization of business schools, and foreigners everywhere study management and firm functions as diligently as they study computer circuity...if they are wise!

PUBLIC AND EXTERNAL RELATIONS

All firms deal with suppliers, customers, governments, investors, bankers, politicians, unions, and others outside the firm. The relations the firm may have with such outsiders may directly influence the performance of the firm through time. A company which has a reputation among its customers for giving a high level of service, for being a good supplier of spare parts and technical advice, and one which keeps its delivery promises, is likely to be in a considerably better position than one reputed to be sloppy or deficient in these areas. A firm noted for its antiunion activities will probably have quite different productivity records than one which deals more constructively with unions. Or a company known to be a consistent tax evader, a cheater on safety regulations and pollution controls, will have quite different regulatory problems than one which is known to be straightforward and honest in its dealings with government. In short, the corporate image is important, not only to salve the egos of executives, but also because poor public relations have direct impacts on firm efficiency, and, in the limit, whether or not it can survive in its environment.

For many years American firms have used professional public relations executives and specialist firms to improve their image, and every major news media is used to being swamped with stories about the virtues of companies and other organizations. The information and media explosion since 1945 has led to the recognition that this public image is important enough to become a factor in corporate decision making in many areas. Few large firms will change significant prices, shift large suppliers, close down obsolete plants, or make other important decisions without some reflection on how these actions will affect the corporation in terms of public response.

MNCs must please many publics. What seems proper and desirable in the United States may not be highly regarded in Ireland or Brazil. In many countries being foreign is in itself a negative image, and often the American, Japanese, or West European firm must go to great lengths to convince a suspicious local population that its intentions are honest, and that it is not some sort of bloodsucking imperialistic exploiter of the local population. Such considerations can assume tremendous importance, in the limit determining if the MNC can continue operations.

The above firm functions are in effect what firms do. These functions must be performed before the enterprise can function at all. In many cases, the firm function is handled casually rather than systematically, and in others specialist firms handle the function for another firm. But one can evaluate the efficiency with which these firm functions are performed. It is clear that in complicated societies producing millions of different goods and services, not all production is carried out with equal efficiency. Some firms are very good at the total production process, while others are very good at marketing or finance. And quite a few companies are so poor at everything that bankruptcies are common in all capitalist countries. But we all can recognize superior performance, and firms which are good are studied carefully to see just how their secrets might be utilized, both locally and in foreign climes.

Managerial Functions

In addition to the above firm functions, an additional set of functions is performed by managers in every kind of production enterprise. These are the managerial functions, which refer to the kinds of activities managers perform as managers. These managerial functions can be performed in any or all of the firm functions noted above, and they are interrelated with them. They are covered systematically below.

PLANNING AND INNOVATION

Managers must set plans for their firms and change them from time to time as changing circumstances warrant. Such plans may range from grandiose general policies covering the entire action of the firms, such as "Our company will generally concentrate its efforts in the earthmoving equipment business," to such minor plans as the location of a new machine tool in an established plant. There are major plans, or overall policies, from which stem a large variety of subplans to be carried out as the result of the initial plan. Thus a decision to produce a new microcomputer (the major plan) would be followed by a series of subplans concerning the production layout of the factory, acquisitions of new equipment, labor training, purchases of component parts and raw materials, the manner in which the general plan will be financed, detailed engineering for the design of the new product, staffing for new personnel, and so on.

Plans necessarily have some time horizon. Managers may plan for fifty years or fifty minutes, depending on the problem and the way in which managers view their planning function. Even no planning (which is common in many enterprises) is a plan of sorts, since implicitly the firm merely waits to see what happens and reacts, which is also a plan. Plans can be flexible or inflexible, can be highly scientific or sketched out on the back of an evelope, or simply carried around in the manager's head. They can be heavily participative, in the sense of involving many workers and junior managers, or they can be dictated from above. They can be presented in such a way as to lead to distortion by workers and managers responsible for carrying them out, or they can be made clear cut and easy to follow. They can be quite risky in the sense that if the plan is realized the odds on the company's success is small, or they can be ultraconservative. They can be scientifically oriented, relying heavily on both social and natural sciences as far as possible, or they can be based on a key manager's visit to his astrologer. They can be very difficult to change, or they can be ultraflexible and subject to modification on the slightest evidence that the original plan and its targets are going astray.

It is clear that variations in the planning process among firms lead to striking differences in the efficiency with which firms carry out their productive functions. Bad planning can lead to inept marketing, inadequate financing, frequent breakdowns of production lines and facilities, shortages of raw materials and components, inadequately trained labor, poor distribution of finished products, poor public relations, and innumerable other results which indicate poor and inefficient management and inefficient production by the firm involved. Good planning can avoid most of these difficulties. Given the always uncertain future, no firm or manager can avoid completely the possible poor results of having to face unanticipated problems, but differences in firm efficiency between good and bad planning by management are profound.

Planning in internationally oriented firms must also take into account the international dimensions of the firm. Planning becomes much more complex, since the MNC is working in many environments with many different possible impacts on the firm. Moreover, it must also take into account in planning new opportunities and options offered in other countries. A firm with a saturated local market can plan to expand abroad, while a local firm faces different constaints. Obtaining lowest cost production must take into consideration all country possibilities, not just one. Variations in all firm functions between countries must be handled with reasonable efficiency.

CONTROL

Firm and managerial functions must be controlled, in that managers must have some method of measuring actual performance and taking necessary steps to correct discrepancies which appear. Historically in capitalist countries, profit control has been a key feedback for private firms. A tacit plan of all companies is to make some profits, usually the more the better. If the firm has an accounting system which indicates that the company is losing money, corrective action is inevitable. The gross profit position is critical, but in complex modern firms the actual location of the loss may be equally important. A firm may have a profit decline, but which divisions and which products are showing the poorest results? The implication here is that the more refined the accounting techniques the firm may have, the better its control job will be performed. In addition to the usual accounting tools available to the firm, it may also use various statistical quality controls, operations research methodologies, and many other control tools developed over the years to help managers find and correct discrepancies as rapidly as possible.

Modern computers, combined with modern applied mathematical techniques and highly developed communications systems, have meant that control can be much more effective and efficient than in prior years. Thus for example, a modern MNC can easily generate daily cash flow reports at headquarters for all divisions in all countries. Space satellites can almost instantaneously transmit information anywhere on earth, and high speed computers can easily perform all necessary mathematical calculations. Or production discrepancies in Belgium can be discovered immediately in New York or Tokyo. It can be argued that the availability of high speed communications and computational capacity has really made the modern MNC possible, since with these aids control is possible anywhere to any degree required.

To correct a discrepancy, one must know that one exists. Thus the control function interlocks closely with planning. A firm is producing parts with a tolerance of plus or minus 0.003 inch, when the requirements are plus or minus 0.004 inch. What action is indicated? Here, nothing is done, since the production is within tolerance. Production and inspection proceedures might even be relaxed a bit, on the grounds that production is TOO accurate! However,if the plan called for tolerances of plus or minus 0.0001 inch, all production is scrap, and drastic corrective action has to be taken.

Such planning/control situations exist in all parts of the firm and in all firm functions. A manager might be allowed to spend up to $2,000 on capital improvements for his division without consulting his boss, which is both a plan and a control. Or a product might be produced if it contributed at least 5 percent above its direct costs to general overheads. Some of the most important modern controls are budgets, which are used by most productive enterprises. Many are never written down, but they do exist! The budget is both a plan and a control. The control technique works only when actual performance is measured against planned performance.

ORGANIZATION

All productive enterprises have some form of organzation, however informal or simple. A small firm may have an owner/manager and a few employees, and the total organization consists of knowing who is boss and who does what. Such organizations are typically quite informal, and as long as they remain small and simple, quite effective. But as firms grow in size, the large numbers of workers, technicians, and middle managers must be grouped in some order so that work can be done efficiently. The more complicated a firm becomes, the more likely that its organization will differ somewhat from other productive firms. One company may find it expedient to organize on a territorial basis; another, in the same industry, may choose a functional plan. It is clear that the way in which the company is organized will have considerable effects on firm efficiency. A highly centralized organization, where an autocratic top management makes all decisions and passes them down to subordinates, will have considerably different productive results than a highly decentralized firm, where middle managers are responsible for making many decisions. It is not immediately clear, of course, which firm would be more efficient in this case, given wide variations in individual psychology, education, and sociological attitudes.

MNCs can have very complex organizational problems. They often are larger, and sheer size leads to organizational complexity. They also are active in many countries, and local problems may vary widely, requiring organizational change. Persons from another culture may prefer authoritarian situations, while workers at home are more comfortable with decentralized situations. Skilled workers available in one country may be unavailable or scarce in another, which may require organizational change. Efforts to force people into molds which they do not fit psychologically or culturally may create many organizational probems.

STAFFING

Firms must obtain personpower of all sorts to perform both firm and managerial fucntions. Recruitment can range from casual hirings off the street to elaborate personnel plans for long term recruitment of thousands of people in hundreds of categories, but in some way firms have to obtain personnel to perform their productive job.

Efficiencies here also can be quite varied. A firm which makes no effort to determine in advance whether or not a person is suited to the postion he or she will fill probably will have greater difficulties with labor turnover, personal conflicts with other workers, and similar problems than will a company which tries to fit men and women to available jobs. In a similar manner, firms which try to train employees systematically for the jobs they hold will probably do better than one in which employees are expected to pick up necessary knowledge informally.

Good people are hard to find everywhere, and an important part of staffing is a systematic search for qualified and able candidates. It is possible to rely on luck, in the hope that the right person will show up, but such informal personnel planning typically leads to inefficiencies.

Staffing is related to the country in which it takes place, and it is clear that any MNC had many additional problems and opportunities in this area. If one country has too few of some type of key personnel, they can be imported; or if some country has a surplus of talent, it may be recruited for use in other nations. Relevant also is the problem of making sure that the selection technques valid in the local culture are valid in the foreign country. Thus, if the firm is accustomed to obtaining certain types of technicians by advertising in trade papers, and no such papers are available, it is clear that the technique will have to be changed.

DIRECTION, LEADERSHIP, AND MOTIVATION

Employees and junior managers must be directed in some manner to perform the necessary tasks in the productive organization. This category of managerial functions deals with the manner in which such direction and leadership is carried out. As with other firm and managerial functions, the way in which this direction and leadership is performed makes a considerable difference in the efficiency of the firm. A plant in which foremen literally beat up workers to make them perform properly has quite a different efficiency than one in which workers and foremen have participative, consultative attitudes toward direction. While leadership may prove quite difficult to define adeuqately, most perceptive observers can immediately detect a situation characterized by weak and vacillating leadership as compared to one in which the leader is strong and competent.

Critical Elements of the Management Process

The above firm and managerial functions in effect answer the question: What do business firms and their managers do? They perform productive work in any society, and the way in which they do their job can be categorized by the above functions. The way which they perform these functions will determine the efficiency with which their firm operates. Given the complexity of modern productive enterprise, it seems clear that no two firms will be exactly alike in terms of their efficiency. Some will be strong and efficient in some of these areas; others will not. Personnel differences can make two firms similarly organized quite different in terms of productive efficiency.

Proper decision making on any or all of the critical elements of the management process tends to become more complex in an international firm as compared to a purely local operation. Usually the range of possible gains and losses is larger when the firm operates in a variety of environments. Possibilities which are irrelevant for a local company become feasible for MNCs, and the dangers of making wrong choices correspondingly increase. As we will see later, the reasons for making particular choices in international operations depend in large part on the kind of environment the firms faces in its multinational activities, but it is clear that the problem is much more complex than for a locally oriented company.

Figure 3-2 categorizes these firm and managerial functions, which are called the critical elements of the management process. These elements are important to both international and local productive enterprise, since every productive firm must, formally or informally, perform these functions in some manner in order to survive.

The reason for presenting this material at this point is that these critical elements are related to the firm's external environment in a variety of ways. For example, staffing clearly depends on the kinds of people available for positions, and people will differ in education, attitudes, stamina, and beliefs as the firms shift from one culture to another. The productive firm is in large part environment bound, and the MNC operates in two or more environments, any of which may have many significant differences from the others. If the way in which managers perform their firm and managerial functions depends on their environment, it is necessary to know what firm and productive functions might be, which is what this section has covered. The next step is to consider how the environment does directly influence managerial performance.

Figure 3-2 lists in considerable detail the various firm and managerial functions. In effect, it is a taxonomy of decision making. If a manager makes a decision, it will be in the area of these detailed critical elements, and often more than one of these will be involved.

Basic Concepts of Nationalism

Since before 1700, the idea of the nation state has assumed increasing importance in world affairs. The basic notion is still with us, and it is likely to remain for many decades to come, even though, from a variety of points of view, the concept may prove to be completely outmoded as a viable political-economic-technical production unit under modern conditions. Manmade institutions change slowly, and generations are required to force even the most essential changes. Indeed, the creation of the modern national state was a long term process which took several thousand years to accomplish.

FIGURE 3-2

CRITICAL ELEMENTS OF THE MANAGEMENT PROCESS

B_1: *Planning and Innovation*

1.1 Basic organizational objectives pursued and the form of their operational expression.

1.2 Types of plans utilized.

1.3 Time horizon of plans and planning.

1.4 Degree and extent to which enterprise operations are spelled out in plans (i.e., preprogrammed).

1.5 Flexibility of plans.

1.6 Methodologies, techniques, and tools used in planning and decision making.

1.7 Extent and effectiveness of employee participation in planning.

1.8 Managerial behavior in the planning process.

1.9 Degree and extent of information distortion in planning.

1.10 Degree and extent to which scientific method is effectively applied by enterprise personnel—both managers and nonmanagers —in dealing with causation and futurity problems.

1.11 Nature, extent, and rate of innovation and risk-taking in enterprise operations over a given period of time.

1.12 Ease or difficulty of introducing changes and innovations in enterprise operations.

B_2: *Control*

2.1 Types of strategic performance and control standards used in different areas; e.g., production, marketing, finance, personnel.

2.2 Types of control techniques used.

2.3 Nature and structure of information feedback systems used for control purposes.

2.4 Timing and procedures for corrective action.

2.5 Degree of looseness or tightness of control over personnel.

2.6 Extent and nature of unintended effects resulting from the overall control system employed.

2.7 Effectiveness of the control system in compelling events to conform to plans.

B_3: *Organization*

3.1 Size of representative enterprise and its major subunits.

3.2 Degree of centralization or decentralization of authority.

3.3 Degree of work specialization (division of labor).

3.4 Spans of control.

3.5 Basic departmentation and grouping of activities. Extent and uses of service departments.

3.6 Extent and uses of staff generalists and specialists.

3.7 Extent and uses of functional authority.

FIGURE 3-2—*Continued*

3.8 Extent and degree of organizational confusion and friction regarding authority and responsibility relationships.

3.9 Extent and uses of committee and group decision making.

3.10 Nature, extent, and uses of the informal organization.

3.11 Degree and extent to which the organization structure (i.e., the formal organization) is mechanical or flexible with regard to causing and/or adapting to changing conditions.

B_4: *Staffing*

4.1 Methods used in recruiting personnel.

4.2 Criteria used in selecting and promoting personnel.

4.3 Techniques and criteria used in appraising personnel.

4.4 Nature and uses of job descriptions.

4.5 Levels of compensation.

4.6 Nature, extent, and time absorbed in enterprise training programs and activities.

4.7 Extent of informal individual development.

4.8 Policies and procedures regarding the layoff and dismissal of personnel.

4.9 Ease or difficulty in dismissing personnel no longer required or desired.

4.10 Ease or difficulty of obtaining and maintaining personnel of all types with desired skills and abilities.

B_5: *Direction, Leadership, and Motivation*

5.1 Degree and extent of authoritarian vs. participative management. (This relates to autocratic vs. consultative direction).

5.2 Techniques and methods used for motivating managerial personnel.

5.3 Techniques and methods used for motivating nonmanagerial personnel.

5.4 Supervisory techniques used.

5.5 Communication structure and techniques.

5.6 Degree and extent to which communication is ineffective among personnel of all types.

5.7 Ease or difficulty of motivating personnel to perform efficiently, and to improve their performance and abilities over time (irrespective of the types of incentives that may be utilized for this purpose).

5.8 Degree and extent of identification that exists between the interests and objectives of individuals, work groups, departments, and the enterprise as a whole.

5.9 Degree and extent of trust and cooperation or distrust and conflict among personnel of all types.

5.10 Degree and extent of frustration, absenteeism, and turnover among personnel.

FIGURE 3-2—*Continued*

5.11 Degree and extent of wasteful time and effort resulting from restrictive work practices, unproductive bargaining, conflicts, etc.

B_6: *Marketing (Policies Pursued)*

6.1 Product line (degree of diversification as specialization, rate of change, product quality).

6.2 Channels of distribution and types and location of customers.

6.3 Pricing (for key items, in relation to costs, profit margins, quantity and trade discount structure).

6.4 Sales promotion and key sales appeals (types used and degree of aggressiveness in sales promotion).

B_7: *Production and Procurement*

7.1 Make or buy (components, supplies, facilities, services, extent to which subcontracting is used, etc.).

7.2 Number, types, and locations of major suppliers.

7.3 Timing of procurement of major supplies.

7.4 Average inventory levels (major supplies, goods in process, completed output).

7.5 Minimum, maximum, and average size of production runs.

7.6 Degree to which production operations are stabilized.

7.7 Combination of factor inputs used in major products produced.

7.8 Basic production processes used.

7.9 Extent of automation and mechanization in enterprise operations.

B_8: *Research and Development*

8.1 Nature and extent of R & D activity (e.g., product development and improvement, new material usages, new production processes and technology).

B_9: *Finance*

9.1 Types of financing (e.g., equity, debt, short term, long term).

9.2 Sources of capital.

9.3 Major uses of capital.

9.4 Protection of capital.

9.5 Distribution of earnings.

B_{10}: *Public and External Relations* (The relationships, attitudes, and policies of enterprise management regarding major types of external agents and organizations.)

10.1 Customers and consumer relations (e.g.: Does firm management regard consumer loyalty and satisfaction as being important, or is it chiefly interested in short run results, quick profits?).

10.2 Supplier relations.

10.3 Investor and creditor relations.

10.4 Union relations.

10.5 Government relations.

10.6 Community relations (e.g., educational institutions, chamber of commerce, business and professional associations, community welfare activities).

The modern nation state has a variety of characteristics which are relevant for international business operations. The more critical ones are summarized below.

1.   Sovereignty. The state is supreme in the modern world, in terms of its ability to affect directly its own people and territories. There is no generally accepted international law which directs national states to behave in prescribed manners in given circumstances. There are many types of agreements, treaties and generally recognized international laws which nations typically observe, but this compliance is voluntary, not forced. Also, such general international principles are partial, not total.

One example may illustrate this point. An American firm may have its property seized by the American government in the United States. Such seizures are common in cases where the state needs property for developments such as new highways. However, an elaborate body of domestic law provides for redress to the injured party.   The state cannot take property without just compensation, and the aggrieved party can go to court and obtain a verdict which is as fair as judicial competence and ingenuity can devise. But an American firm which has its property seized in Cuba is subject to Cuban, not American law, and Cuban law may be quite different. There is nothing to prevent Cuba from passing laws or decrees stating that foreign property now belongs to the state. American owners can complain by going to Cuban courts, not American, and they can complain to their own government, but, short of going to war, the American government can do little to restore the seized property or to recompense the owners. There is no international law which Cuba must observe in such a case unless it voluntarily chooses to do so. The eventual financial results in this latter case would be considerably different than in the domestic case, and the reason would basically be the notion of national sovereignty of each nation state.

There is an international court which is organized to deal with such international legal problems. However, the international court cannot assume jurisdiction over any sovereign state unless that state voluntarily yields its sovereignty in the specific case in question. Thus two states involved in a border dispute might, if the government of each so decided, ask the World Court to decide the issue and agree to abide by the decision, but there is no supranational authority to force the states to do this. If they choose to fight instead, they are free to do so, subject only to their military power, pressures from friends and enemies, the United Nations, and other pressures exerted by sovereign states. The World Court has been effective on occasion, but it is not a total supranational legal authority.

Countries may also decide to give up a part of their sovereignty, but only if they choose to do so. Thus a small Central American state may voluntarily decide to key its currency to the U.S. dollar and maintain it at par with the dollar. It may even use dollars as a local currency.   But it does this by choice, not because it is forced to do so.

In a similar manner, each nation state can have whatever legal system it prefers. Critical legal points affecting asset ownership, labor relations, foreign policy, corporate organization, personal liability, and innumerable other legal situations can be whatever the rulers and people of each national state want them to be. Political organization can also be strikingly different between countries, since each state has its own perogatives in this area.

A national state typically has its own monetary system, organized in whatever manner it finds convenient. The state can control the country's economy in any manner, systematic or not, which reflects the ruling elite's view of what is proper. Economic controls over national and international trade, investments, consumption, prices, outputs, and similar matters critical to firms within the country can be manipulated in any way seen desirable for the national interest.

These problems are not completely new to American firms, since individual American states have different laws and taxes which have considerble impact on firms. But in such cases, federal appeal is always possible, and some legal resolution is usually achieved. In international dealings, this federal mechanism is lacking.

Sovereignty also implies that the country is able to defend itself in any way it sees fit. Each country has some military establishment responsible not only for domestic order but also for defense against external enemies.

There exist generally accepted principles about the way foreigners or foreign firms should be treated, but there is no court of last resort on the international level. Whenever a firm chooses to go abroad, it invariably runs some additional risk because of this notion of national sovereignty.

2. War. Since there is no generally agreed upon mechanism for the settlement of disputes between nations, war is the last resort in cases of violent disagreement. An aggrieved nation can always resort to armed force, taking whatever risks are implied by this action.

War historically evolved as a sort of plunder operation against the next tribe or town, and this attitude persisted into the 20th Century. Both World Wars I and II were partially conceived as operations in which the victor would be able to grab many assets from the vanquished, including large chunks of real estate. In part, the attitude persists today, particularly in border dispute wars that now rage in many parts of the world.

A modern difficulty, which has become increasingly evident since 1945, is that a plunder war is impossible for large, atomically armed major powers. A paradox which has plagued both the Soviet Union and the United States in recent years is that there really is no way of resolving a major dispute between these powers except in an insane way (i.e., totally destroying both parties). But no other effective way of conflict resolution has yet evolved for this kind of situation. Small wars of the Korea, Afghanistan, or Vietnam type have dangerous implications for the large powers, but to date they have been kept in check.

Smaller countries still fight on. Local revolutionary conflicts are still very common, and literally dozens of wars have been fought since World War II. Five or more are on now, and it doesn't matter when you read these words...there are ALWAYS five or six small wars raging on this planet. The participants these days tend to be newer countries in Africa, Asia, and Latin America, where ancient tribal loyalties, modern marxist politics, and border problems still create conflicts. World trade in military equipment is one of the largest single items in the total trading pattern, and poor countries still prefer guns to butter in many, many cases.

The relevance of this point to MNCs is that the international economy is quite chaotic at times, and a company can be caught in a war which can create many difficulties. Lost production, property destruction, and much more can be the lot of a firm caught between fighting factions.

3. National spirit. Many national states go to great lengths to inculcate their citizens with the national spirit, or nationalism. Americans salute their flag, listen to legends of American heroes of the glorious past, sing patriotic songs, and generally are expected to behave as patriotic Americans. To do otherwise makes one suspect in the eyes of his fellow citizens. But Frenchmen do the same with French heroes, French patriotic songs, slogans, and the like...as do Germans, Englishmen, Paraguayans, Indians, and so on through the 150 plus countries of the world. Each national point of view differs considerably from every other one, which leads to misunderstandings, suspicions, hatreds, and war. Americans might study the Mexican elementary school texts on the Mexican-American war with some profit. One is not sure that the same war is being talked about. Similarly the Israeli view of the Arab sitation differs significantly from the Egyptian or Syrian view, to put it mildly.

It takes a long time to inculcate properly the national spirit deemed desirable by many nations. Many national states such as the United States and Western European countries still, after hundreds of years, have many regional and family loyalties which conflict with national loyalty. An American from Mississippi may have certain points of view which are actually revolutionary in their implications, and a Welshman or Scotsman in England may still feel that the English are foreign conquerors after five hundred years. Newer nations often have to try to build up a national spirit from scratch in a generation, resulting in fervent hypernationalistic outbursts so common in the modern world. Such attitudes bear quite directly on foreign owned firms, since the slogan of Mexico for the Mexicans or India for the Indians or whatever is hardly calculated to develop friendly and sympathetic attitudes toward nonnationals. This attitude is made more acute by the long history of colonial oppression in many parts of the world. Newly independent countries treasure the trappings of nationalism, and the UN seat, the modern parliament buildings, and the national flag are regarded very seriously indeed by newer states. Foreigners ignore such feelings at their own peril.

These nationalistic attitudes, which are taken for granted, have curious results on the international economy. Since every state is sovereign, by implication everyone is equally important, and discussions of Paraguay or Ecuador receive careful study and close attention by businessmen, political scientists, and economists. However, the national income of Ecuador is only a fraction of the county income of Los Angeles County, but who cares about that? The state of Indiana has a larger GNP than all but a dozen or so of the nations of the world, yet few persons outside the state are ever concerned, and the balance of payments of Indiana is not even calculated.

A further effect of nationalism is that each country is different, in a variety of ways, and these differences must be studied in order to determine what effect these differences will have on contemplated actions. In our case, the action is international business activities; if firms are going to operate in a series of countries, they must explore how these national differences do affect the internal activities of their companies.

External Constraints on Enterprise Management

The above discussion indicated that a variety of local problems are handled in quite different manners in various countries. The next problem is to determine how these differences might affect the operation of productive firms within a given country.

For example, it might prove impossible for a foreigner to operate a steel mill in a country which prevents production from starting. In a second country, a steel mill might be built, but local law may be such that the actual production must be carried on in ways quite different than those in Japan or the United States. Countries typically have very different business law, customs, economic systems, and rates of change, and firm operations must necessarily adjust to these facts.

This apparently obvious point is often overlooked in studies of business in a single country, simply because the factors which can vary between countries are constant. A Japanese firm whose only operations are in Japan can assume, correctly, that only one antitrust law, labor law, or contract law is relevant. If one knows the law and observes its strictures, this factor can be considered constant; but if this Japanese firm begins to operate in the United States, it will quickly discover that it now has environmental variables rather than constants. U.S. labor law differs significantly from Japanese, as some companies have learned to their sorrow. Since such legal requirements have considerable impact on costs and modes of operation, the differences are important.

Any external factor in the firm's environment which affects the way in which the firm and its management function is important. Such external factors may operate by restricting or changing prices of inputs; by forcing changes in production, marketing, or financial processes; or by restricting price changes of outputs. In any of these cases, the internal operations of the firm will be different than they would be in absence of the given constraint. This is why international management differs from local management. Managers do the same things and think the same way, but their answers differ, since the environments differ.

KINDS OF EXTERNAL CONSTRAINTS

Figure 3-3 presents a systematic list of the critical local external constraints which tend to have direct impact on international firm management and productive efficiency. The four major categories of constraints are those which have maximum direct impact on firms. There are two ways in which thse constraints can affect firm activities. First, they can operate directly on business or firm functions. Thus a law prohibiting child labor presents a legal constraint which operates directly on the personnel and staffing critical business elements. Managers may or may not approve of the law, but they must adjust to it as best they can.

A second major impact is in terms of the decisions and activities of managers. All managers are a product of some culture, and their attitudes and perceptions are based on prior experience, which is in large part determined by the educational and sociological setting in which they have lived. An American manager, faced with a business decision involving subjective risk (such as deciding whether or not to launch a new marketing campaign for a hair tonic), may make his or her decision based on attitudes and premises very different from a French manager in exactly the same position. The reason for the difference would be that these managers have lived in quite different environments.

Figure 3-4 illustrates this general problem. Some constraints, as the child labor law noted earlier, affect the way firm and managerial functions are performed directly, as shown by the arrow from the C´s to the B´s. Other constraints affect managers directly, who in turn affect the B´s, as shown by the arrow from the C´s to the managers. The double arrow from the managers to the B´s indicate that there is a constant interaction of management and the way in which the B´s are performed. Thus the child labor law causes managers to behave differently than they might if the law did not exist, which in turn leads to changes in staffing policies set by management. In the sales promotion situation discussed above, the fact that in France a law may prevent certain kinds of advertising on television may also lead to direct impact of the C´s on the marketing B´s, as well as the impact on manager´s decisions about the campaign in the first place.

EXAMPLES OF EXTERNAL CONSTRAINT IMPACT ON MANAGERIAL AND FIRM FUNCTIONS

The basic idea presented here is that if the environment is different, firms will be operated and managed differently, leading to different efficiency results between similar firms in different environments. Consider an economy which is characterized by high levels of illiteracy. Many Third World countries have between 30 and 80 percent illiteracy rates. This educational constraint would directly influence the types of control techniques a company could utilize effectively. Any control system which required lower level personnel to fill out forms, use written instructions, or report in writing to supervisors would be unworkable. The control system developed in such a situation would be strikingly different than in a firm where all personnel were literate. Such organizational factors as spans of control would be affected as well. A large firm might find that, because workers are illiterate, closer supervision is necessary, and

FIGURE 3—3

ENVIRONMENTAL CONSTRAINTS

C_1: *Educational Characteristics*

    1.1   Literacy level: The percentage of the total population and those presently employed in industry who can read, write, and do simple arithmetic calculations, and the average years of schooling of adults.

    1.2   Specialized vocational and technical training and general secondary education: Extent, types, and quality of education and training of this kind not directly under 'the control or direction of industrial enterprises. The type, quantity, and quality of persons obtaining such education or training and the proportion of those with such education and training employed in industry.

    1.3   Higher education: The percentage of the total population and those employed in industry with post–high-school education plus the types and quality of such education. The types of persons obtaining higher education.

    1.4   Special management development programs: The extent and quality of management development programs which are not run internally by productive enterprises and which are aimed at improving the skills and abilities of managers and potential managers. The quantity and quality of managers and potential managers of different types and levels attending or having completed such programs.

    1.5   Attitude toward education: The general or dominant cultural attitudes toward education and the acquisition of knowledge, in terms of its presumed desirability. The general attitude toward different types of education.

    1.6   Education match with requirements: The extent and degree to which the types of formal education and training available in a given country fit the needs of productive enterprises on all levels of skill and achievement. This is essentially a summary category; depending on the type of job involved, different educational constraints indicated above would be more important.

C_2: *Sociological Characteristics*

    2.1   View toward industrial managers and management: The general or dominant social attitude toward industrial and business managers of all sorts, and the way that such managers tend to view their managerial jobs.

    2.2   View toward authority and subordinates: The general or dominant cultural attitude toward authority and persons in sub-

ordinate positions, and the way that industrial managers tend
to view their authority and their subordinates.

2.3 Interorganizational cooperation: Extent and degree to which
business enterprises, government agencies, labor unions, educational institutions, and other relevant organizations cooperate with each other in ways conducive to industrial efficiency
and general economic progress.

2.4 View toward achievement and work: The general or dominant
cultural attitude toward individual or collective achievement
and productive work in industry.

2.5 Class structure and individual mobility: The extent of opportunities for social class and individual mobility, both vertical
and horizontal, in a given country, and the means by which it
can be achieved.

2.6 View toward wealth and material gain: Whether or not the
acquisition of wealth from different sources is generally considered socially desirable, and the way that persons employed
in industry tend to view material gain.

2.7 View toward scientific method: The general social and dominant
individual attitude toward the use of rational, predictive techniques in solving various types of business, technical, economic,
and social problems.

2.8 View toward risk taking: Whether or not the taking of various
types of personal collective or rational risks is generally considered acceptable, as well as the dominant view toward specific
types of risk taking in business and industry. The degree and
extent to which risk taking tends to be a rational process in
a particular country.

2.9 View toward change: The general cultural attitude toward a
social change of any type which bears directly on industrial
performance in a given country, and the dominant attitude
among persons employed in industry toward all types of significant changes in enterprise operations.

C_3: *Political and Legal Characteristics*

3.1 Relevant legal rules of the game: Quality, efficiency, and effectiveness of the legal structure in terms of business law, labor law,
tax law, and general law relevant to business. Degree of enforcement, reliability, etc.

3.2 Defense policy: Impact of defense policy on industrial enterprise in terms of trading with potential enemies, purchasing
policies, strategic industry development, labor and resource
competition, and similar factors.

3.3 Foreign policy: Impact of policy on industrial enterprise in terms of trading restrictions, quotas, tariffs, customs unions, foreign exchange, etc.

3.4 Political stability: Influence on industrial enterprises of revolutions, changes in regime, stability or instability over protracted periods, etc.

3.5 Political organization: Type of organization in constitutional terms; degrees of centralization or decentralization; degree and extent of red tape, delays, uncertainty, and confusion in industry-government dealings; pressure groups and their effectiveness; political parties and their philosophies; etc.

3.6 Flexibility of law and legal changes: Degree to which relevant barriers to the efficient management of industrial enterprises can be changed and the timeliness of such changes; predictability and certainty of legal actions; etc.

C_4: *Economic Characteristics*

4.1 General economic framework: Including such factors as the overall economic organization of the country (i.e., capitalistic, Marxist, mixed), property rights, and similar factors.

4.2 Central banking system and monetary policy: The organization and operation of the central banking system, including the controls over commercial banks, the ability and willingness to control the money supply, the effectiveness of government policies regarding price stability, commercial bank reserves, discounting, credit controls, and similar factors.

4.3 Fiscal policy: General policies concerning government expenditures, their timing, and their impact; the general level of deficit, surplus, or balance; total share of government expenditures in gross national product.

4.4 Economic stability: The vulnerability of the economy to economic fluctuations of depression and boom, price stability, and overall economic growth stability.

4.5 Organization of capital markets: The existence of such markets as stock and bond exchanges, their honesty, effectiveness, and total impact; the size and role of commercial banking, including loan policies and availability of credit to businessmen; the existence of other capital sources such as savings and loan associations, government-sponsored credit agencies, insurance company loan activities, etc.

4.6 Factor endowment: Relative supply of capital and land (agricultural and raw materials) per capita; size and general health of the work force.

4.7 Market size: Total effective purchasing power within the country plus relevant export markets.

4.8 Social overhead capital: Availability and quality of power supplies, water, communications systems, transportation, public warehousing, physical transfer facilities, housing, etc.

spans would tend to shorten. But this would increase the demand for well trained, literate supervisors, who would be in very short supply. If such supervisors cannot be found, then spans might be very wide and very inefficient, which is one reason why such countries have few large firms. Foreign firms moving into this sort of environment must take into account such educational constraints if they are to operate efficiently.

FIGURE 3—4

EFFECTS OF EXTERNAL CONSTRAINTS ON INTERNAL FIRM FUNCTIONS

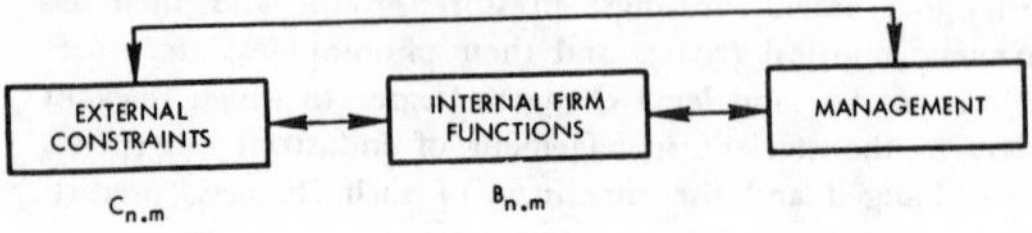

Illiteracy impacts directly on staffing as well. It does little good to advertise in writing for suitable candidates if they cannot read, and therefore other methods of recruitment must be devised. Job descriptions also change rapidly in such a situation, from written to oral presentations. Training programs tend to expand rapidly to make up for basic educational deficiencies of personnel recruited. If they do not, the firm stumbles along operating with considerable inefficiency. The difficulty of obtaining properly trained skilled employees in such an environment leads to use of less qualified people, which leads to everything from high accident rates to low productive efficiency.

Direction is also difficult in such a situation. Communication techniques become oral, not written. Frustration of both managers and employees remains at a high level when communication presents difficulties. Such a labor force is usually sick much of the time, and short time horizons combined with lack of stamina result in high turnover and absenteeism, with corresponding impacts on firm efficiency.

The marketing channels and appeals which can be best utilized in an illiterate culture differ radically from those used in more literate countries. Advertising by the written word is difficult, and other methods must be used. In production, the basic processes used and the extent of automation depend directly on the skill levels of workers, and what is feasible in West Germany may be impossible in such a country. Systematic research and development in such an environment is virtually impossible because of the lack of trained personnel.

A second example taken from the sociological constraints is the operation of a firm in a culture where the view toward wealth and material gain is quite different from that found in the West. Consider firm operations in a strongly Hindu culture, where the majority of the population really believes that large material gains are unimportant and that man's real rewards are in the hereafter. One would expect that in such a situation planning problems would become extremely difficult. Planning implicitly suggests that man can do something about the future; and, in a society which holds that God is largely responsible for future events, it will be quite difficult to interest anyone in the details of good planning. The types of plans utilized and the time horizon of plans in a company in this environment will be quite different than in a society with a different outlook on man's role in the future. The key factor of innovation will probably largely be overlooked, since it will be irrelevant in the view of most workers and managers.

Staffing problems will abound. If few persons care much about life in the present, levels of compensation will hardly be important in determining what job is done and in what way. Other methods of encouraging good job performance will have to be devised. Note here that a manager raised in a Western culture has to change his or her fundumental beliefs about the way people behave before he or she can manage effectively. Cross-cultural situations involving strikingly different sociological behavior can often be totally frustrating to both foreign managers and local workers, and this is one major reason why MNCs find it difficult to transfer their home grown efficiencies. Local firms trying to emulate those companies from very different cultures often find that they cannot, since their local managers behave so differently from those foreigners who developed the system.

In such cultures, production is relatively unimportant. This will lead to low income standards for the population and ulcers for the production manager, who must constantly try to encourage performance in his personnel which they regard as totally trivial. None of the production functions will be performed very well simply because few persons in such a society care much whether or not they are performed at all.

The above example is deliberately pushed to extremes, but cultures exist, along with frustrated managers within them, which are very similar to the above description. The major point is that in such a culture, even if the attitudes discussed are only partially held by a large number of people, they can have a direct and immediate impact on the efficiency with which the critical elements of the managerial process are performed.

When cultures seem fairly similar, it is easy to conclude that they are identical, which can lead to many difficulties. Most Americans seem to feel that Canadians are about like Americans, a viewpoint which deeply annoys Canadians. Hence, all of the above discussion really doesn't apply to Americans working in Canada, or Canadian firms operating in the U.S. But it does, although the constraints impact firms much more subtly. A labor dispute in Canada IS very different from one in the U.S., because Canadians are different! There may also be wide regional deviations within a country. What workers think and feel in British Columbia is quite different than they think and feel in Quebec. Similarly, a labor dispute in California is quite different from one in South Carolina. Those Canadian managers in the U.S., or those Americans in Canada, can get into deep trouble if they fail to grasp this point.

There have been numerous analyses of MNCs that failed in other countries, and invariably such analysis reveals that the MNC managers regarded as constant an environmental variable. That is, they assumed things were the same as at home, and proceeded to manage accordingly.

But if some critical environmental constraint is different, then disaster is certain. This observation is not restricted to managers in MNCs from any one country. Americans have failed in many places; Canadians have failed in the U.S.; Japanese have failed in the U.S. and Southeast Asia; and West Europeans have failed everywhere. But MNC managers have also succeeded brilliantly in most cases. The key is environmental sensitivity, which means in practice taking full account of the local environment when practicing those critical elements of the management process. The B elements are interrelated intimately with the C´s in many ways, and the MNC manager´s problem, along with local managers, is to figure out exactly how. The neater the match, the better the firm will function.

It is possible to go through the legal/political and economic constraints in the same manner as above, indicating just how the external environment interacts with and affects internal firm management. This is the essence of international management. All firm and managerial functions everywhere are essentially the same, but the decisions come out differently, because the environment is different.

The Comparative Management Matrix

All of the suggested interrelationships between the external firm environments and the internal operations of the firm are indicated in Table 3-1. The external constraints are listed horizontally across the top of the table and the critical elements of the management process are listed vertically. The x´s in the table indicate a direct impact of the given external constraint with the critical element. This table is in effect a statement of functional relationships of a given element to various constraints.

This table contains enormous amounts of information. Thus line one in words says that: basic organizational objectives pursued and the form of their operational expression depend on (or is a function of) special management development programs, view toward industrial managers and management, interorganizational cooperation, view toward achievement and work, class structure and individual mobility, view toward wealth and material gain, view toward scientific method, view toward risk taking, view toward change, relevant legal rules, defense policy, foreign policy, political stability, political organization, flexibility of law and legal change, the general economic framework, central banking system and monetary policy, fiscal policy, economic stability, organization of capital markets, factor endowment, market size, and social overhead capital.

It has been observed that even very efficient firms operate at perhaps the five percent level of efficiency. Thinking about this matrix and the above single line may suggest why. It is virtually impossible for even a very well educated and astute manager to know enough about his or her environment, even at home, to get things right very often. Necessarily some selectivity is involved in worrying about what matters in the environment. The perceptive manager doesn´t worry about everything, but rather the constraints that can be deadly. How to figure out what really matters is really the art of management. No text, including this one, can really explain how to choose, but choose

TABLE 3—1

CRITICAL MANAGERIAL ELEMENTS AND EXTERNAL CONSTRAINTS

	C_1 Educational						C_2 Sociological									C_3 Political-Legal						C_4 Economic							
	1	2	3	4	5	6	1	2	3	4	5	6	7	8	9	1	2	3	4	5	6	1	2	3	4	5	6	7	8
B_1 1			x				x		x	x	x	x	x	x	x	x	x	x	x	x	x	x	x	x	x	x	x	x	x
2	x	x	x	x		x	x	x	x				x	x	x	x	x	x	x	x	x	x	x	x	x	x	x	x	x
3		x	x	x					x	x			x	x	x	x	x	x	x	x	x	x	x	x	x	x			
4		x	x	x		x	x	x	x		x		x	x	x	x	x	x	x	x	x	x			x	x			
5		x	x	x					x				x	x	x	x	x	x	x		x	x	x	x	x	x			
6		x	x	x			x		x			x	x	x	x	x	x	x			x	x			x				
7	x	x	x	x	x	x	x	x	x	x	x	x	x	x	x	x						x					x		
8		x	x	x	x	x	x	x		x	x	x	x	x	x														
9	x	x	x	x	x	x	x	x	x	x	x	x	x	x	x				x	x									
10	x	x	x	x	x	x	x			x	x		x	x	x														
11	x	x	x	x	x	x	x	x		x	x	x	x	x	x	x	x	x	x	x	x	x	x	x	x	x	x	x	x
12	x	x	x	x	x	x	x	x	x	x	x	x	x	x	x	x	x	x	x	x	x	x	x	x	x	x	x	x	x
B_2 1	x	x	x	x	x	x	x	x		x	x	x	x	x	x	x	x	x				x			x	x			
2	x	x	x	x		x	x	x		x			x	x	x	x	x	x				x			x	x			
3	x	x	x	x		x	x	x		x			x	x	x	x						x			x				
4	x	x	x	x				x		x			x	x	x	x						x			x				
5	x	x	x	x	x	x	x	x	x	x	x	x	x		x	x			x	x		x					x		
6	x	x	x	x	x	x	x	x	x	x	x	x	x	x	x	x			x	x	x	x							
7	x	x	x	x		x	x	x	x	x	x	x	x	x	x	x	x	x	x	x	x	x	x	x	x				
B_3 1	x	x	x	x			x	x	x	x	x	x	x	x	x	x	x	x	x	x		x	x	x	x	x		x	x
2	x	x	x	x	x	x	x	x		x	x	x	x			x						x						x	x
3	x	x	x	x		x	x	x	x	x	x	x	x			x						x					x	x	x
4	x	x	x	x			x	x		x	x		x			x													x
5	x	x	x	x			x	x	x	x	x		x																x
6		x	x	x		x	x	x	x	x		x				x						x					x		x
7	x	x	x	x		x	x	x		x	x		x			x						x							
8	x	x	x	x	x	x	x	x		x	x		x			x			x			x							x
9		x	x	x		x	x	x		x	x		x	x															
10	x	x	x	x		x	x	x		x	x											x							
11		x	x	x	x	x	x	x		x	x		x	x	x	x						x							
B_4 1	x	x	x	x	x	x	x	x		x	x	x	x			x	x											x	x
2		x		x	x	x	x	x		x	x	x	x			x												x	x
3		x	x	x	x	x	x	x		x	x	x	x			x													
4		x	x	x		x	x	x		x	x		x			x													
5							x	x		x	x	x	x			x						x			x	x	x		
6	x	x	x	x	x	x	x	x		x	x	x	x		x	x											x		
7	x	x	x	x	x	x	x	x		x	x	x		x		x											x		
8				x				x		x	x		x			x											x		x
9							x	x		x	x					x			x	x									
10	x	x	x	x	x	x	x	x		x	x	x	x			x	x					x	x	x	x		x		x

TABLE 3—1 (Continued)

	C_1 Educational						C_2 Sociological									C_3 Political-Legal						C_4 Economic							
	1	2	3	4	5	6	1	2	3	4	5	6	7	8	9	1	2	3	4	5	6	1	2	3	4	5	6	7	8
B_5 1	x	x	x	x			x	x		x	x																		
2		x	x	x		x	x	x		x	x	x	x			x													
3	x	x			x	x	x	x		x	x	x	x			x													
4	x	x	x	x	x	x	x	x		x	x	x	x																
5	x	x	x	x		x	x	x		x		x	x			x													
6	x	x	x	x	x	x	x	x		x	x	x																x	
7	x	x	x	x	x	x	x	x		x	x	x	x															x	
8	x				x		x	x		x	x	x		x	x	x												x	
9							x	x	x	x	x	x				x													
10	x	x	x	x	x	x	x	x	x	x	x	x		x	x	x										x		x	
11							x	x	x	x	x	x				x										x		x	
B_6 1									x				x	x	x	x	x	x				x	x	x	x	x	x	x	x
2									x				x			x	x	x				x	x	x	x	x	x	x	x
3									x				x			x	x	x				x	x	x	x	x	x	x	x
4	x									x	x	x	x			x						x						x	x
B_7 1									x				x			x	x		x			x		x	x	x	x	x	x
2									x				x			x	x	x				x				x	x	x	x
3									x				x			x						x				x	x	x	x
4									x				x			x	x					x				x	x	x	x
5									x				x			x	x					x			x	x	x	x	x
6									x				x			x	x	x	x	x		x				x	x	x	x
7	x	x	x	x		x	x	x		x	x	x	x			x	x	x				x	x	x		x	x	x	x
8	x	x	x		x		x			x						x	x	x	x			x				x	x	x	x
9	x	x	x		x					x						x	x	x	x			x				x	x	x	x
B_8 1	x	x	x	x	x	x							x	x	x	x	x	x				x		x	x	x	x	x	x
B_9 1													x	x	x	x				x	x	x	x	x	x	x	x	x	
2							x						x	x	x	x				x	x	x	x	x	x	x	x	x	
3							x					x	x	x	x	x	x	x		x	x	x	x	x	x	x	x	x	x
4												x	x	x	x	x	x	x	x			x	x	x	x	x			
5							x		x	x	x	x	x	x	x	x						x			x	x			
B_{10} 1										x	x	x	x	x	x	x	x					x					x		x
2							x	x	x	x	x	x	x			x	x	x	x			x			x	x	x		x
3							x	x	x	x	x	x	x	x		x	x					x	x	x	x	x	x		
4	x	x	x				x	x	x	x	x	x	x			x		x	x	x	x	x	x	x	x				
5							x	x	x	x	x	x	x	x	x	x	x	x	x	x	x	x							
6	x	x	x	x	x		x	x	x	x	x	x	x	x	x	x			x	x	x	x							

the manager must.

The general problem is made more complex by interrelationships between the constraints. A country with an illiterate population will have, as a result, poorer legal-political and economic constraints than a country with a highly educated population. Law, politics, and economics are manipulated and managed by people as well, and the more able and well trained these people are, the better managed these functions will be.

Interrelationships also exist between the firm and managerial functions. Marketing is not performed in a vacuum; production, finance, planning, organization, and so on also contribute to marketing results. A common problem in both the external constraint and critical element problems for countries and firms is that of subsystem optimization. A country may have an excellent law which may, because of its ultraprecision, lead to poorer economic results. Or a firm may be very efficient in production at the expense of efficiencies in marketing. Such problems are extremely complex and often very subtle in that it is not immediately clear what over-optimization of a given factor may cost in other constraints or functions.

It is clear that no firm could possibly consider all of the possible interrelationships suggested in Table 3-1. Complete analysis would require more time and money than it would be worth. But consideration of a few critical interrelationships is possible. What is critical for one firm may be trivial to another, but in all cases, some critical element/environmental relationships are important. Thus a firm needing to finance activities in a given country will be quite concerned with economic C's dealing with money markets, while a firm which finances outside the country will not. But this latter firm might be very concerned about the availability of certain types of skilled labor, so the educational C's would be important. What matters depends on the firm and the specific problem, and somewhere in Figure 3-1 one will find the relevant relationships.

It is also useful to examine carefully the relationships in Table 3-1 which are quite different than in the home country. Thus Japanese firms in the United States are advised to ponder such factors as labor law and the behavioral C's, since these can be very different than in Japan. A Japanese firm in California can get into much trouble by acting as if they were in Osaka, which a few Japanese firms have done, and which American firms have often done in other countries.

International Constraints

To this point, we have considered what managers do (B's) and what types of local environmental factors (C's) will affect what managers do and how they might do it. There is another dimension to international business which remains to be explored. Each country is sovereign, and each is able, within wide limits, to adjust its posture toward foreign firms, states, and individuals as it sees fit. It is common for a nation to have special rules, laws, and regulations directed specifically at foreigners, and international companies must take into account such rules and how they might affect their operations within the country. These international constraints, which can differ between countries, often have quite direct impact on the manner in which the firm is managed, and on how it conducts its business within the given country.

It is convenient to divide these international constraints into the same categories as the local constraints: sociological, legal-political, and economic. The educational category is omitted, since no person is educated in an international environment. Education is tied to some country and can be considered as a totally local enviromental constraint. But the other constraints may differ enough between local and international segments of a given country to be analyzed separately.

A second relevant set of local constraints are those which come from the home country of the MNC. A firm may want to invest abroad, but its home country has a law or regulation against exportation of capital. Or tax law might be specialized in the case of profits earned abroad, causing the MNC to change its financial planning.

The total set of environmental constraints which operate on an MNC are indicated in Figure 3-5. The MNC is influenced by its local environment in its home country, as indicated by the C constraints to the left of Figure 3-5. In carrying on international activities, the MNC is affected by its own country's international constraints on such business, indicated by the I constraints. It must also deal directly with the international constraints of the host country (The $I'/1$, $I'/2$, and $I'/3$ sets in Figure 3-5). And as it operates a productive enterprise in the host country, the firm also is directly affected by the local environmental constraints in the host country (the $C'/1$ to $C'/4$ sets in Figure 3-5).

FIGURE 3—5

INTERNATIONAL AND LOCAL CONSTRAINTS AFFECTING A
MULTINATIONAL FIRM

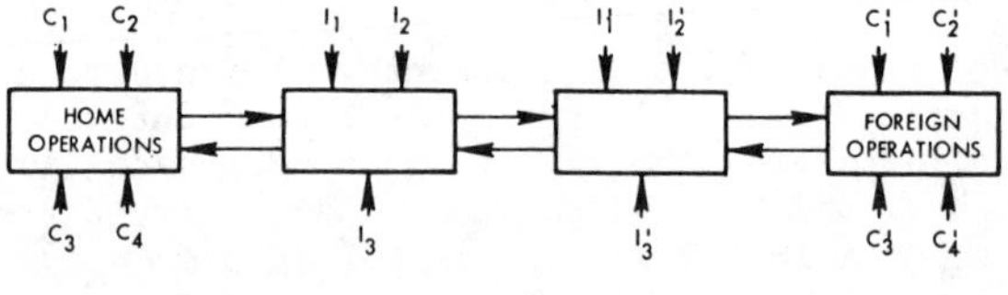

All of these sets are interrelated to some extent. The MNC may find that local educational constraints are such that needed technicians or managers will be unavailable. It may decide to overcome this shortage by importing personnel from its own country. But to bring such persons into the host country, visas must be obtained and legal rules regarding the importation of such personnel must be observed. Here an international legal constraint of the host country is important. Most countries have rules about the nationalities of the people who work within the country, and this solution may prove difficult or impossible. A final international constraint may be that of the home country. Many countries (mainly marxist) have strict rules about leaving the country, and if this is illegal, expensive, or administratively difficult, further staffing adjustments must be made.

In the above case, all four sets of constraints are relevant in determining exactly how the MNC might resolve its staffing problems in the host country. Changes in any of the relevant constraints in any set could have direct effects on the efficiency with which the firm conducted its operations. When firms operate in many countries, the number of potential relevant constraints becomes extremely large. A company with operations in 80 countries would be dealing with 320 different sets of external constraints. While some might be identical or trivial, there would still be a very large number of constraints which would push the MNC into different patterns of varying efficiency in the diverse countries. International business is complicated!

CATEGORIZATION OF THE INTERNATIONAL CONSTRAINTS

Figure 3-6 presents the various international environmental constraints categorized into sociological/cultural, legal/political, and economic. Some of these constraints are quite similar to local environmental constraints. Thus some legal international constraints are actually a detailed sublist of the local C/3.3 (foreign policy). The reason for a more explicit listing here is that the MNC will be much more interested in how this particular constraint works out in practice than a local firm. A foreign policy which excluded foreign firms would be of some importance to a local company, but it would be of critical importance to an MNC seeking entry into that country.

Since the C´s are directly related to the I´s, the I´s also directly affect the B´s. The way in which these international constraints affect firm performance in various countries will be the major focus of much of the rest of this book.

To see how these relationships work out, consider a country with very strong nationalistic sentiments. This attitude is quite common, and national governments are often eager to encourage as strong a feeling of empathy for the country among the population as possible. Such sentiments may be heightened by attacks, either verbal or physical, on foreigners, particularly wealthy, powerful foreigners.

In such countries, marches on foreign embassies (usually the American) by mobs seeking justice and redress from various grievances are common. In the limit, such activities mean seizing of hostages as in Iran a few years ago, or kidnapping or killing of foreign executives, technicians, or even religious persons. Such feelings in themselves are disturbing, but if they lead to legislation banning MNCs, taxing them heavily, or otherwise impeding their activities, then they matter a great deal. Expropriation of MNC assets is not uncommon, and such actions can be very popular in the country, reflecting the view toward foreigners held by a substantial segment of the population.

Such attitudes can have direct impacts on the management of MNCs and even on the sale of foreign products within a given country. Boycotts are common, as are legal prohibitions against products from a given country. Thus Arab countries systematically boycott not only Israeli products, but also the products of all companies in any country that have investments in Israel. An MNC contemplating an Israeli direct

FIGURE 3—6

INTERNATIONAL CONSTRAINTS

I_1: *Sociological Constraints*

    1.1   National ideology: The general collective ideology of a nation as exemplified by their writing, speaking, and other manifestations of a national point of view.

    1.2   View toward foreigners: The general attitude toward nonnationals as evidenced by overt behavior.

    1.3   Nature and extent of nationalism: The manifestation of the collective nationalist feelings within the country as evidenced by actions, writings, and behavior.

I_2: *Legal-Political Constraints*

    2.1   Political ideology: The political viewpoints of existing governments as demonstrated by the prevailing pattern of rule, philosophy of leading political parties, and similar factors.

    2.2   Relevant legal rules for foreign business: The special rules of the game applied only to foreign-owned firms, including special discriminary labor and tax legislation.

    2.3   International organization and treaty obligations: Formal obligations of the country in terms of military responsibilities; political obligations; copyright, postal, and patent obligations; and similar matters.

    2.4   Power or economic bloc grouping: Membership in formal and informal political, military, and economic blocs such as Communist Marxist or neutralist groups; explicit and implicit obligations of such blocs.

    2.5   Import-export restrictions: Formal legal rules controlling exports and imports, including tariffs, quotas, export duties, export restrictions, and similar matters.

    2.6   International investment restrictions: Formal legal and administrative restrictions on investments by foreigners within the country.

    2.7   Profit remission restrictions: Formal legal and administrative restrictions on remittance of profits of local operations to foreign countries.

    2.8   Exchange control restrictions: Formal legal and administrative controls on the conversion of the local currency to any or all foreign currencies or gold.

I_3: *Economic Constraints*

    3.1   General balance of payments position: The general state of the balance of payments, including deficits or surpluses on current account; the flows of capital, both long and short term; long term international financial obligations; and tendencies for chronic deficits or surpluses in the balance of payments.

    3.2   International trade patterns: The usual flows of exports and imports to and from the country. Patterns of commodities and services traded by countries and regions.

    3.3   Membership and obligations in international financial organizations: Obligations and responsibilities of the country toward international organizations such as the World Bank and the IMF; rights of the country as a member of such organizations.

investment has to consider the effect of this investment on sales in Arab markets.

Similarly, in 1981, the U.S. Government imposed special tariffs and regulations on Polish imports, reflecting American feelings about the Polish government, and it has even more stringent regulations about the importation of Cuban products. Most countries have very negative views towards a few countries, and such special discriminatory rules, which fall in the I/2 constraint set, are very common. In the limit the countries are at war, and very little trading or investing occurs.

Political ideology of a country can also have direct impacts on MNCs. One extreme example was the shift around 1960 of Cuba from a capitalist to a Marxist state. The typical Marxist ideologial position is that no foreign firms should be allowed to own or operate enterprises within the country. This attitude is related to the domestic ideology which holds that generally no individual should own productive assets. In the Cuban case, expropriations of American assets in that country were total and extensive.

More recently, countries as diverse as Iran, Angola, Ethiopia, and Vietnam have followed similar restrictionary policies. But other countries, such as Egypt, have moved back to a more accomodating position for MNCs. In all these cases, the special laws and rules for foreign investment have major impacts on MNCs, including very importantly the question of whether or not such firms can operate at all.

Every country in the world has some import and export restrictions, and these have direct effects on both local and international firms. Thus the United States may decide to levy very high tariffs or duties, or impose quotas on imported Japanese autos. Japanese firms now find this lucrative market cut off, and they may decide to invest in production facilities within the United States. If they choose to do so, the planning process of the whole firm is quite different than it otherwise would be. A whole new spectrum of planning, organization, staffing, production, and marketing problems arises as the new investment is carried out. This policy will also have many local impacts. The Japanese firm will require American labor, which will have major effects on Japanese staffing policies. Japanese firms that were largely local are now international. This particular example is extremely common in many countries, and one major reason we now have so many MNCs is that such countries as the United States, Mexico, Brazil, Canada, and many West European countries at one time or another tried to block imports with duties or quotas, but allowed foreign investment. Firms jumped the trade barriers by making direct investments in the country.

A foreign firm may find that the local government has restricted profits remissions because of a shortage of foreign exchange. This restriction will afffect both local and foreign financial planning, since funds may not be available from anticipated sources. The company may have millions of Mexican pesos or Indian rupees, but they need German marks for investments in Europe. Also affected in this situation might be various make or buy production decisions. Instead of making a part in the U.S. and exporting it to Mexico, the MNC can use up those pesos by buying parts in Mexico and exporting them to West Germany. Such decisions will impact any firm in many directions, and it may strongly affect local firms. In this case, the Mexican local firm may get large new orders for parts from an MNC, which impacts the Mexican economy significantly.

A country may have a balance of payments crisis, which means that it does not have enough foreign exchange to meet its international obligations. In such a case, it may impose various types of restrictions on foreign and local firms within its frontiers. Such restrictions appear as legal constraints, although the reason for them is economic. The firm might be unable to import key components for products manufactured within the country, or spare parts may become difficult or impossible to import for key machinery. In such cases, the firm's production activities are directly affected since it must restructure its production operations to fit the new requirements. Make or buy decisions, financial planning, pricing of products, and location of suppliers may all shift as the firm attempts to adjust to this new restriction.

It is quite common for governments to demand as a condition for MNC entry that the MNC earn enough foreign exchange to pay its way. An auto company thus may plan from the beginning to export engines from Mexico, so that it can produce and sell autos within that country. Here, the basic productive structure of the MNC in Mexico will be very different as a result of international constraints imposed by the Mexican government.

The above examples suggest how the international constraints operate directly on foreign firms. Usually the international and local constraints are interlocked, in the sense that a change in an international constraint often brings changes in local constraints as well. This in turn leads to shift in the way in which firms perform the critical elements of the management process. As Figure 3-5 indicates, the usual result for international firms is that there is an I-C-B relationship which cannot be ignored in considering the best ways to operate foreign branches of the firm. Note also that local firms involved in licencing, importing, exporting, tourism, and other internationally related activities can also be very directly affected by the I set.

Table 3-2 indicates how the international constraints are interlocked with the local constraints. As might be expected, most I's are related directly to corresponding local C's. If a three dimensional figure could be drawn in a book, it would be possible to construct an I-C-B matrix showing interrelationships of all of these items to each other. As we noted earlier, the International Business world is complicated! Try imagining a matrix involving about 150 countries' I and C sets, all different, to see why. Moreover, the I set can and does vary between foreign countries. The United States' I set toward the Soviet Union is very different than the I set towards Canada. The resulting multidimensional mess would very clearly suggest why MNCs have great trouble getting things right even a fraction of the time.

TABLE 3–2

INTERNATIONAL-LOCAL CONSTRAINT INTERRELATIONSHIPS

International Constraints (I)		Educational						Sociological									Legal-Political						Economic							
		1	2	3	4	5	6	1	2	3	4	5	6	7	8	9	1	2	3	4	5	6	1	2	3	4	5	6	7	8
I_1	1	×	×	×				×	×	×	×	×	×	×	×	×	×	×	×	×	×	×	×	×	×	×	×	×	×	×
	2	×	×	×		×	×	×	×	×	×	×	×	×	×	×	×	×	×	×	×	×	×	×	×	×	×	×	×	×
	3	×	×	×	×		×	×	×	×	×	×	×	×	×	×	×	×	×	×	×		×	×	×	×				
I_2	1		×		×			×	×	×	×	×	×	×	×	×	×	×	×	×	×	×	×	×	×	×	×	×	×	×
	2							×	×	×	×	×		×		×	×	×	×	×	×	×	×	×	×	×	×	×	×	×
	3							×	×	×	×	×					×	×	×	×				×	×	×	×			
	4									×	×	×	×		×	×	×	×	×	×	×			×	×	×	×	×		
	5												×			×	×	×	×					×	×	×	×			
	6												×	×	×	×	×	×	×		×		×	×	×	×	×	×		×
	7													×	×	×	×	×	×					×	×	×	×	×	×	×
	8												×		×		×			×				×	×	×	×	×	×	×
	9																													
I_3	1																×			×	×	×	×	×	×	×	×	×	×	×
	2																×	×	×	×	×	×	×	×	×	×	×	×	×	×
	3																×	×	×	×	×	×	×	×	×	×	×	×	×	×

Country Constraints (C)

For definitions of *C*'s, see Figure 4–1.
For definitions of *I*'s, see Figure 5–2.

Conclusion

This concludes the exposition of the framework of our analysis of international business activities. The argument is that MNCs are constrained by their local and international environments in a variety of ways. Private profit seeking companies will try to perform the critical elements of the management process as efficiently as possible. But they can only do what their environments permit. In effect, any firm is affected by its environment, and MNCs, operating in and between many environments, are much more affected by them than local firms.

There are two basic kinds of business problems connected with this C-B-I analysis. One concerns the MNC considering new investments in any country. The firm can observe the international constraints to determine if the project should be started or not. If existing constraints appear to present problems that are too formidable, the firm can turn elsewhere, or appeal to the local government to change the constraints. All C's and I's impact directly on planning in this case. The I's and C's present a sort of "go, no go" gauge to evaluate given countries.

A second problem relates to the MNC already in the country and subject to ever-changing C's and I's. Laws and politics change, and their impacts on firm internal operations also change. A new law or economic change can mean major internal firm changes, and it is necessary to evaluate such impacts constantly. The use of the C-B and the I-C-B matrices may help in determining what shifts in constraints may do to the the firm.

Firms can change their environments to some extent, and governments, anxious to gain income and jobs, may also respond to MNC requests. But no company can change its total environment. It must accept and adjust as best possible to many kinds of constraints. The better it can do this, the more efficient and profitable it will be.

The rest of this book will be concerned with the three basic interrelated international business constraints. The next chapter will deal with one critical international constraint system, the international monetary structure. Following chapters will deal with international management issues. And later we will consider both international and domestic environmental constraints which directly affect MNC efficiency.

Questions for Discussion

1. Take another look at the C/3 set in Figure 3-5 (sociological constraints). Rate yourself on each one. Are you a big risk taker; what is your social class; what is your own view toward achievement and work; and so on. How do you think your characteristics would affect your work performance for a big company? Are they good or bad?

2. Are you culture bound, given your answer to question 1? If

possible, find a foreign student and get him or her to rate himself or herself. How does he or she differ from you?

3. Take any country that interests you and look it up in various available sources, such as atlases, statistical abstracts, and encyclopedias. Try to rate the C-4 set (economic constraints) as best you can. Do these look good, bad, or indifferent for a firm interested in investing in the country? Why?

4. Go to any retail store in town and take a good look around. This firm is about to expand into a third world country where personal incomes are around $1,000 per year (as compared to about $10,000 in the United States) per capita. About 30 percent of all adults are illiterate. There is one car for every 40 persons, as compared to one for every two persons in the U.S. What changes do you think this store would have to make to be successful in such a country?. List three of these.

5. We are all nationalists at heart, but we also are all regionalists or statists. What special attitudes do you have which stem from the state or region you come from? How do these differ from more general American attitudes?

6. Sometimes we perceive foreigners differently. How would you describe the characteristics of a young woman from Sweden? From Red China? From England? From the Soviet Union? From Burundi?

7. How would your perceptions from question 6 matter if you were about to sit down and deal with a person from each of these countries? Why?

Supplementary Readings

Baker, James C, and Bates, Thomas H. FINANCING INTERNATIONAL BUSINESS OPERATIONS. Scranton, PA: Intext Educational Publishers, 1971.

Behrman, Jack N. U.S. BUSINESS AND GOVERNMENTS. New York: McGraw-Hill, 1971.

Berge, Kenneth B., Mueller, Gerhard G., and Walker, Lauren M. READINGS IN INTERNATIONAL ACCOUNTING. Boston: Houghton Mifflin, 1969.

Bhagwati, Jagdish N. IMPORT COMPETITION AND RESPONSE. Chicago: University of Chicago Press, 1982.

Brigham, Eugene F. FINANCIAL MANAGEMENT: THEORY AND PRACTICE, 3D EDITION. New York: The Dryden Press, 1982.

Boddywyn, J. (ed.). WORLD BUSINESS SYSTEMS AND ENVIRONMENTS. Scranton, PA: Intext, 1972.

Council of Economic Advisors. ECONOMIC REPORT TO THE PRESIDENT, 1982. Washington, D.C.: U.S. Government Printing Office, 1982 (Or the latest one available).

Dornbusch, Rudiger, and Fischer, Stanley. MACROECONOMICS. New York: McGraw-Hill, 1978.

Ellworth, P.T., and Leith, Clark J. THE INTERNATIONAL ECONOMY, 5TH ED. New York: MacMillan, 1975.

Grosset, Serge. MANAGEMENT: EUROPEAN AND AMERICANN STYLES. Belmont, CA: Wadsworth, 1970.

Halm, George N. ECONOMIC SYSTEMS, 3D EDITION. New York: Holt, Rinehart & Winston, 1969.

Harbeson F., and Meyers, C. EDUCATION, MANPOWER, AND ECONOMIC GROWTH. New York: McGraw-Hill, 1964.

Higgens, B. ECONOMIC DEVELOPMENT: REVISED EDITION. New York: W.W. Norton & Company, 1968.

Koontz, Harold, and O'Donnell, Cyril. PRINCIPLES OF MANAGMENT, 4TH EDITION. New York: McGraw-Hill Book Company, 1968.

McClelland, D. THE ACHIEVING SOCIETY. Princeton, NJ: D.Van Nostrand Co., 1961.

Samuelson, Paul. ECONOMICS, 7TH EDITION (Or any other one!). New York: McGraw-Hill, 1968.

Schultz, T.W. THE ECONOMIC VALUE OF EDUCATION. New York: Columbia University Press, 1963.

PART II

THE INTERNATIONAL

ENVIRONMENT

Chapter 4

The International Monetary System

Introduction

When a company moves beyond its own country's frontiers to conduct any type of business, it discovers the international monetary system. Each sovereign country has the right to issue its own currency, and most do. Each country has a bank of issue (in the United States, the Federal Reserve System) which has monetary control powers for the country.

But a Frenchman normally does not want dollars in payment for goods or services sold to Americans. He prefers French francs. Similarly, the Englishman wants pounds and the German marks. If any international transactions occur, some mechanism for interrelating all national currencies has to be devised. This mechanism is the international monetary system. Exchange rates between various currencies must be determined, flows of money between countries handled, and balance of payments adjustments of different countries covered.

A system implies some logical, ordered structure, but at present the international monetary system is hardly that. It is a mix of international agreements, free currency markets in some countries, blocked currencies, black and grey market transactions in other countries, and numerous activities which have somehow emerged to meet real needs over many years. Moreover, it changes constantly, which means that firms must forever adjust to new problems. But whatever it is, firms must learn to live with it.

In this chapter, we will briefly describe the main features of the system. This exploration requires some history as well, since what the system was a few years ago is not what it is today, although the present one is closely linked to what went before. We also will cover balance of payments questions and implications for MNCs as they operate within the system.

Balance of Payments

A basic concept necessary to understand the international monetary system is the balance of payments. Each country creates its own money, and each has various financial dealings with other countries. Countries import goods and services, and they export these as well. Capital flows to and from countries, often simultaneously, as some citizens invest abroad, while foreigners make investments in the country. Countries can receive gifts and grant them. Even the United States receives gifts (in the form of private donations to various charities and individuals, plus occasional grants from governments), and the U.S. also makes gifts, both public and private. And in a few cases, countries steal assets, as when a war is undertaken successfully, and real estate or other assets are taken from enemies.

All of these transactions can be noted and shown in a balance of payments (BP) for any country. The BP shows total cash inflows and outflows in a structured form, as shown in Figure 4-1. Current transactions include exports, imports, and service sales and purchases. The capital account shows various capital flows in both directions. The money used to denominate the BP can be either the country´s own, or some other country´s, such as U.S. dollars, at some stated exchange rate. The BP is always for some stated period of time, such as a month or year. The statement can be as detailed or general as is needed for users. Thus the capital account could show all flows lumped as a single figure, or could run for thousands of pages, listing in detail each capital transaction.

The current account is the short term flows of imports, exports, and services, and this is the one frequently noted in the business press. Thus if the U.S. has a deficit of $3.7 billions in its April BP, what is usualy meant is that imports of goods and services exceed exports by this amount. Often only the physical trade BP is used, since this one is the easiest to calculate quickly. But the BP always balances; if the U.S. did run this deficit, then in effect it owes foreigners the $3.7 billion, so the total BP will show a capital inflow item of $3.7 billion to balance the total statement. Such capital inflows may be very short term, since bills for imports might be paid in weeks or days, or it may be long term, in that foreigners accept long term debts from Americans. A foreigner might regard the purchase of a corporate U.S. bond maturing in the year 2035 as a wise investment, so such long term debt is not necessarily negative for any country.

Countries are like individuals, in that they cannot create other countries´ monies. A country, like you, cannot spend more than it earns indefinitely. If it spends more than it earns in foreign currencies, then it incurs a current account BP deficit. It can make this up the way you do, by borrowing, long or short term; getting gifts from outsiders; or stealing. This latter case means war and extreme danger for countries, or possible jail sentences for individuals, so it is not advised, but it has happened.

If a country finds itself with a current account BP deficit, and it cannot borrow or obtain gifts, then it must do something. The something involves lowering the standard of living of its citizens, since they have been living beyond their means. Either revenues must be expanded through increased sales abroad, or expenditures must be cut. At this moment (no matter when you read this, since it is always happening), anywhere from a dozen to a hundred countries are faced with a BP crisis in this sense. They must do something, and what they do depends on the international monetary system and the feasible options within it.

FIGURE 4-1
Islandia: Balance of Payments
Analytic Presentation, 1983 and 1984 Provisional
(In Millions of SDRS)

	1983		1984	
	Credit	*Debit*	*Credit*	*Debit*
A. Goods and Services	3,322	4,171	3,587	4,542
Merchandise (exports FOB; imports C.I.E.)	521	2,407	1,715	2,705
Nonmonetary gold		17		26
Freight and insurance on merchandise				
Other transportation	49	52	56	49
Travel	1,583	796	1,646	819
Investment income	66	788	74	805
Other government	26	10	24	10
Other private	77	10	72	128
B. Unrequited Transfers	54	11	73	9
Net Total of Goods, Services & Transfers		806		891
C. Capital (excluding reserves & related items)	564		642	
D. Allocation of SDRs	40		39	
E. Reserves & Related Items		177		210
Net Errors and Omissions	379		420	

One man's debts are another man's assets. If someone runs a deficit, then someone else is running a surplus. There are typically a few BP surplus countries at any time. In 1982-83, Japan was running huge surplusses in the range of $20 to $30 billions per year, while most countries were running deficits. In 1974-81, many oil exporting countries ran huge surplusses, while most industrial and third world countries ran large deficits. But in the end, if the numbers are correct, the world BP should add up to zero. All debts would equal all assets for any given period.

The numbers are rarely counted properly, however. Errors and omissions are huge, since many citizens are not the least bit interested in letting their governments know what they are up to. We have no idea of the BP in cocaine traded in the world economy, nor do we know much about politicians who establish illegal bank accounts abroad. We know little about how much cheating goes on in terms of declaring the value of goods for tariff purposes, and the American who goes to Canada for an evening, spends some dollars, and then returns, is not required to report her expenditures. The errors are large, and only estimates can be made of the data in virtually every item of the BP. Wise students do not take official data too seriously, although when a country runs short of foreign money in the aggregate, the signs are everywhere. One cannot easily convert local currency at local banks; often some form of foreign exchange rationing is applied; black or grey markets in currencies may spring up; and official reserves are known to be low. In a general way, countries can and do know what is going on, but specific individual transactions can be very difficult to trace.

Since a country's BP position effectively measures a country's standard of living, it is watched very carefully all over the world. Large surplusses mean that a country has the ability to import more. Growing exports lead to the possibility of larger imports, thus raising the standard of living locally. Smaller countries that have a large international trading sector watch it more carefully than any other single economic indicator, since one's surplus or deficit determines all economic options.

Evolution of the System

Historically, gold was the international money, and if a country owed another country cash for goods or services, it could pay off in gold. Each country's currency was defined in terms of gold weight. If a dollar was worth one twentieth of an ounce of gold, then gold was worth twenty dollars an ounce. If another country stated that its currency (say a peso) was worth one fortieth of an ounce of gold, in that country gold was worth forty pesos an ounce. The exchange rate between dollars and peso was two pesos to one dollar. If an importer bought an American car for $2,000, he would immediately know that it was worth 4,000 pesos. Banks or other agencies handling the exchange transaction would charge a small fee, so the actual exchange rates would vary marginally from the precise rate, but these variations were always small.

In pre-1914 years, gold often WAS money, and even into the 1930's some countries, such as the United States, issued true weight gold coins. Hence a twenty dollar gold piece contained exactly once ounce of gold. One could settle foreign debts merely by going to a bank, getting gold coins for paper money, and sending the coins overseas. Until 1934, most American paper money was directly convertible to gold in this manner, as were many foreign currencies.

Rarely would anyone actually pay a foreigner in such a clumsy and expensive manner. Shipping and insurance costs were high, and it was easier to buy a bill of exchange from a major bank and send it to the foreign creditor. The actual gold transfers tended to be small and restricted to central banks. But in theory, gold was money, and most banks and firms acted as if this were true.

This historic gold system had fine theoretical virtues, one of which was to provide for automatic adjustment of any foreign payments difficulties a country might have. Suppose that at going exchange rates (determined by each country's definition of its currency in gold), the United States began to have foreign deficits. This would be a BP deficit. As the deficits piled up, foreigners would ask for payment. The payments would be made in gold, shipped by the central bank or large commercial banks. As gold flowed out of the country, the supply of money began to decrease. Remember, in the true gold system, gold was money, and in this case less money was around. As money supply decreased, prices would fall, and foreigners would buy more American goods.

In the gold receiving countries, money supply would be rising. Prices would begin to rise, and Americans would buy less. The overall effect would be to bring the American deficit back into balance. Authorities would do nothing, since the system was self-equilibrating.

This system actually existed in most countries before 1914. Treasure hunters might well pay close attention, since if you are looking for gold, you should find a pre-1914 situation where gold was being shipped to cover an international deficit. Thus if you are interested in raising the Titanic, which sank on its way from England to the U.S. in 1912, the key question would be what the BP situation was between the U.S. and Great Britain in 1911. If Britain owed the U.S. money, then the Titanic should have lots of gold on it. But if the U.S. owed Great Britain money, then...well, is anyone interested in an old ship's hull?

Similarly, a rule for moviemakers is always rob the stagecoach heading east. The Western U.S. was a major gold producer, and it paid for its Eastern imports by shipping gold to the Eastern U.S. The westbound stagecoaches held only trinkets and paper! Sometimes historical knowledge might pay off.

The delightful simplicity of the gold standard, plus its self-equilibrating tendencies, makes it attractive even today, and many thinkers would return to it if they could. Another very nice virtue of the gold standard was that it forced politicians to behave. Having a gold standard in a country meant that if a BP deficit occurred, the political leaders HAD to make adjustments internally to correct the imbalance. But in a practical and complex world, the system suffered from real defects.

The first of these was war. The original system collapsed during World War II (1914-1918), and never really got back in gear. When a belligerent country fought its enemies, it seemed a bit absurd to stop shooting just because the gold supply was running low. If key items such as ammunition and food had to be purchased from abroad, then the whole international economy of the belligerents would be restructured, which in practice meant leaving the gold standard. This was done by refusing to export gold, controlling all imports to meet national needs, and rationing scarce foreign exchange to use for military purposes. Moreover, war usually brought rapid price inflation, which tended to suck in luxury imports from other countries. It was not considered ethical to have workers at home importing perfumes and caviar while soldiers died in the trenches. By the end of the first World War, most belligerents were off the gold standard, and few got back on it afterwards. These countries went to a controlled system, with their currencies being inconvertible to anything without special licences.

A second major reason why the gold standard stopped working was the rapid shift after 1920 to national monetary systems based on paper, not gold coins. Checks and currency became the standard money in most countries, and supplies of both could be controlled by central banks without recourse to gold supplies. Hence money supply did not necessarily change as gold supplies changed, which meant that the simple equilibrium process described above did not work. In the 1920's, as one example, the American economy ran consistent surplusses in foreign trade, and gold flowed into the United States to pay the bills. But foreign countries did not reduce their money supplies to match the gold outflow, and the Americans did not expand their money supply to match the gold inflows. Hence no adjustments occurred, and the system fell apart in the early 1930's.

Third, a true gold standard requires price decreases as well as price increases. Since 1933, prices have gone up nicely everywhere, but they very rarely have gone down. For psychological and other reasons, people feel very upset when THEIR price declines. We know how to live with an inflation rate of five percent in a year when our salaries do not rise, but if there were a five percent pay cut, strikes, sabotage, and lost productivity would be probable. So one very critical element of the gold standard is missing.

A true gold standard would involve some rational and fair distribution of gold among the countries. Adjustments would have to be fast enough so that no one country, or a few countries, would corner the supply. If they could, other countries would refuse to play, and the system would collapse. Historically, the country with an excess share of the world's gold supply thought that the system was a great idea, while those with shortages were not so convinced. The English in the late 19th Century had the gold and supported the system enthusiastically; the Americans at that time objected and politicians argued that the country was being crucified on a cross of gold. Then in the 1920's and on to 1955, when the Americans had the gold, they thought that it was a great idea, while other countries, including Great Britain, thought otherwise. The South Africans, who produce most of the world's supply of new gold, enthusiastically support the gold standard ideal, though few others agree with South Africans on anything. Communist countries have always regarded the gold standard as a tool of imperialism, and have never followed its rules, even though the U.S.S.R. is a major gold producer and sells its gold in world markets for hard currencies to purchase imports.

And finally, the gold system does not require any political management at all. What happens, happens, and politicians can do nothing about it. Most governments since the 1920's or even earlier have felt that they can manipulate and control events, including international events, in a positive way, and they try. Voters, suffering from poverty, inflation, or other ills also feel that their governments should do something. It would be hard to imagine a scenario where a country was deeply depressed because of a gold shortage, and the govenmment announced that of course it could do nothing. Totalitarian regimes might have coups, and democratic ones would change parties in power at the next election. The irresistable urge to try to change one's fate by positive actions could force any country off gold, as it has so many times in the past. And unless everyone goes along, the system cannot work well, if at all.

THE INTERNATIONAL MONETARY SYSTEM, 1944-1971

Because the prewar gold standard (really the gold exchange standard, since gold currency was not used in most countries) had collapsed during the Great Depression years of the 1930's, it was imperative to reconstruct the system after World War II. The 1930's were characterized by foreign exchange controls, economic warfare, and rationing of scarce foreign currencies. Not surprisingly, world trade collapsed as well. In 1944, all allied nations (some 45 countries) met at Bretton Woods, New Hampshire to develop this postwar system. The United States, as the most powerful country in the world at that time, was able to influence most the basic system, although Great Britain, represented by the great Lord John Maynard Keynes personally, also managed to get some key modifications.

The new monetary system involved fixed exchange rates as in the old gold standard. Deviations of plus or minus one percent from fixed rates were allowed. These fixed rates were defined by each country in gold or dollars. At that time, the two were synomymous. The United States had so much of the world's gold, and was willing to sell gold for dollars to any foreign central bank, that dollars were in effect gold, or vice versa. If a country got into temporary balance of payments difficulties, it could borrow from the newly created International Monetary Fund (IMF) to cover its short term deficits. The country was supposed to take deflationary steps at the same time to reduce internal demand for foreign goods and services. If proper steps were taken, export would rise, imports would decline, and the country would no longer have a deficit. If fundamental (structural) disequilibrium appeared, the IMF would agree to devaluation of the country's currency.

We will return to this international monetary order in more detail in Chapter 8, where the role of the IMF will be considered. This international system functioned reasonably well for 25 years, since international trade and investments rose steadily throughout the period, and while many countries changed the value of their money (devalued or revalued), the system did work.

THE INTERNATIONAL MONETARY SYSTEM, 1971 ON

The Bretton Woods system had at least three fundamental weaknesses. First, in spite of the introduction in 1970 of Special Drawing Rights (SDRs, which are bookkeeping entries of the IMF to increase the level of international reserves), the system had not solved the problem of where new international reserves would come from to serve the needs of increased trade. From 1946 to 1971, international trade had increased in real terms by an average of ten percent per year, while new gold supplies increased at about one percent per year. This trade increase was unprecedented and unforeseen, but it led to huge demands for working capital by countries in some world accepted money. Quite often, a country has to import, in the form of raw materials, semi-finished goods, or components, in order to export. How does a country finance these imports? The answer, with a world accepted currency, means that countries need foreign currency or gold reserves in ever-increasing amounts. About the only available currency was the dollar, and increasingly dollars began to be used as an international currency of settlement. Remember that the dollar was considered as good as gold at this time.

Second, the distinction between "temporary" and "fundamental" disequilibria was not clearly defined, so that countries often waited too long to make necessary exchange rate adjustments. And third, there was a lack of symmetry in the adjustment process. Deficit countries were forced to devalue, while little pressure was exerted on surplus countries to revalue.

Such weaknesses, in addition to the burden on the United States as the chief source of international reserves, led President Nixon to take the U.S. off the gold standard in August of 1971, and to introduce an exchange rate system of "managing floating", whereby exchange rates vary daily according to the supply and demand for currencies. In short, the Bretton Woods system had fallen apart.

By 1973, even the managed floating part had ended, and since then the world's monetary system has been characterized by freely floating exchange rates for major currencies. Some countries, most notably developing ones, have clung to fixed rates and exchange controls. This system involves setting a rate, usually in line with the U.S. dollar or with the currency of the country's major trading partner. If the demand for foreign currencies grows larger than supply, the currencies are rationed through use of exchange permits.

The communist countries all have fixed rates and inconvertible currencies. All foreign exchange transactions are performed by the state for the total economy. Since no foreigners can convert a CPE currency to anything else, these monies are not demanded, and whenever black markets function, they sell at deep discounts. A Soviet ruble, as one example, can be purchased in the West for ten or fifteen cents, although the official rate is one ruble equals $1.10 U.S. But even taking Soviet banknotes into Russia is a major crime, so this speculation is not encouraged.

Floating currencies have clean or dirty floats. A clean float is one in which there is no effort by the country's monetary authorities to influence the value of its currency by dealing in it. A dirty float is one in which the monetary authorities attempt to influence its currency values by direct interventions in the foreign exchange market. The "managed float" is somewhere between these two, based on more or less acceptable means of influence.

Finally, some smaller countries merely fix the value of their currency to a major one, usually the U.S. dollar, and ride with it up and down. A related technique is to fix the rate in terms of the dollar and then formally devalue or revalue the currency in terms of the dollar depending on local conditions.

THE EUROPEAN MONETARY SYSTEM

Countries with reasonably strong floating currencies find floating rates difficult to manage. One is never sure of what international values will be. Under the earlier fixed rate system, a good deal of international uncertainty was eliminated. Hence it is not surprising to find that various regional blocs would seek to gain more monetary stability if possible. The European Community (EC) has tried several times since 1971 to develop a stable regional currency, following the lines of the pre-1971 IMF world. In the late 1979 agreement, all of the EC countries except Britain agreed to have a stable regional exchange rate system. In this system, rates are fixed between member countries, and fluctuations of plus of minus 2.25 percent around par are allowed. If market forces drive a currency above or below this range, then a central fund, established by EC nations, will buy or sell the affected currency to keep it within the fluctuation band. The various currencies will float against outside currencies, but not in terms of each other.

As with the earlier fixed rate IMF system, the success of this regional operation depends on no one country getting too far out of line. Thus after 1981, the new French socialist government tried a program of sharp reflation of the French economy, following classical liberal prescriptions of broadening social security benefits of unemployment insurance, health care, pensions, and higher minimum wages. The net effect was to rapidly expand the money supply, which led to price inflation, which led to the franc falling rapidly on world markets. Imports to France rose rapidly, while exports shrunk.

The French government also nationalized several key industries by purchasing their shares with borrowed money. Nervous investors (both French and foreign) tried to get their capital out of France, and little new capital flowed into the country. The increased demand for foreign currency by franc holders further depressed the franc. Rather quickly, the franc dropped to its 2.25 percent bottom, and soon the support fund was exhausted. At this point the franc was devalued, and then, as this scenario continued, devalued again. After two years or so, the French government was forced to impose a new austerity program, involving some foreign exchange controls, sharp tax increases, and decreases in government spending. Readers who have had the depressing experience of finding that they have been carried away by easy credit and discover that they have been living beyond their incomes and their credit is exhausted, will recognize France´s problem easily. When one is in this position, one must cut back expenditures sharply, try to pay one´s bills, and generally suffer a reduced standard of living. Countries have the same problem that individuals have, namely that they cannot create some one else´s money. One must earn, borrow, or be given it.

The above example was exactly what happened in the pre-1971 fixed exchange rate world. A government faced with excess expansion had to cut back. In a floating exchange rate world, a country can continue to expand, but its currency will continue to depreciate on world markets. The depreciation can be extreme...such currencies as the Argentine peso can and do drop to minute fractions of former values if local inflation is huge.

Somehow international trade continues, even expanding in most years. The past few years have seen international stagnation, due more to world recession than floating exchange rates. But the floating system injects a new element of uncertainty into all trade calculations, since no one can be sure what a dollar, pound, or mark is worth. In recent years, we have seen rapid development of currency trading markets, and now it is possible to hedge transactions in major currencies, but even with these aids, there is much more uncertainty in the system now than formerly.

THE UNIQUE ROLE OF THE UNITED STATES

The United States was in a unique position (along with the United Kingdom) in international currency matters. Both the dollar and the pound were key currencies, which means they they were used by other countries as international reserves, in addition to gold. The United States eased into this position during and after World War II, and it has maintained it to the present day. The pound has gradually lost importance in this sense, and today is largely a local currency. Its preeminance before 1946 was in part due to Britain´s major trading and international banking position, and in part due to its use all over the historical British empire.

In 1934, the dollar was defined in gold at $35 per ounce. The U.S. at that time held over half of the world´s gold supply, this reserve being built up over a 30 year period of BP surplusses. By 1946, the dollar was as good as gold, and any foreign govenment could buy all the gold it wanted for dollars at the fixed price. Countries trying to build up their international reserves realized that they could hold dollars instead of gold, and settle international accounts with dollar checks written on New York banks. This was easier and cheaper than shipping gold around, and it had the further advantage that these dollar reserves, instead of being a pile of sterile yellow metal, could earn interest by being invested in short term U.S. government securities while they served their reserve function.

Non-U.S. individuals and private companies, often banned legally from holding gold, soon realized that by holding dollars they had a gold equivalent asset. They could also pay bills anywhere in the world with dollar checks, and rather quickly the habit of using dollars to settle third country transactions grew rapidly. Everyone would accept dollars, but often some would not accept local currencies, even good ones. Thus an Italian importer might pay a German seller in dollars for goods. The German would happily accept the dollars, knowing that they could be used anywhere, including being converted to marks.

After 1946, international trade in the Western world began to expand rapidly, and this expansion continued to 1980 at a rate of about ten percent, in real terms, per year. As trade expanded, the need for liquid international reserves also expanded, and a larger supply of something to use for such reserves was required. There was no international currency except gold, but if dollars were as good as gold, they could serve. Note that this point would hold only as long as foreigners really believed in the value of the dollar. If dollar holders abroad ever doubted that they could not get gold for dollars, they would rush to convert all dollar holdings into gold. Like any individual who is confident that his bank is sound, this becomes a self-fufilling prophecy. Cautious central bankers normally diversified their portfolios in any case, which meant that as dollars piled up as reserves, they would on occasion buy some gold from the U.S. Treasury or the Federal Reserve System. Since they were always able to get it, confidence was maintained, but by 1970, the $35 billion U.S. gold hoard had shrunk to $13 billion (at the $35 per ounce price), while foreign dollar liabilities soared from perhaps $12 billion to over $100 billion. The bank was getting very shaky.

Gold does have considerable value in industrial uses, electronics, and dentistry, but its major historical role has been as a store of value. People think that it is valuable, and it is. Thus an enormous amount of labor and capital is devoted to digging the stuff up wherever it is found, so that it can be reburied in bank vaults and safety deposit boxes. This activity fills a psychological need and in so doing it performed a monetary function, but the end result of the gold standard was to put the world economy at the mercy of the gold producers. If more gold was produced, there was more money, economic expansion, and booming economies. If less gold was produced, there was deflation, unemployment, and an international monetary crisis. This is a hell of a way to run a railroad, but the world happened to run this way for many centuries. Proposals for reform met with passionate resistance.

In effect, the shift to the dollar was an effort to avoid this gold supply tyranny. Fortunately for other countries, the U.S. continued to run a persistent BP deficit in the period 1946-70. Thus in the 1950´s the U.S. created some $20 billion in short term liabilities to foreigners in this manner, while gold stocks declined. But note that the game cannot continue forever. When the U.S. runs out of gold, then foreigners try to cash in and cannot. The game ends, as it did in 1971, when the U.S. went off gold and the present system began. But even in the current system, the dollar is still used as a world currency, even though no one can be sure what the dollar is worth in gold. At this writing, gold sells for about $350 per ounce, but it has been as low as $90 and as high as $850 in the past ten years. In effect, our present international monetary system is one of a dollar based inconvertible paper currency, with a heirachy of "good" currencies being used. The dollar is best, but any reasonably stable, completely convertible currency is nice, such as the British pound, the Swiss franc, the German mark, the Japanese yen, the Canadian dollar, or many others. Less desirable currencies are those with exchange controls, such as the Indian rupee. And at the bottom of the list are communist country currencies, which cannot be converted into anything, no way, nohow.

Note that this creation of dollars in the period 1946-70 was in effect an expansion of world money supply, which coincided nicely with increased world liquidity demands. The average increase also neatly matched demands in most years, so the net result was a rapid expansion of world trade without much inflation. Greatly helping the use of the dollar as a world currency from 1946 to date has been the phenomenal improvement in world communications. It is now possible to transfer billions of dollars from one continent to another in seconds via satelites or cables. As paper transfers became much easier and cheaper, the older method of shipping gold physically declined even more rapidly. It was just too expensive, given the nice dollar transfer options.

After 1971, many countries began to realize that the international game had shifted very significantly, in that with fixed rates, a country with balance of payments problems had to make internal adjustments, while with floating rates, the country could shift this adjustment to outsiders. Consider a common case of a country living beyond its means, typically because of domestic political pressures. Little old ladies NEED higher pensions; workers DESERVE higher wages; the military establisment HAS to have better weapons from abroad; and schools MUST be improved. It is easy enough to print or otherwise create some local money to buy such nice things, and as governments do, prices increase locally. Often, particularly in smaller countries, the little old ladies buy imported commodities; the military gets its latest electronics gear from abroad; the new schools need imported cement and steel to be built; and workers buy foreign stereos and cars. As local prices increase, foreign products are relatively cheaper, so imports surge. Exports decrease or stagnate, since to foreigners they are now more expensive.

Under the fixed exchange rate system, the country would shortly face a BP crisis. Domestic deflation would be necessary, and the pensions would be cut, the military forced to survive with older weapons, and so on. In short, the complete adjustment would be internal.

But under the new floating rate system, the country would do nothing. As local inflation soared, its currency price on world markets would merely decline, meaning that its export prices would stay in line, and foreign import prices would rise. Given any politician's propensity to take the easy way out and avoid the wrath of voters, it made sense to con the old ladies with big pensions. The fact that import prices would rise and local prices would probably rise faster would not (one hoped) prevent a landslide victory for the party in power in the next election.

If one or a few countries figured it out this way, the

international result would be a decline in these countries´ currency prices in world markets. But if most countries followed this strategy, then the net result would be worldwide price inflation, with no one currency falling much in price relative to others. Your prices would rise, but so would prices in other countries. In the end, only minor shifts in currency values would occur, based in large part on relative rates of inflation. Since even the U.S. was happily inflating this way through most of the 1970´s, the overall world result was worldwide inflation, ranging from a few thousand percent per year in really undisciplined countries to fifteen to thirty percent per year in major industrialized nations. Only a handful of countries (Switzerland, West Germany, Japan being the most important) managed to resist this trend. Now, name the three currencies that appreciated the most in the world exchange markets in the 1970´s...

Throughout the 1970´s to date, the dollar has remained the key world currency. This sometimes confuses Americans, since there really are two dollars. One is the local one, used for familiar local purchases. This we understand. But the second dollar is the world reserve currency, used everywhere for third country payments, international loans, private and government reserves, and other foreign uses. The exchange rate of these dollars is one to one, and they are totally interchangable, which adds to the confusion.

In spite of the uncertain international value of the dollar, it remains supreme for the following reasons:

1. The dollar is totally convertible to any other currency freely at some price. Many other countries, including such strong ones as Japan and France, have some exchange controls or other difficulties, particularly with very large transfers. But the U.S. dollar can and is traded freely. Some $15 to $20 billions are traded daily in major exchanges around the world.

2. The U.S. is the world´s largest economy, and it is the freest. Foreigners can invest in almost anything in the country, including real or paper assets. If you hold dollars, you can buy stocks and bonds, make bank deposits, buy real estate or companies, or whatever, and earn money on your money. Most other countries are either very small, making massive foreign investments difficult, or too restrictive for foreigners.

3. The U.S. is regarded as very safe from many foreign perspectives. If one comes from a shaky country full of revolutionary thunder, then parking one´s money in the U.S. for safety makes much sense. Literally hundreds of thousands of political exiles now live comfortably in the U.S. because they were farsighted enough to build up dollar balances earlier. Such lessons are not lost on present politicians and others faced with much potential trouble at home.

4. The U.S. typically has a low inflation rate, which is nice for rentiers. In the 1980´s, the U.S. has done much better in containing inflation than most other countries, and if you have reserves to safeguard, better a country where their value will be maintained. In the 1980´s, the dollar has risen sharply in terms of other currencies,

which makes it very attractive to foreigners. If you invest 100 pesos in dollars at a five to one exchange rate in 1982, and then find that you not only earn ten percent on your money for two years, but that you get back seven pesos to the dollar in 1984, the investment appears very attractive indeed.

5.   The U.S. money market is the best in the world by far, and it is totally interconnected to all markets in all countries. Buying and selling securities of all sorts is cheaper and easier in the U.S. than anywhere, and much less restrictive. Moreover, the U.S. has excellent controls on frauds and other problems involving dishonest brokers and participants.   A foreigner dealing with American firms has much less chance of being defrauded than in almost any other country.

6.   Finally, what else does the world have? It badly needs an international currency to conduct its affairs, but international politics precludes the establishment of any viable alternative to the dollar.   Efforts to establish a world currency have been tried, as we shall see later, but the dollar still is nice to hold, and foreigners continue to hold them.

If foreigners are to hold dollars, they have to obtain them from the U.S.   In effect, the U.S. can run a continuous BP deficit, with foreigners holding IOUs in dollars, which they really want to hold anyhow.   The larger the BP deficit, the more dollars foreigners hold. The U.S. can import much more than it exports, which means that foreigners are paying for the privelege of using dollars everywhere. The American standard of living is slightly higher than it otherwise would be as a result, and Americans can happily purchase autos, stereos, toys, and anything else from foreigners for nothing except another IOU. It is as if you had a credit card you could use anywhere, but never had to pay the balance due, since the company issuing it would happily hold your debt.

This game has been going on since 1946, and astute foreigners have always questioned the ability of Americans to get something for nothing (well, almost nothing...bankers always get a commission!).   General DeGaulle of Franch was particularly incensed in the 1960´s, and France´s eagerness to buy gold for dollars at that time was an important element in bringing the fixed rate system down. But the dilemma here for suspicious foreigners is that if the dollar goes down, they go down too.

Suppose that Japan, a country with a large BP surplus, decides to destroy the dollar. It might be able to do this by converting all its dollar assets to something else, say German marks. It could refuse to accept dollars for payments for Japanese goods. If this plan succeeded, the result for Japan would be mass unemployment, as factories closed for lack of American orders.   Many other countries, holding dollar reserves, would be unable to buy Japanese goods, intensifying Japan´s problems. And Japan would face major external political problems, as other countries accused it of ill faith in its international dealings.   What might happen in the next Japanese election, with all those unemployed workers demanding jobs, is enough to make any America hater pause. Much better to live with the present dollar system...

The paradox here is that if the U.S. improved its BP position to zero, that is, no deficit, the world would have massive international liquidity problems, probably a world depression, and other nasty outcomes. Yet, the U.S. keeps getting something for nothing. Nothing requires that the international monetary system be logical!

A variety of suggestions for reform have been made in the past 25 years which involve somehow getting rid of the dollar as a key international currency. What they all suggest (apart from those who want to get back to gold, period, and deflate everybody) is to create an international money which could be expanded in line with growing world trade. This has already been done domestically in every country, so the proposal is hardly radical. Thus in the United States since 1915, the Federal Reserve Banking System is responsible for expanding or contracting the supply of money to meet the demands of the economy, and these days the Friday report of M/1 (cash and checks) in circulation is closely watched all over the world. Money can be expanded very easily in modern economies because the central bank can either print more currency, or more commonly create more checking accounts, whenever desirable. If a similar system could be established internationally, then the problem of international liquidity would vanish for good.

Discussions and debate on the above point led to creation in 1970 of Special Drawing Rights (SDRs), issued by the International Monetary Fund (IMF). SDRs are a peculiar form of money, since no person will ever see one. They are bookkeeping credits given to various countries by a complex formula interpreted by the IMF. In order for the scheme to work, every IMF member country has to agree to accept SDRs in payments for international debts. The SDRs belong to governments, who do write SDR checks to other governments to settle accounts. Like modern domestic currencies, the SDRs are created out of thin air. They are literally as good as gold, since a country can spend them anywhere. Originally they were defined in terms of the dollar, but as all currencies, including the dollar, floated, they were redefined as a weighted average of a number of major trading currencies, so the SDR floats gently, too.

Thus if the U.S. government owes West Germany $500 million, it can write an SDR check to cover this amount. These international reserves are then switched to the West German IMF account. The West German government might spend them to settle an account with a major oil producing nation such as Saudi Arabia, who in turn might send them to Japan to pay for machinery. No private firm or individual will know or care how such accounts are settled, since each will receive his marks, rials, or yen in his local currency. But the various government books will be neatly balanced.

If such a system worked well, the Americans no longer would have to generate balance of payments deficits to create world economic liquidity. As world production and trade grows, so could the supply of SDRs.

The major objection to this scheme came from two sources. Many Europeans, well aware of runaway inflation, felt that the idea could lead to world price inflation. Under previous schemes, if a country spent too much, it had to get back in line, as its BP deteriorated. But with SDRs, the whole world could have too much purchasing power with SDRs, if too many were issued.

A second objection came from Third World countries, interested in economic development. SDRs were distributed largely to wealthy countries, since they were the most important factors in world trade and economic activity. But if the SDRs were given to poorer countries, they could become an important source of world economic aid. These poor countries could spend the SDRs in richer countries, buying machinery, armaments, and other items needed for economic development. Richer countries, on receiving payments for their goods in SDRs, would have the desired international liquidity.

But the SDR plan came too late. By early 1971, foreigners and Americans were nervous about the value of the dollar, and they began massive conversions of dollars to foreign currencies. Only central banks could get American gold, and a few did so, but any citizen could take his dollars and convert them to other currencies. If the value of the dollar fell, then the speculator could buy back dollars at a new lower price, thus gaining the amount of the devaluation. For a few dollars and a couple of cables or phone calls, literally millions could be made.

The 1971 result was the closing of the American gold window, which meant that foreign central banks could no longer obtain gold for their dollars. It also meant a ten percent devaluation of the dollar in terms of gold. The dollar continued to fall in world markets until in late 1973 it was worth from 10 to 40 percent less in terms of major currencies than it had been in 1971. But as noted above, everyone kept using the dollar for lack of a viable option. Remember that only central banks could use SDRs, and by the mid-1970´s, far more private firms and individuals were involved in foreign markets than governments. The U.S. had in effect created too many dollars for both internal and international use than were needed, so the dollar value declined. In international markets, it fell in terms of foreign currencies; in local markets, this surplus showed up in accelerating price inflation.

Everything depends on everything else. As the dollar cheapened, U.S. export prices in dollars looked very attractive to foreigners, so the U.S. had a vigorous export boom from 1973 to 1981. Literally millions of extra jobs were created in the U.S. as many industries exported more and required more labor to produce for these new markets. But as the dollar rose after 1981, export growth faltered, and then in 1982 exports fell in dollar value. Perhaps a million U.S. workers lost their jobs as a direct result.

The other side of this coin is that a highly valued dollar means cheap imports. As the dollar gains value, prices for foreign goods decline, thus cutting the inflation rate. Perhaps a percentage point or two has been cut off the U.S. inflation rate in 1982-84 as a result of the stronger dollar on world markets.

Foreign governments are very ambivalent about all this. They first accused the U.S. of making the dollar too cheap, thus creating very competitive export conditions. Then, as the dollar strengthened, they criticized the U.S. for overvaluing the dollar, thus allowing Americans to pay far too little for imports. Note that you can't have it both ways, although we all want it both ways. You can't simultaneously have a cheap currency for exports and job creation, with a valuable currency for cheap imports and a highly desired currency. At any moment, the U.S. is under criticism for having too cheap, too expensive, or both dollars.

Cheaper dollars meant that foreign investments in the U.S. are cheaper, while American investments abroad are more expensive. Thus it is not too surprising to discover that from 1973 to 1981 there was a major foreign investment boom in the U.S., while U.S. foreign investments slowed. After 1981, the reverse occurred.

The Amerians rather like their floating rate, since it allows for flexibility in U.S. international dealings. Major West European countries and Japan would rather have fixed rates, preferably at prices which slightly undervalued them. If this happened, exports would be cheap and the local economy would boom, and jobs are a hot political issue everywhere in the stagnant 1980's. But the critical question of how to fix any rate that will stay fixed, given the propensity of local governments to try to spend far too much always, remains. Remember the case of France noted above. If even a few countries inflate too much, then their rates change, and guess what? We are back to the floating system again. To return to fixed rates implies that every country in the world would apply severe fiscal discipline on themselves and always make internal adjustments to external problems. No country in the world could possibly make such a promise, given any conceivable political system. Hence the floating rates are likely to remain.

OIL AND DOLLARS:

In late 1973, the Oil Producing and Exporting Countries (OPEC), a cartel which controls much of the world crude oil production which is exported, increased crude oil prices fourfold, from roughly $3.00 per barrel to about $12.00 per barrel. Since most of the Western countries, including the United States, import large quantities of oil, this move immediately put a huge strain on the world monetary system. Overnight, oil importing countries had to find about $100 billion per year extra to finance critical petroleum imports. Through historic accident, most world oil was paid for in U.S. dollars, so the U.S. was immediately involved in two ways; first as an importer who had to pay its bills, and second, as a provider of world oil currency needed by other countries to pay their oil bills. The oil producing states suddenly began to receive additional tens of billions of dollars per year for their oil.

The world had no sooner managed, more or less, to adjust to this oil price shock when prices were again raised to about $35 to $40 per barrel in 1979-80. Once again, the oil producers piled up huge balance of payments surplusses, while the importing countries had to find dollars to pay for them. As supplies rose in response to these higher prices, world oil prices drifted downward to around $26 to $30 per barrel, where they remain in 1984.

This energy price explosion led to many efforts to reduce imports
of oil, many of which have worked. But for non-oil producers such as
Japan, Italy, Brazil, and West Germany, plus many other countries, these
price increases have meant much larger foreign exchange expeditures for
oil.   In poorer countries, just earning or borrowing the dollars to pay
for oil can be a major financial problem. Somehow, in spite of much
concern and worry about the potential collapse of the system, it has
managed to survive. The critical developments went about like this:

1.   As the OPEC countries acquired new billions of dollars, they
tended to spend most of it. By 1979, all but three of the thirteen OPEC
countries were actually in balance of payments deficit.   The three
surplus countries, Kuwait, Saudi Arabia, and the United Arab Emirates,
are countries with small populations and huge oil reserves.   Oil
exporters with big production and big populations, such as Iran,
Venezuela, Nigeria, and Indonesia, have found ways to spend their new
wealth.   This situation is the same now as it was in 1979, except that
the surplus countries have much smaller surplusses than they did in the
late 1970's.

The result has been a booming trade with all OPEC countries by all
Western countries and Japan.   Many of those petro-dollars were returned
to the advanced countries to pay for food, weapons, consumer goods, and
industrial equipment.   This enabled these coutries to pay their oil
bills without too much trouble.

Poorer countries without exports needed by OPEC were in trouble,
but a few, most notably India and Pakistan, profited by exporting people
to some OPEC countries in the Persian Gulf area to do both skilled and
unskilled work now needed in the industrial and commercial booms
sweeping this area. Worker remittances home in hard currencies helped
pay for the oil needed.

2.   The OPEC states with big dollar surpluses had to do something
with them. They tended to put them out at interest in Western countries,
including the U.S., and these funds were invested largely in government
securities and in certificates of deposit at larger banks. The banks
now had additional new billions to lend. One obvious place to lend at
good rates of return was to countries, and the petro-dollar recycling
took the form of multi-billion dollar loans to many countries, rich and
poor, who could stand up to presumably close credit scrutiny of coldly
analytical bankers. Poland, Mexico, Zaire, Turkey, Denmark, Brazil, and
many other countries were able to obtain dollar loans from private
Western banks.

This lending quickly became a multibillion dollar business,
completely dominating the relatively smaller amounts lent by official
organizations such as the World Bank and the IMF. By 1981, perhaps $700
to $900 billion had been lent in this manner. Bankers tended to regard
countries just as they did individuals or corporations.   Just what
collateral could a country offer? Mexico, with huge oil deposits (and
not an OPEC member), good exports of cotton and industrial products,
looked good.   But the bankers forgot that each bank might make a huge
loan to Mexico looking at the same data, without much concern about
other banks.   Thus the available collateral might be spread far too

thin.   They also chose to ignore the fact that while one can force a
person or company into bankrupcy, you can´t force a country into
insolvency.   If the country doesn´t pay, it can be virtually impossible
to get one´s money back.   Countries are extremely reluctant to default,
since such an action would lead to further credit cutoffs and a rapid
decline in local economic activity, but the lending risk is always
higher than for a domestic loan.

By 1981, the banks were getting very nervous, since these country
loans were getting larger than bank equity. Thus if Mexico and Brazil
both defaulted, the resulting losses would wipe out all stockholder´s
equity in most of the ten largest U.S. commercial banks.   As the bankers
became cautious, the world recession came along, slowing down export
markets for many creditor countries. Oil prices declined, and petroleum
producers such as Mexico had to sell more oil to get the same number of
dollars, which Mexico couldn´t do.   One by one, countries found
themselves unable to repay principal, and some couldn´t even pay
interest on existing debts.   Poland, Brazil, and Mexico are now in
virtual de facto default, although their bankers, by necessity, have
cooperated by extending old loans and lowering interest rates.   But new
loans are very difficult to obtain.

Thus petro-dollars may come from West Germany, who obtained them
from the U.S. by selling Mercedes in that country.   They are paid to
Saudi Arabia for oil, and the Saudis then deposit them in a major New
York commercial bank.   The bank lends them out to Brazil, who uses them
to buy industrial equipment from the U.S.   The U.S. uses them to pay for
Nigerian oil, and the Nigerians use them to pay for Japanese trucks.
The Japanese use them to buy Kuwaiti oil...and the cycling process goes
on, always in dollars.   The game goes on, for a while more at least,
although those debtor countries have to cut back imports dramatically to
save foreign currency to pay back old debts.   As they do, exports from
Western Europe, Japan, and the U.S. slow, and these countries have
unemployment problems.   This was not an inconsiderable factor in pushing
the world into recession after 1980.

3.   As this game proceeded after 1973, the U.S. began to run large
balance of payments deficits.   In part this reflected increasing oil
imports, but it also reflected the more rapid recovery of the U.S. from
the oil price rise induced recession of 1974-75.   As the U.S. economy
recovered rapidly, the country sucked in imports from many countries.
Exports expanded, but imports went up faster. The net result was balance
of payments deficits in the range of $25 to $30 billions per year, as
compared to $2 to $4 billions in the 1950´s and 1960´s.   American
authorities had also discovered the delightful aspect of floating rates
that we mentioned earlier. A bit more inflation in the U.S. merely meant
(they thought) that the U.S. dollar would drop slightly in world
markets.   But other countries saw the same point, and the world began a
decade of rapid price inflation in most countries.   Vastly higher
energy prices didn´t help, since energy costs percolate through the
entire economy, leading to price increases everywhere.

Massive deficits pushed the dollar lower in world money markets,
particularly against the big surplus countries, namely West Germany,
Japan, and Switzerland.   The problem here was that the dollar was being

used as a key world currency, yet its value was declining. Those holding dollars found that in terms of other harder currencies, their assets were shrinking. Hence they tried to shift out of dollars, and the resulting demand for harder currencies pushed the dollar lower than before.

One result was that the harder currency countries got their oil cheaper, since they paid for it in dollars. Japan, whose yen had risen over thirty percent against the dollar, could now buy oil for thirty percent less. This enhanced the Japanese competitive position in the world and made it easier for the Japanese to run still bigger surplusses.

The problem that the world faced in the mid-1970's was that nothing could really replace the dollar. West Germany and Switzerland are relatively small economies compared to the U.S.; if they tried to run massive deficits to provide world liquidity, they rather quickly would collapse, as nervous traders noticed their deficits and bailed out of these currencies. Japan still has many capital flow exchange controls and is not the least bit interested in being a key currency.

4.   By 1980, no one knew what to do but stumble on, but local U.S. politics partially resolved the problem. The election of a more conservative president, efforts to restrain the dollar money supply, and other contractionary efforts aimed largely at the domestic economy began to send the dollar up on world markets. By 1983, it was almost as strong in terms of most major countries' currencies as it had been in 1973, and it was still rising slightly. Once again, the dollar was sound, at least compared to anything else, and it remains the key world currency. Various other hard currencies get used for international transactions, but the dollar is still by far the most important.

5.   Because oil is paid for in dollars, the U.S. can pay for its oil imports (or anything else) by creating more dollars, which is what has happened. As we noted earlier, this annoys many foreigners, but no one can come up with any viable solution to the very real need for a world currency to finance every sort of international transaction. So, we stumble on.

The U.S. deficit shows up in various places as a huge surplus, and the surplus countries typicaly invest in the U.S. in one way or another. OPEC countries typically took passive, portfolio investments, while the Japanese, Swiss, and West Germans tend to make direct investments with their own MNCs taking part. In either case, these countries earn interest or profits in dollars which can flow out of the U.S., or be reinvested there, thus making the investments a good deal in both the short and long term. Remember that you can buy anything, anywhere, with dollars, which is more than can be said for most local currencies.

The first edition of this book (in 1965) discussed the problems of the fixed dollar exchange rate, and the danger that the American balance of payments deficit would lead to problems. We were right...the U.S. and the world did have problems. The Second Edition (1974) looked at those new floating exchange rates and wondered how this new system would hang together. It did, somehow, although many forecast disaster at that time.   The Third Edition (1980) examined wonderingly those huge petro-dollar loans and wondered if collapse might be near. It almost, but not quite happened.   And now in this Fourth Edition, we find ourselves wondering if major banks will collapse as countries fail to repay loans, and if the dollar will remain a key currency, and if it doesn't, what else have we got?

Through most of this period, until about 1981, we got steadily expanding world trade, massive growth of MNCs, both U.S. and others, rising per capita incomes in most countries, falling death rates, more and maybe even better education for more people, and other nice things. Problems we have in abundance, but so far the international monetary system has managed to hang together with surprising efficiency, given shocks that could have easily destroyed it all.

This durability of a screwy system stems largely from the fact that those who might wreck the system, namely the big surplus countries at any moment, realize that if the system collapses, they go down with the ship, too.   Those with power to destroy examine the alternatives and find nothing better than the jerry built system now in place.   Minor reform is possible, and in the future something a bit more reasonable might be constructed.   But for the moment we lurch from crisis to crisis, always (so far) coming out in one piece. Time will tell if the Fifth Edition will require a discussion of some major reconstruction of the international monetary system functionings and structure. We doubt it...having followed this thing for over twenty years, it seems reasonable to suspect that it might endure for a while longer.   But uncertainty is a real fact of life when one examines anything international.

FLOATING EXCHANGE RATES AND SPECULATION

Exchange rates now float, and they can go up or down rapidly on any given day. A problem for all international operators in the 1980's is to figure out how to handle these day to day fluctuations.

Speculators handle some of the problems. One can speculate in currencies as easily as in stocks, real estate, soybeans, or any other commodity.   Foreign exchange spot and future rates are quoted for many major currencies, and one can buy or sell depending on one's instincts. Possible gains (or losses) can be huge. Quite recently futures trading has begun in the U.S. in major foreign currencies, and many speculators not the least interested in international transactions, but very interested in any good speculation, have entered the market.

Traders not interested in speculation also have problems, since if they accept an order for future delivery and payment, they have to figure out how to handle possible changes in value. An American firm may accept an order now for delivery of $300 million worth of jet aircraft two years hence, payment to be made on delivery by a West German firm.   Should the payments be denominated in marks or dollars? If the exporter anticipates the dollar to decline relative to the mark, he might try for marks. But suppose the dollar increases in value? Here an aircraft manufacturer is involved in speculation whether he likes it or not. A sophisticated West German buyer might also have his own ideas about future currency values and try to get on the right side of the market, which merely adds to the confusion.

One way to avoid this speculation is to buy dollars or marks for future delivery, but now the firm incurs a substantial additional cost. This example suggests why many would like stable world currencies. Stability eliminates one major risk of doing international business.

Those who invest in foreign countries also incur exchange risk. They may also speculate. An American can buy a British government interest paying bond, denominated in pounds. If the pound rises relative to the dollar, then the speculator not only gets his interest, but his exchange gain as well. If pounds decline, however, he could lose a lot. All foreign investors face this problem, including all MNCs.

This speculative factor turns our attention to a fundumental question. Just what makes currencies fluctuate? Is it possible to forecast exchange rate fluctuations?

One could propose a forecasting model of this form: A given exchange rate is a function of the following variables...

Many such models have been formulated. We have mentioned one major variable, the relative rate of inflation between countries, but one could add such factors as the foreign reserves a country may have, in hard currencies or gold; the foreign borrowing ability the country has; its growth relative to other countries in critical export sectors; its present balance of payments position (deficit or surplus); capital flows net (in and out of the country); and various psychological factors, such as speculators´ expectations about the country´s future.

The probable answer to our question is that it is about as easy to forecast exchange rates as the stock market. If we all could forecast the stock market, we would all be millionaires...but somehow only a lucky or astute few get rich at this activity. To date, although some very clever theorists have turned their attention to this exchange rate forecasting problem, no one has found a sure fire prediction formula. Many try, however, with varying results.

The demand factors noted above are easy to list, but hard to work with. Remember that countries can also have dirty (e.g., managed) floats. If their currency is rising, and they don´t want it to rise, their central banks can produce more money to sell, keeping the price down. If they want to avoid a fall, they can borrow from abroad or run down reserves. One may be sure a currency is about to fall, but the exact timing of the fall is very, very difficult to forecast.

All of this makes life harder for everyone, but as we said before, what else is there? No one can really figure out a better world monetary system than the one we have, even though any knowledgable observer can easily list dozens of major defects.

IMPROVING THE BALANCE OF PAYMENTS

Normally there are a handful of surplus countries and over a hundred deficit ones. It is typically far easier to spend money than earn it, and politicians everywhere are under pressure to give the voters a free lunch...except in the end, there is no free lunch. Inevitably, a balance of payments deficit gets out of hand, and the country must do something. What can be done?

Figure 4-2 suggests various corrective measures. All have been tried at one time or another by every country in the world. Old hands can remember the frantic efforts of the Japanese in the 1950´s to get their economic house in order, given their huge BP deficits, and not so old hands can remember the U.S. trying to do the same in the 1960´s. Given a relatively dynamic international economy, inevitably any country eventually has problems. One can often find discussions of many of these measures in such business journals as THE WALL STREET JOURNAL or BUSINESS WEEK. The key point is that any or all of them will have the effect of either reducing foreign exchange requirements, or earning or somehow getting more foreign exchange. Impecunious American college students, forever aware of their problems of getting that foreign currency known as dollars, should have no trouble understanding what is being attempted here by countries. The country problem is exactly the same as for individuals for precisely the same reason. An individual cannot legally create his country´s currency, nor can a country legally create another country´s currency. Students need imports from the outside world to survive, and so do countries.

FIGURE 4-2

POTENTIAL BALANCE OF PAYMENTS CORRECTIVE MEASURES

Demand Side:

Current account:
  Restrict imports
    Deflate economy through proper monetary-fiscal policies
    Greater import restrictions
      Tariff increases
      Quota decreases
      Exchange control
  Restrict purchases of foreign services
    Legal-administrative pressures to use local services
    Exchange control
  Restrict tourism by citizens abroad
    Controls on travel abroad
    Controls of purchases of foreign currency for external tourism
Capital account:
  Obtain short term credits
    Government loans
    Private loans
    Force foreign exporters to wait for cash payments
  Obtain long term credits
    Government loans
    Loans from international agencies
    Private loans
  Obtain grants or gifts
    Private grants (emigrant, remittances, charitable organizations)
    Government grants
    International agency grants

Supply Side:

Current Account:
  Expand exports
    Price reductions
    Trade promotion
    Tax relief
    Export subsidies
  Expand sales of locally produced services
  Expand tourism to country
    Promotion activities
    Special price concessions
      Low transport prices
      Special exchange rates
    Relax visa and other administrative requirements
Capital Account:
  Shift loans from foreign to local sources
  Rules controlling loans
    Tax increases on foreign loans

Questions for Discussion

1.   Obtain a copy of the WALL STREET JOURNAL. Someplace in the back pages you will find various international monetary quotations, along with price quotations for foreign bonds.

This book sells for 54 West German marks in West Germany, 126 French francs in France, and 12 pounds in Great Britain.   In which country do students get the best buy?

2.   Many poorer countries have argued that if SDRs are to be manufactured out of thin air, the poorer countries should get most of them.   The U.S. government has so far objected, thinking that this is a poor idea.

What do you think? Is the idea of giving billions of dollars worth of SDRs each year to poorer countries a good idea? Why or why not?

3. Assume that a wealthy (and very obscure) relative of yours has just died and left you 800,000 Indian rupees. What do you have? What can you do with it? Check around and see if you can determine just what this asset really is. Can you spend this estate in the United States without any problems?

4.   Find the quotation for today for gold in the WALL STREET JOURNAL.   Could you buy some if you had the money? Would you?   Does this price have anything to do with the present international monetary system?

5. Since 1980, the U.S. dollar has risen about 30 percent in terms of the West German mark. How would you feel about this in the United States if:

A) You were a Mercedes dealer.

B)   You were an American soldier stationed in West Germany being paid in dollars.

C) Your dear old German aunt living in Berlin wants to visit you, but never quite had enough marks to make the trip.

D) You were a West German student studying in the United States on a scholarship paid in marks.

E) You were a West German student studying in the United States on a scholarship paid in dollars.

F)   You owned a small American company which already had received feelers about being purchased by a West German firm. You are not very interested in selling.

G)   You were an exporter of microcomputers to West Germany, and your German dealers have been complaining that your prices were too high.

H)   You were a Midwestern farmer producing soybeans for export   to West German food oil processors.

I)   You are a member of a brokerage firm which sells stocks listed on   the   New   York   Stock   Exchange, with a branch in   West   Germany   for servicing your West German buyers.

6.   Many observers and thinkers feel that fixed exchange rates are a   good   idea, and that we should have an international monetary   system which   has   fixed rates between all major currencies.   Others feel   that floating rates are better.

What   do you think?   Give two arguments for fixed rates.   Now, give two arguments for floating rates.

Supplementary Readings

Aliber, Robert Z.   CHOICE FOR THE DOLLAR.   Washington: National Planning Association, 1969.

Caves,   Richard   E. and Jones, Ronald W.   WORLD TRADE AND PAYMENTS: AN INTRODUCTION.   Boston: Little, Brown 1973.

Ellsworth,   P.T.   and   Leith, Clark J.   THE INTERNATIONAL   ECONOMY,   5TH EDITION.   New York: MacMillan, 1975.

Harris, Seymour E.   THE DOLLAR IN CRISIS.   New York: Harcourt, Brace, & World, 1961.

Kindleberger,Charles   P.   and Linderi, Peter.   INTERNATIONAL   ECONOMICS, 6TH EDITION.   Homewood, Ill.:   Richard D. Irwin, Inc., 1978.

Kubarych,   Roger M.   FOREIGN EXCHANGE MARKETS IN THE UNITED STATES.   New York: Federal Reserve Bank of New York, 1982.

Michaely,   Michael.   BALANCE OF PAYMENTS ADJUSTMENT POLICIES: JAPAN, GERMANY,   AND   THE NETHERLANDS.   New York: National Bureau of   Economic Research, 1968.

Roosa,   Robert   V.   THE DOLLAR AND WORLD LIQUIDITY.   New York: Random House, 1967.

Root,   Franklin   R.   INTERNATIONAL TRADE AND INVESTMENTS,   4TH   EDITION. Cincinnati: South-Western, 1978.

Tew,   Brian.   THE   EVOLUTION   OF   THE   INTERNATIONAL   MONETARY   SYSTEM, 1945-1977.   New York: John Wiley and Sons, 1977.

Chapter 5

Behavioral Problems in International Business

Introduction

Citizens of any country typically have some sense of national identity. While these feelings may range from passionate expressions and feelings of belonging to a given race, geographic area, or economic or social unit to extremely dim notions that a person does in fact belong to a given country, the act of being a citizen usually does have some implications for international business activities. Peope such as the Dutch, the French, the Swedes, or the Danes usually have a close sense of race, nationality and economic cohesion, while in some of the newer African countries, some tribal units barely recognize that they are members of a new nation state. But in either case, there are national feelings, pride, and attitudes, and MNCs must recognize that these attitudes do affect their operations.

The impact of such sociological attitudes on MNCs is twofold: first, there is the indirect effect caused by laws, rules and regulations which reflect national attitudes. To take an extreme case, the present attitude of the North Korean government in excluding virtually all foreigners, particularly foreign business operations and managers, is not in itself a sociologicl attitude. But the rules laid down do presumably reflect the feelings of the majority of North Koreans, who for several centuries have endured the indignities of foreign governments and businessmen applying economic, political, and military pressure against a decaying Korean culture. The strong reaction at present reflects in part this feeling that foreigners do not really belong in North Korea.

The second impact is direct and unofficial. We are all familiar with the pattern of a mob attacking an American library or American embassy abroad. Terrorists kidnapping American or other foreign MNC executives are found in many countries. Not as familiar, but relatively similar in personal attitudes, is the strike against an American owned firm, or sabotage of a foreign owned plant because it is foreign. Such reactions to foreigners have quite direct results for MNCs. A new investment might not be made because of such feelings, even if the government of the country in question was actively seeking out foreign investment, and the legal rules provided incentives for such investment. Or the internal management of the MNC might be changed significantly because of worker reaction to the foreign devils who are the managers in such an MNC.

Still further direct impacts are seen in the way in which person to person contacts occur in a variety of cultures. In some cases the foreigner is most welcome; in others, the local citizens may be encouraged to throw rocks at him. Awareness of such differences has led to significant shifts in MNC operations around the world.

These international sociological constraints are closely related to local sociological constraints, since personal attitudes and beliefs and the resulting motivations and behavior are typically totally integrated within individuals, though not necessarily in any rational manner. But the way in which local people view the world generally will have much to do with the way they view foreigners, and any analysis of behavior would have to include local sociological constraints. As indicated earlier, the international sociological constraints also interlock with legal/political and economic international constraints. Emotional feelings toward foreigners lead to laws, rules, and regulations which must be taken into account by MNCs.

National Ideology

Nations, like individuals, have dominant ideals, attitudes, and points of view shared by a majority of their citizens. It is obvious that no country has a totally unanimous view of the world by all citizens, but to describe a person as a Frenchman, an American, or an Irishman is to define in part the kind of man being considered. Politics and laws, as well as economics, tend to follow the stereotypes. No one is surprised when the Irish pass a law in line with Catholic religious thinking, but if such a law were to be considered in the United States, impartial observers would agree that the government had taken leave of its senses.

In a similar manner, attitudes toward property rights, contracts, prices, wages, and similar matters are often unique to given national groups. Some countries regard cartels as the only sound and rational way to organize and control large enterprises; others pass antitrust laws, feeling that competition is much more important. Some countries feel strongly that large plants and other industrial assets properly belong to the people collectively, while others abhor such socialist action. Such attitudes tend to be expressed in law, and the law usually must be obeyed by foreign firms.

Thus in India, it is strongly felt by influential persons that the proper form of society is socialistic. This particular belief is apparently built upon a local ethical base combined with English Fabian Socialist thinking and Marxian political-economic thought, combined with various other local and foreign intellectual and ethical influences. It does not do much good for a foreigner to consider this attitude erroneous or uninformed; if one is to do business in India, it must be taken into account as a constraint. Also to be taken into account here is the inevitable criticism with which profit taking will be observed in India. In the view of many influential Indians, any private profits are immoral, and the profit taker is unethical.

This Indian attitude leads to many legal restrictions concerning the types of investment which can be made, the way in which profits can be remitted, and so on. Such rules rarely arise in vaccuums. Sociological and economic pressures combines to make them as they are.

Countries professing and behaving in accordance with traditional communist ideology, such as Albania and North Korea, do not allow foreign business operations of any sort to be performed within their frontiers. One can again point to the given law or decree which prohibits this, but at the base of the law are strong feelings about profits, private free enterprise, and the way in which societies should be organized, all of which are manifestations of this national ideology.

Political leaders, even despotic ones, tend to reflect the attitudes of their people, which is one reason that major speeches of such leaders are listened to with care by foreign politicians and business managers. Spoken hostility can often lead to actual hostility, as happened in Iran within recent years.

But such overt manifestations of hostility often tend to be overemphasized. Political leaders have to play to vulgar popular opinion, and it is usually true that they are realists. A potential foreign investor, scanning the local newspaper, is not likely to realize that while a potentate is publically damning Americans, his development minister is quietly trying to obtain foreign investments. Americans are often surprised at the relatively warm welcome they receive as individuals in countries reputed to be quite hostile to the United States. The question of what public opinion and reaction really are often is a subtle and complex issue, which must be carefully analyzed by the firm to determine what is really going on.

This whole question is made more complex by frequent sharp divergences of opinion within a country. Foreigners often tend to think of a country as a monolithic unit. Thus to Americans, a Mexican is a type of individual which is clear cut. However, there are 70 million Mexicans, and their cultural attitudes, politics, standards of living, religion, and view towards the world diverge enormously. Who is relevant--a Mexican Marxist, working toward the eventual nationalization of all industry; the Mexican peasant; the Mexican government technocrat; or the new organization man Mexican, working as a skilled business technician for a foreign or local manufacturing firm? Numerous examples of all types exist, and it is easy to oversimplify the question and conclude that, "Mexicans generally believe that...", with whatever one thinks they believe filled in. Where a multimillion dollar investment is to be made for a period of twenty years or more, this sort of questioning of attitudes is relevant. If the general Mexican trend is toward nationalization and socialism, one decision might be made. If it is felt that Mexico will mature toward the point of view of the developed Western private property democracies, quite another can be endorsed. The difficulty for MNCs is that much evidence can be accumulated on each side of the question, which makes accurate pulse-taking difficult.

There is an evolving academic field in international business called political risk assessment, which tries to forecast and determine what is really going on. Given opposition parties seeking power, who may have sharply different ideas about what should be done, countries can and have changed in very short times from ones that embrace MNCs to ones that expropriate them and exile them, and vice-versa. Thus Iran went from a strong pro-MNC stance in 1979 to a violently anti-MNC stance within a year, while the People's Republic of China (PRC) went in the other direction within a few years after 1980. An MNC that has a reasonable idea of what is likely to happen can survive much better than one that hopes for the best. Countries often revile some kinds of MNCs, while welcoming others.

Risk assessment includes a variety of factors, but clearly popular and opinion leader's ideas about MNCs and other direct foreign involvements are critical. As noted above, a real problem is to figure out just what people do feel, given wide variations within almost any country. A second problem is to figure out who is likely to have power in the forseeable future, and what their views of MNCs will be. Ideology does matter, particularly if the ideologues control the government.

While ideological considerations most frequently appear as direct constraints in law, it is true that on occasion firms are pressured directly by such factors. Thus the French strongly believe that they should be responsible for their own national defense forces. This implies that as much defense material as possible should be manufactured by French firms in France, and in fact, rarely does a foreign owned firm in France make any serious effort to sell defense materials to the French government. Here the impact is on firm product line, types and locations of customers, and nature and extent of research and development activity. There is no law which prevents this activity, but it is not normally done.

American national ideology often has direct impact on firms operating overseas as well. For many years, the U.S. government banned exports to the PRC. However, many other European countries did not enforce such a ban. An American MNC with a French manufacturing plant could legally sell goods in China, although few did so. The reason was not legal, but ideological. Note the subtleties here. The U.S. MNC might not care much about the moral stance of the U.S. government, but if it did sell goods to the PRC, then it just might be attacked at home in a variety of ways by anti-communist zealots. A federal prosecutor might discover some minor violation of a law, and charge the firm; boycotts might occur, or other unpleasant events might make the sales cost more than they were worth. Or the MNC's management might really feel that such sales were immoral. For whatever behavioral reason, however, those sales were not made.

The implications of national ideology run through all of the critical elements of the management process. Depending on the point of view of the country concerned, literally any firm or managerial function might be directly affected by a point of view held by large numbers of local citizens. In one country, marketing might be affected by boycotts of the company's products; in another production has to be adjusted to take into account local feelings. Thus in a Moslem country, workers will pray five times a day, and production schedules must be adjusted accordingly. It would be unwise to assign birth control research and

development to a company's branch in Spain or Ireland, and staffing with
Jews in Saudi Arabia is not recommended, regardless of how competent the
individuals concerned might be. In one country the purchase of the
stock of a foreign company might be considered a wise, sound investment;
in another a traitorous act to the motherland. Firms unaware of the
proud histories and traditions of the countries in which they operate
may find continuing inefficiencies created by the constant friction
between their managers and the host country citizens.

View toward Foreigners

The outsider is a familiar theme in fiction in many lands and
languages. He or she comes to the close-knit community as a threat,
representing another set of environmental influences, a different way of
thinking, a peculiar type of ethics, and a potential menace to the
stability and prosperity of the local culture.

By definition, an MNC is this sort of outsider. Usually it is a
wealthy outsider, representing tantalizing possibilities of wealth
undreamed of, of potential unrealized, of possibilities overlooked,
perhaps for generations. Its local managers and technicians,
particularly if they come from the outside, are viewed with mixed
emotions by the local populace.

The way in which the foreigner is greeted may well depend on a
variety of complex pressures, propaganda, influence, and information,
much of it old before the people in question were even born. Arabs
still fight, in some elemental intuitive way, the crusades, whenever the
European Christian appears on the scene, and the Chinese intuitively
resent the foreign barbarians, whoever they may be. Village elders
throughout the world resist the outsider, particularly from the affluent
West, representing as he or she does a very real threat to the local
power and prestige structure. Malaysians and Philippinos resent
Japanese businessmen for reasons connected with Japanese activities in
World War II in those countries. One does not expect the local witch
doctor to appreciate the competition created by the new public health
service mobile stations with their hypodermic needles, doctors, and
drugs. In many subtle and not so subtle ways, the harbinger of
unsettling new methods, new thoughts, and new technology is resisted all
over the world.

There is, of course, the opposite side of this coin. Most persons
appreciate novelty, particularly when it appears to offer some advantage
to themselves, and the Western world has brought a variety of intriguing
items to many part of the world, including such diverse things as pickup
trucks, transistor radios, typhoid shots, and antimalaria campaigns. To
many, at least a few of the items brought are well worth while. A man
with a pickup truck can become a leader and a person of prominence,
replacing older animal forms of transport. Everyone's children benefit
from the shots, and the transistor radios are a window on the world for
billions. Perhaps there may be a new job, a new way of life, which will
some along with the strangers. And of course, in many cultures there is
the genuine curiousity about the persons from outside, particularly if
he or she comes unarmed, with intriguing tales to tell, and interesting
personal ways and artifacts about him.

This dichotomy of feelings about the outsiders runs through many cultures, not only including those now considered underdeveloped. Until quite recently, very few persons had ever seen many foreigners, or traveled very far from the spot they were born. Few Belgians had seen many Italians, nor had many provincial Englishmen talked to Japanese. Perhaps few ever cared to, for that matter. Besides, in the older European countries there had always been wars, and the outsiders always represented a real or potential enemy. The rise of nationalism, first in Europe, and later all over the world, tended to reinforce the attitudes held toward foreigners, and legislation everywhere refects this reluctance to allow the outsider a strong foothold in the mother country. MNCs, in their enormous expansion since World War II have been steadily pressing back the meaning and implications of the outsider, but the suspicions still remain in many cases.

In a few places, such as in El Salvador or Iran in 1984, affluent foreigners may be so endangered that MNCs cease to function. Racial and religious biases are often very relevant. Some foreigners may be welcome, as long as they are not Indian, white, or Japanese. Or exactly the reverse may be true in a neighboring country. In this individual sense, the staffing functions of any MNC are directly affected. Regardless of how good a given manager may be, if he or she happens to be the wrong color or religion or nationality or sex, he or she may not be able to function as a manager or an individual in a given locality. The foreign manager may function badly because while he or she is tolerated, he or she cannot manage in the necessary manner.

In other countries, the foreigner may be so common and so unnoticed that literally any person who is not noticeably handicapped by language problems can survive without any difficulty. Virtually any human who speaks passable English and has the necessary skills could manage almost anything in the United States, since this country is so used to diverse racial, religious, and ethnic types. Indeed, this particular point is one reason why the U.S. appears to be such an attractive place for foreign investment. This very point also suggests why firms hesitate to invest in highly homogeneous Japan, where anyone but a Japanese is so obviously different.

One frequent legal manifestation of this attitude is a law requiring a certain percentage of all employees to be local citizens. A part of the law's rationale stems from the feeling that the foreigners (usually Americans, Japanese, or Europeans) will try to utilize their own citizens for work as far as possible. Even when qualified nationals are available, they will not be utilized. While such legislation has quite direct impacts on staffing, even in countries without legislation many MNCs do make serious efforts to utilize nationals, feeling that political and social pressures will become too extreme if this is not done.

A variant of this law is one requiring work visas or permits for all foreigners. Virtually all countries have such legislation, and often it is extremely difficult to get one's key personnel into the country to work. Thus foreign students in the U.S. are typically specifically barred from working, except in a few special situations directly involving their educations. Such rules can be extremely onerous indirectly for MNCs, since these days so many dual career families exist. To ask a capable executive with a professionally trained wife to go abroad, knowing that the wife will be unable to practice professionally, often just doesn't work. The couple stays where they can both pursue their careers. Wives of government personnel can get bored very easily when their husbands are assigned to such places, and foreign students in the U.S. struggle financially when their skilled spouses cannot work. In all of these cases, the notion that somehow the country is run for the benefit of citizens, not dirty foreigners, is strong. We do live in a nationalistic world.

This attitude toward aliens interlocks closely with national ideology, and in fact may be a part of it. Some nations generally don't mind most kinds of foreigners, as in the U.S.; others detest them, as in Iran; and most others fall somewhere between the extremes. The subtle psychology of entire peoples is relevant here, and the kinds of restrictions which the firm may face will depend in large part on how the country views the citizens of other nations.

Another problem in this area facing many MNCs is that in the newer nation states where the feeling of national cohesion is slight, there may be still more resentment of foreigners than in a country where the national identity is well established, and where citizens are not too perturbed by nagging doubts about their own self-importance. A firm may often find quite severe restrictions on the use of foreign workers and managers in such a country, and it also may find linguistic and religious restrictions as well. It may also find rather frequent outbursts of anti-foreign sentiment, as leaders attack foreign devils to provide a sense of cohesion and internal purpose. One can adjust to such a situation, but only at some cost.

The major impact of this international constraint on firms is on staffing, direction, planning and innovation, and public and external relations. When faced with this sort of anti-foreign feeling in a given country, a perceptive firm attempts to alter plans and basic goals in a way which will give local people a feeling of participation. Managerial behavior in the planning process may well be quite different than in a situation where this factor is unimportant. If prominent local leaders spend much time attacking foreigners in the country, new plans may well include potential reactions to the criticism. External public relations will necessarily have to include some attention to the anti-foreign feeling if it is strongly present. The impact on staffing and direction can be quite important, particularly if foreigners are giving the orders. Firms can adjust to such pressures although it is easier to give advice or note the problem than it is to solve it. But in many cases, this many turn out to be one of the most critical problems facing management, and it must be handled effectively if the MNCs' foreign branch or subsidiary is to survive. The most single critical problem for any firm is its legitimacy. If the society it is in declares it illegitimate, the game is over.

Nature and Extent of Nationalism

Nationalism is one Western invention which has been eagerly seized upon by newer states of all levels of political and economic

development.   Nationalistic feelings may in some cases be restricted
only to some ethnic or religious group, real or imagined, or it may
encompass varied groups of tribes, families, or villages, whose only
real communality is that they are all within a boundary line drawn by a
European a century or more ago.

Older states have had the time to develop strong feelings of
national unity. When one refers to a Frenchman, the picture evoked is
quite clear. The wars, revolutions, educational and cultural standards,
cuisine, attitudes toward women, and a myriad of other factors are
etched sharply for all to see. Foreign firms operating in France have
to be ever aware of what these feelings mean in terms of their own
treatment by the French. Firms attempting to operate without well
developed sensitivity in this area will quickly find that their
operations never seem to work well. Documents are lost in government
offices; critical permits cannot be obtained; indeed, the whole of the
country may intuitively reject a firm and its managers who are unable to
appreciate French attitudes. Few MNCs get into trouble this way, since
the French nationalistic attitude is clear cut, and any reasonably
sensitive group of managers is able to grasp quickly the essentials of
the situation.

A different problem is presented in the newly awakened nations,
such as those in Latin America and Africa. Here emergent nationalism
may take the form of "Mexico for the Mexicans", as many American and
British MNCs have learned to their dismay. Xenophobia in its most
virulent form is a common occurrence in such cases, and failure to
appreciate the power behind emergent nationalism has created great
difficulties and considerable financial losses. More recently, revived
religious fervor in Iran has created massive problems for MNCs,
including expropriation and expulsion.   Often such pressures may
overwelm political leaders who may have been responsible for fanning the
nationalistic sentiment in the first place.

Such attitudes result in legislation of the type Mexico now has,
where at least 51 percent of every enterprise must be owned by Mexican
nationals.   It also shows up in controls and limitations on foreign
technicians and managers.

Still another modern variant of nationalism is found in new states
which have had colonial histories, and whose boundaries are essentially
accidents of history, cutting across tribal ranges and ethnic and
religious groupings.   In the case of black Africa, this nationalism
often is tinged with considerable enmity toward whites and Asians,
leading in the limit to expulsion of large groups, as happened in 1973
when Uganda expelled virtually all its Asians. Bahais in Iran now may
face the same dismal fate, and long ago Armenians in Turkey had a very
difficult time. Hitler´s treatment of Jews in Germany and Europe was
only an extreme example of such emotions. The ruling elites are keenly
aware of their country´s relative poverty and lack of knowledge to
survive as a modern state, and such awareness may lead to considerable
feelings of uncertainty, anxiety, and insecurity. One reaction may well
be nationalism of the most virulent sort, which appears to be a
reaffirmation of the nation´s very existence. In the limit, foreigners
and all things foreign (except the guns) are denounced and banned as far

as possible. The usual results are laws intended to discriminate systematically against the hated foreigners and all they represent, and to create as rapidly as possible a local elite capable of handling economic, political, and military affairs. For many decades, such states tended to be Marxist and leftist, but the Iranian experience in recent years suggests that rightist, religiously oriented regimes may follow similar patterns.

Planning is often directly affected by such nationalistic sentiments. Firms considering operations in highly nationalistic environments must necessarily take these feeling into account in formulating their major objectives. The proper response to such situations may involve altering most of the critical elements, since it is difficult to operate in any area of the firm without taking account of local feelings. These nationalistic feelings also present the firm with a new element of risk, in that nationalization or expropriation may be quite real possibilities, and other activities must be adjusted accordingly.

The overt symbols of such hypernationalism may be quite disturbing to foreign firms, including such demonstrably unfriendly acts as expropriation of foreign firms' assets, an avowedly Marxist or religious orientation of government and its leaders, and frequent political expressions of total animosity toward all things Western. One can easily conclude that any foreign business activity in such situations is hopeless.

But such countries usually are badly in need of captial and technology, and their leaders often realize that their survival depends on rapid economic development. They usually need good management most of all, but few recognize this need. The result is that often the image is much worse than the reality. It is also true that the view toward foreigners held by the elites is not the same as those held by nonelitists, who are much more interested in eating, finding housing, and getting jobs than in flowery political rhetoric practiced at innumerable United Nations meetings. Foreign firms who are willing to explore such countries more closely may find not only good business opportunities, but unexpectedly warm welcomes in official and unofficial circles.

There is a recurring pattern here which merits close attention by MNCs. A country goes hypernationalistic, expropriates everything in sight, closes its borders, expels dissidents and nonethnics, and generally retreats into itself. A subtle assumption here is that management is irrelevant. Anyone in the country, even illiterates or political hacks, can easily manage a railroad, a factory, or a retail shop. So such people try, and disaster follows. Radicals everywhere enthusiastically support the struggling new country, finally free of imperial tyranny. The Soviets send aid in the form of guns and tanks, while other Third World countries wish the new revolutionaries well. All will end delightfully in a new socialist (or sometimes religious) utopia where men are finally liberated. The "women" in the last sentence is deliberately omitted, since such regimes are typically either macho oriented or have religious views towards women which are different than modern Western views, to put it mildly. No one much cares what the women do, in too many cases.

After five or ten years of this orientation, the country is either a Soviet client state, propped up by huge subsidies (Cuba), or in more or less total economic disarray (Uganda, Angola, Ethiopia). Utopias can have bad luck too, such as drought (Ethiopia), but now, standing alone, it is hard to get Western support. After all, you just said last year at some major international gathering that Westerners were depraved neo-imperialist maniacs, who should be shot like mad dogs. Coming back this year to politely ask them for foreign assistance may not work, and the Soviets are not strong in agriculture, nor do they lend or give away hard currencies. They import food, not export it.

Of course all foreign capital inflows have long since stopped, except for some Soviet military aid, with perhaps a few industrial projects included. More importantly, many critical knowledge inflows have ceased. Almost no one really recognizes just how much information and technology flows informally within and around an MNC, as its technicians and managers work in a country. Everyone ignores the fact that astute MNCs, following the advice noted in this chapter, have hired smart, well educated local people and often sent them abroad to learn more. When they return, they are more highly qualified, but cutting off one country means that there is no such learning anymore. Foreign salesmen no longer approach local firms with intriguing offers of better and more productive equipment, and after sales service engineers from such firms are seen no more. Those who have never done work in productive enterprises inevitably underestimate the information flows generated by such means.

Perhaps most importantly, such countries suffer brain drains that can really be deadly. The persons with foreign technical, economic, or managerial knowledge get away if possible, never to return. Newly nationalized enterprises run badly, if at all. Who wants to come home to be shot? Those individuals with Western orientations are typically high on the liquidation list. Thus a few thousand Ethiopians, perhaps as many as a million Iranians, many Angolans, and even thousands of Chileans have left their countries in the past decade, to say nothing of those 60,000 or so hardworking and highly competent Asians who were forced to leave Uganda. Often these people were technicians and managers for an MNC in their home country, and when the regime changed, the people went with the MNC, not the new regime, who would have killed them anyhow. The gainers were the MNCs and other countries where such people now work.

You can own a machine, which makes it valuable, and you can expropriate it. Machines don't think or engage in politics, which is even better. But you can't own a human mind, and humans have all sorts of disgusting habits, like belonging to one religious group or political party or another...better to eliminate them, since they have no value. Perhaps the most significant single point about MNCs is that they clearly recognize that their skilled personnel are much more important than the machines. Countries, particularly hypernationalistic ones, always believe the machines are more important than the people. This may well explain their difficulties.

But in the end, most of these countries realize that they are falling behind, either gradually or disastrously. Then the end of this scenario comes when the country recants, quietly begins discussions with MNCs and Western governments, and rejoins the world. The PRC is only the largest and most visible of these recantations in the past decade. MNCs, particularly those with excellent technology, suddenly find the welcome mat out, and their possibilities are very good indeed. The firms that constantly scan the horizon for such possibilities can win big, and not all of them are huge firms either. Often a smaller high technology company can do extremely well in this dynamic situation.

In short, the revolutionary dogma which was so strong in the 1950's through the 1970's has failed. Countries will still have their revolutions, as El Savador and Nicaragua are demonstrating at this writing, but few, except the fanatics, really expect that the revolution will lead to better things. The most likely scenario for such countries is the one noted above. Countries now in their second or third decade of revolution are having those second thoughts. A good Marxist revolution in a poor country can do everything except produce useful goods and servives, which is exactly what MNCs do. Perhaps the prognosis is quite positive for such firms as a result.

Another factor aiding in less nationalistic tension is the rapid rise in wealth in the developed countries, plus the realization that cooperation with previously despised neighbors can increase wealth for all. The extraordinary success of the European Community (to be considered in detail in Chapter 8) has greatly enhanced this attitude. The general relaxation of nationalistic feelings, which existed so strongly in Europe and Japan as recently as 1945, are responsible in large part for the present boom in international business, since the bulk of such activity has involved Europe and Japan during the postwar period.

Questions for Discussion

1. Within the past decade the U.S. government has allowed trade with the PRC. Now American firms can export products to this country without too many restrictions. They can even invest in the PRC if they want.

Do you think that this business of dealing with a bunch of dangerous communist fanatics is a good idea? Does your image of the Red Chinese have anything to do with your answer?

2. The state of Israel is frequently at war with the Arab states. Which side are you on in this struggle, if any? Why? Does your image of Arabs and Jews have anything to do with your attitudes?

3. Already many European and Japanese (and even a few Indian and Hong Kongian) firms have invested in the United States, and many more are considering doing so. As with American firms abroad, it is quite likely that the few key top managers in these firms will be nationals of

the countries from which the investment money comes from, although the vast majority of the employees will be American.

Would it bother you to work for a firm in your state which had a Japanese top manager, to whom you reported? Why or why not? How about a German? A Swede? An Asian Indian?

4. Several states, noting the difficulty of getting plant investments within the state that provide good industrial jobs, have sent delegations to Europe and Japan to point out to various firms the advantages of using cheap American labor in Indiana or Illinois or South Carolina to produce products. The states reason that if they can get such investments, they really won't be any different than getting an American firm from another state to invest locally. After all, a good German or Japanese firm will pay taxes and hire people just like American firms would, and it may be no more difficult to control a foreign firm than one from another state.

Do you think that the encouragement of foreign investment in this way is a good idea? Why or why not? What behavioral attitudes do you have which influence your answer?

6. If you know any foreign students, take a good look at them (If YOU are a foreign student, take a look at your American friends). Do you regard them as different than American students? Why or why not? What special qualities (good or bad) do they have which makes them different?

7. Ask your foreign student friends to comment on the good and bad qualities of Americans they know. Are these qualities the same ones which you might notice in another American student? What special things do foreigners notice which you do not?

Supplementary Readings

American Universities Field Staff. EXPECTANT PEOPLES: NATIONALISM AND DEVELOPMENT. New York: Random House, 1963.

Davis, Keith, and Blomstrom, Robert L. BUSINESS, SOCIETY, AND ENVIRONMENT, 2D EDITION. New York: McGraw-Hill, 1971.

Deutsch, Karl W. and Folty, William J. NATION BUILDING. New York: Atherton Press, 1963.

Farmer, Richard N. INTERNATIONAL MANAGEMENT. Belmont, CA: Dickenson, 1968.

Richman, Barry M. and Copeland, Melvyn T. INTERNATIONAL MANAGEMENT AND ECONOMIC DEVELOPMENT. New York: McGraw-Hill, 1972.

Webber, Ross. CULTURE AND MANAGEMENT. Homewood, IL: Richard D. Irwin, 1969.

Chapter 6

Legal/Political Constraints

Introduction

Each country is sovereign, and each can and does discriminate against foreigners. How countries actually behave toward MNCs and other foreigners is the subject of this chapter.

These international constraints interlock with various domestic constraints, as noted in Table 3-2. This in turn leads to direct effects on the criticl elements of the management process for MNCs operating within the given environment. The focus here is on how these constraints affect firm performance.

The following discussion covers each of the political and legal constraints in turn.

Political Ideology

There is a spectrum of possibilities here, ranging from extreme left wing Communist states such as Albania and North Korea through somewhat socialistically inclined states such as India and many other Third World countries; through nominally capitalist countries such as West Germany and the United States; and on to even more conservative governments such as Iran. The extreme right and left may well meet in terms of rejecting foreigners, since a real problem for any totalitarian state of the right or left is total control, and the more open the system is, the harder political control becomes. Dissidents may leave; information of undesirable sorts enters; and new and potentially unsettling products can undermine authority. The usual pattern in such states is to close the system as much as possible to avoid foreign contamination, and states of both the extreme left and right have many controls over all foreign activities.

The more closed a system is, the more likely that it will be unable to obtain the latest technologies and ideas necessary for economic progress. Even more important, the less able the country will be to gain the latest military equipment, and authoritarian countries are always interested in more guns and tanks and troops. The essence of political control lies here. Moreover, if a contry doesn´t have the best, enemies may easily destroy it. Hence there inevitably is a struggle between getting the best ideas from foreigners and not becoming contaminated.

Communist countries experimented widely in the 1970's with cooperation agreements, which are a way of getting foreign technology without allowing MNCs in as equals. These agreements typically did not work well, mainly because it is extremely difficult to impose the free wheeling, rather flexible MNC private enterprise system on an inflexible planned economy. But such agreements still endure, and a few work well enough to be continued. All nations export and import, because they have to in order to survive. Turnkey projects might be allowed from time to time, since here the foreigners will leave as soon as the project is finished. In the authoritarian regimes, things banned typically involve some long run direct internal contacts with foreigners.

Countries are subject to change on the above points. The reason is simply that if a nation decides to remain totally isolated, it will probably stagnate. No country has a monopoly on ideas, and smaller countries are at a major disadvantage, given smaller and often less well educated populations. As a closed system notes its more open neighbors surging ahead, it is likely to change its mind. One wonders what a PRC official must think when he talks to a resident of Hong Kong or Taiwan. These other Chinese, with very open systems, have raised per capita incomes tenfold in the past thirty years, while the PRC has moved up perhaps 25 to 50 percent. The PRC is ideologically pure, but unfortunately poor, while those improbable open system Chinese states have done better than anyone economically, literally having ceased to be poor countries. It is not surprising that the PRC now appears to welcome foreign investment and contacts.

Socialist states present a more complex picture. These countries are typically quite poor, and they sometimes welcome the chance to obtain foreign investment, managerial and technical skills, and hard currencies derived from new exports. But many kinds of MNCs are excluded. The foreign manager finds his life made quite complicated by an apparatus of control, restriction, and licensing made necessary by the somewhat dubious outlook towards MNCs which most of these countries will tend to have.

These countries also are subject to change. Increasingly, astute elites are realizing that controls mean extra costs, and poorer countries cannot afford them. They also mean that even desirable MNCs, such as those with neat technologies and good export products, may be discouraged, since there are other easier countries to invest in. A common way to avoid controls legally is to set up free trade zones, where the rules resemble Hong Kong (e.g., very few, with very low taxes). The rest of the country is controlled as usual. In these zones, a type of wide open free enterprise can be practiced which can be extremely efficient, but not really acceptable nationwide. Thus both the PRC and India have recently set up such zones. Those in the PRC are next to Hong Kong, and the MNCs using them most are Hong Kong firms owned by Chinese, not European, Japanese, or U.S. MNCs. Such free trade zones have long been common in the U.S. and Western Europe, and they are set up to avoid onerous local controls and tariffs which would discourage both foreign and local enterprise. In the end, someone HAS to produce something, even though production may involve dubious ethics, immoral behavior, and all that. By isolating such things from the country's mainstream, hopefully they will not contaminate the country.

Capitalist countries are still more complex, since each country typically reserves some part of its economic activity for local citizens. Such industries as public utilities, transportation, and defense are typical examples of restricted areas. Often modern capitalist countries have large public sectors, where private competition is not welcome. Thus Japan and West Germany, considered bastions of capitalism, have state owned public utilities, such as railroads and electric power.

Such entry controls reflect varied historic pressures and problems which a given country may have experienced. Any MNC approaching any country needs a good local lawyer to give advice, since generalization on this point is impossible. Inevitably, there is some discrimination against foreigners, but the degree of discrimination varies widely. Countries also are subject to change without notice, as political parties and perceived problems change. In recent years, there has been much more interest in attracting the "right" kinds of MNCs to many countries, right meaning those offering new technologies and high paying jobs, along with good export potential. Often countries will subsidize MNCs through tax concessions; future employee training schemes; construction of new infrastructure, such as roads and sewers; or even cash. It has been increasingly realized that high paying, high skill industrial jobs are very scarce worldwide, and the MNCs offer them.

This ideological position has been changing rather rapidly since the 1970's. A major reason was the observation that countries that do not welcome foreign investments and MNCs often end up in one of two places: either as Soviet satellites, or with very slow growing economies. Virtually all of the fast growth, high technology work occurring in the world is controlled by MNCs from Western Europe, Japan, and the U.S., and failure to have these firms around merely means that the country falls behind. Hence much rethinking is being done, usually leading to attempts to get more foreign investment, not less.

A second critical factor is the observation that countries that give existing MNCs a bad time, through excess taxation, or other punitive measures up to and including expropriation, do not receive new investments, and they often have disinvestment, as MNCs quietly leave. Thus Quebec tried to make the French language mandatory and imposed a variety of mildly onerous restrictions on MNCs (and Canadian firms, too) in the 1970's. Firms then stopped investing and even moved out of Quebec, leading to major unemployment and economic stagnation problems in this province. It became hard to convince suspicious firms to come, and in the end, Quebec too launched a program to encourage investments and began to change its constraints that annoyed MNCs. Any country can do anything it wants, but there may be a large economic, and eventually political price to pay. And in the 1980's, with world recession, economic sluggishness and unemployment everywhere, relatively few countries are willing to pay the price. Hence we see more efforts to attract rather than repel MNCs, although there are still plenty of examples of both types of countries.

The political ideology constraint interrelates with almost all other international and local constraints, in that the types of political philosophies held by ruling elites will tend to be reflected in other legal constraints and economic variables. These politial attitudes also will reflect in part the sociological and educational factors in the given country. Appreciation of the ideology may lead to better understanding of how other constraints work out in practice.

Relevant Legal Rules for Foreign Business

The bulk of legal restrictions in most countries are usually the same for both foreign and local firms, although as noted above, there always are special rules of various sorts for foreigners. Thus the U.S. has special tax legislation which applies to nonresident aliens, as one example, although resident foreigners may be treated like citizens in most respects. A major reason for this is that a foreign firm or individual also has obligations in his or her home country, and it is necessary to give special treatment to avoid extreme discrimination. If a foreign manager in the U.S. had to pay all American taxes and all of his own country's taxes as well, he would be placed in an impossible position, and both countries are usually willing to make special arrangements for such persons or firms. A second reason for special treatment is that of discriminating against the foreigner, in the sense of penalizing him relative to local firms. The major areas of special treatment, apart from the general question of whether or not the firm can operate at all, are in the areas of labor law and tax treatment, and each will be considered in turn.

Labor Law. A general rule regarding labor in virtually all countries is that the foreign corporation treat its employees at least as well as local firms. MNCs are expected to observe all local labor legislation which applies in the country. In practice, this constraint often leads to some discrimination, since the MNC may be a large and powerful corporation, while many local firms are much smaller and harder to police. The result can be that the MNC observes local labor laws more precisely than local firms. The usual effect is to make labor somewhat more expensive for foreign companies than for local enterprises. This extra cost tends to be offset by higher productivity. MNCs typically are MNCs just because they are more productive. An odd byproduct of this point is that often the MNCs can cream the labor force, getting the best people by paying more and offering better working conditions, giving the MNCs an extra advantage.

Local labor legislation varies enormously between countries, depending on a large variety of local political factors. One can find examples of pre-feudal types of labor treatment (and even slavery in a few primitive countries) as well as very advanced social legislation in other states. Unions may be banned, carefully regulated, or legally placed in very powerful positions. As in other international constraints, such laws tend to change over time as local politics change. These purely local laws are local constraints, applying to the domestic economy. But if there is systematic discrimination against foreign firms in legal enforcement, they do become indirectly related to the international constraints.

A second type of labor law is that which overtly discriminates against foreigners or foreign firms. Employees of foreign companies are legally treated differently than employees of local companies. We have already mentioned percentage of nationals and work visa laws which discriminate against non-citizens, along with tax legislation which can discriminate against such people. MNCs frequently have problems in transferring key personnel to given countries, since they have to obtain hard to get work visas or permits.

Such rules can in fact discriminate among different countries. Thus Japan allows any professional to practice in Japan, providing he or she can prove professional competence. However, the law provides that this rule only applies to nationals of countries where reciprocity is allowed. This type of retaliation for real or imagined discriminations against a country's nationals abroad is rather common in such law dealing with foreigners.

Immigration law is relevant here, particularly in countries where people want to go, such as Kuwait, Great Britain, Canada, and the United States. Every country has laws about who can become citizens, and quite a few have laws about who can leave. Thus highly skilled non-Canadians who want to work in this country have to pay attention to immigration laws, as do their potential employers. Race, sex, skills, health, religion, ethnic background, family status, age, political attitudes, and a host of other criteria may determine who is entitled to become a citizen. This point can be particularly interesting for MNCs who need cross culturally skilled people at the home office. Thus an American MNC may well need a few skilled Arabists in their New York office. The obvious candidates might be citizens of various Arab states, but Americans of Arabic descent, including new immigrants, could also be qualified. If the new immigrant has his or her work permit, the personnel problem is much easier for the firm.

Many countries have rather extensive social security and job security legislation designed to protect employees from casual dismissal. Poorer countries often have large surpluses of unskilled labor, and political pressures often have led to laws attempting to protect those fortunate enough to have decent jobs. Wealthier countries in Europe try to protect workers' rights in this way. Only the most serious cause, such as theft, sabotage, or direct refusal to obey a superior, would be sufficient cause for dismissal. If the firm wishes to dismiss an employee, it often must pay an indemnity based on years of service. The discharge of a long term employee is difficult and expensive, and the result is that labor turnover among employees who have achieved tenure is small.

Unanticipated results include large turnover among employees just before they achieve tenure, since firms are unwilling to allow mediocre employees guaranteed employment for life (American university professors are keenly aware of this phenomenon). Another result is that firms are reluctant to invest in or hire many people if these laws are very restrictive. In effect, the country asks them to forecast personnel requirements for twenty years or more, and few firms can do this. If there is a technological change, or markets shift, the firm may be stuck with a very expensive labor redundancy problem.

This latter point leads to still another unintended result, which is to make it very difficult for new labor market entrants, typically women and the young, to get good jobs. In the 1980's, automation and robotization, the decline of traditional industrial markets, and economic recession have led to skyrocketing unemployment rates among these new groups all over the world. Rapid population growth in Third World countries merely compounds the problem, since each year more young people try to enter the workforce. Many MNCs study carefully the implications of hiring new workers, and if the country's laws are too onerous, then some other country will serve. The high technology industries, with their ability to be very flexible in location, are those that can avoid problems most easily.

While such laws are usually applicable to all firms, they may be applied more stringently to foreign firms. In such cases, informal discrimination against MNCs may raise labor cost relative to local firms to a considerable extent.

Jobs, particularly industrial jobs at relatively high pay rates, are a hot political issue everywhere, and the issue gets very heated when cutbacks and redundancies occur. Thus in the 1980's, pressure to guarantee jobs occurs in many parts of the world. In the EC, a proposal has been made to have MNCs reveal much more data about their internal operations than they have ever revealed before. One provision is to give advance notice of plant closures. American states have considered similar legislation for the same reason. Firms object stre uously to such proposals, arguing that the net result would be to give valuable information to competitors, but political pressures may force the EC and some other countries to require more disclosure.

Here again we encounter the limitations of countries. Any country can have any job security legislation it wants, at whatever cost to the local economy. But MNCs, if they find local rules too restrictive, simply do not invest, and local firms, stuck with large extra labor costs, find it difficult to export in competitive world markets. The resulting economic stagnation is not too attractive, yet local political pressures may force the issue. This is one major reason why labor policies are always in a state of flux. Countries try to get a bit too much, find themselves in trouble, and restructure the rules.

The result of these various labor rules and regulations is that staffing policies within firms are directly affected. A law providing for a given percentage of local workers leads the MNC to recruit and train more extensively in the local labor market, which is precisely what the law intended.

Unintended results are that MNCs' planning, production, research and development, and finance may also be directly affected. The usual result of restrictive labor legislation is to make labor more expensive than it otherwise might be. Quite apart from the humane aspects of the question, labor productivity relative to labor cost is a critical question for all firms. High labor costs can lead to disinvestment, or no investment; it can lead to rapid automation, leading to using less labor. Automation changes financial requirements directly, along with production techniques and the kinds of labor used. Research and development efforts may shift also.

Visitors to Third World countries are often puzzled to see highly automated production lines in areas where labor is apparently quite cheap. This sort of production planning results in part from various labor restrictions. The wage rates may appear cheap, but the machines may prove cheaper in the long run. Machines do not agitate, join unions, or strike. They do not require housing, medical care, or garbage disposal either, and these items are occasionally a part of labor costs for an MNC. The unemployed young and unskilled sit outside the plant, while a few highly trained technicians work inside producing the goods. This unintended effect of intricate and restrictive labor legislation has been a familiar pattern in many countries for decades. Here, one´s humanitarian instincts collide directly with economic realities, and the more open the economy is, the more pervasive is the competitition, which penalizes the inefficient. If a country prefers to be restrictive, it will pay a high price.

Finally, there is one aspect of labor law which is prevalent in Europe. Since shortly after World War II, most Northern European nations have required workers´ representation in undertakings over a certain size. However, the constitutions, powers, and effectiveness of these representative bodies vary not only from country to country, but even from one industry to another. In general, there are three distinct forms: workers´ self-management, as in Yugoslavia, where the workers theoretically make every managerial decision, co-determination, as in West Germany, where workers share equal representation on the supervisory boards with the managerial representatives of the owners; and shop-floor industrial democracy, as in Great Britain or Sweden, where the workers´ influence is directed more toward the day-to-day operations of the firm rather than toward strategic management. In each of these cases, the decision making processes of top management are altered considerably, and under such constraints the strategy of the MNC might be reconsidered.

Tax Law. Like labor law, local tax law also applies to MNCs, and firms are expected to pay their fair share of whatever taxes are levied by individual governments. It is often true that tax collectors are more zealous when pursuing MNCs, and foreigners may pay a bit more than local firms as a result.

Where the products of the firm are being sold only locally, the problem of purely local taxes is somewhat less important. Presumably, with the exception noted above, all firms pay about the same amount, and relatively little competitive disadvantage is felt if a given tax is too high. However, if the international firm also sells in third countries, local taxes can be a key constraint in initial investment decisions. A higher local tax on a key raw material or component might raise costs to a level which precludes export sales. Countries, well aware of this effect, and anxious to attract more investment, are often willing to grant special tax deals to both local and foreign firms that might locate in the country, so the tax subsidy question becomes relevant here as well. Subsidies are in effect the reverse of taxes. A country wants something and is willing to pay for it. Usually any subsidy is subject to complex rules, which have to be studied very closely by firms. This problem becomes extremely complex when one realizes that various local taxes (such as property taxes) may be more important than national taxes, and countries may have several levels of government levying taxes. Moreover, in almost any country tax laws will be so complex as to almost defy analysis. Once again, a really good local lawyer is needed.

Countries also levy special taxes on MNCs and foreigners. Such taxes are of a type not levied on local firms, or levied to a different degree on local companies. Thus Saudi Arabia has an income tax which applies only to foreigners; local citizens and firms pay a zakat tax which is of differing amounts. Chile had a special foreigners' tax on MNCs owned at least 75 percent by nonresidents, and many oil producing nations had special concession agreements with private foreign oil companies working within these countries which provided for special payments and taxes in return for concessionary privileges. On the other hand, countries such as France, the U.S., and the United Kingdom make no special effort to discriminate against foreign companies or individuals, although in most cases a special nonresident tax law applies to both individuals and MNCs active in these countries. Countries also often have tax treaties with each other, in an effort to equalize tax treatment for their nationals working in the other country. As a result, taxes may be somewhat higher or lower than they might be for a domestic taxpayer in the same circumstances.

Taxes are important enough to cause firms and individuals to try to avoid them, and whole mini-countries have built up reputations as tax havens. One can put one's money in such places without being taxed, legally, or illegally. Andorra, the Cayman Islands, and Bermuda are examples of such countries. The question of how MNCs and individuals manage to get the money to such countries more or less legally will come up in Chapter 10, but much money does flow to such tax havens, creating various tax collection problems for many governments around the world.

The impact of taxes and tax systems on firms will be extremely widespread and could conceivably affect every one of the critical elements of the management process. Income taxes of various sorts directly affect net profitability, leading to changes in financial planning, new investments, dividend payouts, and similar factors. Sales, excise and value added taxes on final products affect prices, which in turn affect marketing channels, price policies, and promotional methods. Value added taxes affect the costs of raw materials and components and lead to shifts in production in terms of make or buy decisions, choice of suppliers, and procurement timing. Real property taxes affect production inventory levels and extent of automation and mechanization, and procurement timing. Finally, payroll and social security taxes affect the nature and extent of automation and mechanization, production planning, staffing, and union relations. The extraordinary variety of taxes and tax policies pursued throughout the world makes this topic somewhat difficult to generalize about, but it is clear that in each country taxes will be different, and rational firms can be expected to operate somewhat differently than they would in an environment with a different tax structure.

This tax point strongly suggests that an MNC cannot expect to operate in a set way regardless of the environment. Able managers should be expected to adjust their opertions to the constraints they face, not to what happens to be going on at home. If the structure of taxes is quite different in some foreign branch, one would expect the local manager to operate in a considerably different manner than his counterpart at home. He or she may appear to be doing irrational things by the standards of the home office, but the proper criteria to apply are those of his local environment, together with the relevant international constraints the manager must deal with. To do otherwise is to risk serious error.

International Organization and Treaty Obligations

National states have made agreements and treaties with other countries for millenia. Many of these agreements cover subjects relatively unconnected with business activity, such as extradition agreements for persons committing crimes, or the educational or cultural exchanges of citizens. Some treaties have critical commercial interest, such as agreements on trade and tariffs. While national states may (and often do) abrogate such agreements, they probably are in the main observed by signatories, and where direct commercial interests are involved, they may have considerable impact on MNCs. Such treaties reflect a country´s willingness to perform certain duties and accept certain responsibilities in return for similar favors from other parties to the agreement.

Treaties may be bilateral or multilateral. Bilateral treaties between any two countries usually refer only to those countries, while multilateral agreements may cover dozens or even hundreds of countries.

Merely listing every possible treaty would take a book larger than this one. Two major agreements, the General Agreement of Trade and Tariffs (GATT) and the International Monetary Fund (IMF) will be covered later, since their basic subject matter falls under different parts of this study.

Treaties on Property Rights. Productive private firms own many kinds of property which requires protection. Besides the obvious problem of the protection of real property and other real assets, companies often have proprietary rights in patents and trademarks which often are used in many countries around the world. Americans and Europeans may take for granted that the copyright and patent law will be observed, but in some countries protection is difficult. A few nations are notorious for their copying of anything they can lay their hands on, protected or not. Copyright and patent laws vary between countries, and a real problem for any complex firm is to protect such rights for its international operations.

There is an International Convention for the Protection of Industrial Property which is concerned with such property protection. This is a multilateral agreeement among the majority of the important trading nations. It is concerned with such problems as the international rules that will be applied to patents and patent applications, and for filing for trademark protection. An effort is made here to assure that a firm in one country will not lose its proprietary rights in others.

Most advanced countries not only will belong to such organizations, but they usually will make considerable efforts to enforce the provisions of the agreement. The usual exceptions are the Communist states, since such property rights, in their view, are the property of the state, not private firms. In less developed countries, violations of trademarks are common, and bootlegging of proprietary brands, made by local firms without permission, occasionally becomes a problem. Patent violation is less common, mainly because most patents are relevant in industrial situations, and the less developed countries have less industry which utilize patents. But violations do occur.

Thus low cost imitations of Apple II computers were being made (presumably in Taiwan) in 1983, and being sold in many countries. But these could not legally enter the U.S. or many other countries which cooperated in deterring patent violations. Moreover, such piracy leads to potential retaliation, and as countries build up export markets, they tend to join the countries willing to enforce patents. If they do not, they find that most major Western markets (and Japan) may be blocked. Failure to recognize patents is also a reason (but far from the only one) which makes it difficult for Communist industrial goods to be sold widely. If some product violates a patent held by a Western firm, the product cannot enter that country, and that prohibition may be adopted by other countries.

Enforcement, or lack of it, will directly affect the marketing and research activities of MNCs. The kind of market promotion and planning done in a country where proprietary brand names are often pirated will be quite different than in a country such as Great Britain, where such brand names are secure. Research and Development activities will normally be done in a country where managers can be reasonably sure that they will be able to enjoy the discoveries they make. Control activities may also be affected, particularly if the firm feels that it must police its brand names in a systematic manner in a market where pirating is common.

Other Types of Commercial Treaties. Various countries have entered into a wide variety of commercial treaties of interest to businessmen. Perhaps the oldest are those which provide for tariff reductions or other forms of trade expansion, such as the relaxation of quotas or agreement on customs procedures. Such treaties still are being made, but the GATT has been most important in recent years.

Some Third World countries have attempted to reassure nervous MNCs by negotiating non-expropriation treaties with such countries as the U.S. Such a treaty will usually guarantee that the country will not expropriate private investments in the future, or if they do, that some fair and equitable means of compensation for owners will be devised.

Many of the tax problems discussed above are covered in tax agreements entered into by various governments. A country will agree to treat some form of corporation or individuals in a certain manner in exchange for similar privileges for its own citizens in the other country. Countries often negotiate commercial treaties providing for some means of adjudicating commercial disputes. incuding such items as which courts will handle which kinds of disputes. There have been clauses in such treaties dealing with the duties and responsibilities of commercial attaches at embassies and consulates, and other clauses have provided for types of travel possible for businessmen.

Countries also have often made special agreements about given trade problems. The U.S.S.R. and the U.S. have agreed to specific grain sales, and barter agreements are very common between countries which have surpluss commodities. Communist countries particularly favor this type of trade, which involves such activities as trading trucks for bananas at some specific (typically unrealistic) prices. Turnkey industrial projects often involve government to government agreements.

The direct effect of such agreements on international firms can range from minor annoyances and interferences with planning, as when an executives finds it difficult to obtain an entry visa when he or she needs it, to major impacts, as when the provisions of a treaty prevent entry into the desired business. Some agreements can be quite beneficial, as when an American firm finds that it can sell wheat to the U.S.S.R. for a nice profit as a result of this country contract. Virtually all of the critical elements of the management process are affected at one time or another by such treaties and agreements.

Every country has a network of international organization and treaty obligations with other countries and groups of countries, and these obligations do have considerable impact on international business. Since every country not only has a different set of obligations and promises to other nations, but also has a different attitude toward them, each country must be examined separately to determine how the direct effects do influence the way in which international companies operate within the given country. The impact may range from quite serious to trivial, depending on the given case. The problem for the international. MNC manager is to anticipate this impact and adjust his firm so that the effects will be as favorable as possible.

Power or Economic Bloc Grouping

Most countries belong to some economic and/or political blocs, either formally or informally. In fact, there is a bewildering variety of such blocs in the world today. There is a Communist bloc; an Arab bloc; an African bloc; a neutralist group; an informal grouping of the world's developed Western capitalist nations; and so on. There are also formal military and political alliances such as the North Atlantic Treaty Organization (NATO), the Southeast Asia Treaty Organization (SEATO); the Organization of American States (OAS); and many others. These groups may have political, military, cultural, religious, or economic objectives, or some combination of any or all of these. An extremely important type of organization is the economic customs union, which will be discussed in Chapter 8.

Formal membership in an organization such as NATO implies the acceptance of certain national obligations together with the receipt of certain guarantees which may have significant business implications. In this case, countries are guaranteed by other members that an attack on any member will automatically involve all members. The pact also provides for various forms of combined military forces and military cooperation between members. Implicitly, a nation which joins this group recognizes a military threat in common with other members, implying some communality of interests not shared by outsiders. This sort of common interest may spill over, by plan or inadvertently, to such business problems as allowing private investment capital to flow from one member to another. Tariffs and other trading restraints might also be directly affected by such a military treaty.

Firms involved in the design and manufacture of military weapons are quite directly affected by such pacts. NATO has often opted for weapons systems to be used in common by most or all members of the alliance, and firms such as aircraft manufacturers in many countries have competed directly for major orders. Joint ventures between firms in several countries have been formed specifically to take advantage of this propensity toward uniformity. Thus the American Lockheed Company may team up with Fiat in Italy to propose new types of aircraft to be used by the defense forces of England, Belguim, West Germany and the U.S. Often components for the aircraft might be supplied by firms in these countries as well. In such cases, the precise provisions of the military pact between these countries can have quite significant effects on firm organization, marketing, and planning.

Most formal treaties between sovereign states also contain clauses and sections dealing with such matters as expropriation, cultural exchanges, tariff reductions, profits remission restrictions, and similar matters. Some of these items are important enough to be considered as separate constraints, and they will be considered separately from this section. The purpose of specifically noting the general power or economic bloc groupings is to recognize that the general political and economic orientation of a given country may have a great deal to do with the way in which it treats foreign firms within its boundaries. This constraint, like many others, interconnects with many other constraints to form the total picture of the international environment for MNCs.

Import-Export Restrictions

Every country interferes to some extent with trade passing beyond its frontiers. Basically, two problems are involved here. A country may desire to tax imports to gain revenue, and import duties are historically a favored device of tax collectors. Many countries still levy various import duties for this purpose, and a few still tax exports in order to gain revenue.

A second major purpose of import restrictions is to protect a firm, an industry, or the country from some foreign good or service. Protection may be for some highminded purpose such as controlling drug addiction, or it may be quite base, as when a local industrialist bribes some parliamentarians in order to obtain protection from foreign competition. Exports may be restricted in order to achieve a national purpose, as when the United States blocks the sale of certain computers or pipe layers to the Soviet Union. Endles arguments, both logical and ridiculous, have raged for centuries about the propriety of import and export controls, and the resolution of the problem is not in sight. Our purpose here is not to consider the pros and cons of protection, but simply to indicate the major types of devices used to keep some goods out, raise the price of others, and keep still others from being exported.

The basic reason for the long run controversy about export and import restrictions is that presumably, in the absence of protection, costs and prices would be different than they are with protection. This means that some persons suffer while others gain. Americans using sugar in their morning coffee are paying a tribute to American (and selected foreign) sugar producers, which, while small individually, amounts to millions of dollars per year in the aggregate. A new car buyer in the U.S. in 1984 paid about an extra thousand dollars because of import quotas on Japanese cars, which had the effect of restricting supplies of desirable vehicles. Those gaining from such restrictions press for stiff further restrictions which would enhance their advantage. Those who pay the costs may object, but typically producers are more vocal than scattered consumers. But the fight goes on endlessly, with various outcomes, depending on politics and the perceived problems the country has at the moment.

There are basically three major methods used to restrict imports: tariffs, quotas, and exchange controls.

Tariffs. A tariff (or duty) is a tax on imports. Such taxes may be subdivided into protective tariffs, which are designed to keep goods out of the country, and revenue tariffs, which are primarily intended to generate tax revenues. An ideal protective tariff generates no revenue at all, since it is high enough to exclude all imports. Revenue tariffs are typically set to yield maximum returns and often are quite low. It was common historically for countries to collect most government revenues through tariffs, since in many countries ports of entry are few, and the administrative problems of this type of tax collection are simple. Some Third World countries still gain much revenue from tariffs. Most countries, including such advanced nations as the U.S., still have some mixtures of revenue and protective tariffs built into their tax structures. Often the original reason for a given duty has long been forgotten, but the tax is still collected.

As might be expected in a question long considered of extreme importance by businessmen, government officials, and consumers, the practice of tariff collection is a complex situation in most countries. The methods of levying duties, the definition of commodities, and the administrative requirements of a customs police are matters which have developed over centuries, and in most countries an army of specialists is necessary to guide one's goods through complex procedures. An incredible array of documents, licenses, bills of lading, sanitary permits, official seals, and other trivia is required for proper clearance. It has been estimated that the paperwork alone in handling imports adds perhaps ten percent to the costs of foreign goods. Since many local business people, officials, and others have a vested interest in making the procedure as expensive and frustrating as possible, it usually is. Bribery and corruption also flourish in too many nations at the customs house, since a few controllers can hold up anyone needing imported goods, and corruption costs can be very high.

Tariffs of all sorts have direct effects on all firms within any country since they directly affect costs and prices of competitive goods and components. Tariff policy often is designed to pressure both local and international firms to do something they might not otherwise do, and the impacts can be quite widespread for given firms.

Consider a case where a country wishes to establish an automotive industry (as Brazil, Mexico, and Argentina have in fact done). Such countries may begin by establishing differential duties on completed vehicles and components. Thus the duty on a complete auto may be 500 percent, while the duty on unassembled parts is 20 percent. Since it costs less to import the parts and put them together than to pay the extra duty, firms begin to set up assembly operations within the country. Production and production planning is affected, not only in the given country, but also in the home country, because the firm must now send its exports in kit form rather than as completed vehicles.

A next step is differential duties on different kinds of components. Relatively simple items in the vehicle which might be manufactured locally are assessed high rates, while difficult or expensive to make parts take lower duties. Thus the auto firm might find that the duty on upholstery, floor mats, door handles, light metal trim, and similar items rises to several hundred percent, while rear axles, engines, and transmissions requiring long production runs and heavy capital investments take lower rates. This usually causes shifts in suppliers, make or buy decisions, and inventory planning, among other functions. The process can proceed, usually over the manufacturers' protests, until the complete vehicle and most components are made locally. The manufacturer can always decide to give up and leave, but then it forfeits a market to the competition who may be willing to go along with the government.

Tariffs may also force substitutions of all sorts. A high duty on petroleum may lead to more extensive use of coal, as one example. Quite often the duties may have unanticipated effects. A country wishing to protect its cotton spinners and textile industry may levy high duties on cotton products, only to find that the nylon, polyester, and other synthetic imports are rising. Businessmen, both local and international, are extremely adept at evading the intent of the existing tariff law, and the rules perpetually change as a harrassed government tries to keep up with ingenious users of imports and technological change.

Quotas. A more direct method of restricting imports is by means of quantitative restrictions, or quotas, on the amount of a given commodity that can be brought into the country in a given time period. The United States uses this method on such imports as steel, autos, sugar, beef, and textiles, among other items. More recently, a variation of quotas (called "orderly marketing arrangements") have quasi-officially limited the importation of many goods. Many other countries use similar techniques on virtually every product known to man.

Quotas are much more effective than a tariff, since someone may be willing to import a commodity even if tariffs make the price high. A quota of zero will keep out everything, assuming that smuggling can be prevented.   It usually cannot...among the U.S.'s largest imports are illegal narcotics, and cigarets, transistor radios, and other interesting items are often widely smuggled.

Quotas present an additional problem to governments using them.   If the quota is effective, the item restricted then becomes in short supply, and the holder of the quota in effect has a valuable license which yields additional income. If a given type of textile materials is sold in world markets for a dollar a yard, while the domestic price is $1.75, a tight quota on such textiles provides for potential profits of seventy five cents per yard. The license to import is worth that much. he can either import the goods himself, or sell his quota rights to some one who needs the material. This sort of property right in itself creates various distortions in the economy which are hard to rec :ify, and the existence of such valuable rights typically breeds a group of fast buck artists who have the necessary friends in the quota issuing government office.   International businessmen working in quota using countries inevitably meet such individuals.

Young students might be well advised to stop here and study instead the way in which they might get a quota for something. A good quota in the U.S. for sugar or textiles, which are granted to someone, can be worth millions.   Why work, when one can spend a year or two getting a quota, and then be a millionaire? It does not take too much imagination to see how corruption can rapidly spread in this situation, but no country ever figures this into its calculations. In effect, the more dishonest one is, the more likely one will win. Then moralists wonder why people are so cynical these days, in countries of every political persuasion...

In this quota situation, firms usually have problems created by improper planning by government officials. If quotas on key imports are set too high, the result is an ineffective quota and no capital gains to the operators. But if the quota is set too low, firms using the product have difficulties in obtaining enough supplies to keep operating.   A plant using a given petro-chemical technology may find that the quota is used up in October and that no further imports will be allowed until the following year. If this is a critical raw material for production, then the manager must either close down or go to the government offices and argue with the bureaucrats. In either case, his planning is directly affected, and his operations are more costly than they otherwise might be.

Although it is easy to indicate the serious problems which quotas create, governments tend to be quite attached to their use, and there are no indications that they will be abolished in the foreseeable future.   Their attraction stems largely from the fact that they can be used to influence economic activity in ways deemed desirable by government, and firms have to learn to make money in spite of quotas.

Exchange controls.   These controls will later be considered separately because they are important enough for a variety of reasons to merit special attention. However, many types of exchange controls are utilized to control specific imports. A firm may have to obtain permits for using foreign exchange based on the kinds of imports it desires, and foreign exchange will be allocated on the basis of whether or not the imports are desirable. A firm may wish to import cosmetics, only to find that such trivia is on the banned list. Only key capital machinery gets permits easily. Such controls may be used in combination with tariffs and quotas.

Like quotas, exchange licenses usually have a value of their own, and many countries have active markets in them. The usual problem is that the country has a shortage of foreign exchange at the given exchange rate, and the demand for foreign money is greater than supply. Note that one way to avoid this is to have floating rates, but many countries do not like to float their currency. Since exchange licenses tend to be available as the supply of foreign exchange varies, it may take a very adept operator to maneuver through this particular restriction. In one year, licenses may be scarce and expensive; in another, they may be had for the asking. It is also fairly common for a country to have several rates of foreign exchange for different classes of imports. A machinery importer may get a more favorable rate than the cosmetics importer, and armaments tend to get the most favorable rate of all.

One effect of exchange controls is to underprice imports. In effect, the holders of permits are allowed to buy foreign goods at low prices, since the only reason for exchange controls is that the local currency is overvalued. Combine this with preferential handling of such items as capital equipment, and one typical result is that firms are overcapitalized. Since foreign machines are cheap, the firm uses them. Less labor gets used, often in Third World countries with major labor surpluses.

This area of import controls is one which directly affects every MNC operating in the country. The direct impact is on prices, which typically has very direct effects on costs and selling prices of the firm both locally and in international trade. Such price effects can directly impact on virtually all firm and management functions in many ways. Since the restrictions are so direct and visible to most managers, considerable attention is directed to this factor. Even the most casual perusal of international activities will suggest that this trade control is always carefully watched and considered.

International Investment Restrictions

Most countries have some restrictions, which may apply to foreigners and/or citizens, concerning types of investments which may be made in the country. The United States, as one example, has quite restrictive rules concerning foreign investments in air and land transportation, while many countries have restrictions on foreign investments in other critical areas such as armaments and public utilities. MNCs wishing to invest in these sectors will find that various types of government approval is necessary before funds can be committed.

Many Western countries have more detailed investment regulations, often integrated with the national plan for economic development. Thus countries such as India, Pakistan, and France, among many others, have five or seven year development plans of varying detail and complexity, which indicate the general lines of economic advance hoped for in the period stated in the plan. A foreign investor in any of these countries would find that his own plans for industrial or commercial expansion must be integrated into the general framework of development. If not, he may find that the government will refuse to allow the necesary permits for the investment.

Such investment approvals must be made by planning boards, ministers of commerce, or other officials entrusted with this problem. Each country has its own technique of control.

It is also common to find discriminatory restrictions applied to foreign firms, particularly in Third World countries which may fear excessive foreign economic penetration or domination. Thus in Great Britain, MNCs are treated exactly like domestic investors in most cases, while in most Third World countries, MNCs face special rules. Japan, which is an exception to patterns found in highly industrialized nations, normally will not allow foreign corporations to invest in Japan as solely owned foreign enterprises, and even joint ventures may prove quite difficult to form with Japanese firms. Mexico usually requires 51 percent local ownership in joint ventures, while Argentina insists on special permission by presidential decree in each case, which presumably is decided on its individual merits and contribution to the economy.

Countries often indicate which types of foreign investment will receive preferential treatment. In the 1980's, high technology investments such as computers are typically welcomed, while routine investments, which often can be done with local capital, are discouraged. Often investment approvals are contingent on reinvestments and expansions.

The general impact on firm operations here is quite direct, since the usual problem is whether or not the company can begin operations at all. This is a "go-no-go" type of constraint. If the investment is prohibited, nothing else happens. If it is approved, all of the other constraints, both local and international, become relevant. Firms already established may find that expansions are also subject to similar approvals, since countries with national plans may not be interested in expansions of successful enterprises if such expansions channel production in directions unintended by government policymakers. Failure to achieve the necessary permits for investment will have a direct and immediate impact on all of the critical elements of the management process.

The other side of this investment restriction coin is investment subsidies. Countries are often very interested in getting more foreign direct investment, since such investment means jobs, tax revenues, skill acquisitions, and hard currency export earnings. Dozens of countries now offer investment incentives, such as special labor training; tax rebates or tax holidays; special infrastructure investments, such as roads and sewers; and many other items which might encourage firms to locate in the country. Many West European countries have special investment incentive programs for impoverished areas of the country.

Provincial or city governments sometimes offer similar incentives. Thus in the United States, states and cities sometimes try to provide investment incentives of the types noted above for both local and foreign firms. In cases where a major industrial investment is to be made, MNCs can sometimes play off one country or region against another to get the best deal.

Such incentives also alter the firm´s planning, since they affect costs and factor inputs. A given incentive might impact almost any critical element, and the final locational decision has to be made with the various incentives in mind.

Profits Remission Restrictions

MNCs may earn large amounts of local currency in net profits. It is quite common to find inflationary situations where local earnings are easy and where rates of return are quite high on invested capital. But these earnings need to be converted to dollars or marks or yen for remission to the MNCs home country, or to be redeployed in other countries. Where exchange controls are minimal or totally absent (as in Western Europe, Hong Kong, Singapore, Canada, Japan, and the United States, among others, at present), the problem is simple, but many countries have exchange convertibility controls of varying complexity and severity, and often the firm finds that it cannot remit profits easily. Such controls tend to change quite rapidly, both for the better and for the worse, as a country´s foreign exchange earnings rise or fall. In the limits, the firm´s profits are completely blocked, and it is unable to repatriate any profits.

This particular constraint is of special interest to all firms, and often this exchange control is handled separately from others. Countries interested in attracting foreign capital may offer to guarantee profits remissions for some fixed period in the future, or in stated amounts or percentages in order to reassure nervous investors. Special deals may be made for particular investments deemed to be important for the country. Often profit repatriation is an item of special bargaining between government officials and firm representatives.

Before the investment is made, the kinds of profits remissions restrictions which exist may determine whether or not the investment is made. If a country has a history of frequent and severe restrictions, investment risks may be regarded as much less favorable than in a country where this problem has been minimal. In this situation, the usual direct impact on the firm is in the planning area.

MNCs may face new restrictions in existing operations. In such cases, the company´s reactions to new opportunities within the country may be quite different than it otherwise might have been. Firms have often turned to special deals involving barter in such situations, and there is a lively barter broking trade going on somewhere in the world at all times. Communist countries prefer such transactions, and other countries often try to unload surplus commodities this way. An MNC may be able to trade its own product or something it can buy locally for something it needs abroad. However, the extra costs and time involved in lining up such deals typically make them unattractive except as a last resort.

Planning and financial activities will be directly influenced in such a situation. The MNC's marketing and production functions could also be impacted since sales may be easy, but the firm may be unwilling to expand capacity because it cannot enjoy the profits from such an expansion. Hence it may refuse orders or cut back on selling efforts while operating existing plants as close to capacity as it can. As blocked funds pile up, there may be shifts in financial planning, since the firm may now be willing to purchase more items at higher prices in local markets than it otherwise would in order to use up the surplus local currency. Hence an expensive second hand machine available locally might be purchased instead of a more modern one available only with hard currency. The result here may be that production processes will become quite different than they would be if the currency were readily convertible to other currencies.

Exchange Control Restrictions

Profits remissions restrictions are a part of general exchange controls which may be applied to any type of monetary transfer involving conversion of local currency to foreign currencies. Thus a country may have extensive and complicated rules and regulations covering not only profits remissions, but also imports, capital outflows of all sorts, tourism, and other demands for foreign currency. In effect, the government of the country rations out available foreign exchange to some, but not all, persons wanting it. MNCs have trouble here in obtaining currency for critical imports of components, raw materials, and spare parts, as well as in their efforts to move capital or profits out of the country.

Many of the effects of such exchange controls have been covered above in the sections on import restrictions and profits remissions restrictions. This general category is added to include all the other items which may also be subject to controls over the local currency. Countries may choose to maintain overvalued exchange rates, and MNCs must adjust to such controls as best they can. In cases where the exchange controls are severe and foreign currency is quite difficult to obtain, much of the local management's time and effort may go into attempting to convince exchange control authorities that a given need for foreign exchange is critical to continuing production. Since the exchange rate affects virtually all prices and costs of the firm, either directly or indirectly, the impact of such regulations on all phases of managerial activity is hard to exaggerate.

Countries with histories of exchange control and monetary instability don't attract too many MNCs, unless the gains are huge, and whatever being produced can be exported, with the MNC getting its gains in hard currency. As a result, quite a few countries have cautiously moved to a freer stance, wanting to attract more foreign investment. But then as they do, others are forced into exchange controls by events such as too much debt burden, loss of key markets, or even acts of God, such as droughts. As with everything else in international business, everything changes, and not always for the better.

Conclusion

This chapter has indicated how the legal-political international constraints can affect various phases of management and firm efficiency in foreign operations. Since there are over 150 countries, each with its own set of ever-changing legal-political constraints, it is impossible to indicate how these will work out in detail in any given case. The examples were used in an effort to indicate the kinds of difficulties firms might face in this area.

These constraints can range from minor irritants which bother local MNC managers slightly to major impacts which affect the very existence of the MNC. The long and disturbing history of confiscatory taxation, overregulation, expropriation, currency instability and controls, and oppressive labor legislation in many countries suggests that these constraints cannot be taken lightly by any firm. Careful consideration of each is necessary if the MNC is to survive in its foreign environments. However, the other side of the coin shows large profits, fast growth for MNCs, a chance to perform creative and exciting changes within alien societies, and a challege to perform efficiently in a variety of environments. One cannot perform well, however, without knowing a great deal about the kinds of constraints he or she will be facing, and this chapter has attempted to set out the more important international constraints relevant to all types of international firms.

Questions for Discussion

1. Select any foreign country which interests you and do some research in any available sources. Find at least three major legal-political constraints in this country which might affect the direct investments made by MNCs. Are these good, bad, or both, from the points of view of these MNCs?

2. We mentioned in this chapter than many countries have laws which state that some given percentage of all employees in any firm in the country must be nationals. Do you think that such laws are a good idea? Why or why not?

3. The United States has no laws banning the use of foreign nationals in the United States working for foreign owned companies. The country does, however, have quite strict general visa laws which could be used to control working foreigners in this country.

Suppose that many foreign firms invest in the U.S. in the next few years. Should foreign technicians and managers be excluded by these visa requirements, or should such key personnel be allowed to enter and compete with Americans who need jobs? Why?

4. Ask some foreign students about the problems they face in obtaining visas to get into the United States to study. Do you feel that these persons were fairly treated by the Amerian Government? Why or why not?

5.   Many Mexican citizens try to slip into the United States illegally to work, since it is virtually impossible for them to obtain valid U.S. work visas. They come because American wages are so much higher than in Mexico. Are you in favor of tighter border controls to keep such people out or not? Why? What rights should illegally entered Mexicans have in the U.S., if any?

6.   Canada encouraged the migration of American teachers to work in that country for many years. Now, as more Canadians obtain the necessary qualifications, the Canadian government is having second thoughts.   It is possible that many Americans will be asked to leave, even those who have worked for many years in that country and have obtained tenure of employment.

Is this fair? Why or why not?

7.   Suppose that you were asked to advise a small Third World country about which international organizations the country should join, and which they might avoid. Give a short statement explaining your reasoning for each organization.

8.   The United States now has import quotas on such products as steel and autos. Do you think that such quotas are a good idea? Why or why not?

9.   The United States is a charter member of NATO, along with many European countries. One key provision of this treaty is that if any member is attacked by any enemy, all other countries in the pact are bound to go to war.

Do you think that this type of treaty is in the national interest? Why or why not?

Supplementary Readings

Arthur Anderson & Company.   A   series entitled "Tax and Trade Guide...(name of country)." Numerous countries covered.

Bergsten, C. Fred, and Krause, Lawrence B., eds. WORLD POLITICS AND INTERNATIONAL ECONOMICS. Washington: The Brookings Institution, 1975.

Blondel, Jean.   COMPARING POLITICAL SYSTEMS. London: Weidenfeld and Nicolson, 1973.

Crosswell, Carol M. LEGAL AND FINANCIAL ASPECTS OF INTERNATIONAL BUSINESS. Dobbs Ferry, NY: Oceana Publications, 1980.

Nehrt, Lee Charles.   THE   POLITICAL CLIMATE FOR PRIVATE FOREIGN INVESTMENT. New York: Praeger, 1970.

Price, Waterhouse & Co. A series of pamphlets entitled, "Information guide for Those Doing Business in...(name of country). Many countries included in this series.

Robock, Stefan, and Simmonds, Kenneth. INTRNATIONAL BUSINESS AND MULTINATIONAL ENTERPRISE. Homewood, IL: Richard D. Irwin, 1973.

PART III

CHALLENGE AND RESPONSE

Chapter 7

Governments and the MNCs

Introduction

National governments are a critical factor in the whole MNC equation. Any government, in a nationalistic world, can ban, tax, or expropriate any private company. There are enough examples in recent history of such negative actions to convince anyone that the threat is real. Iran in 1979-81 was a dramatic, but certainly not unique example.

Governments can also encourage firms through subsidies, tax rebates, and other assistance, and there are many examples of such programs among countries of many political persuasions. Increasingly in the 1980's countries are realizing that if they want to be in the international mainstream of advanced technology and rapid economic growth, they have to obtain access to the best people and organizations, and these are multinational. If a country blocks off ideas, it has to do everything itself, and no country can. It has been a fairly common scenario in the past decade for a small country to go Marxist, expropriate every foreign company around, close its frontiers, and then stagnate. Such a country typically does interesting things in reforming the local economy, such as increasing educational and health care efforts, but few outsiders pay much attention. Then foreign currency gets very scarce (because these systems necessarily are import substitution ones), the army finds that either it must depend on Soviet weapons or fall behind, and consumption drops as goods get hard to produce or import.

Such countries' leaders posture at the United Nations and make violently anti-American and anti-Western speeches, but no one listens anymore. We have heard it all before from the masters. Speakers from Singapore, Hong Kong, Taiwan, and South Korea are much more interesting. After all, they have moved from deep poverty to significantly industrialized and affluent countries in twenty years, using the open systems approach. None of these countries (and Hong Kong isn't even a country) have much military or ideological muscle. They just got rich. How? For two thirds of the world's population, struggling with intractable poverty, this is the critical question. And the answer, linking up to the older rich countries economic systems in a pragmatic and effective manner, isn't all that attractive. But the options are more dismal.

So the scenario proceeds with the previously radical country coming back to the open game, opening new free trading zones, perhaps allowing foreign investment in key sectors, and generally trying to play the Hong

Kong game. Unfortunately for the latecomers, the world recession of the early 1980´s means that the country gets less than it might have earlier, but perhaps something is better than nothing. In the end, Marxism and closed systems have not done much for smaller countries, and there is considerable doubt that even huge countries like the PRC gained much by following this ideology. We may see, somewhat to our surprise, a much more open world system in the 1980´s and 1990´s as a result, although there still will be many countries that follow the holy grail of closed system planning.

Governments can set any rules they want, if they are willing to pay the price. Historically, the price has sometimes been to risk (and even suffer) an armed invasion by another country, as Grenada learned in 1983; modern prices may also include losing key markets, having incomes drop, or losing future potentially profitable investments. Because historic prices have sometimes been high, governments rarely take extreme actions without some consideration of the total outcome.

We can divide national governments into several groups. One affluent group provides homes for MNCs. This used to be largely the United States, with some West European participation, but Japan has definitely joined this group since the 1970´s. A new phenomena is the MNC coming from a Third World country such as India, Malayasia, Thailand, Taiwan, or South Korea, and while such MNCs tend to be much smaller than MNCs coming from industrialized nations, they are growing rapidly, both in size and numbers. Home countries may also be host countries, as when a British based MNC competes abroad, and faces local British competition from a Japanese or American MNC at home. The viewpoint of a country with strong and growing foreign interests is likely to be somewhat different than a large second group of countries, which are those which typically only receive MNC investments. Remember, however, that the vast majority of MNC investment is in other affluent countries. Most of the attention and concern about MNCs in the Third World really involves the smaller percentage of total investment.

A third group of players could be termed the nonplayers. These are largely Marxist or communist countries which have decided not to allow foreign ownership. Trade is fine, and an occasional cooperation agreement or oil exploration contract is allowed, but ownership and control are not. Eastern Europe, the Soviet Union, Cuba, Vietnam, North Korea, Burma, and Albania are included in this group, joined now by religiously oriented Iran.

These categories change as countries try to maximize their positions. Both India and the PRC are much more open now than they were ten years ago, while Iran has changed from very open to quite closed. MNCs can be sure that the rules will often change, so complete listings of countries and their positions at any one moment would be useless.

But such country attitudes are critical to MNCs, along with the countries´ fates, so we now consider some of the key strategic responses which governments have made to the MNC challenge. We have seen the way firms think through their multinational problems in preceeding chapters; now we turn to the question of how countries perceive the issue, and how they respond to the multinational challenge.

The Eternal Provincials

Any national government, regardless of its political outlook, has as its basic task the optimization of its own people's well-being. In this world we have governments ranging on the right from theocratic dictatorships and kingdoms to communists on the left, with all possible stages in between. We have parliamentary democracies, presidential systems, countries where only men can vote, and countries where no one votes. But whatever the political persuasion, the government tries to optimize as best it can for its own citizens.

MNCs are global optimizers. Many observers perceive them as home country optimizers, but criticisms coming from home suggest that such firms are not pleasing everyone there either. The MNC sees the world as a whole, with interesting provinces here and there raising roadblocks and barriers to doing things efficiently, profitably, and well. If MNC activities help countries, fine, but the name of the game is long term profit maximization, not social welfare for selected persons in certain geographical locations.

This is the nub of the whole world economic problem. No one, until 1955 or so, lived in a world where the part was bigger than the whole. The local government is trying to get something bigger than itself to do something useful for local citizens; the firm, taking a global view, may see the matter quite differently.

Thus the American government, for perfectly sound local reasons, might be interested in getting American firms to invest more money in American fertilizer production. But the companies correctly perceive that there are much higher rates of return to be earned in other countries and other products. Even offers of local subsidies and other temptations may not be enough to shift the balance. Note that the American government can force the issue with laws, takeovers, or government investments in new plants. But such actions may be self-defeating, since firms in other sectors, aware that they may be next, run for safety to Switzerland, Sweden, or the Bahamas. Investment drops sharply elsewhere, and new problems arise.

This scenario could have been presented for Belgium, Norway, or Honduras at any time in the past 40 years, since these small countries had little bargaining power against large foreign firms. The fact that the same scenario can now be presented for France, the United States, or West Germany suggests how far the multinational revolution has already gone. Joining nervous small countries are nervous big ones, since no one is big enough to hide behind its borders, keep its firms at home, and forget the world. As we noted at the beginning of this chapter, those countries that do are likely to find stagnation, not happiness.

Such scenarios would be impossible if the MNCs were simply exploitative mechanisms for skimming the cream off various countries. If this were all the game was, a country could ban them and go on in traditional ways. The problem is that the MNCs have something to offer which the country needs. If the country could have done these things for itself, it would have done so. But it cannot, and when a representative of the MNC comes along with an interesting offer, responsible officials will listen. If the payout is high, the government may well give permission. And in the 1980′s, it is quite likely that government officials will be doing the offering to reluctant MNCs, rather than the other way around.

The Positive Sum Game

Here we find the other side of the dilemma. The only way MNCs can possibly operate in a nationalistic world is to offer more than what already exists. If a country′s wealth rises, then both parties can get a share. If the MNC were totally exploitative, then no sane and responsible government would allow it to exist for ten minutes.

We are so accustomed to zero sum games, where if I win, you lose, that we automatically assume that multinational business is a zero sum game too. But it is not. I win, and you win too, is the correct formulation of the problem. Relative exploitation may exist if I win 90 percent of the gains, and you get ten percent. You might argue that the deal was unfair, and demand redress. Such controversies are very common in deals such as oil concession agreements. But even here you are ten percent better off than you used to be.

This positive sum game is economic. We measure our gains in dollars or yen or marks. But there may well be other less quantifiable costs. How can we measure the costs of losing one′s cultural identity, which has happened when a large MNC swamps a small country with its technology, and implicitly, its values? How can we measure the feelings of uneasiness about losing control of one′s economy, and being linked into some mysterious world system where a minor taste change in Tokyo, New York, or London can wipe out a whole industry in South Korea or Hong Kong? How can we measure the possible loss of power which follows when a previously independent country now finds that its critical armaments producers or transport facilities are now controlled by foreigners, or so mixed up with industries in potential enemy countries that war production would be impossible? How can we measure the feelings of loss that local prime ministers may have when they see that their economy is so controlled by others that they have less real power than the governor of South Dakota? Such costs are very real, yet no one has yet devised a means of weighing them against whatever economic benefits may accrue. Much of the uneasiness about the MNCs′ power is really an effort to sort out thse costs and determine if the gains justify them.

No country, even the most rabid dictatorship, is a homogeneous political unit. There is an opposition, even if it hides in the hills and plots revolution. More commonly, even in fairly monolithic countries, the opposition is quite visible and vociferous. If the ins like MNCs, the outs probably will take a countering position and press for more control or even banning these monsters. Many concerned citizens may feel the same way, and the opposition may eventually gain power. The reverse may also occur. Often these changes revolve initially more around cultural losses than economic gains. Thus Iran felt strongly that the modern world was impinging upon deeply held Islamic values and reacted, while in a more modest way, Canadian Quebec felt that its French language and French culture were being destroyed by foreign influences (including those from the rest of Canada).

Such political maneuverings mean a precarious political life for many MNCs. It may also mean few bother to invest in such places, preferring instead more stable climes such as the United States or Western Europe. The MNC game is so new that we have no conduct codes for either countries or firms, although the United Nations is attempting (for over ten years now) to construct just such a code. Those gains and losses keep being added up by all interested parties, and they shift as the country and its firms evolve. A trade union violently against MNCs today may shift in favor as it sees worker incomes and skills going up rapidly in neighboring countries. The same union may shift again at some later date when those hard won skills become useless as the MNC shifts new production to other countries to take advantage of lower wage rates. No one can make definitive statements about what is going to happen next year, since no one yet has worked out the complex calculus of gains and losses, both economic and psychological.

If the MNC is to operate, it has to make a positive sum deal. There are plenty of historical examples of quite exploitative situations, but the days of banana republics and gunboats are probably gone for good. Many people, conditioned by Marxist thinking from those days, and convinced that the game is really zero sum, see nothing but exploitation in the MNCs´ evolution, but it is quite unlikely that we would have gone as far as we have along this particular road if exploitation were all that was going on.

If the game were exploitative, one would expect that any country, such as Iran or Cuba, that expelled the MNCs and went to a closed system, would immediately show rapid economic gains and faster growth. Exactly the opposite has occurred in the numerous situations where such system closing has occurred. The usual results are economic losses, stagnation, slow or negative economic growth, and decay. What is actually happening in such cases is that the country gives up whatever piece of the positive sum multinational game it had, which of course leads to losses. But millions of influential people believe exactly the opposite, so such closings are likely to continue to recur.

Government Options

As governments perceive the problem, they have several options to follow. We have models of all types in the real world, and we can observe results where various strategies were tried.

The Open Economy. This strategy is allowing foreign based firms about the same rights as local companies. In pure form, the local currency is convertible, profits remission restrictions are nil, tariffs are low or nonexistant (as are quotas), and entry into almost any type of business is allowed. Most West European countries, along with other affluent countries such as the United States, Canada, and Australia follow this strategy in a general way, although every country has a few protected sacred cows which foreigners cannot control. Not surprisingly, given what we have been talking about, such sectors are typically characterized by ineptness, inefficiencies, and high costs. Hong Kong, Taiwan, South Korea and Singapore are examples of small, rapidly growing countries which also follow this strategy, and as we have mentioned, such diverse countries as Mexico, India, and the PRC have trade zones which are similar in orientation.

Another group of open countries are the oil producing states. They allow oil to be exploited and produced, and they import almost everything. Kuwait, Saudi Arabia, and the United Arab Emirates are almost pure models of this type of economy, while other oil states such as Venezuela, Nigeria, Indonesia, and Iraq have local production of many items besides oil, and often protect these sectors.

Japan is very open on both exports and raw material imports, but somewhat restrictive on capital flows, manufactured and agricultural imports, and investments. Increasingly the Japanese are under pressure by other countries to become more open in sectors other than trade, and even in trade the Japanese are accused of systematically discriminating against foreigners in many sectors. Since the Japanese have to have an open world system to survive, they seem to be grudgingly moving toward even more openness. Few remember that the major reason why the Japanese have done so very well since 1945 is that the world trading system has become so much more open than it used to be. If the Japanese had to sell their exports into a 1935 world of beggar my neighbor import controls and huge tariffs, they might be very poor indeed. Of all countries in the world, the Japanese probably need a relatively flexible, totally open world system the most.

The major danger of this strategy is that your local economy becomes an interrelated outpost in the world economic system. The world may sneeze, but Taiwan may fall fatally ill. The key advantage is that your country can attract the world's best experts in almost anything, and your own people can learn to do it themselves very fast. Local managers have long since taken over most Taiwanese MNC operations, and in the oil states many of the skilled jobs are held by locals. A country may want all the jobs for its citizens, but they are only there because some foreigners started the venture long ago.

Often overlooked in this open system is the possibility of linking local firms to foreign markets. Huge retailing chains such as Sears have long bought products from small manufacturers in the U.S., taking over the marketing function. If a company could produce socket wrenches well, then Sears could sell them. What socket wrenches? Well, Sears' very competent marketing people would know. In effect, a division of labor here is to have the production people do one job, with marketing people doing what they know best.

This Sears model works very well in Hong Kong. Most smaller firms are locally owned, and their job is to provide the products that foreigners want. They do this most efficiently, thus becoming a production outpost for Japanese, European, and American marketers. Internationalization here is not so much direct manufacturing investment, but rather effective exporting to sophisticated markets. The model works very well for many products, since the marketer avoids wrestling with all those international and domestic constraints we talked about in previous chapters, while the producer avoids them in complex industrial markets as well. Let a competent Chinese industrialist worry about how to find labor and capital, and get production going in Hong Kong, while the capable Sears marketer can ponder what kinds of T shirts and sandals American teenagers might buy.

One major advantage this Sears model gives is that it forces world class quality control on manufacturers who otherwise might take decades to learn it. If those T shirts or transistor radios aren't up to standard, they are not purchased. The manufacturer learns very fast to do whatever is necessary to produce quality goods. In communist countries, where this pressure is absent, quality is a major, if not the major problem. In Hong Kong and Taiwan, somehow quality gets built in, and the countries surge ahead. Note how easily information gets transmitted in this latter case. If Sears wants high quality merchandise, it can put a firm in contact with whomever in the world knows how to produce it. The firm, well aware that it will go broke if it doesn't come up to par, will listen and learn rapidly.

Increasing Your Share. A common strategy for countries which have big multinational operations is to try to increase their share through legal action or moral pressures. Hence new tax laws may be passed discriminating against sectors dominated by MNCS, or concession agreements renegotiated. Big and profitable MNCs may be asked or forced to build key social overhead capital projects, such as roads, schools, or hospitals. These and other techniques have been tried, often with considerable success.

The key constraint is to not go so far as to jeopardize the MNCs' profitibility, not only in your own country, but relative to others. If the firm can find another place to operate more profitably, it will. It may not leave, but it can run down existing investments through time, thus slowing economic growth. Such situations are very common, as are actual disinvestments, where the MNC sells off its assets to another MNC or a local group, which then is stuck with all these controls, plus losing its information channels to the outside. Rarely does such a disinvested firm do very well, although it can if the MNC really didn't do a very good job of meshing its local operations with the local environment. Such cases have occurred.

A variation on the theme is to try to form a multinational group to press for mutual advantage. Thus the Organization of Petroleum Exporting Countries (OPEC), which is an international cartel of oil exporting countries, has tried to control prices and outputs of crude oil. It had very considerable success before 1980, but it now has serious problems, as we noted earlier. A similar tin cartel tries to do the same with this commodity. Other efforts at cartelizing world production have not typically been very successful, although many have been tried. The usual problem is that not all countries want to play the game, and renegades can wreck the cartel.

MNCs, particularly of the high technology, fast growth type, have tended to gain the negotiating edge in the 1980's. It is relatively easy to control one's petroleum fields, but how does a country control microcomputer production? The product can be manufactured almost anywhere and exported profitably. To get such a firm to invest is difficult, and any onerous restrictions simply mean that the MNC disinvests and goes elsewhere. Some other country will be offering a subsidy, not trying to make life difficult for the firm. That other country will pick up the jobs, the technology, the tax revenues, and the hard currency from exports, and something is always better than nothing, meaning that if the country gets perhaps ten percent of the action, it is still much better off than getting a hundred percent of nothing. Disinvestment in such cases may mean nothing more than transferring a few key technical and managerial personnel, giving up a building lease, and selling off some obsolete machinery. In fields such as computers, the machinery is always obsolete, even if it is a year old. Often those key people are residents of the local country, and they are more likely to go with the MNC and be productive elsewhere than rot at home.

MNCs can of course pick and choose, and there is a competitive pressure by countries to offer the best deal. The pressures we have noted in this section apply more to historic investments than new ones, and remember that if the country gets too picky, the firm simply stops new investment, leading to potential stagnation. The 1980´s have already seen significant increases in both the numbers of countries offering subsidies and the size of such subsidies. More are likely to follow, given the changing bargaining situation.

Limitations and Expropriations. A further step along the restrictionary path is to block entry of most, if not all new firms, and to expropriate older foreign investments. The country chooses to do most of the job itself.

Observers might conclude that expropriations are very common, since such conflict is reported around the world. Actually, major expropriations are rare, and probably getting rarer. One reason is that most logical expropriations have already occurred; a second reason was noted above.

But expropriations are a feasible strategy, and in a few cases they can actually increase local wealth and incomes. They seem to work best under these conditions:

1. When the operation is totally local and fairly simple. An example would be African states nationalizing British owned local life insurance companies, local banks, and local merchandising operations. This works because the country controls the entire operation, from marketing to production. If the investment has been around for years, local citizens have acquired most of the skills needed to make the system work well. The company taken over cannot do much internationally, such as block foreign markets. Unless the home country wants to send in the marines, little can be done except to ask for compensation. Often, after years of dickering, such compensation is actually paid, since failure to do so could cut off foreign credits, and the home country could seize any assets the expropriating country had in the country. Thus even now, Cuba cannot hold any assets in the U.S., since it has never compensated owners for expropriations made in the early 1960´s, and within the U.S., the courts have made many judgements against the Cuban government. If a Cuban ship showed up in an American port, it would be seized under court order and sold to meet creditors´ demands. Such problems can be very awkward, so in the end the expropriating

country pays compensation. It may not be as much as the MNC wanted, but at least something is gained.

2. Where raw materials are consumed locally, the same situation applies.   Peru took over its oil industry, and virtually the entire market was in Peru.   Hence the ex-owner was limited in terms of international pressure. Long ago, in 1937, Mexico did the same thing and got away with it.

In these cases, the country may actually add a bit to wealth, or at least not lose too much. What happens is that the MNC's profit is a payment for critical managerial and technical services, and if the country's own citizens are capable of supplying them for the same of less money, the country may gain. Here again, the country in the end usually pays compensation to the expropriated owner, for the same reasons noted above.

The expropriation strategy works worst when:

1.   The investment is a piece of a more complicated international whole. This would be the case where an auto firm has an assembly plant, plus the manufacture of perhaps a few hundred of the thousands of parts going into a car or truck within the country. If the country grabs the plant, the owner simply stops shipping the other pieces in, and all you own is a factory full of half finished vehicles which cannot be finished, ever.   Egypt, Chile, and Iran have all expropriated such plants, and they all lost a lot as a result. The workers, who could not be fired for political reasons, received full pay while they lounged around the idle plant. In the end, all three countries had to recant in order to get some vehicles in a deteriorating situation.

Other major auto firms were not the least bit interested in taking over such problems. Any inventory wouldn't fit, and the perceived risks were very, very high. Once again, the home countries had their courts make judgements against the country,   which   meant the loss of international credits and the inability to own anything in the MNCs home country.   After a few years of local jubilation and excitement about taming the foreigners, deals were quietly struck to get them back in, often with better terms than the MNCs had in the first place, given extra risks. One could even argue that for major MNCs, one really nice country to go to was one which had performed such expropriations a few years earlier. Leaders are usually much sadder and much, much wiser.

2.   Where international marketing is involved. If the product is being sold in foreign markets by the MNC, then expropriation can mean loss of the marketing function. It can also mean endless lawsuits about patents and trademarks in all countries that observe such things internationally.   It looks easy to sell copper, machines, or toys abroad, until one tries it for the first time with totally unskilled people.

The usual result in such cases is for the MNCs to come back in after a few years, often with some political face saving. Thus now the copper mines belong to the people, and the MNC is paid to market the commodity worldwide. Again, the MNC can often get a better deal than it originally had, given all country's desperate need for foreign exchange.

The more complex the market is, the more difficult it will be to succeed on your own. A raw material sold in competitive world markets will be easier to sell than a complex machine or components for someone else's products. A further problem in complex items is that some product inputs invariably need to be imported, and if they come from the expropriated MNC, they won't come. This makes production difficult.

3. Where brains and knowledge are the key assets. If a country takes over a local branch of an international bank, all it gets is a few microcomputers, some leased office space, a dead Telex machine, and the desks. The skills, in the the form of foreign banking experts, go home. In almost all cases of expropriation, the foreign staff gets out. In most cases the expropriating country is most happy to get them out. Since the company was selling specialized skills, these are now not available. Such firms are usually locked into intricate international information networks, and all these linkages are immediately broken.

An unnoticed aspect of such expropriations is that the expropriating country often loses lots of local talent as well. The local employees of the MNC, given a choice between a rabid hypernationalist radical local government and a chance to work abroad with the MNC, will typically take the latter choice. Again, the country is typically happy to see such decadent capitalists leave, thus giving to the MNC and other countries millions or even billions of dollars of human capital. This is one major reason why any expropriation leads to income losses, not gains, but few leaders interested in expropriations have ever thought about the point.

Since MNCs have reasoned this through, typical results are that the company hedges in dubious countries by investing in systems with these last three characteristics. A variant on this theme is to perform turnkey projects, or obtain management contracts without owning the assets. If the country is upset, it sends your personnel home, but nothing else is lost. Another variant is to have the local firm do production, while the multinational does the international marketing, and possibly supplies such key ingredients as technical assistance, licensing of processes and trade names, and financial support. Crafty MNCs often manufacture a few critical and high technology components at home and export them to the branch. Come the revolution, and the auto example noted above is replicated, since once these components are used up, production stops.

An MNC cannot do this in raw materials production, since it has to go where the oil or copper or tin is. But options include performing drilling, exploration, and production under contract with the local government. If oil is found, the MNC can also market it abroad for the host government. Modern oil and other mineral exploration has many such examples, including operations in such countries as the PRC and Vietnam.

Negotiation Strategy

The negotiation process is ultimately a function of the relative bargaining power of MNCs and countries. If an MNC has little to offer a country, there is no reason why the country should allow it to operate. But if the MNC has something the country wants, then entry is easy.

Countries are getting smarter in bargaining because of the rapid spread of knowledge about MNCs, along with growing wisdom of what can and cannot be done by local governments. Sophisticated government bargainers have watched those expropriation experiments too, and they are aware that if they get too tough, they may lose more than they gain. MNC bargainers are also more sophisticated (many may even have read earlier editions of this book!). Negotiators on each side can more readily evalute correctly their bargaining power. MNCs have shown great adaptibility to many different situations, and there is no reason to suspect that they will not be able to continue being adaptable in the future. But they will have to do much more thinking about what their real advantages are than in the past.

As we noted earlier, the MNCs that still are expanding may have more power than MNCs did historically. One major reason is that older investments were in oilfields and mainline manufacturing, and these industries are now not expanding much, if at all. Very few auto or heavy equipment manufacturers anywhere in the West are expanding. Most are trying to figure out how to cut back and disinvest. Moreover, any logical, and many illogical expropriations have already happened, and there are very few privately owned oilfields in Third World countries at present. New ones will be owned by the country, with MNCs performing contract management, production, and marketing. The new pattern is high technology and labor intensive light industry, and these shift the bargaining power back to the MNCs, for reasons noted above. Moreover, given the great difficulties expropriators have had if they act without compensation, modern expropriations tend to be buyouts at reasonable prices, which defuses the politics somewhat.

No major MNC (and virtually no smaller ones either) ever went broke because of an expropriation. Somehow these companies manage to thrive elsewhere. Moreover, most MNC assets and activities are in affluent countries highly unlikely to expropriate anything, unless it be a piece of land to run a new road through, and then adequate compensation will be paid. If Ethiopia expropriates all foreign assets (as it did a few years ago), no one much cares, including the MNCs who lost perhaps two minutes gross income as a result. Once again, the bargaining power shifts to the MNCs, against the countries, and it is likely that this shift will remain for some years to come. Countries and politicians might not like this, but they will have to live with it.

A further new development which shifts the balance is the rapid growth of those MNCs from smaller or closely controlled Third World countries. A country such as India may find to its dismay that highly competent Indian entrepreneurs are investing abroad rather than at home. If India makes its business controls tighter, then more skilled Indians will leave and invest abroad, leading to still more losses. These new MNCs tend to be concentrated in older and more technically sedate industries long ignored by huge, modern Western companies, and often the Indians or Singaporians or whatever prove to be very efficient indeed, even in countries such as the U.S. India certainly does not have as formal policy the rapid creation of wealth in the United States, yet hundreds of thousands of Indians now live (and often invest) in the U.S., and the ethnic group with the highest per capita family income in the U.S. is Asian Indians (second place belongs to Americans of Japanese descent, and WASPs are third). Over a million Iranians, 400,000 El Salvadorians, tens of thousands of Chileans, Lebanese, Ethiopians, millions of Cubans, and many others now contribute to U.S. wealth, not that of their home countries. The price of being morally right can be much higher than most government officials realize.

The World Government System

None of the above government options are attractive for countries proud of their own identity and culture, and the options are probably getting worse. Each option contains risks and costs. And, running through the problem in subtle and critical ways is the phenomenal competence of the MNCs. If the MNCs were merely expoitative, or if they provided services and goods which could just as easily be created by local citizens, then the problem could be easily solved. The difficulty is that too often they provide the real keys to rapid economic progress. Whatever our politics, rapid income growth rates are desired, since they provide the wealth to do what we want, be it build more churches, increase armaments, build highways, or improve schools. Wealth also is what counts in the world pecking order. Few persons pay attention to poor men or poor countries, but many listen respectfully to the rich, particularly the new rich.

We need a world political system with some real power. If the MNCs are global, the regulators should be global too. But in this nationalistic world, the possibility of global government which really works does not seem too probable in the near future. The United Nations studies MNCs and makes suggestions, but it does not have the power to control any country's policies as yet. By the turn of the century (we are not sure which century!) we may see such an organization.

We do have regional groupings which are beginning to affect multinational firms. The European Community is beginning to coordinate the policies of its members, but very slowly. OPEC also coordinates its members' policies toward oil production and prices, but only with extreme difficulty. Total coordination and control on a global level is still far away.

Meanwhile, the MNCs, with their impressive productive advantages, infiltrate the world economic system. Their major interests are in affluent countries which are willing to bear the psychic costs to get the economic benefits, but they also work anywhere they can to their own advantage. They can offer something to everyone, because they really are positive sum gameplayers. Nations fret, but as yet they do not quite know what to do. The world system is turned upside down, and our political institutions are not yet organized to handle the problems they face. Perhaps some day they will be.

Questions for Discussion

1. In recent years, various communist countries, including the PRC, have begun cautiously to open their local economies. Now there is talk of agreements by American firms to have major cooperation agreements with the PRC to manufacture such items as diesel engines in that country, using American MNC technology and managerial skills.

The American firms will provide the technology and get paid with diesel engines made in the PRC, which will be sold in other countries. Why do you suppose the PRC would be willing to consider this type of international business? What advantages will accrue to them? What costs?

What will the American MNC gain? Why?

Do you think that this is a good idea for the United States? Why or why not?

2. Many nationalists and Marxists in poorer countries argue that it is preferable that their countries be closed systems. In the limit, this means being like Albania. If one major goal of any country is very rapid economic development, what does a country lose by moving to this closed system pattern? Why? What does it gain? Why?

3. Many keen observers of the struggle for power between large MNCs and governments have argued that the only solution to the problem is to have some sort of world government to control such companies. This would mean that local governments such as the United States would have to give up sovereignty in key areas, such as antitrust, industrial location, investment decisions, and similar matters.

Do you like this idea? Why or why not? What advantages might such a supranational control authority have? What disadvantages might it have?

4. A major MNC wants to locate a factory in a suspicious country to manufacture electronic components for its computer line. This plant would employ about 3,000 local citizens, most of whom would work on assembly lines. Gross revenues are estimated to be around $30 million per year, and net profits before taxes about $8 million.

What might this firm offer to this country which might make the deal more attractive? Why? What might seem unattractive to the country about the deal? Why?

5. Some years ago, a major automotive firm wanted to build a $200 million plant in France to make automatic transmissions. This plant would produce such equipment for all cars manufactured within the EC by this firm. Under EC rules, these transmissions would be shipped anywhere within the market duty free. The concept was similar to an American company building transmissions in Indiana for use in cars made in Michigan and sold in Illinois.

France at this time was rather suspicious of big foreign firms, so it refused permission for plant construction. The firm then went about thirty kilometers north to Belgium, where it was welcomed. The Belgian plant now makes the transmissions, exports them to France and elsewhere for installation in new cars, and sends the cars to be sold around the EC. They also are exported worldwide.

Analyze this situation from a power standpoint. Who had the most power here? What could the government of France have done? Should a sovereign state be treated as shabbily as this by a mere private corporation?

6. When a country gets tough with foreign firms, as when it nationalizes some of them, or raises taxes to prohibitive levels, the usual result is a sharp decline in foreign investment in the country. Often this causes rising unemployment, declining incomes, and much economic trouble. The tougher the country gets, the more economic trouble it usually has.

Is this fair? What power does a small country have in such a situation? How can such countries possibly avoid such problems, if they feel that it is important to them to be more independent?

7. A major American MNC is considering investments in manufacturing cars in a somewhat unstable foreign country. The company realizes that at some future time, politicians in favor of expropriation of all foreign assets may rise to power. Yet the profitibility of the new investment looks terrific.

What strategy might this company take to minimize the expropriation risk? Be specific.

Supplementary Readings

Behrman, Jack. NATIONAL INTERESTS AND THE MULTINATIONAL ENTERPRISE. Englewood Cliffs, NJ: Prentice-Hall, 1970.

------------- U.S. INTERNATIONAL BUSINESS AND GOVERNMENTS. New York: McGraw-Hill, 1971.

Bergsten, AMERICAN MULTINATIONALS AND AMERICAN INTERESTS. Washington: The Brookings Institution, 1978.

Dunning, John H. STUDIES IN INTERNATIONAL INVESTMENT. London: George Allen and Unwin, 1970.

Faith, Nicolas. THE INFILTRATORS. New York:E. P. Dutton and Co., 1972.

Hartshorn, J.C. OIL COMPANIES AND GOVERNMENTS. London: Faber and Faber, 1967.

Hellmann, Ranier. THE CHALLENGE TO U.S. DOMINANCE OF THE MULTINATIONAL CORPORATION. New York: Dunellen, 1970.

Kindleberger, Charles B. THE INTERNATIONAL CORPORATION. Cambridge, MA: MIT Press, 1970.

Levitt, Karl. SILENT SURRENDER: THE AMERICAN ECONOMIC EMPIRE IN CANADA. New York: Liverwright, 1971.

Long, Frank. RESTRICTIVE BUSINESS PRACTICES, TRANSNATIONAL CORPORATIONS AND DEVELOPMENT. Boston: Nijhoff Publishers, 1981.

Servan-Schreiber. Jean-Jacques. THE AMERICAN CHALLENGE. New York: Atheneum House, 1968.

Turner, Louis. THE NEWLY INDUSTRIALIZED COUNTRIES, TRADE AND ADJUSTMENT. London: Allen and Unwin, 1982.

Vernon, Raymond. SOVEREIGNTY AT BAY. New York: Basic Books, 1971.

Chapter 8
Development of the
International Order

Introduction

We still are a long ways from having world government, and the MNCs are sometimes bigger than the governments which try to control them. Moreover, the MNCs can jump national boundaries easily in accomplishing their tasks. As a result, it often is not too clear just who does control any firm engaged extensively in international business.

Because governments have long had problems in intergovernmental relations, from time to time efforts have been made to create international organizations which pull countries together to resolve a common problem. Many of these organizations have quite limited powers and functions, but at least they represent the beginnings of a truly international structure for business, commerce, and trade. Firms interact often with these organizations, and they are important in determining some specific problem outcomes. These organizations determine a portion of the international constraint structure. For this reason, they are worth examining. They are also interesting as examples of multinational cooperation which could serve as a pattern for still more integrative efforts. We seem to be unable to stand still in our world order. We stumble forward toward still more cooperation, often in fits and starts, with considerable backsliding. As change occurs, so do opportunities and options open both to firms and countries.

INTERNATIONAL FINANCIAL ORGANIZATIONS

Membership in various international financial and monetary agencies rarely directly affects firm operations within a given country. However, such memberships are extremely important in determining the kind of economic environment in which the firm will work. Each international organization has rules which the member countries have agreed to observe; such rules can have rather direct effects, most commonly favorable, upon firms within such countries. Some of these organizations are potential sources of foreign capital, which have very direct impacts on the country´s balance of payments, and hence on the legal rule directly affecting international firm operations within the country. Others provide for support of the local currency in time of crisis, which again has direct impacts upon the firm. Hence in the International Monetary Fund (IMF), a country can receive help to support its currency in return for certain obligations on the part of the country; and both the obligations and the help will affect foreign firms quite directly, even if management never comes directly into contact with the international organization. There often is a significant difference between the actions feasible for a member, as compared to a non member country.

THE WORLD BANK

The World Bank, founded in 1945 as the International Bank for Reconstruction and Development, had as its basic initial purpose to provide a pool of capital for lending to war torn nations for reconstruction. When this task was largely completed in the early 1950's, loans for economic development became its primary purpose.

The World Bank was one of a triumvirate of agencies conceived at Bretton Woods in 1944 to assist in critical reconstruction of postwar world trade and finance. A second organization, the IMF, will be considered below; the third, the International Trade Organization, never became operational, because few governments were willing to ratify its basic treaty. It was replaced in 1955 by the General Agreement on Trade and Tariffs (GATT), which also will be covered below.

The IMF deals with problems of currency stability; GATT deals with tariffs and other barriers to trade. The World Bank basically deals with the problems of international flows of capital. The basic organization is that the member countries contribute capital to the World Bank, roughly in proportion to their incomes and political importance. In effect, countries buy shares in the World Bank and have voting rights in a manner analogous to any joint stock corporation. Any nation is free to join, provided they abide by rather simple and straightforward operating rules, and over 130 nations, including the United States, are now World Bank members. Yugoslavia, Romania (since 1972), the PRC (1981), and Hungary (1983) are the only communist bloc members.

The Bank also sells bond issues in various countries to obtain additional funds for lending. It has in recent years successfully floated issues in West Germany, Italy, Canada, the Netherlands, Switzerland, the United Kingdom, and the United States. Its bonds are highly regarded, since there have been no defaults in the Bank's history, and its financial position is extremely sound.

The Bank lends at commercial rates of interest to public or private customers who qualify in a commercial sense for loans. Only member nations and their dependencies are eligible for loans. There is no subsidy involved in Bank operations, since loan applications are carefully analyzed, both in terms of potential profitibility of the project and the potential balance of payments problems which might arise as a result of repayments of the loans. The unique feature of the Bank's actitivies is that it routinely deals with large scale international loans to borrowers who may have no other source of funds domestically or internationally. Third World countries are now the only customers, since more affluent countries have other borrowing options. Infrastructure loans for such projects as irrigation, electric power, roads, harbors, and water supplies are most common. India, being both a Third World country and having over 700 million people, has long been the major borrower, but dozens of countries have taken loans.

While all World Bank loans must be guaranteed by the country's national government, many loans are to private firms. A private electric power company may obtain the loan, but only after its government has guaranteed repayment. Like a commercial bank, the World Bank does not normally advance all the capital; the country or firm involved is expected to contribute substantial equity. The Bank may also only lend the amount of money needed for foreign exchange. A major electric power project may require, say, 60 percent of costs in foreign exchange, with the balance of costs incurred locally. The Bank would not normally lend money for the domestic costs.

Loans are not made in any particular relation to the size or wealth of member countries. The ultimate loan criteria is the desirability of the project presented. An important byproduct of the Bank's activities has been research and advice to Third World countries on the types of activities for which they might be best suited. The Bank has published over 30 country studies under its own auspices, indicating what kinds of economic development policies and programs might prove most desirable in the given country. It also works closely with such United Nations organizations as the Food and Agricultural Organization (FAO), coordinating studies and knowledge in particular countries. Many of the Bank's reports and studies contain invaluable information for MNCs, since they deal with economic and business information and problems.

International contracting firms in particular are very interested in World Bank projects, since they are the contractors which do these jobs. A billion dollar plus project to build roads in some Third World country is an attractive piece of business for qualified bidders. Equipment suppliers, such as turbine manufacturers, suppliers of roadbuilding equipment, and even cement manufacturers can gain large orders from World Bank projects. Moreover, payments are in hard currencies, often in countries without such currencies. Firms in all industrial countries, including such newly industrialized countries as South Korea, have benefitted from Bank projects.

Still another impact on MNCs is the incremental hard currency a World Bank loan presents to the capital account in the balance of payments of many Third World countries. Mexico or Brazil might eventually be able to finance a major power project, but with World Bank loans, the projects can be undertaken years ahead of expected internally financed dates. The result can be rising incomes and production within a few years, instead of a few decades. As development proceeds in this way, the balance of payments does not deteriorate impossibly. MNCs are indirectly benefitted by not having to face more capital remittance and other exchange controls, which might be necessary if World Bank capital were not available.

Until the 1970's, many countries could only obtain large amounts of hard currency capital from the World Bank. But then, as we noted in Chapter 4, private bank lending rose very rapidly, and by 1980 was much more important to Third World countries than World Bank funds. As the private lending boom collapsed, the World Bank becomes relatively more important, but it still is not large enough to handle all credit demands. Its capital is limited by the amounts that richer countries choose to invest, plus whatever bonds it can sell.

The World Bank has an affiliate, the International Finance Corporation (IFC), which was formed in 1956 in recognition of the fact that in many cases private firms could not expect to obtain the guarantees of their governments for World Bank loans. The IFC initially lent only on fixed interest, bond type loans; in 1960, this provision was modified to allow for equity participation by the IFC in industries in member countries.

Like other World Bank loans, IFC loans are essentially commercial in nature, and are typically made to firms in Third World countries without well developed money markets. The IFC insists on large equity participation by borrowers, and as a result, for each dollar of loans made, three to five additional dollars of capital eventually get invested. The cautious approach to lending, including extremely close analysis of the firm and its loan proposals, tends to be an educational experience in itself for firms who have not been in an environment where such money management is taken for granted. But the IFC remains a small part of total World Bank activities.

The World Bank and the IFC operate generally on commercial lending principles. This has been one of the major complaints about these agencies, since one major barrier to expanded lending has been the inability of Third World countries to come up with economically viable projects. There is a far greater shortage of financial planners, feasibility report writers, engineering consultants, and professional management people than there is capital, and really poor countries often do not have the capability even to prepare detailed loan requests, in spite of much World Bank assistance.

A second World Bank affiliate, the International Development Association (IDA), was begun in 1960 to answer this criticism. The initial capital subscription, since increased substantially, was a billion dollars, and was contributed by member countries. Unlike the Bank, countries were divided into developed and underdeveloped categories, with special easy subscription terms to the less developed.

The general purpose of IDA is to make subsidized developmental loans to Third World countries. Capital is provided to such countries at zero interest, payable in 50 years, with a 10 year grace period at the outset of the loan. While IDA maintains that it carefully selects its loan projects, it is clear that it is willing to make a wider range of loans on much riskier projects than the World Bank itself.

IDA will lend to either public or private organizations, and government guarantees are not required. The developed country members also are not eligible for loans, and these countries´ contributions to IDA can be considered a part of their developmental aid activities.

Unlike the World Bank, IDA cannot count on selling its securities in various developed countries, since it has no income from interest earnings. It must rely on the willingness of hard currency countries to keep it supplied with funds. This multilateral aid is often viewed with suspicion by such countries as the United States, since the rich country cannot control where the aid funds go. Given a choice, The U.S. might elect to give funds directly to countries for projects it prefers. IDA is forever scrambling for funds as a result.

The impact on MNCs of the IDA are quite similar to those indicated for the World Bank. Direct sales of capital equipment, large international construction contracts, enjoyment of social overhead capital projects built in part with IDA funds, and easing of balance of payments pressures are among the advantages.

REGIONAL DEVELOPMENT BANKS

A number of regional development banks have been established following the general World Bank format, including the Arab Development Bank and the Inter-American Development Bank. The general idea behind these banks is to provide public capital for given regions which may have common political, cultural, religious, or military interests. All function reasonably well, although their combined capital was swamped by private bank lending in the 1970's, as noted above. But the Third World needs enormous amounts of capital, and any net additions to supplies are welcome. Now that private banks are extremely reluctant to lend again, it is likely that the World Bank and regional development banks will again receive more attention. Efforts to expand their capital in the end depend on the willingness of richer countries to fund multilateral aid programs. As noted above, such countries often prefer to give aid bilaterally, since they can control who gets what, what it is used for, and where it gets spent. Not all gifts are benevolent; often the giver expects much in return, and multilateral aid leads to loss of control over funds.

The educational impact of all of the lending agencies also cannot be underestimated. Nothing improves governmental or private firm performance more quickly than a suspicious banker asking embarrassing questions about the details of a project which emotionally looks good to its promoters, but which may in fact be a hopeless economic proposition. The act of seeking out such loan assistance may in itself give considerable indirect benefit to MNCs, who must also deal, hopefully in a rational manner, with the same public servants and private local businessmen who seek outside assistance. If the net result of the lending activity is some improvement in business performance, the effort may be well worth the cost.

INTERNATIONAL MONETARY FUND

The IMF was the second major institution to come out of the Bretton Woods Conference. This organization deals with problems associated with sudden changes in the balance of payments for member countries. Before the IMF, a country might have a crop failure, leading to serious short term pressures on the balance of payments. The only recourse of a country in this position would be a devaluation, imposition of exchange controls, or possibly a quick international loan from another country or private bank. Since such short term disturbances also affect other countries, any quick moves to correct such disturbances may affect them even more, it was felt that some mechanism should be created to deal with such problems. The experience of the 1930's in most countries suggested that such reform was badly needed.

The basic idea behind the IMF is to provide for short term.drawings of foreign currencies needed to shore up the balance of payments in the drawing country. Each member is levied a quota of funds to be paid to the IMF in gold (25 percent) and its own currency. By mid-1979 the 138 member countries had contributed a reserve of over $39 billions to the IMF. Member countries have an almost automatic right to draw on the first tranche (or the 25 percent of their quotas in gold), and successive tranches are increasingly difficult to obtain. Thus a country in temporary balance of payments difficulties has an immediate source of capital available to cover the first shock of its deficit, and if it can convince the IMF of the validity of its position, it can draw considerably more to cover deficits.

The ability to obtain more credits from the IMF basically rests on the ability of the country in question to convince the Fund that its plan to restore equilibrium in its balance of payments is sound. One immediate effect here is to insure that a country in trouble, for whatever reason, will be forced to consider meaningful economic alternatives at home to solve its problems. The country also has available a great deal of very high skill technical advice about what corrective steps might prove desirable. For a country which may not have this kind of technical assistance available locally, this can be a major advantage.

Historically, the IMF required that member countries have fixed exchange rates defined in dollars or gold, but this part of the system ended in 1971, as we noted in Chapter 4. But countries still have balance of payments difficulties, mainly because they try to peg rates to the dollar or other hard currency, have crop failures or runaway inflations at home, and then run out of foreign exchange. The IMF still operates effectively to assist in such situations.

One major advantage the IMF gives countries with local political problems is its aloofness and insistance on unpopular measures that countries find difficult to carry out. As we noted in Chapter 4, the usual problem is too much money creation locally, leading to price inflation, leading, with any sort of pegged exchange rates, to a balance of payments crisis. The IMF experts come, gravely examine the situation, and recommend that those pensions be cut, government spending be reduced, military expenses diminished, and so on. Such steps usually make much sense, but local politicians cannot really take them without losing the next election (or being deposed in the next coup). They can blame those evil, unfeeling IMF experts for all the country´s troubles, and indeed, quite a few elections have involved such accusations. The IMF makes a fine whipping boy, and it is used to this role. In the end, their advice is taken (in part), the money supply is brought under control, IMF loans are made to the unhappy country, and the crisis is resolved.

Given the huge private bank loans outstanding to so many Third World countries, the IMF is playing a larger role than ever in helping resolve balances of payments problems. At this writing (1984), the IMF has asked its members for large increases in funds, and it is possible that if a few countries default on private debt, the IMF may well take over some of this debt. During most of the 1970's, the IMF's role was dwarfed by large private international lending, but now that the bankers are reluctant to lend more to Third World countries, the IMF's role is again quite important. It has been a most useful institution for both affluent and poor countries over the past 35 years, and it will undoubtedly continue to play a critical role on the world stage.

GENERAL AGREEMENT ON TARIFFS AND TRADE

This organization has over 95 members and is basically concerned with the reduction and elimination of tariffs and other trading restrictions between member nations. The ultimate goal of GATT is to structure a multilaterally oriented, totally free trading system between all countries.

In general, GATT members are unable to use quotas, but, as usual, several loopholes exist in the rules. The major one is where a country has balance of payments difficulties. Here a country may levy discriminatory quotas against countries where it lacks foreign exchange to buy. Such discriminatory quota rules are to be elimated by consultation with the IMF, and many have been reduced or liquidated in this manner. All GATT members are also IMF members.

GATT operates through annual meetings, where members negotiate, usually bilaterally, to reduce tariffs on selected items. This is a sort of horse trading operation where one country gives reductions in exchange for reductions from the other country on items which might be exported to it. When agreement is made between the bargainers, the most favored nation principle is applied. This means that any reduction made to one country applies immediately to all other nations (less those specifically omitted from the given country's legislation). Thus if the United States agrees with Great Britain to reduce American automobile tariffs by 10 percent, every other exporter of automobiles to the U.S. receives the same concession. If in return for this concession Great Britain has reduced the tariff on computers by 15 percent, then other computer exporters to Great Britain also get this reduction. The result has been fairly far reaching tariff and quota reductions for a variety of exports from many nations.

The United States is typically other countries' largest single market, and this most favored nation principle applies to all but a few communist countries. Thus in 1981, Poland, which did have MFN status, lost it because of its internal activities that the U.S. did not favor. Immediately, tariffs on Polish goods reverted to the Hawley/Smoot level of 1930, which typically range two to tenfold higher than those MFN rates negotiated through GATT. The result for Poland was the closing of many critical markets and a major economic loss, which is exactly why the U.S. can use this MFN threat quite effectively against other countries' policies.

GATT is a rather informal organization compared to the IMF and the World Bank. The formal foundation for GATT, the International Trade Organization, never was formally ratified by enough countries to become operational, and as a result GATT has no permanent secretariat or elaborate rules of operation.

UNCTAD AND THE NIEO

The United Nations, and within it the Conference for Trade and Development (UNCTAD), has become a forum for an ongoing debate between the developed countries (DCs) and 117 less developed countries (LDCs). By mid-1979, the LDCs were pressing their demands for a "New International Economic Order." The term itself is unwarranted, since the issues involved are not so new, and since the demands are as much political and social as they are economic. Also implementation of the NIEO would possibly create chaos rather than order. Furthermore, realization of the NIEO is highly improbable. However, our consideration in this chapter of the development of the international order makes it advisable to focus briefly on the issues involved.

The demands by the LDCs that an NIEO be established stem from their perception that a poverty curtain separates the LDCs from the DCs, both materially and philosophically. Specifically, the LDCs contend that the present world order systematically discriminates against them in as least six ways:

1. There is an imbalance in the distribution of international monetary reserves, and a few rich nations are said to control credit facilities.

2. The distribution of value added to the products traded between the DCs and the LDCs is heavily weighted in favor of the DCs.

3. DC protectionism prevents the LDCs from receiving their due share of wealth, whereas the poor cannot afford the luxury of protectionism.

4. Unequal bargaining power between MNCs and LDCs results in the inequitable sharing of benefits.

5. LDCs have only pro forma participation in the important economic decision making bodies at the international level.

6. Unequal relationships pervade the intellectual world as well, so that the value systems of the DCs are being forced on the LDCs.

Thus, from the perspective of the LDCs, the causes of their poverty can be traced primarily to factors external to their societies, in particular, to the exploitation and inequitable dependence relationship imposed on them by the DCs. Lingering neo-colonialism is obviously a major factor in this explanation, and most present LDCs were historically colonies of major European countries.

Affluent country representatives, however, obviously perceive the situation quite differently, and contend that the basic causes of poverty are internal, and can be explained though cultural, political, social and economic factors within the LDCs. The bill of particulars noted above contain some germs of truth, but some LDCs have become affluent, and others are becoming so, which suggests that all blame does not lie with the DCs. This debate has raged, often in extremely derogatory terms, with much name calling, accusations, and ill feeling, through many years at many international conferences.

But it is unlikely that dramatic changes will result through the continuation of the North-South dialogue, in spite of certain concessions which the DCs have made, particularly on trade in labor intensive commodities, such as textiles. This is partly due to the fact that most of the LDC demands are clearly unacceptable to the DCs. For example, one proposal calls for an orderly settlement of all past debts, which means in most cases wiping the slate clean by debt forgiveness. Another suggests renegotiation of all MNC contracts. A third suggests the redistribution of world reserves on the basis of need, ignoring the credit worthiness of the countries involved. And a fourth calls not only for increasd powers of the UN in economic affairs, but for greater voting strength of the LDCs within the IMF and the World Bank.

These demands appear unrealistic at present, and indeed, given world recession in the early 1980´s, even more unrealistic than they appeared in the 1970´s. MNCs have more, not less bargaining power now, and LDCs which try to control them carefully end up with the usual one hundred percent of nothing. The MNCs simply invest in more tractable countries. OPEC once seemed to be able to force the afluent countries to their knees, but now OPEC is in disarray, and its bargaining power much less than as late as 1980. It is hard to imagine a country like the U.S. voluntarily raising taxes to pay funds to LDCs, even if for moral reasons this course seemed wise. And the U.S. announced in early 1984 that it will withdraw from UNESCO (giving the required year´s notice), one UN agency that has spent much time trying to prove the U.S. is a devil, at the U.S.´s expense. While LDCs do have many legitimate grievances, trying to change the world through the NIEO has not proved a fruitful way of achieving reform.

However, UNCTAD has served the purpose of focussing attention on the issues involved in the world economic system which LDCs find distasteful or unfair, and UNCTAD does provide a forum for debate to focus on the differing perceptions of rich and poor countries. Readers of this book from wealthy countries perhaps do not realize the intense feelings of unfairness that most persons from LDCs feel. The U.S. and other affluent countries are regarded as insane, mad dogs, able to rape the world by force. The helpless LDCs are impotent and outraged. Such feelings, for better or worse, do matter in the international order.

CUSTOMS UNIONS

The very rapid development and outstanding economic success of the European Community (EC) since its formation in 1958 has focused much attention on this type of economic union. Both persons within the EC and those interested in doing business with it have followed its evolution and development with great interest. Other trade unions, such as the European Free Trade Association (EFTA), the Latin American Free Trade Association (LAFTA), and the Central American Common Market, among others, have been organized in large part because of the obvious advantages of the EC, although none of these have managed to attain such success.

What occurs here is that many of the international and local constraints change rapidly as a result of the formation of such a union. Rules and regulations, as well as economic and social policies and attitudes which have taken centuries to mature to their present form are suddenly altered, and businessmen both inside and outside the market area have to make major adjustments in internal management to take proper advantage of the shifts. Given the typical complexity of the changes, the proper internal enterprise changes are not always so obvious, and considerable attention is paid to the way in which given constraint changes will alter established ways of do.ng business and managing productive enterprises. The EC is particularly interesting to outsiders, given its huge wealth and incomes.

TYPES OF CUSTOMS UNIONS

Variations are numerous in customs unions. Agreements can range from an agreement to eliminate trade barriers on a narrow range of products, as Canada and the U.S. have done on autos and components, to complete political and economic integration. Actually, complete integration is a well established idea, since this is exactly what the United States is. When one trades between New York and Illinois, he or she is trading in a totally integrated customs area. The formation of European national states followed a similar pattern, as Germany, Italy, the United Kingdom, and other countries were formed out of a mass of petty states, each with its own trade restrictions, tariffs,and local sovereignty. The present trend to unity in Europe is a part of a continuous, albeit often interrrupted movement toward larger free trading areas.

A general division of customs unions is as follows:

1. A free trade area: Here tariffs and quantitative restrictions are abolished between member countries. However, each country maintains its own duties and restrictions against outsiders. The EFTA is this sort of free trade area. Thus Sweden and Portugal have agreed to abolish trade restrictions between each other, since they are both members, but each country maintains trade restrictions of its choice with all outside countries.

2. A customs union: In this case, tariffs and quantitative restrictions are removed between all members and also external trade restrictions of all members are brought into unity. Each country gives up the right to levy its own trade restrictions.

3. A common market: Here the customs union principle is followed, and additionally, factor mobility is permitted betwen members. This means that capital and labor can flow freely between member countries. This is the form of the EC. In this case, it is not necessary to have identical labor, money, and political policies, although these must be at least partially harmonized to the extent necessary to make the free flow of goods and factors workable. If West Germany had a severe depression, while Benelux had an inflationary boom, it is unlikely that the EC could continue to function. Some degree of cooperation between member states would be necessary in such a case.

4. Total economic integration: Here the area is unified as above,

but in addition, monetary and political policies are totally integrated.
The United States or any of the present European countries individually
represent this type of unification. While we tend to regard present
national states as immutable and fixed, many are not particularly old.
The U.S. is actually one of the oldest, since countries such as Germany
and Italy did not emerge as nation states until the middle of the 19th
Century. World War II brought about many nation state changes (i.e.,
Poland, East and West Germany), while most present Third World countries
were formed after this war (i.e., India and Pakistan in 1947; most
African states in the 1960´s). Nation making has been going on for
several centuries, and there is no particular reason to expect that the
process has ended.

ECONOMICS OF CUSTOMS UNIONS

The formation of any of the types of customs unions described above
has two basic effects on firms. First, input costs may change, usually
downward, since inputs of all sorts are now available from larger areas.
In the case of a free trade area, a firm manufacturing washing machines
which purchases its electric motors may find that it can now obtain such
motors more cheaply from member countries. If the agreement also
provides for the free flow of factors, a company may find that it can
borrow money more cheaply from a bank in another member country, or it
may be able to obtain workers or technicians more easily and at lower
cost.

Second, markets typically expand, since firms can now sell in
several countries on an equal basis, as compared to one in the past.
The actual gain for any given firm will depend in large part on the
types of restrictions which existed historically. If markets in other
member countries were sharply restricted by high tariffs or quantitative
controls, the impact may be large. The complexity of tariff and other
restrictive legislation in any country precludes any generalizations
without detailed study of the given case.

The general results will thus typically be a reduction of costs and
an expansion of sales. As might be expected in this very favorable
situation, the usual results of economic integration have been a period
of years of economic expansion, high levels of new investment, and
general economic buoyancy for the countries concerned. Thus in the EC,
the period 1958 to 1974 was a golden age of very rapid economic gains
unknown in earlier times.

The losers in the new situation are typically the inefficient local
firms which require much protection and subsidy to survive. Every
country has its sacred cows, firms which are regarded as so critical to
national welfare that they have to be protected regardless of cost. The
consumers pay the bill for their inefficiency in the form of higher
prices and low quality products. It was widely feared that such firms
would collapse in droves as the EC came into effective operation, but
this did not occur. Even moribund enterprises have shown a striking
vitality when finally exposed to the harsh winds of effective
competition, and even inefficient companies have typically managed to
survive. Nothing focusses the minds of managers in an ineptly managed
family firm so totally as the prospect of bankruptcy and disgrace. When

such firms had to become more efficient, they did what was necessary to become so, and many thrived and grew. The general economic expansion in the EC also allowed many modestly competent firms to survive easily.

The combination of potentially larger sales and lower costs has far-reaching secondary effects as well. A firm which formerly might have had difficulty in competing at home may now find that it not only can compete in the common market, but also in other export markets, because of its newfound efficiency. While some inputs are available locally in the market, others may be imported from countries outside the customs union, leading to economic expansion there. The usual effect of significant cost reductions, regardless of how achieved, tends to percolate steadily through the world economy, resulting in far-reaching changes in economic efficiency.

In the EC case, most European firms perceived the new situation as ripe for export expansion. As the EC countries' economies grew, these firms expanded locally and exported to other EC countries. But American MNCs perceived the EC as a sort of new United States, where they could operate easily much as they do between various American states. They expanded into the EC in a multinational sense, taking full advantage of the new rules. As American firms, they knew all about common markets! The EC countries became a major new investment target for many U.S. MNCs, and most of these expansions were successful.

Economies of Scale. An extremely important consideration in any economic integration for all firms is the economies of scale which may be realized by firms as their sales increase. Economists have long pointed out that a firm's relationship of unit cost to output depends largely on the scale of production, which in turn depends on market size. Figure 8-1 shows this general relationship. A firm may have built the smallest efficient plant known to produce a given product, and still have a market so small that the plant cannot be fully and efficiently utilized. This would be output OQ in Figure 8-1A. If the market expands somewhat in the short run, the plant will experience lower production costs, since as output increases, unit costs will decrease. This follows from the ability of the firm to utilize fully all available equipment and personpower. This output might correspond to output OQ in Figure 8-1A. One possible outcome of an economic integration would be this sort of cost reduction made possible by such increase in production with a given plant.

A more impressive effect could be created by a customs union as well. In the long run situation, where a firm has a chance to vary the size and capacity of its plant, it might find that still larger plants would result in even lower production costs. This could follow from technical improvements developed since the existing plant was built, or it might indicate that, given the small market at the time the first plant was built, it was uneconomic to build a much larger plant and operate it at still lower capacity levels. Figure 8-1B suggests this long run situation. Curve ATC represents the cost curve of the short run plant in Figure 8-1A. But there is a larger, more efficient plant, ATC , which could be built if the market was large enough. The ATC curve is the total long run average total cost curve, which forms an envelope around all of the possible short run curves.

FIGURE 8 −1

SCALE ECONOMIES

A. Short Run

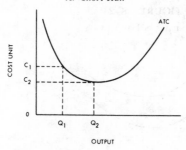

OUTPUT

B. Long Run

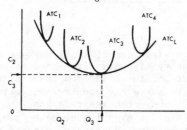

If the market expands beyond the capacity of the initial plant, the firm may build a new plant with the cost curve ATC . In this case, unit costs will be reduced below those of any possible situation in the existing plant (from OC to OC in Figure 8-1B). This new low cost level can only be achieved if the market is significantly larger than it was under earlier conditions. If this case occurs, there will be an investment boom as well, as companies build their new plants, which is exactly what happened from 1958 to 1974 in the EC.

If input costs also decline, costs will be still further reduced. The cost curves in figure 8-1 indicate what would happen if input costs stayed the same. Changes in unit costs here depend entirely on changes in output levels. One still might be paying the same prices for labor, machine hours, and capital, but because all of these inputs can be more efficiently utilized, costs fall. But consider a case where some input costs also fall, as would happen in a new customs union. In the washing machine case noted above, the manufacturer might find that some component costs have fallen by 30 percent. His entire cost function would then shift downward, as shown in Figure 8-2. If the firm could produce the amount OQ at cost OC under earlier conditions, it now can produce the same output for unit cost OC , since it now has cost curve ATC instead of ATC . This point applies both to local and multinational firms within the common market, and both will respond with extensive new investments. The combination of these two potential cost reductions of many firms in the EC explains much of the dynamic changes in the EC countries since 1958.

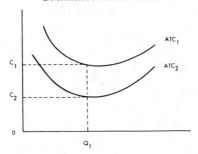

FIGURE 8-2

DECREASES IN INPUT COSTS

Plants built to take advantage of local markets under old rules may be inefficient. A country may have given concessions, in the form of trade and tariff protection, to an international firm which was willing to build a small plant to serve the country. But with the major changes in the rules, all of the above becomes relevant, and the MNC will build new, larger plants, often not even in the same country, if some other common market member offers some advantages in costs or markets.

Marketing economies of scale may also arise in an economic integration. Prior to integration, the firm may have had to maintain a separate marketing organization in each country, or it might have only operated in its country of production. But there are many fixed costs in marketing, as the firm invests in sales outlets, channel design, and sales promotion, and the small market may mean that distribution is expansive. Physical distribution economies also may be absent, as the firm must handle the distribution of its finished product by inefficient, less than carload lot methods, and utilize small and inefficient warehouses for storage.

As the market expands, it is possible to spread marketing fixed costs over more units sold, resulting in lower distribution expenses per unit. The combination of lower production costs plus lower marketing costs can lead to lower prices, higher margins, or some combination of the two, which in turn can lead to explosive growth of firms and economies.

Financial economies of scale are also possible. A larger firm may get its money more cheaply, given its increased volume. If the economic integration includes some enhanced capital mobility, firms can now have access to foreign sources of funds in the same manner as they previously could only tap domestic sources. Large loans also cost relatively the same to evaluate as small ones, and some savings in administrative expenses can be expected. The rapid growth of the Eurodollar market was not unrelated to EC growth.

In addition to these internal scale economies, firms may also enjoy enhanced external economies of scale. These are events and costs incurred external to firms. An example might be the development, after economic integration, of improved, coordinated rail transport facilities between major centers in two or more countries, or more efficient port facilties. Before integration, such services could not be afforded, given low traffic flows. But with the increase in volume, the railroads and ports may be able to improve service, lower rates, and generally reduce transfer costs. Not to be forgotten is the sharp reduction in customhouse costs, if the goods no longer have to be inspected, tested, stored, or otherwise delayed in transit. Time is really money!

The development of specialized service firms, such as advertising agencies and financial brokers, may also be a sort of external economy for firms. Prior to integration, the market for such activities may have been so small as to preclude development of a host of such specialized activities; after integration, they become economically feasible, and any company can take advantage of them.

The general effect of a major economic integration can be visualized by Americans by considering what would happen if each state in the union had its own currency, customs officials, tariffs, and restrictions on trade. In terms of short run advantage for local citizens, such restrictions may appear sound, since they force production of everything to be done at home, at higher costs. But the real costs of trying to do everything yourself are enormous, and, in effect, the modern economic integrationists are trying to achieve what has already been achieved in the United States. As the size of the market expands, firms find that they can reduce costs, expand sales, and still make more money than they did previously.

This sort of basic revision of the international rules of the game has a major impact on virtually all of the critical elements of the management process. Planning shifts dramatically as new cost and price relationships are formulated; organization changes as firm and plant size changes, and as the production functions of the firm change rapidly; marketing, production, and finance change in character; research and development may well change to focus on new opportunities in an expanded and quite different market; and public relations assume a broader focus. One of the major reasons for the intense interest in economic integration by productive firms is that these changes are recognized as inevitable by everyone, and the problem is one of determining how the firm's management can optimize the company's position under the new situation.

Factor Mobility. Americans take for granted the fact that they can travel the length and breadth of the land without passports, customs inspections, or visas, and that they can easily shift liquid or real capital from region to region without restrictions. For the rest of the world, however, this situation would represent a utopia. Factor movements are sharply restricted between countries all over the world, and most countries are too small to take advantage of economies of scale in factor use as discussed above. The EC is making a major effort to remove the restrictions on the free flow of labor and capital between members. An immediate result is to lower costs, as noted above.

Labor mobility across national boundaries raises many problems for countries and firms. Each nation has its own local laws and regulations governing hours of work, social insurance benefits and taxes, safety rules, and similar matters, and governments of the countries concerned usually press for good treatment of their citizens working abroad. Employers using foreign workers have problems of adjusting to two sets of government pressures, rather than one. The effects on staffing and direction are direct here, since the firm encounters such legal problems, as well as language and cultural differences, which present new difficulties in making most effective use of the labor force.

If free flow of factors is so efficient, why do countries resist so tenaciously? The answer lies in control. If anyone can ship capital abroad, then when the government does weird things, the country stagnates or collapses. If anyone could go anywhere, then protected workers could be under tough competitive pressures. There is inevitable political pressure to keep out all foreigners, as we noted in other chapters, and if the pressure succeeds, factor mobility slows. People stay poorer, too, but few citizens are sophisticated enough economically to appreciate why.

Transfer problems. Before the economic integration takes place, a firm has locational choices which are restricted to one country. But with economic integration, the entire union is now a market, which can be supplied from any point within the market.

This change requires a complete change in locational planning. Instead of considering locational factors peculiar to one country, the entire market as a unit must be analyzed, and plans must be adjusted to take account of this fact. This point can even be important when a single tariff is removed, since if a company can ship product into a market without extra costs, then other countries are potential productive locations. The U.S. and Mexico have agreements relating to free flow of components into Mexico and tariff free imports from Mexico on many items. Hence many U.S. firms produce in Mexico, near the U.S. border, using components from the U.S., and then sell the product back into the U.S. If a tariff wall existed, Mexican locations would not be considered.

Locational theory is a complex problem in itself, and the locational factors for even a small plant could fill a book. Such questions as the location of major markets, transport costs, warehouse facilities, communications facilities, local taxes, unit labor costs, and many other factors are relevant in seeking an efficient location, and most of these will shift as integration occurs. Of particular importance in a customs union is the question of transport adequacy between member countries. The EC has the advantage of possessing excellent facilities, but other customs unions suffer from serious defects in transportation facilities between member countries. Tariffs are one transfer cost, but transportation is another, and if these are high, nothing much moves anyhow.

Where member countries have traditionally exported raw materials and imported manufactured goods, as is the case in Latin America, most roads and railroads lead to the major export ports, not to nearby countries. It is often easier to export to Western Europe, Japan, or the U.S. than it is to move goods around in the interior. Effective economic integration presupposes that the countries in the union are able to transport commodities between the member countries, and it is this lack of facilities which makes the potential short term impact of economic unions outside of Europe somewhat less promising that they otherwise might be.

Balance of Payments Problems. All recent economic integrations have not changed the position of national currencies. Each member of the union is allowed to maintain its own currency, typically allowing it to float as it pleases. The EC does have its ECU, as noted in Chapter 4, but not all EC members are ECU members, and even here, the stronger currency countries tend to have upwardly moving currencies, while weaker members occasionally have to devalue to remain within the 2.5 percent float limits. Relatively free capital movements between member countries can also contribute to wide currency fluctuations.

If currencies were to be integrated, member countries would have to give up much sovereignty, as states have done within the U.S. There actually are 12 U.S. dollars (one from each of the 12 Federal Reserve districts), and these dollars always exchange at $1 equals $1. Why? The reason is that the U.S. states cannot impose any controls on the flows of goods, people, services, or capital. If a state gets into trouble, its citizens can leave to work elsewhere. If local industries become uncompetitive, they go bankrupt and close. If interest rates in Chicago are higher than in New York, capital flows to Chicago. Each region has to make internal adjustments to external forces, which is exactly the reverse of the international situation, where governments try to push adjustments outside the country. No customs union has been able to get as far as the U.S., except those new countries, such as India, who in effect did internally what the U.S. did long ago, namely force all domestic states to give up sovereignty to the central government.

As noted earlier, the intent of any customs union is to take advantage of the free flows of everything across national boundaries. The basic model is the United States; the problem is to figure out how far suspicious countries are willing to give up sovereignty and control in order to gain the economic benefits. The EC has been by far the most successful customs union in history, mainly because its member countries were willing to cooperate on so many matters. But the EC has been unable to do much with national currencies, and its agricultural policies (typically leading to high price supports for inefficient producers) are in disarray. Whenever a problem pops up which historically was solved by a local government, as when a major industry gets into economic difficulties, it is tempting for that country to regress to its nationalistic ways and try to resolve the problem in traditional, local ways. The usual results are disasters compounded in the long run, as inefficient industries stagger on with huge subsidies, or farmers get large incomes at the expense of consumers. Costs soar, incomes stagnate, and unemployment grows, as the nation tries to save its economic dogs. Voters like it this way, but the long term cost is stagnation and inefficiency.

A major reason the EC worked so well was that Western Europe went on the oil and natural gas energy standard in the 1950´s. Until this time, most of Western Europe had used coal as a primary fuel. This energy shift led to cars, trucks, and all the economic activity associated with them, as well as low cost electric power provided by burning cheap oil in boilers to generate that electricity. The beginnings of the EC coincided nicely with this massive structural shift of Western European economies, and a large proportion of those new plants were connected with production of diesel engines, autos, trucks, roadbuilding equipment, and numerous other items associated with a liquid fuel economy. American MNCs in these areas benefitted extensively, given their experience at home with such production. In one sense, the EC from 1958 to 1974 was a catching up and replicating, in a more efficient manner, what the U.S. had already experienced in the period 1925 to 1955. It was more efficient because both the MNCs and the Europeans could take advantage of new technology and build better facilities.

But Western Europe was a major oil importer, and the OPEC events after 1973 hit the EC economy very hard. Just as the Europeans caught up, and even exceeded the U.S., the era of cheap energy ended, at least temporarily, and EC history since the mid-1970´s has been one of rapid price inflation, economic stagnation, and increasingly bitter struggles within the EC about its many problems. More integration seems delayed, as the various EC countries struggle with internal problems. Yet Greece has just joined the EC, and Portugal and Spain want to join. The gains are large, even if countries must give up a lot to take advantage of them.

Not to be forgotten in the consideration of formal customs unions are the huge gains made possible through GATT negotiations and other efforts to reduce tariffs. The U.S. has been relatively consistent in its support for freer trade, in spite of occasional setbacks, as when the steel or auto industry gets into trouble. One result has been the rapid expansion of such unlikely places as Taiwan, South Korea, and Hong Kong, all of whom have taken advantage of specific trading opportunities to develop new industries and expand old ones. And Japan, more than any other country, has thrived brilliantly in the new economic world of freer trade. World international trade expanded at about ten percent per year in real terms from 1948 to 1980, and we are all richer as a result. Whenever a country goes back to isolation, the inevitable result is stagnation and decay, not advance, and a surprisingly large number of perceptive government officials know this. In 1984, prospects for expanded customs unions and lower tariffs and other trade controls seem dim, given world recession, excess capacity, and obsolescent industries in need of protection everywhere, but we may yet be surprised. No one ever thought that the EC would get started either, back in 1956.

The economic advantages of economic integrations tend generally to outweigh the costs and disadvantages of not integrating. The modern industrial world requires large markets and large production units to allow a country to perform efficiently. The last historic developments of nation states, occurring in presently affluent countries roughly from 1600 to 1870, created countries which in modern terms are too small to perform effectively as economic units. The wave of creation of the present Third World, with the possible exception of India and the PRC, also created too small countries to stand alone. Integration appears to offer major advantages to these countries, and given other dismal closed system options, we may see still more integrative efforts in the next decade. We hope so. The option may well be World War III, which isn´t much fun to contemplate. An often overlooked problem for closed systems is that they tend to generate wars, and wars, particularly big wars, only mean the end of the world. If nothing else happened as a result of economic integration since 1945 but to postpone World War III for a while, it was worth whatever it cost anyone, anywhere!

One can see the antiwar nature of integration by pondering how Germany and France might fight yet one more World War. They can´t. Their economies are now so integrated that any serious military effort would fall apart in months, as the Germans realize that critical items are now partially produced in France (or Great Britain, or Italy, or wherever), and vice versa. But both France and West Germany are now unable to go back to being closed systems, to do it all themselves, to prepare for that war. They would be so inefficient as producers that they could never get started. Open economic systems scramble production so thoroughly that no one can stand alone, which means that no country can fight a major war. If only we could get the Soviets into the game...

Customs unions may be the forerunner of a still broader trend to a one government world, in spite of current difficulties. The EC was so successful for so long that others ponder possible similar options, and there is also the considerable success of GATT to ponder. If not world government, at least we might be able to loosen up the trading system a bit more. But why not, after a decade or so, Canada and the United States, joined together with an expanded EEC, and further linked toward the Pacific with Taiwan, South Korea, Australia, New Zealand, and Japan? We can speculate rationally about some larger customs union encompassing most of the world´s affluent countries before the end of the 20th Century. Closed system options do not seem all that attractive, and the mind boggling potential for our (whererever you are) firms if they could only tap totally markets in Japan, the U.S., or wherever, moves people everywhere to consider the what ifs...

And while the affluent countries ponder such options, the Third World examines its alternatives as well. Those Third World countries that joined the world, such as Taiwan, have done so well, while those that stayed closed did so poorly. India and the PRC cautiously experiment with mini-open systems called free trade zones, where Hong Kong rules apply, and Sri Lanka and Mexico try similar experiments. Even Eastern European communist states dispair over their closed system stagnation, and wonder how they might get into the rest of the world and grow. As always, the struggle is between those who want to control everything, and those who would just as soon try anything once, and maybe get rich. One can find numerous examples of both types of countries in the world today, and it is certainly not clear what the general outcome will be.

One point is clear. The world has been totally reconstructed since World War II, and a number of important and critical institutions have helped open the world trading and business system. This opening has led to the rapid expansion of MNCs everywhere, to growing incomes and wealth in most countries, and to revolutionary changes in the way we live and our expectations. Like it or not, things are very different. Like any revolution, this one has led to much concern that things are changing in the wrong direction, that what we need is to return to some glorious past, some time and place where things work out the way we want. Iran is a classic expression of this position, just as Hong Kong is a classic expression of the new order, and the EC a classic example of new efforts to integrate previously independent states. The past was tough, the future bleak, so Hong Kong went out and adapted to the new world, for better or worse. No one argues that Hong Kong is a utopia, but it probably is in better shape, even humanistically, than it might have been if it tried any other option. In the end, we may be stuck with each other on this One World, and we may have to figure out how to live together a lot more closely than we have historically.

We could go the other way. Many provincials would like to do their own things in their own ways, and for every two forward steps, the world backs up one. We will have to wait and see if our new international order is just one small anomaly or the wave of the future.

Questions for Discussion

1. Some Americans, observing the great success of the EC, have suggested that the U.S. consider joining this organization. If such a common market could get economic growth up to over six percent a year, it might be a good idea.

Would this be a good idea? Why or why not? What would the U.S. gain by joining? What would it lose?

2. The U.S. government has given billions of dollars to IDA. These dollars are lent on very easy terms to poorer countries, who use them to buy foreign goods anywhere for their development. Do you think that this is a good idea? Why or why not?

3. An optional form of aid to poorer countries is through AID, which is the American government agency responsible for foreign aid. AID loans are usually tied to the United States; that is, the dollars must be spent in the U.S. for American goods. Would you prefer this type of tied aid compared to the untied IDA sort? Why or why not?

4. The IMF liked fixed exchange rates for major currencies. But now the dollar and most other currencies float around. A dollar's value in international circles is exactly what anyone is willing to pay for it.

What are the advantages of a fixed exchange rate system? What are the advantages of a floating rate system? Be specific.

5. As a member of GATT, the U.S. is involved in tariff reduction discussions when this organization meets. Shortly another major meeting is planned, and it is anticipated that Americans will offer still more tariff reductions to major trading nations such as Japan, in exchange for similar reductions on American exports to these countries.

Do you feel that still further tariff reductions at this time are a good idea for the U.S.? Why or why not? Are they good for Japan? Why or why not?

6. The governments of Canada and Mexico have suggested to the government of the United States that perhaps the time is ripe to discuss a customs union in North America following the pattern of the EC. While it is clear that much hard bargaining would be done before any agreement is reached, these countries would like to begin preliminary discussions. Do you think that this customs union would be a good idea? Why or why not? What would the U.S. gain? What might it lose? How about gains and losses for Canada and Mexico?

7. European observers have pointed out that some of the major winners in the formation of the EC are American MNCs. These companies know how to take full advantage of a multicountry trading area, since they have had a lot of practice with such things at home. What kinds of American company experience would be useful in operating within the EC? Be specific.

Why would European large firms not have such experience? Be specific.

Supplementary Readings

Bain, Joe. BARRIERS TO NEW COMPETITION. Cambridge, MA: Harvard University Press, 1956.

Balassa, Bela. THE THEORY OF ECONOMIC INTEGRATION. Homewood, IL: Richard D. Irwin, 1961.

Beloff, Max. THE UNITED STATES AND THE UNITY OF EUROPE. London: Faber and Washington.

Biersteker, Thomas J. DISTORTION OR DEVELOPMENT: CONTENDING PERSPECTIVES ON THE MULTINATIONAL CORPORATION. Cambridge, MA: MIT Press, 1981.

Cole, John P. THE DEVELOPMENT GAP. New York: Wiley, 1981.

Dillard, Dudley. ECONOMIC DEVELOPMENT OF THE NORTH ATLANTIC COMMUNITY. Englewood Cliffs, NJ: Prentice-Hall, 1967.

Drew, John. DOING BUSINESS IN THE EUROPEAN COMMUNITY. Boston: Butterworth, 1979.

Haas, Ernst B. THE UNITING OF EUROPE: POLITICAL, ECONOMIC, AND SOCIAL FORCES. 1950-1957. Stanford, CA: Stanford University Press, 1958.

Lehmann, David. DEVELOPMENT THEORY. London: Cass, 1979.

Lortie, Pieire. ECONOMIC INTEGRATION AND THE LAW OF GATT. New York: Praeger, 1978.

Reed, laurence. EUROPE IN A SHRINKING WORLD. London: Oldbourne, 1967.

PART IV

MULTINATIONAL CORPORATIONS

Chapter 9

MNC Strategies: Management

In the 1980's, perhaps 1,000 American and 1,000 other privately owned firms could be classified as large MNCs. These companies operate facilities in more than one country, and their overall orientation is toward the world, not toward one country. Each has to be managed. How they are managed, and how their top personnel view the world and their companies, is the subject of this chapter.

Millions of other companies, public and private, are engaged around the world in some international business, typically as exporters or importers. They may also sell licenses, patents, or copyrights to foreign firms, or build turnkey operations in other countries, but they do not own and operate facilities in other countries. Their orientation tends to be local, rather than international. While these firms are important for their various local economies, our major focus is on the truly multinational firm. These companies are shaking up the entire world with their success.

Such MNCs are not new. The old Singer sewing machine company was an MNC in the late 19th Century, along with a number of German, Dutch, Swiss, and English firms that operated throughout Europe and occasionally in the United States. The Fuggers ran a sophisticated international banking operation in the 15th Century throughout Europe, and every European colonial power had firms that had many branches throughout the colonies. Both Ford and General Motors had extensive foreign manufacturing activities in the 1920's.

However, until the 1950's, relatively few firms had grown enough in their home country to exhaust all local possibilities. Going abroad is more difficult, and requires much more sophisticated management, than staying home, and firms do what they can locally before they get interested in foreign ventures. Companies would export or import goods to sell or use as components of their own production, but such activities were seen as a modest extension of purely local business activities.

By the late 1950's the environmental stage was set for massive multinational business expansion. The Americans led the way, since this country had most of the larger firms who had taken full advantage of local options. The American dollar was strong, and foreign investments were encouraged by the U.S. government as a good way to get dollars abroad and contribute to world development. Formation of the EC in 1958 also provided an interesting challenge. The EC set up a sort of mini-United States in Western Europe. European firms, still trying to recover from the damaging effects of World War II and hypernationalism, saw the EC mainly as a device to expand exports; American MNCs saw it as a chance to develop pan-European systems following the typical American model. Other West European countries were willing to allow foreign investment as a means to create jobs, gain American technology, and assist in rapid economic development. So the multinational rush was on, and we began to see rapid evolution of the MNCs.

A second parallel development also occurred. The industrial nations needed raw materials and oil, and many of these deposits were in far off poorer countries in the Middle East, Africa, Asia, and Latin America. As American deposits and wells were exhausted, firms sought out new sources. Firms obtained local concessions to find oil, develop copper mines, and obtain bauxite. While this type of activity expanded dramatically after World War II, it also was not new, as MNCs from the U.S. and Western Europe had followed a similar pattern for decades before the war. Where firms were successful, they prospered, as did their host countries, who received a rentier's share of royalty or tax payments. In this international business, the foreign firm acted as a local producer and world marketer abroad.

This type of MNC has declined in numbers dramatically, since most of the countries involved have taken over the local raw material assets, typically by purchase. MNCs are still in the game as marketers, refiners, exploration teams, and management contractors, but they rarely own the local raw material assets any longer. However, public perception of the MNCs changes so slowly that many of the alleged nasty behavior of present MNCs is supposed to occur in situations which no longer exist. If there is exploitation in the oilfield, it is highly probable that the local country's public company is doing the exploiting.

These two developments were often closely linked. As Western Europe gradually shifted from a coal energy system to an oil base, Middle Eastern and African oil, produced by English, French, and American MNCs was refined and marketed in Europe by those same MNCs that discovered and produced the oil.

Still another form of MNC activity was encouraged by governments themselves through tax policies. Brazil applied high tariffs on finished motor vehicles and lower tariffs on parts in the early 1950's, and American and European firms responded by building assembly plants in that country. Later, tariffs were raised and quotas imposed on key parts, so the firms had to build them locally. Then local content laws provided that perhaps 90 percent of the vehicle by value had to be made in Brazil. By the 1970's, Brazil had its auto industry, and MNCs had a major stake in the country. Similar laws and innumerable forms of tax exemption and relief have encouraged local investments in many countries around the world. The companies went international not because they wanted to but because they had to, given local governmental pressures.

The Canadian model, now about a century old, has been used by many countries and encourages MNCs. It is the policy of having relatively high tariffs on many goods, plus an open foreign investment policy. Many firms thus build small local production facilities in Canada to avoid the tariff. Such a pattern can lead to small, inefficient plants, which have plagued Canada for 80 years, but it does create multinational firms. Henry Ford I assembled his first car in Windsor, Ontario, in 1906 because of these Canadian constraints, thus starting the Ford Motor Company on its MNC path.

And finally, in the 1970's and 1980's, we are seeing another kind of MNC, often based in a Third World country. Many of these firms are relatively small, and many are totally unknown. Many prefer it this way. Instead of having worldwide brand names and attempting to create public consciousness about the firm, owners are often quite anxious to avoid attention. Each branch may have a quite different name, and often the product lines in every country are unrelated. Ownership is sometimes hidden in a fuzz of holding companies based in Andorra or The Bahamas, with the intent of obscuring who owns what. These invisible MNCs often are semi-legal, in the sense that funds for initial investments may have come out of countries with very stiff exchange and capital export controls. They may even belong to criminal elements, such as the Mafia. Many may be quite respectable, but owned by ethnic minorities, who are not anxious to attract public attention.

These MNCs operate in a different world than the high technology, mass marketers most people think of as MNCs. They may own apartment houses in Cincinnati, condominiums in Los Angeles, motels in Wyoming, coffee shops in London (England or Ontario), or bicycle plants in Bolivia. Owners may be Asian Indians, Taiwanese, South Koreans, Mexicans, or Taiwanese. Individually such investments tend to be small, but collectively they total many (uncounted) billions of dollars.

Motivations for these new MNCs vary, but one major one is to avoid onerous monetary and exchange controls at home, to say nothing of taxes and rapacious governments. An astute El Salvadorian, surveying his country's present prospects, and concerned for his children's future, might well contemplate establishing a small firm in California or New York. If the revolution succeeds, and Salvadorian properties are expropriated by the new government, all will not be lost. An Indian, facing the problem of how to pay in dollars for his numerous childrens' educations in the United States, might well start a firm in Singapore or Hong Kong, since these countries have convertible currencies and open foreign investment policies. If the foreign branch has a positive cash flow (never mind profits), then his hard currency problem is solved. He might surprise himself by being very profitable and successful with this branch, and expansion to the U.S. or Canada might be a logical next step. Such expansion also offers the possibility of emmigration, which may also be attractive for relatives.

Americans of Asian Indian descent have the highest per capita family income of any other ethnic group in the United States, including native white Americans. It figures.

Many of these new MNCs also operate in areas that larger MNCs have forgotten. Very few big MNCs makes bicycles, and few make flashlight and transistor batteries, but such light industry is alive and very well in the Third World, and a clever Indian or Taiwanese firm may go to other Third World countries to manufacture such items. Such branches may be small, but they can be very viable. And competent overseas Chinese these days are being welcomed back to the PRC to develop new industries, so many Hong Kong investments are in those free trade zones of the PRC. MNC activities are much larger than most people realize, and focussing on the Fords and IBMs of this world can lead to error.

A curious possible outcome of this new type of MNC is a more open attitude on the part of many Third World countries. Nowadays, the MNC activity is not just a one way street, and if the suspicious Indian government realizes, as it is beginning to do so, that if it squeezes foreign firms in India, retaliation is both painful and possible, then perhaps Indian MNC policies will not be so restrictionary.

High Payout Strategies: As many companies expanded abroad, the payoffs were usually higher than at home. If risks and costs were higher, so were returns on investment. The trickle of investment in the 1950´s became a flood in the 1960´s as firm after firm discovered this.

The critical obstacle to even greater MNC expansion has been the provincial orientation of top managers. Everyone comes from some local environment, and until the mid-1950´s, most business was totally local. A successful manager, long accustomed to operating in Illinois or New York or Manchester, was hestitant to move into uncharted international waters. where there be monsters everywhere, and unknown monsters at that. Not only Americans feel this way. It is not too attractive to a successful Japanese or West German executive to ponder moving to a state called Indiana where no German or Japanese has ever gone before. How about schools for the children? How about one´s wife, who can´t speak English? How about the appalling food? American managers, considering a move to Liverpool in 1955, had the same sinking sensation. Better to stay home and be comfortable. But if you want your firm to be among the world leaders, you go, like it or not.

Other factors also pushed firms abroad. Transportation and communication makes control of distant factories and sales offices easier. As more managers practice abroad in different environments the ability to use strange foreign institutions to the company´s advantage has expanded. Few American firms could have raised money from European banks or money markets in 1955, but now such activities are routine. If pools of good, skilled labor exist anywhere, it becomes easy to lock them into the world production system.

In recent years, some major firms have diversified their political risks at home by investing abroad. Tax considerations also can be a major factor. Thus many European firms have invested in the United States, fearing that conditions at home might lead to socialism, communism, or worse. Local constraints about the use of labor, labor costs, political turmoil, and other negative factors have also been important. Rapid development of European and Japanese managerial competence has contributed to this reverse investment as well.

Take a wealthy, professionally managed company, with objectives of increasing profits, growing rapidly, and staying ahead of rivals, and place it in a world where firms got bigger than their own nations could accomodate, and add freedom to maneuver internationally, and you get the world of MNCs. The top managers now have to manage the global company efficiently. How can this be done?

What is International Management? Those who have observed managers in many countries have noted that management looks about the same everywhere. The things managers do seem, like the things physicists do, not to be culture bound. A manager plans and controls his operations; he finds funds; he does market analysis; and he organizes production. Figure 3-2 of Chapter 3 (the critical elements of the management process) listed these managerial activities. The taxonomy of management does not vary from place to place.

But the outcomes in various places are very different, because the environment does matter. One does a market study for his soap anywhere. But if the firm is selling to a group which has peculiar demographic or cultural characteristics, then the best marketing plan will be different as compared to some other group. The variables are the same, but their values are different. Similarly, a firm may have labor troubles in any country, but if labor law in Great Britain differs from the United States, then the bargaining strategy changes. What is legal in one place may not be in another.

Here we find the basic concept of the environment/management interlock. The environmental constraints, both domestic and international, do influence the critical elements of the management process (the B's in Chapter 3). The clever manager is one who can sense when to be different because he or she now has a different environment. If this interlock is done poperly, then the firm can be more efficient and profitable.

But no firm or manager can possibly consider all 44 domestic and international constraints, or all 77 critical elements simultaneously. Moreover, it is sometimes possible to bend the environment to meet your conditions, rather than the other way around. The international management process becomes a subtle selection of what to change within the firm; what not to change or ignore, because it really doesn't matter that much; and what to plan to change in the future, because environmental and internal changes are constantly occurring.

A manager might perceive that in the foreign country money markets are quite differently organized than they are at home. If he is interested in loans, he must operate differently than the home office. But at the moment, his funds are ample, and there is no need to worry. On the other hand, local educational characteristics are such as to create major production problems because of shortages of certain types of skilled labor. If this problem is not solved, disaster is certain. Back in Chicago, the company never worried much about these labor skills, and hence never built a training program, but here this is the key priority. The foreign branch might spend considerable time, money, and management skill solving this skills problem, because this is the key variable. Later on someone can worry about financial problems.

Now this may seem self-evident, but it is common to find home office provincialism creating problems. If the company has never had a skills shortage problem at home, why should the manager in Uguland constantly be spending company cash on useless training programs? Telexes fly back and forth, the local man is called home to explain, and only with difficulty do the home office managers see what is going on. Companies with iron-clad procedure manuals written for the home country are always in difficulty, since their branch managers are always up to something odd which has to be explained, or worse, which is not allowed.

At the same time, the view from the field tends be be somewhat provincial. The local manager, seeing only his or her operation, is convinced that the company´s best interests are served when the branch prospers. He or she has a hot new project ready, and she even may have lined up local financing. The payout rate will be 25 percent per year after tax, and success is highly probable. Not incidentally, this success is likely to enhance his or her reputation and prestige in the company, and shortly ensure promotion to bigger things. Then the roof falls in, in the form of a Telex from headquarters instructing the local manager to make the local loan and remit the entire amount to the home office. Such incidents can drive a good manager to consider resigning.

But what the local manager does not know is that in another country a still better and bigger project has come to fruition, which will earn 35% after taxes on investment. Top management, taking the global view, is investing in the best globally, not locally.

Companies with highly decentralized operations discover that local suboptimizations will often occur if key controls and plans are not made globally. The international management trick is to make sure that whatever happens will benefit the entire company, not one local office.

It was only a few years ago that the above observations became relevant to the larger and more progressive MNCs, so it is no surprise to discover that many companies still continuously suboptimize in their management. Moreover, they still fail to take into account the subtleties of the local environments, and make some little effort to adjust their local operations to reflect local realities. As a result, even top firms are perhaps ten percent as efficient as they really could be. One major reason that MNCs are so successful is that their competitive local firms are likely to be only eight percent efficient, given the problems of obtaining good local managers anywhere. But most companies still have a long ways to go to achieve the efficiencies they are ultimately capable of.

A company starts abroad, and fumbles around with new and unknown problems, such as taking foreign exchange risks and dealing with unfamiliar labor forces in strange cultural settings. Gradually its local managers learn to live with the new environment, and the firm learns to mesh its activities with critical local customs. At the same time, top management back home begins to take a global view, seeing that optimizing in England or Japan alone may not be the best solution for ten other branches in as many countries. Staffs appear to track key variables, such as foreign exchange fluctuations, money market changes in key countries, political risks, and patent protection rights in important branches. With each new workable adaptation, new managers are trained to do still more complex tasks. Focus is on what works, not on interesting academic exercises. And latecoming firms discover that they nave much to learn which other competitors already take for granted.

The Global View. Top managers in MNCs are among the few people who truly take a global view of what is going on. Their attitude is one of the spaceman, floating far off from spaceship earth, examining from afar all the interesting features of the total terrain. Their job is to optimize the MNC's activities on a global basis, to take advantage of whatever is happening anywhere. Individual countries, including big ones such as the United States, are seen as interesting provinces, full of booby traps, strange but intriguing tribal rites, and bigots whose local interests predominate.

Note how this role differs from politicians, military men, union leaders, and even many religious prelates. Such men and women are responsible to the province or to the country, not to the world. Our world organizations, such as the United Nations, have relatively little power, or, if they do, tend to hold it in extremely limited areas. An example would be the world air traffic control system, or the iceberg patrol. Such international activities are important, but hardly broad enough to control the world's destiny.

The provincials, such as the president of the United States, or the chancellor of West Germany, are charged with protection of their province. Activities which might cause losses in the province are resisted. But the MNC manager is optimizing globally. If the new plant logically should be built in Brazil instead of New York, it goes to Brazil. The politicians object, but unless they are willing to risk giving up their share of the MNC's gains, there is little they can do. In the weird world of multinational business, the controlled (the MNCs) actually are above and beyond the reach of the controllers. No one is sure what to do about this problem, although many countries have seen the issue. To date, solutions are worse than the disease, typically involving punitive local controls to drive the MNCs out. This would be fine, except that the MNCs are often the sort of high wagepaying, high technology, high taxpaying organizations the countries want.

It is a strange world when persons few even know, such as the chief executive officers of major MNCs, actually have more real power than politicians and generals. Dozens of major MNCs have more income and wealth than all but a handful of sovereign nations (General Motors would be among the ten largest countries in the world). When a country tries to control such a giant, it discovers that the country is being controlled, not the firm.

Thus a small country may be dubious about a new MNC investment for any number of good or bad local reasons. Perhaps pollution is feared; perhaps the company could wipe out local competetitive firms; perhaps locals dislike the idea of having too many foreign executives around to control the country's destiny. So the country has the right to ban the investment. The MNC simply shifts its investment to the next country. Now the first country has lost income, training possibilities for its citizens, and the foreign currency earnings from exports that the investment might have provided. It is still sovereign, but the cost is high. After a few years of stagnation, when the next opportunity comes along, the local government may not be so recalcitrant, and the country, like it or not, is drawn still more into the interdependent global production net.

This MNC power has increased sharply in the 1980´s. World recession and the secular decline of many important major industries have led to most countries finding that high paying industrial jobs are very scarce and often declining in numbers. If an MNC offers such jobs, resisting them is tough. MNCs are often major exporters to hard currency countries, and the possibilities of having new or expanded industries gaining such foreign exchange is also difficult to resist. Closed economies have done poorly since the 1960´s, and open ones have done very well, and politicians are not unaware of this point. And MNCs seem to control much of the high technology industries of the future, so if a country wants in on this future, the MNC many be the only vehicle which offers it. No small country has enough technicians, scientists, adventurous firms, or even organization, to allow it to get into this high tech game on its own. Even giants such as the U.S. and Japan do not have enough critical resources to do all high technology work alone.

Not unrelated to all of this is the observation that truly gifted people, when blocked at home, simply move to countries which offer a future, often working for an MNC. The brain drain from Third World countries is often debated, but even wealthy countries lose some of their best people to countries where the action is. If you choose to stay where you are, you may lose more than hard currency or tax revenues. You may lose your very best citizens as well.

The obvious solution to this MNC domination problem is to have a world governnment with real power, but such an organization does not appear likely for some decades yet, if ever. Meanwhile, the MNC managers continue to be the integrating global force for the whole world, whether anyone likes it or not. Already thinkers are talking about a world crisis on this point, and they are probably right. We have never seen a world where the subset controls the set, but we are approaching such a world now. It will be interesting to see how the problem is resolved.

Another peculiar dimension of this new world is the power created by business, as compared to traditional armaments. Japan has no military power of any importance, but its commercial power is awesome, and modern Japan scares other countries far more than the historic militaristic Japan ever did. Countries such as Denmark, Sweden, Switzerland, and even Hong Kong are not among the military powers, but they are critically important commercial countries, and they matter a great deal. They also pose a modern dilemma for power seekers. The PRC can easily take over Hong Kong, but what do you get when all the human resources leave, or are prohibited from taking part in their own peculiar form of wealth creation? Owning some decaying office buildings and other real estate is not exactly interesting, yet this is all Hong Kong would be without its human resources. Historically, and right on to this day, the way to make people behave was to conquer them militarily, but somehow these modern, open commercial countries can´t be dominated this way. It is a puzzle which no one has even begun to resolve, and it may be an extremely important puzzle for the next 50 years. The MNCs, along with the related open world economy, have really changed the world, in ways which traditional power seekers as yet only dimly perceive.

MNC Advantages. The MNC got into this power position by being in the right place at the right time. Such firms tend to be large, competent, cash rich operations in their home countries, and they have usually exhausted their major high profit opportunities at home. But they do have cadres of top personnel, both in management and technology, and they do possess huge assets of knowledge, trade names, patents, technical know how, and managerial skills. They also own lots of assets such as machine tools and factories, but as noted above, increasingly these things are seen as of second level importance. IBM or any other major MNC is more a skilled labor system than an asset ownership system.

As the MNC expands around the world, its ability to tap its own resources wherever they are is a major advantage. A local firm having problems with a given production process may not even know that firms in other countries have already solved the problem. But the MNC´s local manager contacts home. Within a day or two, some expert elsewhere in the firm is on the plane to help out. Or a sticky financial point in a major loan deal comes up. Perhaps even headquarters may not know the answer, but a quick call to one of the firm´s major banks produces the necessary experts to resolve the issue. The MNC is linked up to all the world´s expertise, and its managers know how to locate this knowledge. Few local firms have much chance competing against such linkages.

But note that in an open system, the local firms are much better off than in a closed system. If the local Hong Kong firm has a problem it cannot solve, it can contact its customers, its suppliers, its equipment or component vendors, or local banks. Many of these firms will be in other countries, and many will have knowledge and linkages similar to those noted above. Perhaps the equipment supplier in Japan has the answer; perhaps the American customer knows, or can find out quickly. That local bank will have foreign correspondent banks who will help out. When the expert arrives, he gets into the country, since visa requirements are minimal. Many local firms in such situations are suppliers to MNCs, which means that they also can tap into the expertise network when necessary. After all, the MNC gains when its suppliers are good.

Now ponder the plight of the Rumanian manager with a similar problem. Unless he can find someone locally to help, he is in trouble, because it is extrmely difficult to get outside help. The local suppliers do not know, and cannot find out; the Soviet buyer is uninterested in the problem; and the local bank does not have many external contacts. In the unlikely event that an outside expert is located, he may wait for six months for the right visa to be obtained. Most external contacts are discouraged, and a manager making many trips abroad, even if he could, might become politically suspect.

The Rumanians are noted for turning out quantities of low quality goods, unsalable on world markets. Hong Kong is noted for its quality, steadily improving industrial goods, its fast learning rate, and its ability to adjust quickly to changing world conditions. It figures.

Perhaps most importantly, the MNC knows exactly what it wants to do. It has a goal of long term profitability, and in considering any specific local project, the key question is how this will contribute to profits. If other projects pay off better, then they will be done first. Every company loses a few, since no one can always forecast correctly, but if a small group of companies pursues profits all the time and gets them most of the time (because its managers, workers, and technicians are good), then these firms will be growing faster than any average, and these firms will be the huge MNCs of tomorrow.

The country may have a persecuted minority which it strongly feels should be helped. It requires its local firms to invest in activities which will help this group. But unfortunately, these investments only pay two percent on capital. The MNC happily lets local companies tie up scarce capital in such projects and invests its own in some other country where the payout rate is 30 percent after tax. Then we seem surprised to discover, in five or ten years, that local firms are growing very slowly and having competitive difficulties abroad, while the multinationals are growing very fast, paying better wages, and threatening to take over the whole country. If the name of the game is growth in incomes and productivity, then the way to get this is to always invest in the most profitable sectors, be they government or private.

We are all culture bound, and we all have our own local values which make those two percent (or worse, minus 30 percent) investments necessary and desirable. Perhaps we want more churches or mosques; perhaps more housing for the poor or milk for babies; perhaps more military gear; or you name any good cause you choose. In any country many such examples can be found. But above the local pushing and maneuvering for advantage sits the MNC's headquarters, with its top management making decisions on a global basis for greater profitability. Hence what may happen is nothing. That is, a key local investment will not be made. Few will know that in some distant foreign city such a decision was made. But this decision could slow a country's growth rate for a decade, leading to the ironical result that the country may not be able to afford that milk for those babies at some future time.

The MNCs are profit oriented, which is to say output oriented. Most non-profit systems tend to be input oriented, and this point, plus the usual lack of knowledge about what production really involves, leads to total confusion and often very high costs on many such moral issues. Thus we decide that our children cannot read. The usual remedy is to improve inputs (i.e. give schools more money, raise teacher's salaries). Crime rates rise, so we raise inputs (i.e., hire more policemen). This strategy uses up more resources, but does not necessarily improve output. Just what those teachers and policemen are supposed to do remains unclear, and far too often, after inputs go up, children still cannot read, and crime rates continue to rise. A profit making firm would begin with a totally different notion of what is happening. Crime rates are up. Now, how can they be brought down with minimal inputs? One very obvious answer is to legalize some things, such as making some drugs legal. If this happens, then with no additional inputs, you improve output. But note the moral question. People shouldn't use drugs! Some children have great difficulty learning to read; therefore, forget them and use your resources to improve the performance of those children who can and want to learn. But again, ALL children should be able to read!

The profit seeker is ammoral; most of us are moralizers. The usual result is that we don´t really much care what important things cost, and they often cost a lot. This is another way of saying that we stay poorer than we might be, but we are willing to pay the price. Most of the time, we have no idea what this price is, although we pay anyhow. This is exactly the biggest strength and weakness of the MNC. It doesn´t care about our local morality, although it will normally be polite about it. Because it doesn´t care, and because it is interested in output, the MNC works better than anything else in the productive job. It simply ignores things that don´t matter.

This is also the MNC´s biggest weakness, since sometimes people care a lot about something, and if there is a conflict with the MNC on this point, the MNC goes, not the country.

MNC managers sometimes appear as immoral monsters, sucking the blood of ....(fill in anyone you choose. The managers have been accused of it before). But an overlooked point is that managers tend to be quite moral in their internal dealings, as well as their external relations with various unions, buyers, suppliers, governments, and customers. The reason is simply that you cannot get a group of superior people to work together without trust and respect for each other. If everyone is a crook and immoral, too many good people leave. Obviously there are enough exceptions to this statement to fill ten books this size, but note how often dubious firms have great difficulty in growing and obtaining profits. Few good people really like to work for idiots or criminals, or even people of dubious morality, and if such persons manage any organization, then really good people tend to go elsewhere. They can, too. Superior people always have options. Really efficient firms rarely have to bribe people, cheat on labor, cut corners with suppliers, or even corrupt governments. Poor firms sometimes feel they have to, and they are the ones that get into trouble.

It is ironic that publicly owned firms have just as much difficulty with this point as privately owned firms, and often they have more. The reason may well be that such firms really have no particular incentive to be honest. If they are not, perhaps someone will bail them out.

Any successful MNC will also have a lot of political knowhow. Given the real and perceived dangers of foreign domination, any organization operating from afar has to know what it is doing all the time to survive. In recent years, this necessity to know has led to the field of political risk assessment, which is the systematic analysis of political conditions in countries of interest to the MNC. If an MNC can forecast political difficulties, it can take the necessary steps to withdraw without loss, or possibly adjust to whatever local conditions exist and stay. In either case, the problem is one of survival, not necessarily in any one country, but globally.

We noted in Chapter 7 that the basic defense of the MNCs is to play a positive sum game. If the MNC is able to offer more than the country feels that it costs, then it can survive.

Organization for the World. As firms begin to move into international affairs, they attach a department to handle this odd business, usually called the export department. From time to time the export manager received new duties, such as handling licensing sales to foreign companies, or perhaps managing a few small branches abroad.

As this international business grows, the firm expands the responsibilities and duties of the export or foreign department. At this stage, we usually find a vice president of international affairs handling different geographic regions. The manager has under his or her direct control traditional functional activities such as personnel, production, and marketing, though not as often finance. The top manager still wants to control the purse. But the international VP may raise money in foreign capital markets and analyze trends in major countries, reporting directly to a home vice president or the chief executive officer. Thus at one time the Ford Motor Company had an English Ford, a German Ford, and a French Ford organized along these lines.

Most companies, even large MNCs, are still at this level of organization. If the various country branches are relatively distinct units, each with its own problems, product lines, and marketing complexities, such a system works reasonably well. It also works well when the international part of the company is small compared to the home office. But it has the disadvantage of encouraging suboptimization in each of the foreign units. Each regional or national manager can win by maximizing for his or her piece of the operation, yet such tactics may make the corporation as a whole less profitable.

Pressures for reorganization come when foreign business gets mixed up with domestic, and when the various foreign branches also get intermingled. When the EC was formed, it became possible for the West German branch to ship duty free to the French branch, and vice versa. MNCs saw that intermingling might present the same options and opportunities as have long occurred in the United States. It does not make much sense to have an Indiana branch, a Michigan branch, and an Illinois branch in the Amerian Midwest, so why have a French, German, and Italian branch? Moreover, various European branches export components or products to the United States, while at the same time importing other items from the home country. Unless the organization can track such transactions carefully, trouble is certain. Both marketing and production problems get badly mixed up, and local managers may unwittingly suboptimize.

As finance becomes more international, still more trouble arises. A West German branch manager may find that he can raise cash easily at nine percent interest, while the British manager is faced with tight money markets and twelve percent rates. Yet the next good project is in England. Unless the financial system is coordinated, the company can wind up being squeezed financially in Great Britain while West German funds are underutilized. But if the operation is organized globally and well coordinated, then the money can be borrowed in West Germany ind invested in England.

As the MNCs recognized such problems, the very rapid development of really efficient world communictions networks proceeded apace. It is now possible to have virtually instantaneous communication with any branch anywhere in the world. Hence a firm can have global cash flow information available at the home office every morning for a thousand branches and offices, and it can also have exchange rate information for all currencies within seconds. This communication efficiency leads to internal information efficiency, which makes possible new forms of control, organization, and planning.

Recognition of these organizational problems has led to the next organization step, which is to integrate foreign units into sub-global activities. Now Ford is Ford of Europe, with all European functions under one management. The concept is relatively new in Europe, where suspicious countries have long stayed separate, but quite common in the United States, where multi-state operation is taken for granted.

A possible next step, which few MNCs have undertaken, is to organize globally for key functions. This is presently most common in finance, since large short term gains can be made by global integration, but world wide market organizations are also possible. A Ford or Toyota or General Motors might have a small car division, organized globally, which handles this product everywhere in the world. Or a computer manufacturer could be organized by total markets (say, for research computers), instead of by territories.

No organization chart ever works, or even reflects reality, since it shows only the direct functional relationships between managers. As the firm grows in size and complexity, managers are required to check out key points with more and more people who have necessary expertise. Few of these experts have any line authority over managers, but they can effectively veto the act. Hence one European manager might be interested in obtaining a ten year lease on office space for her European operations. Technically, on the organization chart, all she has to do is get the approval of her immediate superior, the Vice President of International Operations. But practically the problem is very different. She might have to consult with her local attorney to determine if the lease is properly drawn; local real estate staff personnel might also have to approve the deal. She would consult with headquarters financial experts to determine if the financial terms were proper, and the company architectural staff might also have to give their approval. The financial staff which deals in foreign currency values might look at the contract to see if some advantage could be gained by having clauses dealing with money value changes, or possibly paying in the currency most likely to decline in value through time. The long term planning committee at the head office might be consulted to see if a ten year lease under these circumstances meets the long term objectives of the company.

The capable professional manager does all of this in advance, so when she presents her proposal to her nominal boss, the deal is as good as made. Yet note that any one of these experts or groups could have changed the deal, probably for the better, by suggesting logical changes. In almost any case, such staff experts probably did change it. Who was boss? In the end, the manager may have many bosses for a given problem. This example suggests why organization is so different and often so subtle for any given problem. Unless one knows the company very well, it is easy to arrive at quite mistaken conclusions about how it is organized.

As the company becomes more internationalized, this question becomes even more difficult. Suppose that some of those staffers were Europeans, others Middle Easterners, and still others Americans? In addition to the usual expertise questions, cross-cultural communications become critical. Does our manager react to those Middle Easterners in the same way as she might react to Americans? How does a Middle Eastern male react to a female line manager? Such questions are common in MNCs, but relatively rare in local firms, where all managers and staff share a common cultural heritage.

This point suggests another reason why MNCs can be so good. That Middle Eastern staff expert is there because he is so very competent, and he somehow has managed to overcome whatever prejudices which might be used against him. A local European firm might try to get the best European, or even the best Swede, or German. But the MNC gets the best, period. The ability to select staff from wider talent pools is one major reason why the MNC is efficient.

Control Issues. Somewhere in the history of any MNC is the beginning single plant, with the owner running everything. Control was relatively easy, because the firm was concentrated in one place, and it was not too large.

By the time the company had expanded to national size, its managers had already experienced considerable troubles. How can a person manage and control plants he or she may have never even seen? The answer really gets at the very basis of modern business management. Such control is done by building really good management information systems, which develop timely and relevant information to send to the top managers. Such a system also involves careful planning and target setting for key indicators, so that when deviations occur, managers will know about them. Until such a system is developed, no one can manage any large organization well.

Such a planning/control information system is easy enough to describe, but it takes years to develop one properly. Not only does one have to know what is important, and hence worth reporting, but reasonable and efficient plans have to be followed. The B-1 and B-2 elements shown in Figure 3-2 of Chapter 3 taxonomize the critical parts of this problem.

As the organization grows in size and complexity, considerable decentralization is critical. No top manager can possibly handle all the details. He or she has to let subordinates do most things and make most decisions. But they cannot do it all, if the organization is to hang together. Total decentralization would mean total chaos.

So again we find an easy palliative. Decentralize what is unimportant, and centralize what is. Easy to say, yet it may take some of the most brilliant people in our generation a decade or more to achieve for a firm which operates in forty or fifty countries and has 100,000 or more employees. One reason is that what is important is not always so obvious, nor does it stay the same. Something trivial in 1973 is critical in 1980, or vice versa.

This point also suggests why the often predicted decline of smaller firms, including many local ones, never seems to happen. The costs of control can be huge, and all those experts and staff people are very expensive. A small firm, with a handful of creative managers and technicians, can sometimes produce much cheaper, with minimal control costs, than bigger firms. In the 1960´s, pundits were forecasting that by 1984 there would be only about 500 firms in the world. Somehow, this forcast turned out in error. One major reason was this cost of control problem; another was an unexpected technological development in many fields toward fewer economies of scale, which also is in part a control problem. The microcomputer makes complex controls easier and cheaper for smaller firms, and much modern capital equipment is quite efficient at low levels of production. This means that the giant MNC can only thrive in some, not all areas. Moreover, as creativity becomes more critical and highly educated professionals proliferate, MNCs cannot always get them to work for the firm. Why labor for an MNC in a tightly controlled situation, when one can set up one´s own firm and do much better, both in terms of income and psychic satisfaction? Not all good ideas come from big companies; indeed, a significant share of the new technologies and improvements on older ones come from smaller firms, or even individuals.

The part of the organization most tightly controlled is finance. We find branches and subordinate units preparing their budgets (both of costs and revenues) and gaining approval at higher levels. But things change rapidly. With floating currencies, controls on the types of monies held are relevant, and new centralized controls are introduced. As price inflation continues, some older controls requiring approval of of capital expenditures above certain amounts should be changed, and as inflation slows, controls allowing automatic growth in key expenditures become obsolete. Deals with communist countries in blocked currencies have to be examined with special care. Perhaps three years ago, there were few deals with communist countries.

MNCs have lost whole branches through expropriation, because they miscalculated local political sentiments. Does this mean that local public relations should be handled at higher levels? Perhaps so, but perhaps a good local manager can do it better. And how about such a simple thing as whether or not to use common metric standards throughout the company, including the United States? Many American engineers might resign if this decision were dictated from the head office, yet on such a seemingly trivial point may depend $500 million per year of manufacturing economies in the 1990´s, or control of key foreign markets in the PRC or Japan.

All of us, including chief executive officers, have only 24 hours a day. If all the important things go to the top, then they either don´t go to the top, or they don´t get done. So, we decentralize. So, we are back to the original question. What is important? Companies that can´t get this seemingly innocuous point straight have grave difficulties, and

one can point to literally dozens of big MNCs in trouble right now
because of this issue. Getting it right is perhaps the most difficult
problem of all. This question also gets at the very critical problem of
selecting the right subordinates, which we will turn to in Chapter 13 on
personnel. If you have terrific subordinates who can do their jobs very
well, then it is much easier to decentralize efficiently.

We will be returning to these control points in later chapters on
functional management problems, because they are so critical to overall
success. Yet no one really knows for sure what to do in any given
situation. The concept of decentralizing most things and centralizing
what is REALLY important from the center is recognized, but the details
are killing. If top management fails here, then trouble is certain.

From One Country to One World. Most private firms began as small
companies on one country. A few dynamic, well managed firms keep right
on growing, particularly if they understand management functions well.
They grow right out of their home countries. After ten or fifteen years
of international expansion, the dynamic firms discover that perhaps a
quarter to a half of their sales, investments, and profits are abroad.
At this point, management begins to change rapidly. Managers still plan,
control, and organize, but now these functions have to be considered in
a global context.

Initially, top managers have problems with this international
orientation, since they all came from some local environment. It is
hard to realize that staffing considerations now must take account of
all of those good managers from other countries. It is difficult to
grasp that direction and motivation problems now involve many cultures,
not one. Organization across national boundaries becomes much more
complex than organizing within a single country, and control problems
multiply geometrically as distance and national frontiers intrude.

But none of these problems are unsolvable. Gradually managers
learn that environmental differences do matter, but that these
differences can be handled. Managers are empirical people, and they are
willing to do what works. What works best in the multinational world is
the global view of the corporation. The final step is dispassionately to
view the world as a whole, as we described earlier. The company now is a
world citizen, not a local one.

Few firms have come this far yet. Most are still local, and the
MNCs are just beginning to realize their true potential. Many firms
remain locked into local patterns. Yet these patterns change rapidly.
We SHOULD have an American in that post, but our best man happens to be
a Brazilian. Why not try him? The competition is keen, and second best
won't do. Next year, when that capable Brazilian has proved himself,
staffing will have gradually shifted to looking for the best man or
woman, not the best American. And buying American is all right, except
that our competitors are buying where components are cheap and good, and
they are gaining a major edge. We have to shift policy, because if we
don't, a whole market will be lost. So the change is made, and after a
few years, the procurement function is very different.

Firms can stay home, and many do. They can even be very efficient and well managed. Their growth rates will be determined by their local economy, not the world, and their managers will be local, with local hang ups. If these do not bother the firm, nothing horrible will happen. But if the provincialism does matter on critical managerial issues, then the MNCs will run away with the markets and profits.

In the end, the local firms may be right. We may see nationalistic resurgences that ban foreign investments, and force firms to stay home. We may see even more development of technologies and management that permit smaller, local firms to compete very effetively with the giants. If we are forced to stay home because of nationalistic feelings, we will all be poorer, and firms that have gone the multinational route are in for grave difficulties.

But a good manager who has seen the world will also end up as a good local manager, because he or she can see through local emotional problems. Such heated domestic issues as whether to hire blacks or women in key positions will not be bothersome, since he or she has seen it all before in some other country. He or she will know more about motivating different kinds of young people, because the international manager has already had much experience in motivating various people from different cultures. His or her firm will win big at home, too.

The field of management is just beginning to grasp this multinational thrust. Most texts still discuss management as a one country problem, with the United States as the most frequent model, since most scholars and writers are Americans. One can go through good American business schools and never know that international management problems even exist. The environmental/firm interrelationships are not noted or discussed. Slowly the scene changes, and more people each year realize that this new global system is what is really important. All the trends point to still more international materials being used.

Conclusion. Chapters on management or international management usually spend more time than we have here on planning, organization, control, and direction questions. But international management at this stage is probably more a state of mind than a nice organization chart or a policy manual. Today, only a few thousand organizations have grasped the global principles we have ennumerated here. Even in this select group, the majority are still locally oriented, with some interesting things going on in other countries. Those that have perceived, correctly, the truly global nature of their task, and who have managed to that end, are among the fastest growing and most profitable companies in the world. Top management in virtually all major world corporations is moving rapidly far beyond any country, and taking full advantage of the world economy. Such firms have left our national governments and world organizations far behind. Even the Soviets have to come to terms with such productive systems, because there really is no second choice. We are stuck with these multinational companies, whether we like it or not, and we like it because they are so productive.

For those who dislike total views of the world, there will always be plenty of provincial activities to take part in. The really big corporations cannot handle everything, and smaller local firms will continue to thrive. As MNCs get richer and bigger, their local suppliers will prosper too, and most of world business will still be essentially domestic business administration, oriented to the small culture bound firms all over the world.

Such local business is interesting and important, and it merits close and continuous study. But this is not where it's at. The MNCs are changing the whole world, not just some small city in Thailand or Denmark. Through historic accident, institutional evolution, nationalistic development, and technological progress, we find ourselves, somewhat to our surprise, stuck in the middle of some new kind of world that no one really wanted. It will be around for quite a while.

The top managers who run such MNCs have become important. They know how to mesh their internal firm activities anywhere with whatever environmental constraints exist. They have learned to go for big payoffs wherever they are to gain at the expense of those who get bogged down in local, low payoff activities. They have learned that to get in the game, you have to offer other players a piece of the action, so the game has to be positive sum. They have learned, and are still learning, how to control their far flung empires, and how to get them organized so that once in a while something works out the way it should. They have learned to avoid the more obvious suboptimization routines which local managers, in good conscience, try to carry out, and they have even learned to make such good and conscientious men and women aware of the broader interests of the total corporation.

No superman does all of these things perfectly all the time, so it is easy to find plenty of examples of international management blunders. The surprising thing, given the tremendous complexity of the task, is that international managers get anything done right, let alone all of it. Because they do as well as they do, they are admired, feared, hated, and examined closely by many interested parties. But MNCs could do the job better. One way to do better is to learn more about management of the various business functions in an international context, and our next four chapters will cover these topics.

Questions for Discussion

1. Consider any business functional course you may have taken, such as marketing, finance, or accounting. What parts of this course might be useful to you if you were managing a firm in Egypt? Which parts might prove useless? Why?

2. In 1947 it took 18 hours in a slow propeller driven plane to get to Europe from New York. It cost about $1,500 in money worth four times more than today. A three minute phone call to Great Britain cost $40, and you took hours to make a connection. Now it cost $6 to $10, and you can even dial direct.

Do these facts explain something about the willingness of firms to expand abroad? Why?

3. Do you personally play any zero sum games? What are they? Do you personally play any positive sum games? What are these?

4. A major American MNC has two requests from governments to consider. One is from the mayor of a large midwestern city. He would like the firm to spend around $4 million in training high school dropouts from the ghetto. If the company did this, it is possible that losers could be transformed into productive citizens.

The second request is to spend $4 million to buld a new hospital in a very poor country in which the firm operates. Infant mortality rates are ten times as high as in the U.S., and if this hospital were built and staffed, literally thousands of children who now die will live. The company feels that it really only has $4 million to spend for such projects. Which one would you support? Why?

5. Assume that you have just been hired to be a plant manager in your company's new operation in Saudi Arabia. Your job will involve planning, staffing, and developing a new factory in that country to assemble automobiles.

What would you start learning before you got on the plane to go to your new job? Why?

6. Foreigners often object to the fact that critical decisions about their future are made by American managers far away. Now the shoe may be on the other foot, as foreign firms invest in the U.S. Would it bother you to work for a foreign firm in your state, when you know that your very job and livelihood is determined by men living in Zurich, Stockholm, or Tokyo? Why or why not?

7. Do some research on a recent expropriation of any American firm in any foreign country. What key errors did this company make in this situation? In your judgement, could the company have done something to avoid the problem? What?

8. Recently a major American MNC was asked by one country in which it operates to build a new $80 milion factory to manufacture arms for defense. This country has real enemies, and a war has been fought within the last ten years with the country's neighbor. The rate of return on this investment would be around six percent per year on invested capital.

The MNC has many other projects in other countries paying thirty percent or more, so it politely declined the invitation. Moreover, its scarce and valuable key technical and managerial personnel were in such short supply that even some projects paying over twenty percent have to be postponed.

The immediate reaction in the country was annoyance and disbelief. The company was pilloried in the local press as being cruel, insensitive to local values, financed by the C.I.A., and potentially dangerous. Was this a good decision by this company's managers? Why or why not?

Supplementary Readings

Berenbeim, Ronald, MANAGING THE INTERNATIONAL COMPANY. New York: The Conference Board, 1982.

Davis, Stanley M. COMPARATIVE MANAGEMENT: ORGANIZATION AND CULTURAL PERSPECTIVES. Englewood Cliffs, NJ: Prentice-Hall, 1971.

Dunning, John H., Ed. ECONOMIC ANALYSIS AND THE MULTINATIONAL ENTERPRISE. New York: Praeger, 1974.

Fayerweather, John. INTERNATIONAL BUSINESS STRATEGY AND ADMINISTRATION. CAMBRIDGE, MA: Ballinger, 1982.

Hays, Richard D., Korth, Christopher M., Roudiani, Manacher. INTERNATIONAL BUSINESS: AND INTRODUCTION TO THE WORLD OF INTERNATIONAL BUSINESS. Englewood Cliffs, NJ: Prentice-Hall, 1972.

Hennart, Jean-Francois. A THEORY OF MULTINATIONAL ENTERPRISE. Ann Arbor: University of Michigan Press, 1982.

Kapoor, A. and Grub. Phillip D. eds. THE MULTINATIONAL ENTERPRISE IN TRANSITION. Princeton, NJ: The Darwin Press, 1972.

Neghandi, Anant R. and Prasad, S. Benjamin. COMPARATIVE MANAGEMENT. New York: Appleton-Century-Crofts, 1971.

Ouchi, William. THEORY Z. Reading, MA: Addison-Wesley, 1981.

Phatak, Arvind V. INTERNATIONAL DIMENSIONS OF MANAGEMENT. Boston: Kent, 1983.

Richman, Barry M. and Copen, Melvin R. INTERNATIONAL MANAGEMENT AND ECONOMIC DEVELOPMENT. New York: McGraw-Hill, 1972.

Richardson, Bradely M. and Ueda, Taizo. BUSINESS AND SOCIETY IN JAPAN. New York: Praeger, 1981.

Vernon, Raymond, and Wells, Louis T. Jr. MANAGEMENT IN THE INTERNATIONAL ECONOMY, 3D EDITION. Englewood Cliffs, NJ: Prentice-Hall, 1976.

Chapter 10

MNC Strategies: Finance and Accounting

INTRODUCTION

Finance is finance is finance, the world around. Any competent financial executive will be using his or her professional analytical tools wherever he or she is. If the problem is an investment decision, then existing financial tools will be used for analysis. If the problem is one of speeding up collections, much practical and theoretical material exists to show the executive the way to greater efficiency.

Yet international finance is different. As with so much of conventional business materials, the analysis is the same, but the values of variables will be different as a company moves from one environment to the next. And, since the world is organized into nation states, each with its own laws and monetary systems, finance is directly affected. Particularly in finance the environmental/firm interrelationships have to be handled properly if the company is to perform efficiently.

As we suggested in the last chapter, such international thinking is relatively new for most companies. Only ten to fifteen years ago, most financial problems were purely domestic. But when a third to half of gross revenues come from abroad, international finance is not a minor point. It may well be critical to the firm's profitability and survival. Moreover, even large domestic firms can take advantage of the world money market to raise funds, and many have. An electric power company in Canada, operating entirely within that country, might well float a Eurodollar bond issue in Europe to fund new investments, or an American private railroad might do the same. Many of those private bank loans to Third World countries were in fact designated to large local firms, often publicly owned, for domestic investment purposes.

THE MULTICURRENCY WORLD

As a company moves from one country to a global position, the first obvious financial problem is that each country issues its own currency. As sales and purchases are made in various countries, the firm faces conversion problems. Since each country can set any value it chooses on its own money, along with any rules it pleases for conversion to any other, the firm has to understand the international monetary system, which we covered in Chapter 4. Previously esoteric subjects such as balance of payments problems, exchange controls, relative rates of inflation in numerous countries, devaluations, and revaluations, become a routine part of corporate financial planning.

The company will be receiving and spending many currencies, and one immediate question is what values are actually involved. Because a country says that its currency has some value does not mean that this is true. The currency might be under tight exchange controls, and it may be inconvertible. To carry accounts receivable of $100 million in money which cannot be used may give some comfort to the treasurer, but it will not be very useful. Even to state that the company has $100 million in a foreign currency infers an exchange rate.

It may be hard to determine real values of various currencies, but revaluations and devaluations also occur. Many currencies now float on a daily basis, so values are unstable. If that $100 million happened to be in West German marks in recent years, and the firm needs dollars, then a considerable loss has occurred, since the mark has dropped sharply in terms of the dollar. But if the firm holds U.S. dollars and wants to invest in Canada, it is far ahead, since the Canadian dollar also has fallen in terms of the U.S. dollar.

This discussion points to one critical difference in international finance, which is foreign exchange risk. Firms, even local ones which might export or import, face a risk which purely local transactions do not have. Strategies for minimizing this risk are at the very core of international finance.

Many parts of the local environment also can affect financial activities. These would include any international constraints a country might have on profits remissions and exchange controls. Local interest rates and inflation rates also are critical, as are local money markets and funds availability. Perhaps some capital needs can be met locally if the local banks or financial institutions are understood. And even the local postal service might become important if a financial planner is pondering how to speed up collections. Some countries have organized postal giro systems which enable firms and individuals to transfer cash rapidly and safely; others do not have such systems. What is a giro system? Americans might be puzzled, since they do not have one. But if the firm operates in Great Britain, detailed knowledge of how the system works could speed up average collections by several days. With interest rates at ten percent or more, this could save millions of pounds or dollars every year.

Historically, the usual manner in which MNCs found out such things was the hard way. That is, they went abroad, operated for some time, and only much later realized that international financial problems were special. Some firms, a few years after going abroad, had efficient staff personnel who could handle most international financial problems; others, after a decade or more abroad, still wondered what a devaluation was. In more recent years, international finance expertise has grown geometrically, and it is much more common for MNCs and even local firms to have a good working knowledge of their problems, but even now, competence levels in this field are very uneven.

An enormous amount of detail must be known to do the international finance job properly, since every critical local constraint must be known in depth. Legal, economic, social, and technical details vary widely, even between fairly similar countries. An American might casually assume that Canadian constraints are roughly the same as in the U.S., but close examination of Canadian law and customs would suggest many criticl differences. About the only way to do the job right is to find the experts who know or can find out. Consultants, local lawyers, local brokers, bankers, tax attorneys and accountants are needed. Such personnel are costly, but payouts can be very high.

GLOBAL FINANCE

Once the company begins to perceive its total international financial operations as a total system, possibilities of global optimization emerge. Some MNCs have gone this far, and more are moving toward the global approach, but many still are quite provincial in their orientation, particularly American ones, where the dollar is still perceived as something very special, and other currencies some kind of funny money. When the MNC begins to think in global terms, the following considerations are highly relevant.

Types of Financing. American firms have an advantage here, since the American money market is the most sophisticated in the world, and large firms already have had much experience in choosing between bonds, stocks, short or long term loans, loans from banks or insurance companies, and so on. By the time a firm begins to go international, it normally has worked intimately with the American money market for many years. And because it has, it often continues to do so for its foreign activities. It is easier at the outset to float bonds in Wall Street than in France. Personnel know all problems; underwriters are familiar; and terms and conditions are well understood. Similarly, internally generated funds from profits and depreciation will be larger from the parent than from newer subsidiaries.

Twenty years ago, this would have been the end of the discussion, since money markets, even in quite sophisticated European countries, were relatively underdeveloped and not worth exploring. But starting in the early 1960´s, the U.S. began to experience its balance of payments problems, and one early control was on capital exports. Expanding American MNCs were sometimes unable to obtain dollars to send abroad.

These controls led to increased interest in European money markets, and bigger American firms began to raise capital there. Firms discovered that they could sell bond issues to Europeans, placed in various European money centers. The range of issue types became about as long as any American list, as convertible debentures, stocks, preferred stocks, and bank loans were floated. Since each country has its own laws, customs, and peculiarities, every issue became an education for American financial executives.

At this time, there were few European or Japanese MNCs, and only later did these companies get into the world money markets, including the U.S. money market. Japan to this day is not a major international financial center, mainly because of various capital controls and restrictions the Japanese government places on the yen, but over the years, virtually all MNCs based everywhere have used the U.S. money market.

Larger American commercial banks have long had foreign offices, and they also were expanding rapidly abroad after 1955. It became possible to use one´s own banker in far off places, and bank lending, often with foreign deposit money, became common. All those surplus dollars we discussed in Chapter 4 belonged to foreigners, and many of them were deposited in American and European commercial banks. These banks, starting in the early 1950´s, began to loan these dollars to American and European firms for commercial purposes, and the Eurodollar market was born. A Eurodollar is a dollar deposited in a bank outside the U.S., and lent out to a customer for commercial purposes, or to any good credit risk (such as a government) who can use dollars. Unlike domestically owned dollars, which are subject to U.S. bank controls, these Eurodollars were very hard to control. An American branch bank in London might make a loan to a French firm to expand its Norwegian activities. Since the dollar was at the time as good as gold, borrowers were happy to get them, and the borrowers´ suppliers also readily accepted dollars instead of Norwegian funds. American local lenders were not allowed in this Eurodollar market because of American restrictions on dollar outflows, but tens of billions of foreign held dollars were in the market by the late 1960´s, and literally hundreds of billions are available now. Control by any government turned out to be difficult. In the above example, the French, Norwegian and U.S. govenments all were involved, but none were able to control the total transaction.

As the dollar weakened and finally fell, other Eurocurrency loans emerged. An American firm in Europe could borrow 200 million West German marks to finance its new Greek plant, which came from Great Britain. The English suppliers would happily accept the marks, since it was a strong currency. Again, local control of such markets turned out to be very difficult, since too many companies, banks, and countries were involved. This Eurocurrency lending continues to date, at ever larger amounts each year.

Private commercial banks from Japan, the U.S., and Western Europe have been among the most rapidly growing MNCs in the past 30 years, and one result has been to develop and refine money markets everywhere into a global system. The Bank of America or Citicorp have offices everywhere, and they handle loans and deposits from everyone, in virtually all currencies. A huge pool of professional expertise has been built up in such banks, and one result has been the rapid international financial education of many of these banks´ customers. If a creditworthy firm seeks a loan, it is an easy step to introduce this firm, even if it is totally local at the moment, to the world of global finance. Given where it is and what currencies it does business in, the bank can suggest a credit package which very probably will be global, not local.

Thus many an American local firm may borrow money in Illinois, perhaps not even realizing that the dollars it gets are owned by a Middle Eastern country, and are a part of the petrodollar recycling system we discussed in Chapter 4. Sophisticated firms, knowing much about interest rates and financial conditions in a dozen or more countries, may well do much global financial analysis itself. Such an MNC may well choose the types of financing which is cheapest and most available, which could be almost anywhere in the world.

The idea of using one country´s currency to finance activities in another historically was only done in dollars and pounds sterling, but there is no reason why any currency cannot be used. Borrowers may well get a better deal in some other convertible, strong currency, and many have over the past decade.

Sources of Capital. As we suggested above, sources for MNCs can be anywhere. The new problem in such a system is conversion costs from one currency to another. Even inconvertible currencies can be moved, though at considerable cost. To get out of some currencies, the MNC might resort to the black market (unusual for larger firms) at big discounts from par, or it might work some barter transactions. It can buy something available in the local blocked currency and sell it (probably at low prices) in a convertible currency country. Many barter brokers now operate around the world to assist, at a nice commission, in such transactions. Costs of conversion here can be very high, which means that the financial experts will have to be careful before getting into such deals. In some cases, firms stumble into such deals, in that some country in which the firm operates imposes exchange controls, and the firm now has inconvertible currencies to worry about.

A possible pattern for the MNC is to shift all funds to central office control, though not necessarily converting them to dollars or any other currency. Then each branch gets its needs reallocated per local budgets. This system is also a control system, since headquarters is always in complete command of cash. Quite a few major MNCs have already developed such systems, and more are likely. This system also forces the firm to think globally, since requests for fund use necessarily are accompanied by reasons. Unless the local branch gains approvals, it cannot spend the money.

Many governments pass out cash to private firms and give credit guarantees. Such payments usually are subsidies for doing things governments want done, such as building factories in depressed areas, or hiring handicapped workers. If the company is in an area interesting to government, it can explore such possibilities. Many governments also have loans available, usually connected with socially desirable projects. On occasion, some historical factor leads to having cash available. The United States has a Cooley loan program, which is the lending of certain soft currencies owned by the American government in countries where agricultural products were sold for these currencies. If an American firm is investing in India, it can, under specified conditions, borrow Indian rupees to finance parts of the local Indian activities. As is typical of such programs, the conditions are relatively inflexible, but at least some firms qualify.

Funds can be obtained by speeding up collections and slowing down payments. Local customs and practice may be different than at home, and detailed knowledge of local constraints is useful. Often an American based MNC, long accustomed to planning rapid collections and fast transfers, can innovate in countries where collection practices are more leisurely. Acceptable times for payments of bills vary widely also, and funds can sometimes be expanded by taking advantage of slower payoffs. The problem is knowing enough about each country to be able to do the right thing in ways which benefit the firm, without getting into local troubles. Here again, steadily improving communications and banking systems make fund transfers anywhere in the world extremely fast (like seconds) as compared to earlier times.

MNCs are getting increasingly sophisticated about sources of funds on a global basis. The real problem is accumulating enough detailed knowledge about sources, and then analyzing this knowledge in terms of what it will do for the company. Since the supply of sophisticated financial experts who can do this well is limited, expertise spreads fairly slowly. But payoffs can be huge.

Perhaps the most efficient changes in financial planning for uses of funds in MNCs is in taking a global view of all possible investment opporttunties. Big firms are constantly generating new investment possibilities, and a viable and efficient company has dozens of larger projects which can be invested in at any moment. But only a few can be attempted, not usually because of lack of money, but because of lack of skilled managers and technicians. Companies tend to run out of skilled people long before they run out of cash.

So some priority scheme has to be considered. Which projects are done first, second, or third? Which are deferred to next year, or three years from now? The MNC will deploy its funds so that the highest payout projects are done first, while others wait. If an efficient company does this consistently, it is likely to be a fast growth company which seems to run ahead of its competitors. The best British investment possibilities may now yield fifteen percent on capital, after tax; the local British firm is stuck with this maximum rate of return. But the MNC can put its cash (including British funds) into thirty percent payouts in Thailand or Brazil, and defer British projects for a while.

This investment process is subject to many exceptions. Perhaps social objectives or political considerations force investments in lower return projects; perhaps the company is not yet a totally global firm, with a global point of view, so the home country comes first. But if a company does manage to invest in higher payout projects even occasionally, it will outrun its rivals. This point is one major reason why national governments are so nervous about MNCs. They cannot be sure that what is important locally will be done, even by locally based MNCs.

Protection of Capital. An MNC can lose or gain huge chunks of cash through currency value fluctuations. In recent years, firms receiving dollars have done extremely well, since the dollar has risen sharply on world markets. But if an MNC received dollars in the mid-1970's, it would have lost much of its capital, since the dollar fell steadily at that time against such currencies as the Japanese yen and the West German mark. In effect, anyone involved in more than one country faces an exchange risk, and this is one unique factor in international finance. There has been enormous interest in this topic since 1971, when currencies began to float, simply because the currencies floated so far. To lose perhaps 30 percent of one's capital simply because the firm was in the wrong currency for a few years was a major problem for firms. Moreover, since the early 1970's American (and some other countries') accounting rules call for stating exchange gains or losses in the firm's annual audited report, and it is downright embarrasssing for a major firm to admit that it lost perhaps $60 to $100 million in a single year this way, as has happened often to major MNCs.

The floating exchange rate system, along with increasing world trade and finance, has led to an explosion in currency trading, both for commercial and speculative reasons. In one sense, any currency that is convertible and floats can be seen as a commodity to be bought or sold for a profit, much like hog bellies, silver, or wheat. Indeed, the Chicago Board of Trade has had currency futures options for sale for a number of years, and other foreign exchange markets around the world also deal in these monies. Some $15 to $20 billions of foreign exchange is traded daily in the United States alone, mostly for speculative reasons. But banks and MNCs, along with governments and non-profit organizations, also buy and sell foreign currencies constantly.

Many exchange risks can be hedged by buying and selling in the forward exchange markets, which exist for most major world currencies. However, hedging costs money, often lots of it, and many firms prefer to assume the exchange risk themselves. In some currencies, and for some large transactions, hedging is not yet possible.

Assuming an exchange risk leads quickly to consideration of exchange rate forecasting, which we covered in Chapter 4. Some major firms, such as Ford, have been forecasting for over twenty years, and most major companies at least dabble in this critical area, or buy advice from banks or consultants. If a company can anticipate currency values, it can arrange to be on the right side of the market, thus gaining considerable profit. But scholarly studies of major currencies suggest that the market may be close to perfect in the theoretical sense, which means that it may be about as easy to forecast as the American stock market, which is to say you really can't. Many try; few come out ahead.

The gnomes of Zurich, those international speculators, are well known, as are the Middle Eastern oil sheiks who shift funds rapidly from country to country to take advantage of expected currency value changes. But there may be gnomes in Chicago and Cincinnati too, who are nothing more than corporate treasurers who are protecting their stockholders' money by shifting it to the best currencies. Such gnomes may be accused of not being very patriotic (in England, Brazil, or the United States), but they do have the legal responsibility of protecting the owners' cash. If they do not, they are remiss in their duties. As with so many other things in international business, we have not yet even raised the moral questions involved, let alone answered them. If the American government is trying to protect the value of the dollar, should a treasurer, who is pretty sure the dollar will fall, keep his firm's money in the U.S.? If he does so, he may well face stockholder suits, since he is in effect giving away their cash.

Losses from expected exchange rate shifts can be minimized by a system of leads and lags in international payments. Suppose that a company expects the dollar to fall in value and the mark to rise. The company can accelerate all payments to West Germany, and slow payments to the United States. In a large firm, with thousands of customers and suppliers all over the world, and with many internal fund transfers, hundreds of millions of dollars per month can be shifted in this manner. When the expected increase in the mark occurs, the firm will have more of its funds in marks, and hence will profit accordingly. If many major players in the foreign currency game see the problem the same way, these leads and lags can accelerate the expected dollar decline, as demand for marks rises rapidly, while demand for dollars falls.

As we noted earlier, MNCs are concerned with political risks, since expropriation can lead to major capital losses. The various techniques used to avoid expropriation noted earlier are relevant here, as is the art, or perhaps science, of political risk forecasting. It would not do for a major company to invest $50 million this year and lose it next year. The American government has expropriation insurance for unstable countries, but the cost is high and benefits are uncertain. Firms can minimize, but never totally avoid, expropriations or other negative political actions.

We mentioned in the last chapter that an efficient MNC might be ten percent efficient, and this financial discussion suggests one reason why the figure is so low. Even the problems are as yet ill-defined, and solutions, which are firm oriented and specific to given problems, are still further away. But the move is on to much more sophistication, and companies are likely to improve in the future.

TAXATION

Firms end up paying taxes everwhere, but tax avoidance is a highly refined art. An MNC, operating in dozens of countries, faces more tax collectors and taxing agencies than any other institution. Even in the U.S., there are thousands of taxing agents, and any modern country will have almost as many.

Because the MNCs link countries, every government has to consider its taxes relative to taxes in other countries. If the U.S. levies a 40 percent corporate income tax, and country A levies a 65 percent tax, the firm would be wiped out if tax offsets were not allowed. One occasionally reads that some major American firm pays very little American corporate income tax, and these offsets are why. In such cases, foreign taxes may well be higher than the American.

For a firm facing varying tax rates, one attractive possibility is to shift income to lower rate jurisdictions. A company can do this (maybe) by arranging its internal affairs such that expenses pile up in the high tax area, while staying down in the low tax system. Thus a pharmeceutical firm may license its own branch in a foreign country to manufacture a patented drug. What should the fee be for use of this patent? If the country using the patent has very high corporate income tax rates, the answer is high enough to wipe out income. Now the income is in the home country. If taxes are high here, have some engineering consulting work done for the parent by a subsidiary based in a low or zero tax country, and charge the parent enough for the consulting to wipe out profits there. This is a question of intracorporate transfer pricing, and if tax collectors are not diligent, it may be possible to pile up net income in some tax haven.

Such intracorporate transfer pricing problems extend to components and materials as well. Consider a firm which makes its engines in a European country to put in cars manufactured in Canada for sale in the United States. The price it charges itself (e.g., applies to the varying divisions) will depend in part on relative tax rates. In this case, the firm would consider not only income taxes in the various countries, but also Canadian and American tariffs. Other local taxes might be relevant. Since perhaps as much as $300 million per year in annual sales might result from this one deal, it pays to analyze the tax situation very carefully before setting any price. Just to confuse the issue, cost considerations might include marginal, or out of pocket expenses only; total unit costs; or some variant of these. And since the engines would be a proprietary item, it would be difficult to set a price based on market value, since there is no external market.

Tax collectors will be watching such transactions very carefully as well, since revenue losses could be very serious if the firm could minimize its tax bill. In Third World countries with blocked currencies, that pharmeceutical example noted above could be used as a way of getting profits out of the country, and officials often watch such transactions, along with other royalty payments, very closely. Much negotiation and consultation are likely for such big items. Because such problems can result in literally millions of dollars of extra profit, and because fairly high level government consultation may be involved, it is normal to find such pricing policies set at the highest managerial levels. If local managers, anxious to make a good profit showing, were able to set such intracorporate prices, suboptimizations would be certain.

This point may also suggest why some MNCs might be interested in staying relatively unknown. If Firm X in country A actually belongs to the same group as Firm Y in country B, but tax collectors do not know this, then intracorporate transfer pricing can yield great potential tax avoidance. Why doesn't the tax collector know? Because both firms X and Y are held by unknown persons in Andorra or The Bahamas. No one has any idea of how big such activities are, but the potential for serious, and potentially illegal, tax avoidance is very large when even small firms go multinational.

There are taxes, but there are tax exemptions and subsidies too, and firms spend a lot of time analyzing how to take advantage of them. A common practice in poorer countries wanting industrial development is to offer tax holidays for specific periods for new investment. The firm may not pay corporate income taxes for the first five or ten years the plant is in operation, or local property taxes may be forgiven. The usual problem with such lures is that they are offered in places few want to go, but on occasion they can be very attractive. American states, provinces in many nations, and various foreign countries occasionally offer various inducements, including property tax holidays, infrastructure investments, and whatever else those in power think will attract investors. Sometimes such inducements can be quite attractive.

Jobs, particularly good, well paying jobs, are so scarce around the world these days that any firm thinking of expansion only has to mention this fact, and it will be besieged with offers of help. In one sense, what is happening is that various countries and communities are buying industrial and office jobs, feeling that such jobs lead to major income gains. MNCs, or local companies, can usually get something for nothing in any location they feel is desirable.

Some unanswered ethical questions arise here. Should a company be responsible to its home country, its stockholders, the world economy, or whatever in considering tax and subsidy options? Countries usually assume that the foreign based firm is favoring its own home country in tax payments, but there is no particular reason why they should. And the home country often is bitter because the firms pay taxes someplace else. In this nationalistic world, who pays what to whom can get rather emotional.

Some firms, less ethical than most, manage to evade most payments to all countries. This is easier done by those smaller firms who are not yet noticed by tax collectors. With a bit of juggling, and possibly a bit of chicanery here and there, all profits and cash flows end up in some zero tax haven country. Few governments have enough skilled accountants and tax auditors to cover every firm in every situation. But even such evasive firms create jobs and income, and those workers spend the money locally. What is ethical here is an extremely subtle question.

Those fabled Swiss numbered bank accounts come from someplace, and tax evasion is one source. It is possible, with considerable wit and ingenuity, to get away almost free if you try, particularly if you operate transnationally, and some do.

This tax area is incredibly complex, where firms have to study in detail all their operations and plan their strategies. Even to list the tax laws of a small country would take a longer book than this one, and existing tax treaties between countries (or their absence), special rules, intracorporate pricing policies, and a host of other problems will be with the MNCs forevermore. One can only note the problem and observe that the experts in this field should be at the highest competence level.

FINANCIAL CONTROL

It is a lot easier to lose things in an MNC than in a local one, simply because the problems are much more complex, and the rules and procedures are also much more complex. In both internal and external audits, the personnel have to be good. Moreover, few firms as yet have built a really global financial and informational system, so various items get lost in the crannies of the system. Who can evaluate a strange request for funds in a far off country which may be perfectly logical under local circumstances? One author once saw a request for cow's blood, which was critical to use for blessing a new plant. It was pretty expensive, too. The local budget controller in Indianapolis might be pardoned for wondering just what was going on.

Local accounting practices also can lead to control problems. Accounting is not uniform, and unless sophisticated people understand how to compare disparate reports, confusion and loss of control is certain.

The way to develop proper control procedures is to perceive the global view of the corporation. Only when every financial transaction is seen in relation to all transactions does anything make much sense. A global financial plan and system, where all funds are focused at the center, can lead to really effective control proceedures.

ACCOUNTING

Accounting provides the data and information system for both auditing and financial planning. But accounting is often culture bound, and firms which move to other countries quickly discover that whatever rules apply in the United States or France, or any other country, either through accepted accounting practices or law, may not be the same rules which have to be applied. In order to understand and use foreign accounts, one has to be very sophisticated about what rules are being used.

Thus in the United States, assets are rarely, if ever, written up in value to account for inflation, but in some countries, such practices are condoned or even required. An American might be puzzled as to why his assets seemed to increase steadily in a foreign country when no investments have been made. Inventories and similar asset items could be treated the same way. Some countries allow for various reserves which can be used to offset net income; others do not. An income statement might be very different as a result. American accounting rules call for certain systematic depreciation allowances; in some countries, the firm can write off the entire investment in the first year, while in others, completely different rules apply. Governments often require certain precise accounting procedures to compute taxes due which would be illegal in the United States.

If a country has had a history of extreme price inflation, it is likely that its accounting rules will allow accounting for inflation. American rules do not. Such inflation accounting can get very technical and extremely complicated, but firms operating in such countries will have to understand these rules and how to convert reports to American practice.

Translation of accounts is an important accounting concept. If an American company has accounts in more than one currency, then the ideal would be to translate foreign currency statements into dollars as accurately as possible. In the fluctuating currency world we live in, this translation process is extremely difficult. No matter what rate of exchange is used, it will be wrong shortly, as rates change. What exactly is the value of a West German plant, which cost 85 million marks to build in 1978? One could use the mark/dollar exchange rate of 1978 and get one value. But if the current rate were used, the value would be much lower, since the mark has fallen about 25 percent relative to the dollar since 1978. Such fluctuations in value can dramatically affect a firm's assets, sales, profits, and other critical values.

A company which wanted to look good could select the exchange rate, actual or historical, that made profits the highest. But in the United States, very precise accounting rules govern such translations. For foreign currency translations, FASB-52 is the key rule. This is the translation rule issued by the Financial Accounting Standards Board in 1981, which is the rulemaking body for American accountants and auditors. FASB-52 replaced FASB-8, originally promulgated in 1974, and abandoned after a few years of heated protest. The reason for concern was noted above. No matter what rules are used, values will be confused. Since even minor changes in foreign translation can mean variations of tens or even hundreds of millions of dollars in reported net profits, controversy is certain.

FASB-52 excludes adjustments for currency exchange rate changes that do not impact cash flows and requires adjustments for those that do. It presents standards for foreign currency translation that reflect in consolidated statements the financial results and relationships as measured in the primary currency in which each firm conducts its business. The primary currency is the one in which the firm mainly operates. FASB-52 also provides guidance for choosing this primary currency.

For most American firms and many foreign ones, the dollar would be the primary currency. FASB-52 goes on to delineate translation adjustments and other technical problems of extreme importance to firms, including the critical questions of transaction gains and losses. Since these gains and losses are included in determining net income for the period in which the transactions existed, just what is included and what is not can dramatically affect net profits. One major intent of FASB-52 was to avoid sharp value fluctuations in a company's financial position which actually had little to do with what was really going on, but as we noted above, no matter what translation techniques are used in a world of rapidly fluctuating currencies, problems will arise.

Each country in the EC has different accounting standards, and there has been little progress to date in coordinating accounting practices. The result is again confusion, since standards can vary widely. What a published income statement or balance sheet really means can require a sophisticated international accounting expert to determine. Other countries are equally diverse in their accounting requirements.

It is quite proper for an MNC to have three to five sets of books as a result of these considerations. One set might be prepared in accord with local tax law, for tax computational purposes; another set might be prepared for local stockholders, using local accounting rules and conventions; still another set might be modified to reflect American rules and practice, for tax purposes at home; and yet another set might be prepared for managerial purposes. Which set is correct? It depends on what they are used for.

One overlooked gift of MNCs, along with other international organizations, to the world has been good accounting. It is easy to ignore accounting, until one´s organization is a disaster of defective control systems, stolen assets, and lack of control. Insistance on proper accounting, applied as effectively as possible to complex (and not so complex) organizations, has resulted in more internal firm efficiency gains than anyone, except perhaps harrassed accountants, realize. Only with really good records can any firm managers know what is going on, and manage effectively. Such proper record keeping is just one of the many reasons why professionally managed MNCs have such superior performance.

Because accounts are used for so many internal and external purposes, and because even a simple change in procedure can result in millions of dollars of changes in net profits, accounting procedures are carefully studied by tax men, public accountants, managers, government securities control organizations, stock exchanges, and stockholders. Reality in accounting depends on too many variables to be casually considered. One result is that international accounting is a rapidly growing field, with the usual shortage of top level experts able to help firms.

CONCLUSION

This brief chapter can only begin to describe the complexities of international finance and accounting. Increasingly, this field is beginning to see a global potential for the firm. Instead of perceiving the company as a group of disparate pieces, the modern MNC is viewing its activities as a single, integrated unit. One major result is that the large MNC can utilize its funds in the most productive way on a global basis; another is that it can obtain funds from the most advantageous source. Local firms, trapped in whatever provincial problems they have, are unable to do nearly as well, unless they are very lucky.

Accountants are also beginning to see the world as a whole, but much more slowly. In part this reflects the need for accounting procedures and rules to be tied to nation states; in part it reflects real intellectual differences about what the rules should be. But any firm operating in a dozen countries has to be aware of these rule differences in order to integrate its own activities and records.

Questions for Discussion

1. A rapidly growing American manufacturing firm with annual sales of $95.8 million has recently set up its first foreign manufacturing venture in Denmark. As is common in such cases, the company´s financial vice president is not an expert in international finance. He arranged initially for the firm to set up a Danish bank account in kroner, and this branch used this account to conduct its business. Each quarter the subsidiary remits profits to the home office.

The company is now planning its second foreign venture in

Singapore, since the first one has proven very successful. The firm will put up an initial $12.5 million in capital for this project. The financial vice president now realizes that he will be dealing in three currencies, with considerable exchange risk, and he is concerned that he should begin to plan to coordinate more closely the financial activities of all branches. Moreover, it appears as if the firm will be expanding into several other countries in the next few years, since this company now sees that its major expansion path and most likely successes will be in this international area.

Help this vice president by laying out a good general financial planning/control system for his present operation. What kinds of exchange risks are likely in these three countries the company now operates in? If necessary, do some research and find out how the Danish kroner and the Singapore dollar have behaved in recent years.

What other kinds of experts and institutions might this vice president consult to help him? What kinds of financial services are available for this firm?

2. Do some research and find out what has happened to the value of the American dollar relative to the West German mark since 1971. If an American firm had a West German subsidiary which generated an average profit of 9 million marks per year during this period, what would this have meant in dollars to the company?

A West German firm has a branch plant in North Carolina which has earned an average net profit of $3 million per year for the past five years. How did this company fare as the value of the dollar and mark shifted? Which company was better off in the past five years? Why?

3. Your boss has asked you to forecast the value of the British pound in terms of the dollar for the next year. What key factors would you begin to look at to determine what might influence this value? Why?

4. During 1982-83, the dollar rose rapidly in value in terms of major European currencies. One major British MNC, foreseeing this rise, successfully speculated against the pound. The company did this by putting most of its excess cash in dollars; by borrowing at the prime rate in London and shifting these funds to dollars; and by paying all U.S. bills very promptly, while delaying payment of pound accounts due from their British suppliers. As a result, this company earned over $86 million in exchange gains in these two years. Throughout this period, the British government called for patriotic defense of the pound.

Another major British company in a similar position took the position that as a British firm it was unethical to speculate against the pound. The company did nothing special about the problem, and as a result took an exchange loss in these two years of $27 million. Both companies have sales of over a billion dollars per year, with net profits of over $300 millions per year.

Which company did the right thing, in ethical terms? Why?

Would your answer be different if these companies were American based? Why or why not?

5.   An American company noted for its conservative accounting practices has a branch in a foreign country which allows for total write offs of certain new investments in the first year. This firm invested $4 million in new equipment in this country this past year, and the investment qualified for the fast write off. Actually, the equipment will be useful for at least eight years.

The corporate income tax in the country is 45 percent. By writing off the asset this year, instead of writing it off over six years as required under American law, the comany will save about $1.9 million in tax payments.

The chief accountant for this firm argues that the company should follow American rules in writing off this asset. He feels that if the company begins to use different accounting concepts of depreciation abroad, even if they are allowed, the company's books will really not reflect the true facts. In as far as possible the company should have all its books follow exactly the same rules and a foreign branch should be treated exactly like the American parent.

Do you think that this argument is a valid one? Why or why not?

Supplementary Readings

Arpan, Jeffrey S. and Radebaugh, Lee H. INTERNATIONAL ACCOUNTING AND MULTINATIONAL ENTERPRISES. Boston: Warren, Gorham and Lamont, 1981.

Eiteman, David K. and Stonehill, Arthur I.   MULTINATIONAL BUSINESS FINANCE. Reading, MA: Addison-Wesley, 1973.

Gilman, Martin G.   THE FINANCING OF FOREIGN DIRECT INVESTMENT.   New York: St Martin, 1981.

Henning, Charles N., et. al. INTERNATIONAL FINANCIAL MANAGEMENT. New York: McGraw-Hill, 1978.

Kelly, Maria Wicks, FOREIGN INVESTMENT EVALUATION PRACTICES OF U.S. MULTINATIONAL CORPORATIONS. Ann Arbor, MI: UMI Research Press, 1981.

Miller, Elwood L. ACCOUNTING PROBLEMS OF MULTINATIONAL ENTERPRISES. Lexington, MA: Lexington Books, 1979.

Mueller, Gerhard G. INTERNATIONAL ACCOUNTING. New York: Macmillan, 1967.

Nehrt, Lee C. INTERNATIONAL FINANCE FOR MULTINATIONAL BUSINESS, 2D ED. Scranton, PA: Intext Eductional Publishers, 1972.

Zenoff, David B. and Zwick, Jack. INTERNATIONAL FINANCIAL MANAGEMENT. Englewood Cliffs, NJ: Prentice-Hall, 1969.

Chapter 11

MNC Strategies: Marketing

Introduction

Marketing executives are fond of pointing out that if the company cannot sell what it produces, everything else is a waste of time. Success in the market will determine which firms die, and which grow and prosper. We now have total marketing concepts well established, which cause a company to begin at the market and work backwards through its other functions to get desired results. The concept makes sense, since if the company produces what is wanted, at the right time, place, quality, price, and quantity, it will succeed.

Historically, international marketing was something the export department did, selling a few products to foreigners. Such orders were often looked upon as a nice marginal business, but hardly worth getting worked up about. The real action was at home. Even today one can find many companies which try to avoid export sales, since they are somewhat more troublesome to make than domestic ones. This attitude is particularly common in large countries such as the United States, with huge domestic markets and historic isolationist attitudes. Smaller countries such as Switzerland and Sweden have always seen exports as critical to local prosperity, and questions of tariffs and other trade controls have long been crucial to the country's economic success.

But few firms like to give up a market, and occasionally because of shipping costs, tariff increases, or possible new business, a company would invest overseas. Possibly volume was growing nicely, and the country concerned raised import duties sharply. The firm had to invest in the country or give up the market. It chose to invest, and it was on the road to being a MNC. And as this happened, problems of marketing products within strange countries and cultures emerged in sharp focus. It was one thing to ship an occasional order to Brazil from the Dayton, Ohio plant, but when the new plant in Brazil was completed, with much more productive capacity than exports ever were, just how did one sell in the country? If this problem were not solved satisfactorily, the new investment was in jeopardy.

This new kind of international marketing has grown dramatically in the past forty years, but the older form of exporting and importing has grown even faster. The world created at Bretton Woods in 1944 led eventually to relaxation of trade barriers everywhere, and the EC and other customs unions only enhanced this trend. The move to the oil standard, with huge volumes of petroleum being imported by many countries, and huge volumes of goods exported to pay for the oil, also accelerated the trend. GATT really worked, and tariffs and other trade barriers gradually came down all over the world.

Perhaps most importantly, the United States began, in the late 1940´s, a long term trend to lowered trade barriers. The U.S. imported about a thousand foreign cars in 1938; by 1983, over two million were being imported. In effect, the U.S. decided to allow others to compete in the local market, if they could. They could and did. What the U.S. received in return was access to foreign markets for American agricultural products, aircraft, machinery, computers, and ten thousand other items. One cannot underestimate the power of this idea, where anyone can trade anywhere (well, most places).

Now, Americans take for granted Japanese cars and consumer electronics, French wines, English leathers and scotch, Taiwanese clothing, Hong Kong toys, West German Mercedes, and even Brazilian steel. Old timers from 1950 would marvel at the incredible variety and low costs of consumer goods in the U.S. today. The best color TV sets now retail for less in absolute dollars (which are worth about a sixth as much as in 1950) as a clumsy, inefficient black and white set did in 1950. It is common to find real prices for consumer goods from one tenth to one half as much as they were twenty years ago. And other countries happily buy Apple microcomputers and Boeing jet transports in return. In effect, the law of comparative advantage is being tested, and it is correct. By specializing in what you are good at, you maximize your income.

All of this leads to strange sights, such as high powered American ad agencies managing sales campaigns for Japanese producers, and the growing trend of consumers in many countries, including the U.S., being totally uninterested in where the goods come from. What is important is whether the price and quality is right. In effect, all of marketing is becoming internationalized, and it is not only the Americans that are interested. Virtually all countries face intriguing marketing questions in other countries, and while the past few years have seen the slowing of the growth trend, it seems highly unlikely that we will return to autarky at any time in the near future. If one is going to sell any good or service, it is likely that some international dimension will be involved, sooner or later.

Governments love production, which usually results in good jobs, huge factories, and power. Consumers love products and services, the more and cheaper the better. For some reason, a steelworker or auto assembly line worker is usually perceived to be more important than a sales clerk or an ad writer. Hence marketing is usually seen politically as something to be endured, not admired. But the past 40 years has seen an explosion in international marketing, as country after country has yielded to political pressures and let those accursed foreign products in. After all, if the country doesn´t, it can´t export, and those lovely production jobs will disappear. Moreover, happy consumers mean more votes for those politicians astute enough to allow those delightful products to be sold. In the end, we may be witnessing a new kind of world, where marketing really matters, even if official policies and marxist philosophies regard the whole field with considerable distaste.

Marketing is Marketing

As firms moved into strange cultures and experimented with proper marketing methods, it became clear that marketing is marketing, wherever you are. As with other international business firm functions, it turns out that the basic methodology useful in the United States is the same as in Brazil, France, or Egypt. What does change is the environment. The variables are the same, but the values are different. Successful firms match up their internal marketing activities with whatever environment they find themselves in. Because these environments are so different, the marketing solutions turn out to be very different on occasion.

Major MNCs increasingly tend to regard their various markets from a global perspective, with each country, region, or product line seeking out some market segment which is most profitable. Moreover, they have discovered that products, sometimes with adaptations to local conditions, can be sold almost anywhere, but sometimes in some different market segment. Thus detergent soap powder was developed in the U.S., but rather quickly could be sold profitably in Western Europe, Canada, and Australia. Some years later, this market could be expanded to Third World countries. After all, cleanliness is next to godliness in many, many cultures!

But what might be a low cost, economy product in France might be an upscale, luxury product in a poorer country, at least at the outset. Here, market segments differ, yet the basic product stays the same. Large four door sedans made in Detroit might be upper middle class family cars in Canada and the U.S., but they can (and do) find minor markets in many countries as luxury vehicles for officials and taxis. Note that in these cases the costs of expanding markets and finding new segments is relatively small. One can conceive of the world as the market, beginning in Japan or the U.S., and then gradually expanding all over the world.

Here is one major reason why American MNCs have some major advantage in world markets. These firms can work in their home market for years or even decades, developing considerable distribution and marketing expertise, then move abroad, either as exporters or, more commonly, as MNCs. As new products are developed in the U.S., they become potential future products abroad. Thus a major toiletry manufacturer might be selling a thousand products in the U.S., 900 in Western Europe, and 25 in Mexico. As the Mexican market develops and grows, such a firm has a very good idea of what happens next. The local Mexican firm does not. A Dutch or Swiss firm, with a very small local market, may have to expand into exports almost from the outset, which can be more difficult than selling locally, which gives such firms many problems. Japanese firms, with relatively large home markets, also are in a strong position, and they may have the further advantage of being able to bring to market products already developed by American or European firms. The Japanese firms can offer improved products, better quality, and superior after sales services, and, given low American trade barriers, often succeed. Note how critical trade barriers are in this case. If the U.S. market were tightly protected, this game could not go on.

Note how such marketing concepts as mature markets, market segmentation, superior sales promotion, and physical distribution all are completely relevant in the international marketing question. Nothing really is different, except that from time to time one encounters environmental barriers or differences, such as tariffs, quotas, differing customs, or whatever. But such problems can be overcome in many cases, often with direct investments in the country being served.

KEY MARKETING VARIABLES

The basic marketing problem is to sell the goods. What key variables affect sales anywhere? Price, as economists have pointed out for centuries, is one key variable. High prices lead to lower sales, and vice versa.

But here the environment enters. What is "high" in Bangkok may seem low in London, and at the same price, different volumes of goods can be moved. Price itself is a complex variable, involving quality of product, delivery dates, credit terms, and after sales service (or lack thereof). Some of these elements are culture bound, and seemingly identical prices (at going exchange rates) may be quite different. In one country, price includes some implicit or stated after sales services; in other countries, such items are quoted separately. A provincial marketer may discover that things are not always what they seem when he or she begins to analyze the company's pricing policies in various countries.

One company's price relative to another is also relevant. Customers tend to compare relative prices and make purchase decisions based on such data. Substitute goods prices may be relevant, as when customers consider buying butter or margarine. Firms discover that in foreign countries traditional differentials may not apply, or that people respond more to smaller (or larger) changes in relative prices than they do at home. In very poor countries a small shift in the price of margarine relative to butter may have major impacts on sales, while in other countries similar changes would hardly be noticed. Brand names may mean more or less abroad than at home, allowing for higher or lower price differentials. Many American and Japanese firms have discovered that insistance on quality control means more abroad than at home, and sales stay high even though much cheaper foreign goods are available. Others have discovered that treasured home brand names mean little abroad, and prices have to be lowered to meet competition. In such cases, customers are reacting differently to the same data as local buyers would, so changes in marketing strategy are necessary.

Income levels are critical in marketing, and per capita incomes range from perhaps $100 per year in some very poor African countries to over $10,000 in affluent West European countries and the United States. If a company is selling electric appliances costing two to three hundred dollars, it will not find very lucrative markets until per capita incomes climb above $3,000 per year. Poorer countries cannot afford such luxuries. But if one is selling soap, transistor radio batteries, rice, or laxatives, even very poor countries may offer lucrative markets.

We sometimes find rather unexpected changes in markets because people get a bit ahead as incomes rise. Thus one detergent marketer did very well for years by spotting poor, but growing countries. When the company first entered the market, incomes seemed so low that detergents could not be sold. But within a short while, incomes inched up a little, and as soon as basic food, clothing, and shelter needs were met, thrifty housewives began to buy good soap, which only cost a few cents a day. Sales would skyrocket within a few years. The trick was to spot just that time when a growing country was getting off the bare subsistence floor, which required some close analysis of income and income trends, along with some good hunches about when the breakthrough would occur.

There are many relevant income measures, such as the gross national product, personal income (before or after taxes), supernumery income, and so on. Sales of various products are related to these in different ways, and marketers use different measures to get the results they want. The concepts are the same, but the numbers are very different. So are results.

A real problem for all marketers is lack of data or poor data. Experts accustomed to working in affluent countries with excellent data often find that poorer countries have very poor data, and while one needs to know gross national product, the estimates available are very poor. One sure sign of economic development is the steadily increasing quality and quantity of data available.

Demographic variables are numerous and important. If you are selling toothpaste, you have to know how many people have teeth to brush (not just the population figures, incidentally, since some people have false teeth, and many are babies without teeth). If you are selling shoes, estimates of both population and sizes of feet are critical. Capital goods manufacturers have to know about electric power generation, voltages, and line capacities; ad agencies have to know how many newspapers, magazines, and TV stations accept advertisements; razor blade makers must know a lot about the numbers of males and their shaving habits (along with how many females are likely to shave their legs); and textbook publishers must know how many students are around, and in what levels and courses. Such data defines the total market and can tell any seller much about sales potential. As noted above, good data is often very hard to find, so marketers may often work in ignorance in many markets.

Finally, taste variables are critical in marketing. People like things, or learn to like them, or they learn not to. Advertising tries to influence tastes and behavior, and most discussion of ads and their ethics revolves around this point. Ads also give useful information as well, which few object to, and which can be very important in many markets. Knowing about prices, qualities, and availability of products cannot be taken for granted in many markets.

The taste variable is the tough one, since the marketer runs into cultural and educational variables which are often very difficult to figure out correctly. How will Indians react to certain ads? Will an Italian family respond to a soup ad in the same way a Swedish family might? Knowing for sure can mean tens of millions of dollars in extra sales. Moreover, all cultures are changing all the time, and appeals which wouldn't work ten years ago might be very successful now. It is alleged, as one example, that West European markets are coming much closer together in basic tastes as affluence spreads and as families acquire the same types of consumer goods packages. This basic package includes such items as refrigerators, radios, stereos, TVs, vacuum cleaners, and similar consumer durables. The precise package may vary with the physical environment; Italians will buy air conditioners, while Swedes will buy heaters, but most consumers seem to like the same general durables. If true, firms can save large sums by having all European advertising campaigns much the same way that they now have total American campaigns. But it is not yet proven that Europeans are similar. A marketing executive responsible for European sales will spend much time trying to get the answer to this fundamental question.

International marketing is full of stories about how certain products failed because of these cultural differences. It is also full of stories about great successes which occurred because a good marketer correctly assumed that perceived differences really didn't exist. Thus Sears has done very well in several Latin American countries by following its basic North American selling policies. When they began these ventures thirty-five years ago, most Latins and Americans predicted disaster. But Sears policies of quality, fair market prices, money back if not sastisfied, and credit fit Latin cultures as well as the North American. Testing such assumptions about cultural differences led to large profits and growth.

The reason marketing is so complicated is that all of these basic variables are changing simultaneously, often in quite confusing ways. One can observe that for one company, its prices are raised. But at the same time, competitive prices went up faster, while the key demographic variables turned against the firm. It may be in a baby oriented market, and the number of births is declining. Also, real incomes are going up seven percent per year, while mothers seem to be much more concerned about their children's health. What will happen to sales, given this data? The usual answer is that we are not sure. Even the most careful research into all the variables may leave a confused picture, and even the most refined computer multiple correlation techniques may not catch the nuances of taste changes or reactions to comparative price cuts.

International marketing, or marketing in various cultures is even more complicated, because each environment yields different values for the variables. In our next country, taking the same baby oriented firm, births are rising; relative prices are declining; and real family incomes are going up only two percent a year. What is going to happen? We find ourselves guessing about the relative importance of key variables, unable to say precisely what will occur. And if we add that the data are of very poor quality, and those numbers may be off by plus or minus twenty percent or more, our confusion is compounded.

The environmental constraints discussed in Chapter 3 are important, since they taxonomize the environment along lines similar to the above variables. Thus price changes are caused by shifts in the legal constraints or economic factors (C-3's and C-4's), along with possible changes in key international constraints, such as tariff increases (I-2's). Demographic and taste changes are closely related to the behavioral and educational characteristics of the population (C-1's and C-2's). Firms that understand the environment and how it affects their key marketing variables will do better than firms which merely hope that their home country strategies will work.

The United States has long led the world in marketing expertise, and when foreigners sell in this market, they typically hire Americans to do it. Thus Japanese car makers hire American ad agencies to develop sales campaigns, and Hong Kong manufacturers sell products to American distributors, often using their own brand names, to sell at retail. Such strategies are usually more effective. Moreover, American ad agencies go abroad, and they can often sell their services in other countries. Knowing how to market effectively is one of the trickiest parts of business to learn, and only the very expert can expect consistent success.

International Marketing Problem Areas

As firms move abroad, marketing problems which are easy at home can get complicated. For example:

Distribution channels: These channels are quite environmentally determined. An American firm may be able to sell directly to major retailers, since their volume is so large. But in smaller countries, the economic method of distribution may be through wholesalers, jobbers, exclusive agents, or some quite different channel. Legal differences also can affect channels. In some countries, exclusive distributorships, owned by local citizens, may be encouraged, or even mandatory, while in the U.S. such distribution patterns could lead to antitrust problems.

Custom and tradition also play a major role. It is expected that certain wholesale/retail patterns be maintained, and firms which violate tradition can get into trouble. They can also revolutionize marketing patterns, if they change at the right time and place. The trick is to know when to innovate and when to observe local customs.

There are no simple channel rules. Many MNCs have found out the hard way that each culture and country is different. The MNC has a major advantage of even knowing about channel theory, since local firms may just do what always has been done. The typical MNC is an MNC because its marketing expertise level is so high.

Product mix: American, Japanese, and European firms, accustomed to dealing with affluent and sophisticated markets, typically have elaborate product mixes. In more restricted markets, the most economic product mix tends to be much simpler. Consumers have less income, and often less knowledge about options. This point also relates to

production.   If the market is small, factories may only be able to
produce limited ranges of products economically.

Companies can be too sophisticated as well.   The Japanese car
makers do very well in the U.S. with a limited range of options, while
American manufacturers may have too many options that cost too much.
Choosing the right product mix can be a tricky business, since too
simple a mix can miss important market segments, while too complex a mix
can cost more than it is worth in terms of inventory costs, production
expenses, and customer confusion.

Trademarks: Consumer oriented firms invest millions of dollars in
their brand names, and they also try to protect them in foreign markets.
This involves intimate knowledge of local copyright law, as well as
which countries belong to the international copyright convention.   Local
firms sometimes bootleg brand names or copy movies or books, taking
advantage of good will and market power built up over many years by
reputable firms.   This has become a major problem for many American firms
producing high quality branded merchandise in recent years.   One of the
authors once discoverd that the Lockheed brake products being used as
replacement parts in the Middle East were imitations of dubious quality,
made in some unknown Eastern company.   The copied boxes were perfect,
although the product was not. The cost of having defective brakes in
large trucks in crowded traffic conditions could be very high.   The cost
to this reputable firm in terms of customer goodwill and reputation for
reliability was also high.

Because so many major companies literally survive by their brands,
this is considered top priority.   Yet on occasion a company can get into
serious competitive trouble because of too much reliance on brand names.
This will occur when a country has tight retail price controls on
consumer products.   Firms without established brands can change names,
offer somewhat different products, and thus raise prices.   The branded
products are stuck with fixed prices, and governments are not likely to
be too sympathetic toward rich foreign firms.   Such price controls
usually occur during rapid inflationary periods, which also present
serious cost problems and cut margins sharply.

One major reason American and Japanese firms have done so well
abroad is that they have tried to build product reputation in much the
same way as they do at home. This concept is quite new in many
countries, and customers appreciate quality and reliability more than
most American critics realize.   One only has to spend some time in a
foreign country where caveat emptor is the rule to understand how
important this is.   Even communist countries have problems on this
score.   The idea of advertising extensively, selling the idea that brand
Y really is superior, and then trying to make it superior, works in most
cultures.   The Americans worked out this idea initially; Western
European firms also use it extensively; and the Japanese have applied it
brilliantly, most notably in the U.S.   Marketing executives, well aware
that it works well everywhere, spend a lot of time and money protecting
brand names and copyrights.

Publishers, as well as movie and TV producers have lots of trouble
here, since it is easy to copy their products, and it is getting easier

all the time, thanks to modern technology. Pirating a TV tape or movie is very common in many countries, and pirated books are equally common. Thus popular business texts are often reproduced in English in Taiwan or other countries without permission. A certain status symbol by low paid text writers is to have one's textbook pirated in this way. Few authors (including us) ever get rich writing texts, and it is nice to know that someone abroad thinks so highly of one's work that they will pirate it. Alas, as far as we know, no one has pirated this book...which may say something about its popular cross-cultural appeal. But to pirate a movie such as STAR WARS can be a big business proposition, and copyright owners try to protect their property internationally as best they can.

Data Availability: We mentioned this point briefly above, but it is worth stressing. Modern marketing lives by data, and American data is the best in the world. When a company goes to other countries, even fairly advanced ones, the problem of how to get relevant market information can become frustrating. Data costs money, often lots of money, and the American government and other institutions provide it to anyone at low cost. Specialized data processing firms also provide much specific data for given uses, as in television ratings. But firms abroad may find that they either change their marketing analysis methods or spend a lot of money obtaining their own data.

One result is that marketing in foreign countries often is not as efficiently done as at home. Executives know what they need to do, but it just can't be done.

Warranties and After Sales Service: Americans and Europeans are used to complaining bitterly about problems with merchandise, but in many countries the concept of warranty is virtually unknown. The buyer is stuck to work out problems as best he or she can. Agencies for more complicated products such as appliances and cars also are unaccustomed to providing parts, maintenance, and repairs. Here is another major American revolution percolating throughout the world, now joined by West European and Japanese firms. The American MNC reaction to lack of after sales service for complex products is to try to find agents and representatives who will perform such tasks. In effect, the old image of the merchant who buys low and sells high is transformed into that of the sophisticated seller with a well organized parts warehouse and repair shop who stands behind the product sold.

Such revolutions never happen in a hurry, and the translation of the idea into practice in countries totally unaccustomed to such strange ideas is very difficult, but many MNCs try. If the MNC is moving into a country like the U.S., which takes such after sales service for granted, an early step is always to develop good distributorships and dealers, plus parts warehouses and other necessary investments to keep the product operating. Many major foreign firms have failed in the U.S. because they did not appreciate this point. A European auto firm might sell its cars fairly well for a few years, but then when breakdowns occurred, few (or no) parts were available, and skilled mechanics did not exist. Then sales nosedived, and the product was withdrawn. Much of the success of Japanese electronics and auto firms in the U.S. came because those firms appreciated the need to have very strong service organizations behind their products.

Language can be difficult. The Japanese have to translate not only ads and sales brochures, or have them prepared locally, but, much more importantly, they must have repair manuals and parts lists translated into various languages. A major industrial firm might have several hundred thousand pages of manuals, covering endless details on all their equipment, translated into perhaps 40 to 60 languages. When good technical translation from English to Arabic might cost one to three hundred dollars per page, this cost is not trivial. One option here is to teach various technicians and mechanics basic English, and then translate the manuals from engineeringese to basic English, but the costs are high as well, since a major MNC might have several thousand distributorships employing tens of thousands of technicians. For complex, advanced technology products technical words may not even exist in many languages, and technical translators have to invent them.

This point is almost completely overlooked in scholarly literature, perhaps because most linguists are more interested in literary problems than technical ones, and few technicians are bilingual, or otherwise aware of translation problems. But to try to figure out which electric wire goes where on an Italian Fiat, when the manual is in English, but the wiring diagram is in Italian, can be fun. Even more fun is trying to assemble a Japanese model kit in the U.S. when all instructions are in Japanese. The pictures helped, though. Failure to communicate can inhibit sales dramatically, and most MNCs have large numbers of highly skilled people working on such technical translation problems.

Worker training is also a real problem. Third World countries do not have large numbers of highly trained technicians, and those who also can speak English or Japanese or German are very, very scarce. MNCs typically end up training their distributor´s technicians, including bringing such people to the home country for advanced training. Firms do this because it helps sales enormously. When a local contractor might lose one to five thousand dollars a day because his bulldozer is inoperative, he will tend to buy the product which can be easily and quickly serviced. Often he won´t, but his competitor will, and after a decade or so, the only survivors will be those firms that offer the best after sales services.

Advertising: Pushing products gets very emotional everywhere, and as the company moves from one country to the next, the rules change dramatically. Some countries have quite elaborate truth in advertising laws; others have none. Many countries have state radio and television networks which either accept no advertising or limit it under stringent rules; a few have rules similar to the United States. Many countries have special restrictions on most advertising which make this practice quite different than it is in the United States.

The usual problem is that most countries do not have as elaborate a communications/publications system as the U.S., which means that it is harder to present advertising messages. Media common in the U.S., such as local papers, may be much smaller or nonexistent in other countries. Specialized personnel who know how to do advertising well are in short supply.

But American firms have managed to live with all limitations and legal constraints, as have other MNCs from Western Europe and Japan. Historically, non-U.S. based MNCs followed the Americans, and then most MNCs took these practices to other countries. Much more advertising, and better quality work, is now done than occurred even a decade ago. Advertising is indeed culture bound, but innovation is always possible when inventive executives go to work.

Sales Promotion: Other than advertising, firms have many sales promotion possibilities. Giving away free samples, demonstrations via trade fairs and displays, and salespersons' demonstrations would fit this category. As with advertising, such promotion is culture bound, and different rules and regulations make it necessary to modify customary American practice. Free samples are banned in some countries, and fairs for private firms can be sharply restricted. In communist countries, public trade exhibitions and fairs may be the major way of displaying and promoting products, and hence used more extensively than in the U.S. Firms may have to work out their promotions specifically for each country.

Market Research: No foreign market has been researched as thoroughly as the United States, which is a major advantage for MNCs coming to the U.S. American firms going abroad often find that no one knows very much about given market characteristics. This ties back to data availability, since often a company cannot get the data it needs to do relevant research.

American companies have done much pioneering research in many countries, and many foreign firms have followed their lead and developed much better research efforts after watching the Americans in action. Not surprisingly, many major American ad agencies and other market research organizations are MNCs themselves, since they can sell their knowledge profitably in many countries. Marketing is one area where Americans are very strong relative to rivals, so many foreign companies pay close attention to what they are dong, and American marketing literature, both applied and theoretical, is closely studied abroad.

As with most marketing problems, this is typically seen as a capitalist plot. But good marketing research can be useful in any society, including very especially communist and marxist states. If the crucial economic problem is getting the right goods to the right customers, regardless of who makes them, then state owned companies need some good market research too. In such countries the price system rarely works very well, so firms really need more good research than many capitalist companies. This point is slowly being realized around the world, and even state owned firms are beginning to think about marketing problems.

The British State Railways, Air France, Lufthansa, and Amtrak are examples of public firms that do considerable marketing research, and need more. Because marketing is so often viewed as a plot to exploit customers, such organizations move cautiously on this point, but it makes no sense for a state railway to use up resources running trains no one rides. Who wants what trains, and why? Note that the railway may be local, but many potential customers are foreign tourists, which gives even this problem an international flavor. What might entice Canadian tourists to travel by British Rail? Knowing such information can lead to much more efficient public operations, and more customer satisfaction. Hence market research becomes increasingly important. Even a few firms in communist countries have cautiously experimented with finding out what customers want. When more communist firms do market research, they will be using techniques and methodologies developed for privately owned firms, and they may even buy such information from private MNCs.

Licenses and Franchises: Many firms organize their marketing system through the use of independent franchises and licenses. Coca Cola is one example, while hotel chains are another. Here the question of legal contracts and valid agreements in very different legal systems becomes important. What changes need to be made in a soft drink franchise, when the franchisee is a communist company in Bulgaria? Such agreements can be made, but they are likely to be modified from typical Western practice. Under Napoleonic legal codes, what kinds of contracts and terms are valid and binding? Local lawyers in France or Spain are needed to give advice. Can a brand name be protected, and how, in a given license agreement with a foreign manufacturer? New problems will arise as the company goes to other countries.

It is very common for the franchisee to be a local company. Thus in the United States, all of the local dealers for Japanese cars are American owned local firms. Employees and owners are Americans, which is nice politically, since for widely distributed products, literally hundreds of thousands of local citizens have an economic stake in high sales of foreign products. Thus when American auto firms pressed for import quotas on Japanese cars, many other Americans objected, knowing that they might lose their jobs and incomes if such quotas became too severe. The American government found that its problem was not a simple one of protecting American auto manufacturing jobs, but a much more complex one of trading off such jobs for other jobs in distributorships for mechanics, salespersons, and bookkeepers. The net result often is to scramble up previously simple protectionist problems to the extent that it may be virtually impossible to return to the older system of autarky. Too many locals have a stake in imports to simply cut them off. From the MNC point of view, such scramblings make their political lives easier.

Marketing Organization: An organization suited for a huge American market may not work well in smaller countries with special environmental problems. MNCs are good at working out practical marketing organizations wherever they are, because failure is fatal.

Organizational possibilities are extensive, ranging from a globally oriented company with a total marketing approach to entire world markets to special situations in countries that require them. One might find that in Western Europe the organization resembles the United States, since the mass market is similar. But in Jordan or Ghana, quite special organization is required. Here an exclusive agent who imports the product might be used. How distributors are locked into the marketing structure is a very complex topic, since these local distributors are so important in gaining sales.

One can spend an interesting lifetime exploring this topic, and we can only barely indicate the the extent of this problem. As with so many things in marketing, the complexities of making proper environmental/firm interlocks require extensive and detailed work.

Physical Distribution Management: Goods have to be distributed by transportation systems, and they have to be inventoried until used. The field of physical distribution management deals with commodities flow and storage.

Transportation is closely related to marketing, and it is a vast field. The intricacies of freight rates, demurrage charges, costs of truckload or less than truckload lots, port and airport fees and facilities, materials handling equipment, refrigeration demands, bulk product handling, and much more is involved. This is a world of specialists, quantitative methods experts, and systems analysts. Much model building and quantitative work is done, since many of the variables and parameters are subject to rigorous, quantitative analysis. The actual design and construction of transportation equipment, ports, airports, and warehouses is a huge field involving engineers, contractors, and economic experts.

One major reason for the rapid expansion of world trade lies in the dramatic development of transportation systems. In 1973, the Japanese could not ship cars economically to the U.S., given then existing facilities and transport costs; by 1980, new techniques of shipload lot shipments and drive on, drive off loading and unloading had cut costs dramatically and made mass marketing of Japanese cars in the U.S. economically feasible. The world could not have gone to the oil standard and imported billions of barrels of Middle East oil annually without the development of supertankers and highly sophisticated offloading systems. Hong Kong could not have sold its consumer goods efficiently everywhere in the world without the rapid development of containerization systems, and the Philippines could not have joined the electronic world of producing tiny components without modern air freight transport developments. Real transport and materials handling costs have declined dramatically in the past thirty years, making possible a world trade explosion.

In many countries, physical distribution facilities are not very good, and questions of building new ports, airports, highways, and railways are always important. This is one area where the World Bank, along with many private banks, have lent vast sums for improvement. It is not uncommon to find in some Third World country that more locally produced grain is eaten by rats, destroyed by rain, or rotted in the fields than is actually consumed. The richer the country, the more likely it will have excellent warehouse facilities, highways, rail networks, and good ports, to say nothing of excellent phone systems and cable networks for computers. But physical distribution practices must be adapted to available facilities. A firm marketing frozen foods might find that its market is restricted because of shortages of proper warehousing and transport equipment. In this market, canned goods would get more attention.

Countertrade and barter: Many countries have exchange controls, and many do not have hard currencies available to buy foreign products. But such countries do have some products, and they may offer firms these products in trade for some needed item. Thus Indonesia has traded oil to West Germany for industrial plants, and Lebanon once traded oranges to the Soviet Union for trucks. This barter is now called countertrade, and larger firms often find themselves faced with the decision of whether or not to involve themselves in such trade. If the MNC does, it has the problem of what to do with the commodity it receives. This can be easy. A petrochemical firm using large amounts of oil might find a deal attractive that offers it oil. It can be very difficult, as when a moviemaker is offered chrome ore for the rights to various movies. Few moviemakers know much about the market for chrome ores!

Governments often get involved in such transactions. Communist countries like countertrade, and a capitalist country hungry for exports and jobs might be offered something to trade. The capitalist country might encourage some firms to trade, which can be nice, since the local government may well pay in cash, and try to dump the received commodities itself. Variations on this theme are common and growing in the 1980's.

A real problem in countertrade is that the products offered typically are overpriced. It is common to find trades occurring where both sides inflate the prices enormously. If the price were right, the product could be sold for cash. Only when someone (usually a government) keeps the price too high do the goods fail to sell. But countertrade is enormously attractive to government planners, because they often don't trust markets. Product quality is also a big problem, since one reason the goods offered might not sell is that they are of low quality. Those trucks Lebanon received from the Soviet Union many years ago were real dogs, and virtually unsalable at any price in Lebanon, which at that time could afford to import high quality products from Western countries, and did. But the deal was politically popular, since it disposed of surplus oranges at apparently high prices.

Influencing Key Marketing Variables: The above marketing areas are problems because they affect the critical marketing variables. Thus we want more market research done to know about demographic variables which affect sales. We want to streamline and improve our physical distribution network to provide lower costs and prices, and to provide better services for customers, which will lead to sales gains. Our distributor agreements are important because they will affect prices, product availability, and customer tastes and preferences. If we can build up well known and reputable brands for a given market, we may well develop loyal customers. The basic idea is to get these marketing problem areas structured in a way which will optimize sales. To do this, each culture and country presents special problems, and each solution to marketing problems will be somewhat different as a result.

Export Marketing

The traditional form of international marketing was the sale of goods to foreigners. It is still extremely important, and a major world growth area. Since World War II, governments of every political persuasion have agreed to lower trade barriers and open new markets. In return, they obtain access to foreign markets for their own goods. All of this would be very encouraging to David Ricardo and other early English economists who first worked out the theory of comparative advantage. This theory suggests that if each country specializes in what it is good at, and imports what it does not do so well, then all countries will be better off economically. The parallel growth in world incomes as international trade increases suggests that these early theorists were correct.

The key constraints are international. Tariffs and import quotas are most important, and balance of payments considerations influence government decisions. Because these constraints can be changed by any government, there is endless intercountry horsetrading. No government will give an advantage to foreign sellers unless it receives something in return. Thus when the EC was formed, the member nations agreed to reduce tariffs and most other trade barriers to zero, in return for all other EC countries doing the same. Each country gains access to five others at the beginning, and now each has access to eight others.

Other customs unions have attempted to do the same, and GATT is another example of an international organization devoted to reducing trade barriers. Countries also often make bilateral agreements with other countries to increase trade. Because exports generate foreign exchange and help the balance of payments, most countries are interested in expanding them, although the return price of allowing imports is not too nice. But it must be paid.

Exports generate employment, while imports reduce local employment. In periods of world recession, as 1981-83, it is not surprising to find new efforts at protectionism, since the classical view of the world is so production oriented. The ideal situation, if one listened to such classicists, would be to export everything and import nothing, thus starving to death in a short time. But wow, all workers would have jobs! A more sophisticated view might hold that consumption is most important, and if some crazy country was willing to sell you everything (on credit), and take nothing in return, you would be much better off. These comments are not irrelevant to the United States at present, since this country runs about a $50 to $100 billion deficit in commodities trade per year. In effect, foreigners are willing to take dollars as credit to provide Americans with a higher standard of living. Of course American auto workers are unemployed...there really is no free lunch. But few Americans are aware that because so many other countries are desperately trying to create employment, they live perhaps one to three percent better than they otherwise would. No one ever argued that the world is logical.

Countries usually have some government body interested in expanding exports, given their perceived importance. In the United States, the Department of Commerce has international field representatives and produces much information, including publications designed to help American firms export. The American government, like all developed country governments, also has an export guarantee program which provides export credit insurance. Since smaller firms often do not have the expertise to make foreign sales or to maneuver through the very complicated export documentation jungle, such assistance is necessary. Private firms get involved as export marketing representatives, freight forwarders, documentation experts, financial services, and many others. Examination of the yellow pages of a major port phone book will show dozens or even hundreds of such specialists.

Countries may reduce tariffs, but paperwork goes on. One estimate puts the added cost of exports at ten percent of total shipment value. Much of this cost is in extra paperwork, since through the centuries an incredible array of special documents has been created to cover foreign shipments. Export declarations, sight drafts, bills of lading, consular invoices, special sanitary certificates, and thousands of other special documents are required. Most require special clerical and technical expertise to get right, which costs lots of money. Remember the classical position which holds that local consumers really shouldn't buy imported products. If costs are high, imports will be lower, which is terrific. This is one area where it is easy to add costs and very difficult to reduce them, since most governments love the mess. An often undiscussed problem is that corruption flourishes in such an atmosphere. When no importer can possibly comply with all requirements, a tip to the relevant official gets one's goods through customs.

Thus in one large African country, over 90 percent of the future civil servants in the training institute wanted to work in customs. A cynical local observer noted that for those fortunate enough to be assigned there, at a pay rate of about $200 per month, millionairedom was assured within two years. He could prove it by noting how many junior customs clerks lived in $100,000 per year luxury apartments and drove Mercedes. Officials making perhaps $100,000 per year on the side are not likely to encourage reform. It perhaps is not irrelevant that in late 1983 this country had a military takeover, the goal of which was to get corruption down to some workable levels.

Many smaller firms are active exporters or importers. Virtually any manfacturer can get into the export business, although relatively few do, given the problems noted above. Foreign customers also know little about the thousands of small speciality firms unless each company makes some effort to inform them. Governments usually help, through trade fairs and foreign publications.

The actual marketing problems encountered, once the goods are in a foreign country, are very similar to the ones we have already discussed in this chapter. In many markets, one curious asset foreign producers have is the steady internationalization of the total market. Thus surveys suggest that younger Americans don't much care where things come from, as long as they meet the consumers' needs, while older Americans, remembering long gone wars and hypernationalism generated by them, still prefer American made products to some extent. As the years go by, it is more important to provide proper products than to declare where they come from. A good foreigner can win. In effect, consumers' preferences have shifted to the advantage of the best, away from country of origin. Such major behavioral shifts suggest that the future may be even more international than the past.

Tourism

Another important element in any country's balance of payments is tourism. As foreigners visit your country, they spend money for transportation, food, lodging, and gifts. A nice part of this business is that it requires little new investment if the country is blessed with interesting historic monuments, ruins, churches, or spectacular scenery. Facilities used by tourists, such as buses, trains, and airports will be built in any case, and only additional hotels are needed. Countries as diverse as Spain, Norway, Brazil, Switzerland, The Bahamas, and Egypt have long benefitted from such tourist expenditures. One could argue that the Egyptian pyramids were the best business investment ever made. What other investment has paid off steadily for over 5,000 years?

Much tourism marketing is done by governments, and most countries now have a department of tourism, which promotes the country abroad. Often such country organizations will hire the best American or European advertising agencies to promote the delights of a trip, and ads look much like similar materials in private fields. Countries will also spend much time and money making sure that the quality of a trip is satisfactory. Hotels should be clean and reasonably priced, and no one likes to get mugged or otherwise be inconvenienced when travelling. Officials even try to be polite, and local propaganda stresses being nice to foreigners who provide so much local income and employment. Note the subtle political question here. A foreigner who goes home and talks to friends about how nice the local citizens were is in effect an informal ambassador for a country, and officials are not unaware of the implications of such positive impressions.

Many private firms are also involved in tourism and do their best to promote it. Airlines, both public and private, have a major interest in foreign travel, as do shipping companies and hotel chains. Marketing efforts take familiar forms, with special emphasis placed on influencing local behavioral patterns. An ad for a sunny beach in Trinidad placed in a Chicago or Bremen paper in January can definitely influence behavior!

All key marketing variables are involved in this problem. A country with a cheap currency and good climate can sell on a price basis; more affluent persons with high incomes can gamble on the Riviera or take safaris in Kenya; and some areas gain customer favor, while others lose their attractiveness. A good marketer has the same problems in market research, taste changing, and organization problems as other firms. And marketing success typically doesn't just happen. It is cause by hard work and efficient activities.

Conclusion

We can barely scratch the surface of this broad area here. We have tried to suggest some of the major problems in international marketing, but each point would require considerable involvement and research to cover well. The key problem is to mesh the firm's internal marketing plans and activities with whatever environment it faces. Since much marketing involves legal, behavioral, and economic constraints, changes in any of these will lead quickly to internal firm changes to make the company perform more efficiently.

Perhaps more than in any other functional area, marketing is keenly studied and changed frequently to meet market realities. Firms have very quick and accurate marketing feedback, since they know almost immediately if marketing techniques being tried have any effect on sales. If they do not, or if sales increases are not as large as can be reasonably expected, then change is certain.

Questions for Discussion

1.   Your company is considering the possibility of introducing its television sets into a European country. If the market seems good, the sets will be manufactured in the country.

What demographic data would you want to know before you decided to go ahead with this project?

Would your answer be any different if this new market were the United States? Why or why not?

2.   A major Japanese fast food restaurant chain is thinking about starting a similar chain in the Midwestern United States. The initial plan calls for ten such restaurants in major cities. They would serve Japanese style food. The company has noticed that American tourists in Japan enjoy this food very much, and it figures that if Americans would buy the Japanese style food in Japan, they will buy it at home.

Do you think that this is a good idea? Why or why not? How would you evaluate American taste for Japanese type food in the Midwest?

3.   A successful New York advertising agency is thinking of setting up a branch in Paris. They feel that by now, French and West European tastes are so similar to the American that they can successfully use the same kinds of sales promotions and advertising that they now use in the United States.

Do you think that this is a correct assumption? Why or why not?

4.   A major American cosmetics firm with branches in many countries has noted that even in very poor countries, its lipstick sales seem to take off just as soon as the country gets just a bit above the base subsistance level. Why do you think that this is true? What kinds of personal tastes are being demonstrated here?

5.   Your company is selling agricultural machinery abroad.   It manufactures these specialized machines in the United States and exports them.

Pick any country which interests you and do some research about the kinds of documents you might need to export one of these machines to this country.   Consider such items as bills of lading, export declarations, financial documents, import permits, and other necessary items.

Now consider selling a similar machine in the next state. What kinds of documents do you need? Which sale is the easiest?

6. Your own state is very interested in promoting exports, since sales mean more jobs and income for local residents. Pick any local industry which interests you and consider the problem of promoting sales in Great Britain. What kinds of market data would you like to obtain before you started selling? Why?

7. Now you have made the sale in Great Britain (Question 6), you have to get it there. What transportation options do you have from where the factory is to the final destination in Manchester, England? Which options seem most economic? Consider all movements, from the plant door to the customer's loading dock in Manchester.

8. An American margarine manufacturer built a small plant to supply its Turkish market. Because the Turks rarely used American style bread (theirs is a flat disk about the size of a small pizza), and because Turks were unaccustomed to spreading anything on bread, the company felt that the market would be limited to a few sophisticated Turks who had lived in foreign countries, plus local European and American residents.

To the company's surprise, sales skyrocketed within a few months. The company had to expand the Turkish plant seven times in five years to meet demand. It turned out that Turks bought cubes of margarine and cut off slices to eat with nothing. They liked the taste, the product was attractively priced, and it was easy to carry for long distances while traveling on pack animals in the interior.

Analyze this incident from the standpoint of consumer tastes. What did this company miss when it first took a look at this market? What key behavioral facts turned out to be different in Turkey as compared to the United States?

9. Another American company had a $50,000 shipment of paper towels seized and burned in one Arab country. The company's symbol was a six pointed star. Arab customs officials argued that this was the Jewish star of David, which represented Israel. Since all Israeli products were banned in this country, the shipment was destroyed.

How could a company spot such problems in advance? Take any foreign country you choose and see if you can figure out what types of symbols, tabus, or words might be considerd offensive. Is this an easy task?

Supplementary Readings

Carson, David. INTERNATIONAL MARKETING: A COMPARATIVE SYSTEMS APPROACH. New York: Wiley, 1967.

Cateora, Philip R. and Hess, John M. INTERNATIONAL MARKETING, FOURTH EDITION. Homewood, IL: Richard D. Irwin, 1979.

Fayerweather, John. INTERNATIONAL MARKETING. Englewood Cliffs, NJ: Prentice-Hall, 1965.

Heck, Harold J. INTERNATIONAL TRADE: A MANAGEMENT GUIDE. New York: American Management Association, 1972.

Kahler, Reul and Kramer, Roland L. INTERNATIONAL MARKETING: 4TH EDITION. Cincinnati: South-Western, 1977.

Keegan, Warren J. MULTINATIONAL MARKETING MANAGEMENT. Englewood Cliffs, NJ: Prentice-Hall, 1974.

Robock, Stefan H. and Simmonds, Kenneth. INTERNATIONAL BUSINESS AND MULTINATIONAL ENTERPRISE. Homewood, IL: Richard D. Irwin, 1973. Chapters 13 and 19.

Root, Franklin R. ENTRY STRATEGIES FOR FOREIGN MARKETS. New York: AMCOM, 1977.

Terpstra, Vern. INTERATIONAL MARKETING, 2D EDITION. New York: Dryden Press, 1978.

Terpstra, Vern. INTERNATIONAL DIMENSIONS OF MARKETING. Boston: Kent, 1982.

Wiechmann, Wrick E. MARKETING MANAGEMENT IN MULTINATIONAL FIRMS. New York: Praeger, 1976.

Chapter 12
MNC Strategies: Production

Introduction

International production management is not widely discussed. Few universities have courses in the subject, and only a few writers have examined the problem. Apparently most people regard production management as being similar to physics or mathematics, namely a precise, scientific field which is universal in application. If a firm buys a machine tool to cut metal in Taiwan, then there is no difference in cutting metal in Chicago. Hence a student who knows production managemement well in the United States can immediately move to Taiwan and do exactly the same thing with the same efficiency.

The truth is a bit different. Production management is to some extent culture bound, and because it is, firms make environmental adjustments to do as well as they can. Often, particularly if the cultures are widely different, efficiency can vary enormously. The authors have personally seen cases in Third World countries where the same machines produced perhaps one tenth as much as they did in their home country. Such production differentials merit examination.

Global Optimization in Production and Procurement

A company which is looking at the whole world can take full advantage of every opportunity each country offers. Some countries may have low cost, disciplined labor; in this case, it makes sense to locate labor intensive processes here. Others have highly skilled work forces; here, automated and capital intensive processes can be located. Another country may have low cost supplies of some key input, such as electric power or proper components; here will be located processes which heavily rely on such inputs. Where most, but not quite all inputs are available, the situation can be corrected by importing the key missing item. Where most types of labor are available, but certain technical knowledge is not, skilled men and women can be sent to cover the deficiency.

Few firms have completely realized the potential of such a global system, but many are moving in this direction. One major problem is that this entire area is subject to change without notice, as various countries apply new tariffs and quotas to imports, or restrict the flow of key personnel through changing visa requirements. Moreover, changing markets for many products require constant change in the production system. But the rapid move toward global systems now means that purely domestic production systems are becoming obsolete in many fields. The new car you buy, which is an American or German product, may have axles made in Brazil, electrical components from Taiwan, an engine from Mexico, and be assembled in Canada. Often very large profits can be made by planning the firm's production system in this global manner.

This spells trouble for many purely local firms. If there really are economies of scale, and if major companies are in a position to take full advantage of them, the local firms will be unable to compete. Such considerations make governments very nervous, since they lose control of the companies, but the gains in terms of employment, tax revenues, and export earnings are often so large as to tempt the governments to go along. Moreover, even local firms can buy foreign made components from intermediaries, and they often do.

One example of this new thinking is Ford's efforts to produce a light vehicle for Asian markets. The potential market is huge, but no one country in the market area is large enough to handle the entire production and procurement job. Moreover, each country has (or had) high tariffs to encourage local manufacture of motor vehicles. Ford suggested that a number of countries cooperate in a joint venture, financed and owned by Ford, to produce this car. One country would have the transmission plant; another the body stamping plant; a third the electrical components production facilities; and still another the engine plant. Since each plant would be producing at relatively high volume, it would be quite efficient.

But in order to make the plan work, each country would have to agree to allow free trade in all other components and finished vehicles. Ford proposed that each country make the necessary constraint modifications so that all could benefit by not only having new production facilities, but also by having cheaper vehicles. The amount of bargaining which this proposal led to was extensive, but now the vehicle is being produced. Here a regional plan by a private firm is pushing nominally independent and suspicious countries into a regional production system, for their own (and Ford's) benefit.

American auto companies are far along in this global concept, but European and Japanese firms are following the same path, in part because it makes economic sense, and in part because they have to. Thus in 1984, Japanese auto production has stagnated, since other countries will not allow unrestricted penetration of their markets by Japanese producers. The companies have a choice: they can stagnate, or they can build production facilities and integrate along the lines noted above, including using many components built in other countries. So the Japanese companies are now setting up local assembly plants, manufacturing facilities, and prodding local components suppliers into meeting Japanese quality control standards. Joint ventures are also common. Ironically, American Motors is now controlled by a French auto producer, and General Motors and Toyota at this writing are considering a major American joint venture.

Another automobile industry example of possible large international production integration is the development by several major companies of a world car. Historically, autos designed for the European or Japanese market were very different than those built for the American markets. But rising gas prices and government mandated mileage figures in the U.S. have gradually pushed American design closer to the European. Now a major company can design a car for all markets, and it also can produce the vehicle, or any of its components, in any economic location. Possibilities for cost saving through worldwide production integration are potentially enormous. Various components can be produced in the most economic location, shipped to other countries for assembly, and sold in still other countries. Only the biggest firms can afford the multi-billion dollar development costs of such vehicles, and quite possibly this development may eliminate many smaller auto producers from major world markets.

Production Management

Behavioral Production Management Problems: While the machines may be identical or similar, the workers, managers, and technicians are not. Educational and behavioral constraints are very different around the world, and as a result things which can be taken for granted in one place may be very different in another.

One simple illustration is in basic literacy. Labor is usually cheap in countries with large percentages of adult illiteracy, and companies have taken advantage of this fact by installing major mass production, assembly line type operations in places where cost advantages can be gained. But as the assembly lines are set up and labor hired, just how do you run a line with illiterates? The problem at first glance seems trivial. After all, workers only tighten a bolt, or rivet one piece. But how do you pay illiterates? Checks won't work very well. So the payroll department, along with necessary guards for cash, begins to look different than in the United States or Japan. Some machines have instructions printed in English or German, but the workers can't read, and if they could, these languages would not be the proper ones. Foremen have new tasks in instruction as a result. Try finding the men's room in a country with a non-Latin alphabet, and you will perceive the problems of an illiterate trying to find his way around a large factory with lots of warning signs, such as HIGH VOLTAGE, KEEP OUT, DANGER, INFLAMMABLE, and innumerable others.

Even in wealthier countries, foreign workers may create problems. The West Germans employ many Turkish workers, and these men and women must be specially instructed or a mechanism must be set up for translations. In the United States, millions of workers' first language is Spanish, and similar problems arise. Such problems cost money, and this means that those cheap wages aren't really so cheap after all.

Safety is a very real problem in such situations. It is common to discover that industrial accident rates are closely related to the education and training of the work force, and laborers with low educational achievements have very high accident rates. Few people aside from skilled safety engineers and government workmen compensation experts pay much attention, and these people are very culture bound. What may work well in Indiana may fail in Wuhan, with the result that many men and women are maimed and killed. Yet proper safety precautions in many countries have not yet been thought about very much. MNCs tend to have much better safety records than local firms, largely because they have had much more experience at home with proper safety precautions. This is yet one more example of technological transfer that few know or care about.

All of this adds up to major productivity problems in many countries. Machines are machines, but people are not the same. It is common to find that taken for granted activities, such as oiling machinery regularly, is not done in some foreign country, and what would be a twenty dollar expense in the United States or France becomes a five thousand dollar expense abroad. Why? Not because the worker was not conscientious, but because he did not know. His ability to relate cause and effect was much below expectations for French or American workers.

One result is to find very highly automated plants in countries with very low wage rates. A few key technicians, often imported, do most of the work, and machines do the rest. When firms are asked about such activities, we hear stories about how unreliable the local work force is. What the company is really saying is that the costs of training workers up to minimally acceptable levels, in terms of being reliable and not breaking up the equipment, is higher than the cost of buying very expensive automatic machinery. Such attitudes have very important implications for poorer countries that are trying to modernize and develop local human skills.

One reason such uneconomic input mixes can happen is that production is perhaps the least well understood firm function by most politicians. Few technologists or engineers hold political power, and many leaders are fascinated by imageries of machines in action, by replacing men with highly automatic equipment, with dreams of being a major industrial power. Often import controls have the effect of making machinery cheap (after all, this is what industrialization is all about), and local laws make labor relatively expensive. After all, common humanity makes minimum wages and expensive pension benefits necessary. But such laws and taxes means that only a few favored locals get good jobs, while the rest lounge around outside the new plants. Far too often, the politics of production leads to uneconomic and unrealistic results.

A major advantage MNCs have over local firms is that they can select from the whole world the proper mix of productive resources. If a local firm lacks certain key technicians, it may be unable to get production lines running smoothly, but the MNC can bring in the experts from other countries to solve problems. If critical patents of technologies are held by only a few major firms, small local companies may be unable to buy what is needed, or they may be unaware even that solutions to their problems exist. The MNCs can obtain what they need, wherever in the world it is.

Procurement

Procurement is one of the most rational firm activities. The company needs raw materials, power, components, and other items to manufacture its products. For such complicated items as machine tools or trucks, literally tens of thousands of items must be manufactured or purchased. The problem is one of buying at the best price, consistent with quality and reliability of supply. Many people do not realize that even industrial giants buy huge quantities of components from outside suppliers. Thus a typical modern Japanese auto firm will buy over 70 percent of the value of the finished vehicle in this manner. As the firms move to a global orientation, the supply sources can be anywhere in the world.

One cultural problem is to determine what a supplier means when he makes a promise. Anyone can promise anything to get an order, but missing some minor component can shut down an entire factory, and a single poor quality component can make a vehicle totally unreliable. Hence reliability and quality, rather than price, may be determining, and foreign firms which can do a job for less might not get the order unless they can demonstrate that they are totally reliable. Political and economic uncertainties also can prove irksome. One makes a good deal with a foreign supplier, only to discover that the country's currency has risen in world markets, or a strike by a union has disrupted shipments at the port. Few procurement experts are also expert in forecasting events in far off countries as yet, but many are learning.

Behavioral patterns also matter. It is quite common these days for Americans to discover, to their dismay, that Japanese buyers simply do not believe that they can produce components for cars and trucks at high quality levels consistant with Japanese quality control standards. While this is statistically provable (or disprovable), much of the annoyance stems from simple lack of confidence, and the need for proud American engineers and technicians to prove their competence, which has always been taken for granted in the U.S. Japanese buyers shouldn't behave like this! Such irritations are extremely common all over the world, and many a proud Indian engineer has gritted his teeth when some arrogant American implied that no Indian manufacturer could possibly produce to exhalted American quality control standards...

There is no guarantee in this very competitive world that if you say you're good, you're really good. Having to prove it can be a sobering experience.

Foreign procurement is heavily dependent on international constraints. If tariffs are raised, or new quotas imposed, the firm can get into supply trouble. Such uncertainties, when added to the usual supply problems procurement executives face in domestic dealings, also make firms hesitate. But if potential gains from foreign procurement are large, it may be worth taking the extra risks.

Foreign procurement can be used to minimize risks in certain situations as well. Some critical component may be produced by only one or two local firms, and strikes, monopolistic price increases, or natural disasters could cause prices to rise or supplies to be cut off.

By developing an optional supplier abroad, the firm can hedge against
such disasters. It is common in any case to have several suppliers for
important items, and having them in various countries can be a major
asset. Such a policy can also keep a government in line. A new tax
might not be imposed, if the government knows that the firm can shift to
outside suppliers, or union monopolies might not be so onerous.

Where large firms need huge quantities of raw materials, they can
be forced overseas to develop supplies through lack of resources in the
home country. American multinational oil companies got into many
countries for this reason, as did steel manufacturers looking for iron
ore, and copper fabricators seeking low cost supplies. Since raw
materials are where you find them, the company often has to work with
governments and cultures quite different from those at home. Perhaps a
majority of American and European operations in Third World countries
began as a search for supplies by integrated companies.

As with other firm functions, procurement is about the same
wherever a company operates. As it moves abroad, new risks emerge, as
noted above. As always, the firm must adjust to its environment, and
this means changing strategies and plans to reflect the different
situation, which leads to results somewhat different from those
experienced in a single country.

Procurement needs can also be used to advantage in working with a
variety of governments. Most countries want more manufacturing
facilities, and they are willing to trade various concessions to get
them. If an MNC has supply options, it can offer various countries
manufacturing facilities which fit reasonably into the company's plans.
In return, tax breaks, tariff reductions, and other concessions may be
obtained.

Research and Development

MNCs typically have major advantages in R & D work. These rapidly
growing firms historically were the most advanced, both in use of new
technology and in development of it. This is why the companies now are
MNCs. The typical MNC will have a long history of technical competence
and development of new products and processes, and it also will own many
patents and possess enormous technical know how.

Such firms also will have the necessary financial resources to
finance additional R & D. They are large enough to spread risks over
many products, processes, and areas, so if some research does not pay
off, the firm is not ruined. Local firms often are in an all or nothing
position on this point. If their one or two key developments do not
work out, the company can be destroyed.

The MNCs also are professionally managed, and the managers know
what is needed. They already have a long history of focused R & D,
where the company works on items that are needed and which can be sold
profitably when developed. An occasional inventor may stumble onto some
useful product, but bigger firms typically are working only in areas
where the highest probability of payout exists.

MNCs can also draw on all the world's talent for their projects. If a brilliant young Mexican scientist looks promising, he can work in New York or Brazil, or wherever the company needs his or her talents. If a project is having trouble in Nigeria, experts from other countries can come and do the necessary development work to get things moving properly.

Because the MNCs are so good at R & D work, it is common to find that one of their major assets is knowledge. Local firms, and even other MNCs, have to buy the necessary knowledge, in the form of manufacturing licenses, patent use rights, and sometimes renting key managers and technicians. Most countries feel that this technical work is of the greatest importance, and it makes them nervous to discover that so much of it is done in the United States and Japan. Even the postwar successes of Western European firms is not that impressive. What is needed is R & D work in the home country.

But R & D work tends to be located where the trained minds are, and this usually is in affluent countries, most notably the U.S. and Japan. It is not surprising to discover that these two countries have over 40 percent of their 18 year olds going on to university and college training, while in Western Europe, this figure ranges from 8 to 15 percent. In Third World countries, it ranges from 1 to 3 percent. It is difficult to attract any significant R & D work to a country which lacks such educational advantages, and American firms are often accused of intellectual imperialism. They also get accused of contributing to brain drains from poorer countries, since if that Mexican scientist does go to New York, Mexico has lost a highly skilled and creative mind, possibly for good.

Companies can use their R & D capabilities as a bargaining tool. If a country feels that it needs the technology badly, the firm can present a case for investment by noting how much the country will gain technically. In some cases, only a handful of firms will have the necessary knowledge and ability to carry out successful operations. The computer industry is a case in point. If you want this industry, you will have to deal with a handful of American and Japanese firms to get it. There are no other meaningful options.

A relatively new recognition of an old idea is also shaking up a world anxious to gain the benefits of the very latest technologies. Often smaller firms, most notably American ones, are the leaders in the very latest technologies. Quite a few creative geniuses don't want to work in large firms, and they don't have to. The American venture capital market is so well organized and anxious to back future winners that it is relatively easy for a brilliant scientist or engineer to obtain capital and develop new ideas. At the moment, the future seems to lie with silicon chips and genetics, and in these fields, a surprisingly large number of innovations come from these smaller, local firms. If the idea works, the founding genius is not just an MNC employee...he or she is a millionaire owner of a fast growing firm. If the firm fails, the genius can always work for a bigger firm, or try again.

The result is that non-Americans are frantically trying to figure out just what the magic is. They also try to beg (via aid programs), borrow (via buying patent rights), or steal (via industrial espionage) these new ideas. Even the diligent Japanese have been unable to match the creative outburst coming from the U.S. in the past decade, and Western Europe is far behind. The magic seems to lie in a totally open society, a good venture capital market, and many brilliant, trained people willing to take big risks. Easy immigration of hard working and well trained people from all over the world also helps. Many of the new high technology American firms were founded and developed by first generation immigrants. No other country has quite the same combination of favorable factors.

One could also add that many of these high tech ventures are started by women and minorities, who might be discriminated against in larger organizations, openly or subtlely. The numbers of Asian Americans that have succeeded in this way is quite large. Countries that spend much time and effort making sure that only the "right" people win may miss a lot of talent, and the homogeneous Japanese may have troubles with wild eyed nonconformists with weird ideas. Ironically, many of these adventurers were literally forced out of their native countries by wars, revolutions, or other discriminatory acts. The Vietnamese, Cubans, Iranians, and even Ethiopians now living in the United States make a huge contribution to American wealth, and their own countries do not want them back.

One postwar surprise has been that very few good R & D ideas have come out of communist countries. The U.S.S.R. and Eastern Europe, with large numbers of well trained engineers and scientists, should be able to generate many new industrial ideas, but they do not. The structure of closed societies apparently inhibits innovation, and with the possible exception of Soviet weaponry, virtually nothing comes out of the communist bloc which is desired by anyone else.

We tend to focus on high tech industry, but R & D can be at any level. Those new MNCs coming out of Hong Kong and India do not typically have the most advanced industrial ideas, but they do know how to produce bicycle parts efficiently in Bangladesh, or hand tools in Mexico. Such knowledge is far from trivial, and such firms also contribute to the spread of relevant technology. But few countries care much about such practical things. It is more fun and more dramatic to figure out how to start a new computer industry, even if the lower level technology is more relevant to local conditions.

It is widely forecast that we are at the edge of some new revolution created largely by those high tech industries. What might happen can only be conjectured, but it may well be true that within twenty years, those countries that control these new technologies will dominate the world militarily and economically. They probably will dominate it socially and informationally as well. For such prestige, many countries will strive mightily, and many will try to restructure their economies to match up with the new world to come. Already we have seen major changes in attitudes toward MNCs as a result of this point. Countries that a decade ago would have banned MNCs now welcome the high tech ones, and educational reforms occur everywhere.

No one is quite sure what the benefits of advanced technology may be, but most countries are eager to obtain their share. The advanced industries are where it's at in this modern world. MNCs, as usual, are in a position to get ahead of local firms in most countries in this field, since they have all the necessary assets to continue development.

Technology Transfer

Poorer countries, trying to analyze the causes of their relative poverty, often conclude that a major reason is their lack of modern technology. No visitor to a modern European, American, or Japanese factory can fail to be impressed by the remarkable technological processes, nor the obviously large technical knowledge companies operating these plants have. It is easy to conclude that if only this remarkable know how and technology could be transferred to poorer countries, they would no longer be poor. East Euroepan countries, along with the Soviet Union and China, examining their relative backwardness in many industrial areas, have reached the same conclusion.

The problem is thus seen as one of technological transfer. If the hardware can be transferred, all will be well. However, often missed is the more general organization and management dimension of these complex factories. A factory or a power plant is a visible, highly exciting object, worthy of close analysis. The products produced can be seen, touched, and enjoyed. But the personnel department is dullsville, as is marketing, purchasing, finance, and many other components of the modern corporation. Nothing much happens here except some routine paper shuffling. The machines and technology are what is needed!

Only when the hardware is transferred to another country and works badly, or doesn't even work, do people realize that production is just one link in a complex chain. Those machines have to be operated by trained people. If you can't find such persons, nothing happens well. The products have to be distributed and sold. If your marketing is done poorly, you end up with useless inventory stacked outside the plant. Working capital must be found and used properly. If it is not, the firm goes broke, has to obtain huge government subsides, or often discovers, far too late, that some insiders have stolen the money. If you can't buy the right components and get them delivered on time, no production occurs. In modern terminology, the countries often buy the hardware, forgetting that the software is equally critical. Hardware is easy to get; complex software, in the form of management knowledge, marketing, finance, and so on can be very difficult to obtain or learn.

What is often called technological transfer is more often management information transfer, and this is a much more difficult concept to grasp. Even if the machines are in place, it often is difficult to manage their use properly, and quite often a single factory is just one link in a very long and complex chain of production. The problem is made much more difficult by the imputed ethics inherent in this situation. Machines are value free, but finance, marketing, and other managerial functions are not. Countries that happily buy amoral machinery hesitate to use modern marketing or financial techniques, since these things reek of capitalistic decadence and decay. But if they do not utilize the latest software techniques, those machines just don't work very well.

Increasingly it is being seen that if you buy the capitalistic machines, you have to buy the software as well. Third World countries that bought it all, such as Taiwan and Hong Kong, do very well, while those that bought only the machines, such as Algeria and Cuba, have done rather poorly. East European communist states that tried cooperation agreements have largely failed to get full benefit from them. One major advantage of having MNCs all over your country is that they do bring it all, and one can learn much from seeing what they do. Open systems just work better, and in periods of rapid technical and scientific advance, as we now seem to be entering, those open systems work very well indeed.

But myths die hard, and many countries still stay closed, and they still try to buy the hardware and use it in their own way. Spies everywhere steal the blueprints and smuggle the chips into countries that then try reverse engineering, which is to work back to production from the product. Some of this works, but it rarely works well, and of course by the time the thief figures out last year's chip, some new and improved model will come out of Silicon Valley in California which is much better, or perhaps from some research operation in Tokyo. There is much debate and discussion now that those closed system countries, particularly those that are somewhat backwards technologically, will fall even farther behind if they persist in their current ways. Who would expect Iran to develop any new technology?

Country Production Problems

The Flight to Low Wages: In many industries, processes require mass production techniques, using many workers. Automation may be technically feasible, but economically impractical, given robot costs. Such things as sewing baseall covers and assembling TV tuners are examples of these situations.

In the past 30 years or so, a number of poorer countries have analyzed their advantages and concluded that about all they had to offer the world was a large supply of relatively cheap, disciplined labor. By allowing free access to these workers by foreign firms, it was possible to get some labor intensive industries in the country, and something is better than nothing. A job at forty cents an hour is a lot better than being an agricultrual worker and forty cents a day.

This strategy worked so well for many of the countries that their economies moved to ten percent per year income growth rates. Taiwan used to be one of the poorer countries of the world; now it is approaching the poorer European countries in income per capita. The companies which tried the technique found their costs falling rapidly and made money. In the end, everyone came out better off.

Everyone, that is, except the American, Japanese, or West European workers who used to do these things. In Japan, the very low unemployment rates created few problems, but in Europe and the U.S. objections were strenuous. American trade unions began to shift from their historic support of free trade to demands for more restrictions. At present, most American trade unions are pushing for higher import duties; tight quotas on labor intensive items such as textile manufactures, electronic components, and toys; and new taxes levied against MNCs who make profits in foreign countries. As heavier industries such as steel and autos came under similar competitive pressures in the 1980's, still more support for trade restrictions came from more unions.

West European countries have responded with higher quotas and tariffs against Japanese products, and some efforts to cut off labor intensive products from the newly industrializing Asian countries. Sluggish growth rates in Western Europe, plus some productivity gains in most industries, have led to the problem of absorbing new young workers into the workforce, and teenage unemployment has reached historic highs in most countries. Complicating West Europe's problems are the carefully constructed worker welfare measures, which translate into job security and reluctance to allow firms to discharge workers, plus the lack of extensive new high technology industries to absorb new workers. The teenagers in most West European countries do rather well by living on the dole, but there is very considerable concern that Western Europe may be creating a class of nonworkers, younger people who don't have and may never have jobs. Both the U.S. and West European countries have fairly high minimum wages as well, which makes firms reluctant to hire inexperienced workers. And in Western Europe, the extreme difficulty of firing workers makes both local firms and MNCs very reluctant to hire new workers. The result in the 1980's has been much higher levels of unemployment in both Western Europe and the U.S. than have existed historically.

Trade unions legitimately are concerned about their own workers, who are local. But their efforts to protect their own miss the possibility that by winning, they may lose. Suppose that the U.S. tries to be autarkic again and goes back to making home radio sets, an activity now virtually extinct. Costs, given American wage rates, would be extremely high. Americans will buy many fewer transistor radios at $59.95 than those now made in Taiwan and sold at $15.95. The U.S. can block off these Taiwanese sets, but they cannot block off Taiwanese sales to Brazil, Thailand, or anyplace else, so U.S. exports will be nil. The number of manufacturing jobs created will be far below expectations. It may well be that there will be a net decline in U.S. employment, since with these blockages, American port workers, truck drivers, salespersons, distributors, and others that used to handle those Taiwanese radios are now unemployed. The same phenomena may be observed in the Japanese auto imports to the U.S. American jobs saved in auto manufacturing could easily be offset by job losses in other parts of the economy.

In effect, unions, like others in any economy, have come face to face with the new open world economy. Historically, the U.S. was a semi-closed system; now it is fairly open. The more open it is, the more likely it will be that all Americans will discover the rest of the world, often in painful ways. The inevitable response to such pain is to try to return to our old ways, to cut off all foreign contacts, to go back to the days when our economy and our culture was unique and isolated. Unfortunately, it is highly unlikely that we can, given the scrambling of economies that has occurred in the past forty years.

About all one can say for the scrambling is that it helps avoid major wars, since these days, you probably have to negotiate with your potential enemies rather than fight them. Avoiding World War III may have been one odd result of Bretton Woods and those dreamers who built the postwar world economic order.

Exporting Jobs and Importing People: Countries such as the United States and Japan have very restrictive immigration laws, and few unskilled immigrants get in legally. In the U.S., millions get in illegally across the long Mexican border, but much effort is spent minimizing this flow. In Japan, there is serious discussion and planning for totally automated production systems, using only skilled technicians for planning and maintenance. Japan leads the world in robot use and production, which follows from its low unemployment rate, its efforts to upgrade people skills through education, and its immigration restrictions.

As noted above, when both these countries have labor intensive work to do, it is exported. In effect, the jobs are sent to places where such workers exist. This can create serious problems for the unskilled and semiskilled workers at home, as we noted above, but it does lead to a multinational firm pattern, together with the pattern of using local Hong Kong, Taiwan, and South Korean firms as suppliers of labor intensive products. The U.S. was well into this pattern in the 1950's, which explains why there are now so many American based MNCs, while the Japanese got into the pattern in the 1970's, when Japan began to run short of unskilled labor.

Another way to solve the problem of obtaining unskilled and semiskilled workers is to move the people to the jobs. Locals will tend to get the best jobs they can, and if there is a shortage of labor, it will show up first in the dirty, monotonous, and disagreeable types of work. Western Europe, suffering in the 1960's from wartime loss of people, and enjoying a runaway economic boom, began to import people. West Germany, at that time the most successful economy in Western Europe, first began in the late 1950's to import East Germans; few remember that the Berlin wall was built largely to prevent most East Germans from moving to West Germany. After the Wall was built in 1961, West Germany turned to Italy. The EC pact provided for free flows of workers, and there was a surplus of Italian labor at that time. Going to West Germany and earning West German wages was an attractive option for ambitious, unskilled Italians.

What Western Europe was doing at that time was replicating, in a superior manner, the American mass production pattern. The EC and booming exports provided the new mass market, and the Europeans had the American model to use. This model requires large numbers of industrial workers, which the Americans got off the farm in the 1920's and even earlier. Immigrants also did their part. But Western Europe in 1965 had few surplus farmers, and as the boom continued, country after country imported workers from poorer areas. The Italians were all absorbed by 1970; the West Germans then went to Yugoslavia, Spain, Portugal, Greece, and finally Turkey to get more workers. France relied on Algerians, while Benelux, Switzerland, and Sweden relied mainly on Yugoslavs and Turks. Before the boom ended in the late 1970's, perhaps eight million guest workers were involved in production all over Western Europe.

These foreign workers, usually unskilled and poorly educated, came to work. Typically they did not bring their families, signing one or two year contracts. The host country normally assured them and their own government that they would receive standard pay for the job they did, and they were entitled to all workmen's benefits, such as medical care, unemployment compensation, and pension rights. This was a very attractive option for a young Turk, who might have earned a few dollars a day at home, but could earn five to eight dollars an hour bolting Volkswagens together.

But problems inevitably arise, and older Americans, having seen the flood of immigration before 1920, know all about them. Ghettoes arise, as the foreigners cluster together; vigorous, young unattached males chase local girls; housing is poor; and food is strange. In the plants, safety records deteriorate as foremen struggle with translation problems for men who read only Croatian or Turkish, instead of German. Some men eventually bring their families, and children have troubles in school with unfamiliar languages and customs. Americans can only nod, reflect on their own melting pot experience, and forecast more difficulties.

European trade unions did not protest much about these guest workers for two basic reasons. One is that the recipient countries had very low unemployment rates until the 1980's, often going below one percent. There were plenty of better jobs for good Germans when the assembly lines filled up with Yugoslavs and Turks. The second reason is fear of inflation. Many living Germans can remember two major hyperinflations (1922 and 1948), when prices increased several thousand percent per MINUTE, wiping out everyone. When companies run out of labor, wage rates skyrocket, and even union men are destroyed in the inflation which follows.

MNCs and local firms live with government policy on this point. If the country allows immigration, Ford and General Motors will recruit Turks and Yogoslavs along with Mercedes and Volkswagen. If the country restricts immigration, then quite likely the MNCs will go abroad in search of the right kinds of labor. It is likely that serious immigration restrictions will be a powerful force pushing bigger local firms abroad, since they cannot obtain certain key conditions in the home country. The overall effect of these West European immigration policies in the 1960's and 1970's was to encourage big local firms to stay home and import labor. They got what they needed locally. American and Japanese firms went abroad. If rapid growth and expansion of MNCs turns out to be crucial in the next twenty years, one odd result of this West European labor policy will be to penalize those countries that followed it.

Large scale importation of cheap labor also helps exports and international competitiveness. It perhaps is no accident that West Germany, the Netherlands, and Switzerland, all major labor importers, are among the most efficient industrial exporters. Wage rates do not rise as fast, and inflation rates stay lower than in rival countries.

Whether a country has a policy of importing labor or not is a question far beyond the usual study of production management. Yet this policy will have powerful effects on labor supplies and costs, which in turn will directly influence all of the critical business production elements. Here is one example of how the international constraints directly affect all firms' planning.

Note also how these labor policies subtly ' affect industrial policy as well. Western Europe did extremely well until the late 1970's following this labor import policy, meaning that there was no particular pressure to develop new technologies or new industries. But when the new high tech world began to develop in earnest in the 1980's, the Europeans were far behind. The older American model, based on cheap energy and semi and unskilled labor, looks very weak compared to the silicon chip and genetic world to come. But semiskilled workers are not a major factor in this new world, and Europe is even more vulnerable to industrial competition from lower wage Asiatic countries than the United States or Japan. Their major industries are simpler and easier to replicate than those new high tech industries.

As the world recession continued in the 1980's, and as unemployment rates rose rapidly in Western Europe, many guest workers went home, but millions remain. European countries have an obligation to these people, and their governments are not anxious to deport men who have worked hard and well. Moreover, many come from other EC countries and have a right to remain. In the end, the labor import policy may turn out to be a millstone for many countries, although it led to enormous economic progress just a few years earlier.

Conclusion

Once again, we observe how the globally oriented firm has major advantages. Instead of being trapped in one country, with whatever advantages and disadvantages the culture may have, it can plan its production operations globally. If one country offers something attractive, the firm will take advantage of it. Provincial firms can get into serious trouble because they cannot do this.

But such global optimizing creates opposition from local forces. Trade unions, seeing jobs being lost, will object; governments, seeing investments and jobs going to other countries, get very nervous; and other countries, seeing new investments which might dominate the country or link it to an unstable world economic system, might also object. Even international agencies, such as the United Nations, study the problem, aware that benefits and costs are being distributed around the world in a somewhat random manner. But this is the only world we have, and it was not stuck together in any rational, well planned way. The key roleplayers, given their own interest and constraints, have to work out their futures as best they can.

Looming murkily above all of this is the possible massive restructuring of industry created by new technologies, most notably in electronics and genetics. Most governments feel that without high tech industries, they will fall behind, but few countries have the necessary conditions for creating such industries. MNCs, well aware that creativity can exist in very small companies, often very local, also are nervous, since so much of their advantages stem from massive economies of scale. If the microcomputer and other new technological developments wipe out many economies of scale, where will the MNCs be? Trapped with obsolete technologies might be one answer that is unpleasant. No one, not even powerful MNCs, are exempt from rapid change in production and technology.

Questions for Discussion

1. Many union leaders would like to see American legislation which would prevent "runaway" plants. They propose that American firms be prohibited from going to cheap labor countries with new plants. If such legislation were passed and enforced the net result, among other things, would be to bring back to the U.S. many dreary, monotonous, hard production line jobs. As was mentioned in this chapter, there would not be as many as the unions might like, because all export production would continue in the low wage countries. If someone is willing to do a job for thirty cents an hour, and you have to pay $5 for it, your external competitive position will not be good, unless your productivity is very high. In these cases, it is usually not.

Since these foreign countries which do not have the American plants would have fewer dollars to spend, we could also anticipate some decrease in demand from abroad for such American exports as jet engines, computers, trucks, diesel engines, earthmovers, and so on. These exports are produced by quite highly paid and skilled people. We would in efect add quite a few low skilled assembly line type jobs in labor intensive industries, while slowing the rate of growth in high skilled, high pay industries.

Do you think that this strategy is a good idea, given the present and future composition of the American work force? At present, we have a shortage of highly skilled people in many sectors, but a huge surplus of unskilled workers. The teenage unemployment rate is over 20 percent.

2. Suppose you were given the job of teaching an illiterate, but quite intelligent adult from a poor country how to drive a car. This person, after you finish your job, should be able to follow traffic signs, get a driver's license in your state, be able to control the car properly, and be able to perform simple maintenance operations, such as check the oil and water.

Another part of your job is to train a young American high school graduate in exactly the same thing.

What extra things would you have to do to complete the training job on the illiterate, as compared to the American? List every extra step.

Many poorer countries have adult illiteracy rates of from 20 to 60 percent. Their labor is very cheap compared to American labor. Is it REALLY cheap? Why or why not?

3. Some people in your city are beginning to press for changes in the American immigration laws. They would like to make legal Mexican immigration, in order that they can hire such people to do the dirty

jobs around town. If this were done, such nasty jobs as garbage collection, dull assembly line jobs, household help, short order cooks, agricultural labor, and so on, could be done for about a dollar an hour. The Mexicans would be better off, since wages in Mexico average less than two dollars a day. Americans would be better off, since not only would the dirty work by done by someone else, but it would be cheap.

Would you support this effort to import Mexican workers? Why or why not?

4. The West German government has recently decided that they just cannot allow more foreign workers in the country. Already there are so many that the whole country is beginning to look a bit like a Mediterranean country instead of Germany. But because they will not import more labor, this means that their firms will have to expand multinationally, much like American firms have done.

A midwestern American state, observing this trend, has set up an office in West Germany to try to encourage such reverse investment. The state reasons that if the German firms want to invest in the U.S., the investment might as well be in this state. The sales pitch offered is similar to that presented by any Chamber of Commerce toward getting American firms to locate there. The state gives data on tax rates, power supplies, transportation facilities, labor costs, and so on.

Do you think that this is a good idea? Would you, as a taxpayer, support this German office?

As a matter of fact, many parts of the Midwest now have hourly wage rates lower than those paid in West Germany right now. Should the state advertise this fact, or try to hide it? Why?

5. An American friend of yours who studied accounting has been offered a job in Australia at a salary ten percent higher than he could get at home. The job is with a major Australian firm.

Should he take this job? Is this un-American to turn your back on your country like this? Why or why not?

Is this case any different than the case of an unskilled Turkish worker who takes a job in West Germany at twice the wage rate he could get at home? Why or why not?

6. A small country with a per capita GNP of about $1,000 per year is interested in developing research capabilities in nuclear physics. The country feels that if it does so, it can sell such technology to other countries for use in power generation in the coming years of energy famine.

What kinds of skilled people, production facilities, research institutes, universities, and other assets would this country have to develop it it wanted to be successful in this field? What are the odds against success, if these facilities are not now in existence?

7. A major American tractor manufacturer now buys most of its

axles in Brazil. The price is right, and quality is excellent.

What new risks does this company face in buying from this foreign source, as compared to a local one? Why?

8. What possible hedges might you suggest to the tractor manufacturer in question 7 to avoid serious supply disruptions?

Supplementary Readings

Baranson, Jack. AUTOMOTIVE INDUSTRIES IN DEVELOPING COUNTRIES. Baltimore: The Johns Hopkins Press, 1969.

Baranson, Jack. THE JAPANESE CHALLENGE TO U.S. INDUSTRY. Lexinton, MA: Lexington Books, 1981.

Baranson, Jack. TECHNOLOGY AND THE MULTINATIONALS. Lexington, MA: Lexington Books, 1978.

Buffa, Elwood S. MODERN PRODUCTION/OPERATIONS MANAGEMENT. New York: Wiley, 1980.

Hirsch, Seev. LOCATION OF INDUSTRY AND INTERNATIONAL COMPETITIVENESS. Oxford: Clarendon Press, 1967.

Hufbauer, G.C. and Adler, F. M. OVERSEAS MANUFACTURING AND THE BALANCE OF PAYMENTS. Washington, DC: U.S. Treasury Department, 1968.

Kamin, Alfred. WESTERN EUROPEAN LABOR AND THE AMERICAN CORPORATION. Washington, DC: U.S. Treasury Department, 1970.

Sandman, William E. HOW TO WIN PRODUCTIVITY IN MANUFACTURING. New York: AMCOM, 1982.

Chapter 13

MNC Strategies: Personnel

Introduction

Both authors frequently encounter a modern version of the young American dream. A bright young Spanish major drops by to ask about international opportunities. This young person has heard about American MNCs, and he or she wants in on the game. They want the name of the man to write to in order to obtain a twenty-five to thirty thousand dollar a year job in Latin America or Spain, preferably in one of the more interesting capital cities. Since the person has studied Spanish and the Latin culture, it is obvious that all she or he needs is a few addresses, and the job will be gained. Then, after working hours, one can sit in subtropic splendor, romancing local girls or just absorbing the local culture. After all, Americans know everything, so they obviously will be hired as soon as their credentials are established.

It isn't quite this easy. If either of us knew of any such jobs, we would take them and forget the students...

We mentioned earlier that the really important bottleneck for most large corporations is the shortage of skilled personnel. When one considers that any job advertised in the WALL STREET JOURNAL for managers or skilled technicians offering over twenty thousand dollars per year will receive thousands of inquiries from reasonably well skilled people, this seems surprising. With unemployment rates in the U.S. hovering between eight and ten percent for most of the 1980's, it is even more surprising. One would expect that in the U.S., with its extremely well educated population, any firm could easily hire all the good people it needs. But such is not the case, particularly for the very top people. In this chapter, we will try to indicate why. We will also comment about other dimensions of international personnel work, including problems MNCs based in other countries may have.

PERSONNEL IS PERSONNEL

As with every other firm function, the international personnel problem is about the same as the local problem in many dimensions. The same techniques used in the United States or Canada or Japan are used abroad. If a firm needs to test job applicants, plot a labor union strategy, or recruit new accountants, the methods used will be based on much good local work which has been developed over many decades. If productivity and morale is a problem, the company's personnel experts have much expertise and knowledge to draw upon.

But as usual „in any international or comparative problem, the values of the key variables will be different. Because local personnel are subject to the local educational and behavioral constraints, they will be very different people than those at home. As a result, the training programs and recruitment standards may be very different. Laws governing work rules, employment benefits, tenure, women's rights, hours of work, safety standards, and many other personnel matters also may be different. And if the local economy is booming and unemployment rates are under one percent, the recruiting situation will be different than if 20 to 30 percent of the work force is unemployed. Both situations now exist in different countries.

International constraints may also create problems. A real advantage in an MNC is to bring in foreign experts and managers to help out when problems arise, but quite a few countries have very tough work visa requirements, and such men and women may not be able to get work permits. Less skilled local personnel may have to be used.

But those interested in international personnel work are best advised to study American or other local personnel work first. Once one understands the complex fabric of modern personnel practice, he or she can move on to international problems. These are much more complex, since one now looks at many cultures and countries instead of just one.

INTERNATIONAL PERSONNEL

Before 1910, in banana republic days, every worker in an American firm abroad might be imported. Even the janitors and laborers were American. To this day many Central American countries have stringent requirements about the percentage of foreigners which can be employed as a percentage of the total work force, reflecting their concern that all the good jobs would go to foreigners. Many other countries have similar restrictions, and all have work permit or visa requirements which apply only to foreigners, including the United States and other industrial countries. One total discrimination which is universal is against foreign workers. Locals are always preferable, in every country. The only exceptions are when local people lack critical skills which are absolutely necessary.

But as MNCs evolved, they have steadily shifted to the use of local personnel. Two basic reasons are relevant. One is that local citizens are cheaper, even if they are paid the same wages. The company does not have to worry about the costs of home leaves, transportation expenses for wives and children, and special schooling allowances. The second reason is political. If local governments want good jobs for their citizens, and if they are qualified, then why not hire the best local people? Firms do, and many jobs that Americans used to have are now held by foreigners. When one author was in Saudi Arabia 25 years ago, there was hardly a Saudi citizen who could qualify as a good accountant, but now there are thousands. If good men are available, then it pays to use them. MNCs based in all countries follow the same policies.

The initial move is to use good locals at home, but as the MNC evolves and grows, the third country expatriate emerges. This is a person from one country working in another which is not the home of the MNC. An example might be a Mexican technician working for an American MNC in Peru. If this person is the best the company has, it makes sense to utilize him wherever he can make the most contribution to the company. American based MNCs probably have more third country expatriates than other MNCs, simply because most of them have been at the international game longer. It takes time to develop good people anywhere, and many European and Japanese based MNCs haven't got this far yet.

Top management of the MNCs typically is from home, although even this is beginning to change in the American based MNCs. Virtually all top managers in Japanese and European firms are still locals from the home base, again perhaps because of time factors. It may take twenty to thirty years for very capable people to work up, and most major non-American MNCs simply haven't been in the game that long.

But another discriminatory factor may be at work here. Few MNCs have come far enough to avoid various kinds of discrimination, be it against races, religions, sexes, countries, or whatever. Moreover, few foreigners, however brilliant and capable, could operate effectively in a totally alien top headquarters environment. Ponder the number of Americans who might be able to go to Tokyo, speak fluent Japanese, and understand totally the local culture, both for management of a given firm and the general Japanese one, and it might be concluded that it will be a long time before any American gets to top management ranks in a Japanese MNC. Moreover, the Japanese might well hesitate to promote such a superperson, even if he or she could qualify. The question simply has not come up yet.

American based MNCs have a different problem. English is spoken all over the world, and many foreigners are fluent in this language. We have our specific corporate cultures, but the U.S. is a polygot nation, and deviants of all sorts live in the U.S. and are accepted. A brilliant black manager from Ghana, working up through the ranks of an American MNC, would not seem particularly unusual if he were transferred to the New York office. A capable Frenchwoman would seem even less odd. Asians, blacks, Indians, or whatever are already a part of the American culture. These foreigners already would speak fluent English, with accents no one would find strange in any American city. And they also would have a much better idea of the general American culture than most Americans would have of the Japanese culture.

Assisting the foreigners here is the American equal rights act, which specifically bans most types of discrimination. It does not apply to foreigners, but no one is perturbed when a minority person or female has a good managerial or technical job, and the companies are used to odd types. Many managers in other countries are not.

What this means is that foreigners may have much better options in American based MNCs than they might have either at home with local companies or with MNCs based elsewhere. Already a few of the most capable have achieved major top management jobs with American MNCs, and probably more are to come. The firms, well aware of how hard it is to get truly supperior personnel, are willing to use the best. The net result is that we may be seeing the development of much more of a meritocracy than we have in the past in U.S. And if the firms can pick winners, this just means that the firms will be more efficient.

This point also means trouble for young American white males. These people face new competition, not only from American females and minorities, but also from superior foreigners. It is tougher to get ahead, which means some people try harder, which means firms get superior people...and in the end, American firms may have a curious advantage over foreigners stemming from their willingness to use the best, instead of those selected from a more narrow demographic base. If you want to win, select from the broadest possible talent pool, which is what the Americans are doing. American firms that play the game the old way, trying to hire only WASP males, are in for deep trouble.

This point already is causing trouble for Japanese MNCs in the United States. The Japanese MNC invests in the U.S., hires excellent Americans, promotes them to the top of the U.S. subsidiary, and then loses them to the competition. Americans, well aware that they will never get promoted out of the U.S., simply go to firms where they can keep advancing. Remember, we are talking here about very superior managers and technicians, not the average ones. Superior persons never lack for job options. Historically, many American MNCs lost first rate locals in exactly the same way. If they play the game the old way, they still do.

Another pressure keeping Americans home is the American government. Unlike most other countries, Americans abroad pay U.S. income taxes. Local taxes paid can be offset against income, and certain major deductions exist which are not available to Americans at home, but there is a tax penalty which can be large for high income managers. For a few years in the late 1970's and until 1981, the tax penalty was so huge that expatriate Americans were forced to come home, but some relief was granted in 1981.

Americans, reading ads promising vast employment opportunities abroad at high salaries, sometimes think that many opportunities abroad exist. But the only Americans who now get overseas are the highly skilled and experienced executives and technicians who cannot be replaced easily. Most of this hiring and staffing is done at the head office, not out in the foreign branches.

Many young Americans, observing American social and economic problems, seem to think that other countries offer better opportunities than at home. But the sad fact is that American wage rates and working conditions are much better than in exotic foreign climes. A few European countries might pay higher wages (depending actually on the dollar exchange rate at the moment), but one would have to obtain a work permit in such a country, which these days is almost impossible, unless one has a spouse or some close relative in the country. And of course the person would have to know the culture and speak the local language fluently as well. Women are often bitter about discrimination in the U.S., but virtually every place else is worse, ranging from lags of a few years in West European countries to a millenia or more in some Middle Eastern countries. The sad fact is that the world is an imperfect place, and there really is no place to go to obtain one's utopia.

CHANGING THE WORLD

American firms have had a very significant impact on foreign personnel practices. The success of the American based MNCs has caused many local firms and non-U.S. MNCs to study carefully the American companies' methods. Where they work well, foreigners copy. One place where a real and unnoticed revolution has occurred is in personnel selection practices. Americans are used to their system, which is a meritocracy. The best qualified individual usually gets the job. Many top managers have pointed out that if anything else is done, long run trouble is certain. Suppose that a big company selects key men (only, no women) because they are from the right families or countries. Better men and women, being excluded, go to other companies. If there really is some significant difference in abilities, then the company choosing the best men and women wins.

No one really believes that this will happen every time. Family, race, sex, national origens, and religious qualifications will sometimes count, often a lot. But firms which do not try to get the best, choosing from the largest possible talent pool, tend to be the static companies, those who cannot seem to get their own houses in order, the ones who lag while those firms which hire for results move ahead. Moreover, remember the high tech discussion in the last chapter. If really good people can't win in big firms, they start their own companies, and in many sectors these days, there are few major economies of scale. Those new firms may well cream the big, clumsy ones with second rate managers in the future. There is considerable evidence to date to suggest that this has already occurred to some extent.

Meritocracy is not revolutionary in the United States, and our equal rights laws try to make the situation even more meritocratic. Americans typically expect the best to win, even in the Civil Service, Universities, and other non-business sectors. No personnel expert is perfect, but the more a company works on such problems, the more likley it will do a good selection job. The more favoritism and discrimination any firm is perceived to practice, the less likely the firm will be able to recruit winners.

When a company moves abroad and begins to practice this philosophy in foreign cultures, the result can be revolutionary. Most countries, like the United States at an earlier period, rely heavily on a genetic sort system, that is, the man (and very, very rarely a woman) with the best family gets the job, even if he is unqualified otherwise. It is not surprising to discover that American companies can out compete many British firms in England. Some British firms hire from the stud book (Burke's PEERAGE), while the American firm tries to hire the best British marketing executive. When the competition gets keen, the Americans do better.

Similarly, in Japan, highly qualified young women just graduated from the finest universities somehow never get hired for fast track junior executive positions in major Japanese firms. American banks in

Japan, observing that they had great difficulties recruiting the best Japanese young men, now hire the women. One American executive noted that the Japanese were simply throwing away some of the cream of their talent, and the Americans might as well pick it up. In ten more years, take one guess as to which banks in Japan will be winning...those Japanese ones which fight fiercely for an occasional superior young man they can lure away from Japanese manufacturing companies, or those American banks, who have the pick of some of the finest young minds in Japan? Next question.

Note the revolutionary implications of the preceeding paragraph. The Japanese can continue their present personnel habits, and let the foreigners win, or they change. Either way, the revolution is brewing. Things will never be the same, and a previously discriminated against group will have options and opportunities that never existed before. In a world full of hate, discrimination, and distaste for anyone even a bit different, the power of this nondiscriminatory idea is potent indeed. If you don't do it the nondiscriminatory way, the only question is how long it will be before you drift back to second or third rate status, with no prestige at all. The world needs all the talent it can get, and the Americans seem to have led the way to exposing this point.

Foreign companies, realizing the implications of such personnel practices, shift to the American pattern. This is easiest to do in situations where output and performance can be accurately measured, as in production, data processing, accounting, medicine, and similar work. Evaluation is more subjective in general management and higher level jobs, but it still can be done. Those who do it get the best managers and skilled persons. After five or ten years, they are the winners.

This concept, particularly in Third World, non-Western cultures, is really revolutionary, and few people realize how important it is. If applied on a country wide basis, it means better efficiency for all companies, including local ones, faster economic growth, and greater improvement in the general well-being of the population. It might even mean much less social tension in countries torn by ethnic, religious, tribal, or racial rivalries.

This point is so badly misunderstood that countries regularly exile or otherwise expel literally millions of top people, because they are somehow not nice. Uganda dumped its Asian Indians; Cuba and Vietnam their capitalists; and Iran its pro-Westerners. These gifted people come to the West, learn the language, and make enormous contributions to the United States and other countries astute enough to let them in. One could argue that the U.S. has gained more in taking in political refugees in the past twenty-five years than it has spent in aid programs since 1776. The irony is that the expelling countries want it this way.

Even communist countries have qualification trouble. Their usual selection criteria is not genetic, but political reliability. If a good working class communist competes for a job with a middle class skilled person, the communist gets the job. But in complex business work involving finance, production, or anything else, being a good communist has little to do with being a good manager. The Soviet Union also discriminates against its non-Russian citizens, women, Jews, and some intellectuals, which is good news for anti-communists. The more complex the world becomes, and the more important competence is, the more likely it will be that the Soviets will fall behind.

All those new high tech industries have no room for the not quite good enough. Those countries and firms who expect to cash in on the new technological revolution by using only the politically reliable, the males, the right religions, and so on, are probably doomed to fall behind. Even trying to make bicycle parts in a remote Peruvian province will be difficult unless the best people around are hired to do it. Failure to understand this point will probably cause many countries and firms to fall behind and lose.

THE MNC EXPATRIATE

If young people with language and cultural knowledge don't go abroad, who does? Various studies of successful Americans and other nationalities abroad have been made, and we can construct a success profile to see if the shoe fits. Many want to go, but few make it.

The followng profile is average, not total. We know of young people who were on a plane to their first foreign job 48 hours after being hired; we also know of odd types, such as hippies, 72 year olds, and many others performing real services for many MNCs. Anyone may get abroad, although the odds are against a person who does not fit this profile closely. And remember, the game constantly changes, usually in the direction of the most competent, so next year it may be a bit different.

First, the person is usually male, although this is beginning to change as highly qualified women get into the managerial game. We have only had large numbers of really well trained women in American business for less than ten years, and it often takes a while for a person to work their way overseas. But for non-Americans working for non-U.S. based MNCs, maleness is almost total. For American MNCs, a good guess is that there will be many more women in the overseas game before too long.

Second, the person is typically very well educated. Advanced degrees in law, business, engineering, or the sciences are common. Managers are typically very high skill persons, and one way to acquire skills is to obtain a good education. Moreover, graduate training is normally restricted to persons of quite high intelligence, and our man or woman abroad will be very intelligent indeed. This point applies both to Americans and foreigners.

We know of third grade dropouts who are abroad, along with others who have doctoral degrees. Less educated persons tend to be older, getting their education on the job. Business, unlike law or medicine, does not require formal professional education, but a good education helps, and younger people find it difficult to even get in the game if they do not have excellent educational qualifications.

Third, our expatriate knows his company well. He normally has had years of training and experience within the company, and he knows who really has power, who can do things, and how the informal organization

works.   One thing formal training cannot do is to teach organization
politics, such as whether the boss realy listens to his wife or not, and
who really listens to which subordinates, or whether the finance vice
president holds more informal power than his title would suggest.   Such
things are learned by working with the organization for many years.
Normally one needs five or more years of local experience before going
abroad.

We   know of plenty of exceptions to this rule also.   One major one
is when a brilliant young scientist, such as a chemist, is sent over to
straighten out a specific technical problem.   If your detergent plant is
producing garbage, what the boss does with his wife is irrelevant.   You
get the plant fixed technically.   Another exeption is in firms which
have more technically oriented functions to perform, and where the cost
of being corporate culturally wrong may not be so great.   Branch offices
of banks might be in this category. If a younger person understands
banking and finance very well, he or she can do the job abroad even if
one does not yet quite understand the inner workings of his or her own
bank.   The job is largely technical, not social or political.

But it is nice, when a foreign based manager is far away, for him
or her to know that if a Telex is sent to good old Sam at the Cincinnati
office, the problem will be taken care of in a few days. The formal
approach would be through the New York Office, but Sam and our foreign
manager have worked together in the old days out in Los Angeles, and
they know how to get things done...

Such   factors explain why there are few young people abroad.   It
takes a while to figure out how thing really work, as compared to how
they are supposed to work.

Fourth, our expatriate is a very tolerant and patient person.   He
or she observes strange foreign cultural outlooks, which foul up his or
her operations something awful, yet with tact and patience he or she
gradually straightens out the mess.   His wife and family, if any (and,
given the usual age and sex of the expatriate, there usually is a
family), are the same.   A good man married to a girl from Iowa who only
wants to go home, because the bugs are terrible and supermarkets
nonexistent, will not be much use.   His children will be going to
strange schools, and they should be able to enjoy them.   Culture shock,
which is the inability to relate to very strange situations, is minimal
in such a family.   Instead of finding the local culture alien and
threatening, they find it interesting and exciting.   If our expatriate
meets a charming Moslem gentleman with three wives in the course of his
business dealings, he does not get upset about it, but rather is
interested in this cultural variation.

Such   tolerance and empathy for local sensibilities is rarer than
most people realize, and it is particularly rare among persons who aré
accustomed to ordering things done.   It can drive a good manager crazy
to give orders and find them bogged down in local cultural molasses.
Even such trivia as the inability to complete a telephone connection can
drive a capable person to mumblings and drink.

Fifth, the expatriate knows very well what we have been talking about all through this book, namely, the real need to make environmental/firm interlocks. He or she understands that what was good practice in New Jersey or Paris or Tokyo may not work at all in Mexico City or Buenos Aires, and he or she also knows what will work well. More importantly, he or she knows how to sell such strange ideas to top management, who may not realize the importance of local environmental impacts on their foreign operations. The expatriate may suggest policies which violate every rule in the book back home, but make good sense where he or she is. But to carry the day, the expatriate has to argue the case persuasively to intelligent senior managers who have heard it all before. Remember that the senior men are very concerned about local suboptimizations, and the local expatriate must sell the idea that this new policy is not just a device to make the local managers, including himself, look good at the expense of the overall company.

Sixth, our manager abroad will be very well paid. Salaries range upwards of fifty thousand dollars per year, often way up. By the time the company adds in fringe benefits, overseas allowances, vacations with pay, housing costs, and educational allowances, any American abroad will cost over $100,000 per year. Non-Americans in other countries will be equally expensive. For that kind of money, our expatriate had better be very productive.

Here is another reason why very young peope are rarely found abroad. By the time they learn enough and gain the experience to be WORTH $100,000 per year, they are no longer very young.

Seventh, the expatriate is typically an American citizen if he or she works for an American based MNC, although this pattern is slowly changing. For expatriates from other country MNCs, they will almost always be citizens of the MNC home country.

Eighth, our expatriate may not know the local language. If his or her MNC is operating in forty countries with perhaps twenty major languages used, he or she may not have had time to learn the right one. Interpreters are cheap, but efficient managers are scare and expensive, so lack of language and specific cultural orientation is not as serious a problem as one might suppose. If the manager does know something about his new local culture, fine. Moreover, the international business language is English, and if a young Frenchman or German wants to move up in an MNC, he would be well advised to study English.

Because management is harder to teach than culture and languages, many young people miss this point. They assume that they need the language, and not the managerial skills. It is terrific if the manager has both, but a linguist will never be hired for a managerial position, while a manager may well be hired for a job where he or she has no knowledge of the local situation.

And finally, the expatriate will be a good independent operator. At home he or she might call the boss for advice on a sticky problem; abroad, the manager has to make his or her own decisions. If he or she does, they have to be right most of the time. Everyone makes mistakes, and a manager who never does is too conservative for the company´s own good. But too many mistakes leads to early retirement, or a sinecure at home in the head office where the manager can perform routine tasks. Few firms will fire failures, since almost good people can perform many useful tasks. But such people rarely get promoted, either.

This point leads to the modern trend, which is quite different from the old days. Twenty or thirty years ago, a manager sent abroad could not rise to the top easily. By missing out on headquarter's action, he could not ever expect to be chief executive officer. But now overseas management in a big MNC is critical for taking on more responsibility at the home office. If half or more of the firm's business is done abroad, a key man who has never been there is not qualified for top positions. It is common to find that the new chief has had years of experience managing abroad. If he has had such experiences and done well, he may be the man you need to run the global corporation.

Wait about ten to fifteen years, and we can probably use the feminine pronouns in the above paragraph as well. At present, virtually all the executives with the age and experience to become CEO's in the near future are male. But this too will change, at least for American based MNCs.

With all of these qualifications in mind, it is clear why good people are the key bottleneck for so many firms. People who meet even the minimal qualifications described above are rare, and firms find that profitable projects languish because they cannot obtain enough good managers to staff every key position. Many persons feel that they qualify, but few are chosen. We might add that we did not even mention that our hero should have proper managerial and technical competence as well, since this was assumed.

OVERSEAS MANAGERIAL PROBLEMS

Firms operating far flung branches have special problems. Here are some of the more important ones:

Every company has too few really top rated managers. We suggested above that these days the top people probably have had some overseas experience, but every company still faces the problem of priorities. Which good managers should go where? It is tempting to ship a second rater off to a quiet branch which has few problems. The image he will carry of the company as he plods along may not do much good, but at least he won't clutter up headquarters.

The problem is one of potential. A small foreign branch with good potential may never realize it with a second rate manager, but present profits and sales are too small to require a top flight person. Now the good managers are needed elsewhere. The problem is forecasting where really good opportunities are, and then sending the best managers to take advantage. Not every large company has been able to forecast great possibilities in far off places.

A further problem is to figure out who is second rate. Images and impressions can be wrong, and many a perceived second rater blossomed very well when presented with new challenges. Indeed, one way to test a potentially good manager is to send him or her to some minor branch to see what can be done. Evaluators can be surprised.

Perhaps a third of the top managers in American MNCs abroad are American, but use of nationals grows steadily. American firms can still get into difficulty with good local managers in cultural conflicts. The local man is good because he is very much like American managers. If his country has quite different values, he may be in conflict with them often. Other countries have the Chambers of Commerce, their Red Crosses or Red Crescents, and other charitable and socially acceptable local institutions. The Americanized local man may mix as poorly as any American with other local elites, because he represents a cross cultural type. Few American firms can evaluate how well a local citizen will do, since few understand the subtleties of any foreign culture. In some Third World, non-Western cultures, an American or a third country expatriate might be accepted more readily than a local citizen who has peculiar values.

This problem is so complex that no easy answer is possible. American firms usually welcome any local citizen who is also a competent manager or technician. Rarely does a company worry about how well he or she might fit in with local elites. We have seen Third World managers who were extremely competent, yet who clearly had problems in their cross cultural roles. Some role confusion may be inevitable.

Executive compensation is always a tricky problem, but it is even harder to work out for foreign branches. One problem is in getting relative pay rates correct between nationalities. Americans often get more money at home than local citizens do in their home countries, so it appears natural to pay overseas Americans more than locals. But good local managers may be doing the same work for half as much money, and many will feel aggrieved. Third country managers may be paid even different rates, which complicates the problem. A British manager working in Thailand for an American company may earn more than a Thai, but less than an American. Sorting out pay problems equitably is very difficult. The basic problem is that expatriate pay is based in some way on home country pay, and salary scales are widely divergent around the world.

American top managers often are rewarded with bonuses and stock options, but these may be difficult or impossible to apply in foreign branches. Only rarely does an American company have local stock sold on foreign exchanges, so stock options cannot be given. Legal problems may also be relevant, since various countries have different option laws. Even bonuses can be harder to compute than in the U.S., particularly if the branch is not a complete, self contained unit. Some of the profits or output may be the result of activities beyond the local manager's jurisdiction. Many American firms feel that incentive schemes get managers to produce more, but few have worked out usable foreign incentive plans.

Personnel appraisal techniques are well developed in the United States, Japan, and Western Europe, but these may not work well in different foreign environments. Appraisals often are based on continuous, close observation over months or years, but the overseas manager may only be observed briefly once or twice a year. As with many other problems in a rapidly changing international environment, few firms have yet worked out good systems, and much appraisal abroad is more casual than at home. Cultural factors can play a major role here as well. A Japanese top manager trying to figure out his American executives (or vice versa) might find it very difficult to make objective appraisals.

Management training presents problems for distant branches. Few countries have extensive management training programs common in the United States, and foreign based managers have fewer opportunities to take part. Branches are often smaller than home operations, and in house training activities are also difficult, since fewer managers are to be trained. They often cannot be spared from their current duties, and even if they can, there may be too few for economic training. Many U.S. based firms solve this problem by bringing foreign managers to the U.S., and here excellent knowledge of English becomes critical. If the foreigner cannot communicate well, he or she may have real troubles. Note the problem for Japanese firms here, since few of their foreign managers are likely to speak Japanese.

Even the informal training which goes on through interactions between working managers is less overseas, since fewer good people are involved. A good manager can become second rate if he or she is isolated abroad too long, yet if managers are transferred too often, valuable continuity is lost. If a new manager is sent every year or two, the foreign operation may never take advantage of the practical local knowledge that a long term manager will have.

Dismissals are always awkward, and they can be even more difficult abroad. For home country nationals, the problem is easy. The manager is recalled. But for local citizens, tenure laws, local traditions, and local resentments must be considered. Rather than face such difficulties, it is easy to let the poor manager fumble on, thus losing valuable time and opportunities.

All of this relates to management skills transfer. Good managers practice their art and craft properly wherever they may be. This involves the ability to make the necessary environmental interlock with managerial and firm functions. Historically, during the colonial period, firms tried to change the local environments to fit home country conditions. If the colonized area had environmental problems which made company activities difficult, then the country got changed. Now companies try to change management to fit the local environment, and they do not have any guns. This is more difficult and subtle to accomplish, and managers have to be better than ever. No company has enough good people to handle all its activities, so problems are certain.

LABOR RELATIONS

We have discussed management personnel extensively, but local labor forces are also quite significant. Virtually the entire work force will be local, and the firm has to observe all relevant local laws and customs. This single fact makes labor relations quite different abroad.

Some countries have tough unions; in others, unions are illegal. Quite a few countries have politically oriented unions, more interested in politial power than in traditional American wage and benefit bargaining. Virtually all countries have extremely complex labor laws and welfare legislation, since an easy and popular political action is to pass such legislation. The usual effect is to raise the cost of labor, but those not employed don't know what they missed, and those working strongly favor such legislation. Whatever the local situation may be, the firm lives with it.

Local workers often see MNC plants and offices as highly desirable places to work, particularly in poor countries. Managers see labor as scarce and valuable, and safety and work amenities are important. Hence plants have more labor saving equipment and personnel amenities than local firms. Plants often are newer, and may have air conditioning and clean cafeterias. Few really dirty jobs exist, since these have been automated out in the home country, and they probably are abroad too. And pay rates tend to be somewhat higher than local wages. Remember that the MNC is there because it is more productive than typical firms.

But such benefits do not preclude strikes, union demands, and labor unrest. Since the head office will not be intimately knowledgable with local labor problems, this personnel function is likely to be delegated to field management. Decentralization makes sense when some obscure local question is critical.

Labor relations is an area where local expertise is necessary, and often the top personnel manager, or key advisors, will be local citizens. This is often the first functional area to go local, since the experts are likely to be available sooner than in production, finance, or marketing. If the firm goes to court on labor matters, the lawyers will always be local. When distant home country managers get involved in local labor problems, the usual result is trouble, since few of them will know much about the details of local legislation. Thus a Japanese MNC ended up in a U.S. court on a discrimination charge because this firm had hired more Japanese Americans than anyone else. Hiring such people might have seemed sensible in Tokyo, but the policy probably violated American equal rights laws. One author got into trouble in the Middle East by hiring a Shia Moslem in a key position when only Sunni Moslems normally filled this post. The author did not even know at that time what the difference was, and it cost his company dearly. Such ignorance leads to trouble, often big trouble.

Conclusion

We have barely scratched the surface of a very complex problem. Firms trying to staff their global operations will find enough problems to keep them busy forever. Globally oriented firms have the advantage, since they can effectively tap the world personpower pool, while local firms are trapped with whatever local talent is available. Global firms can even tap the local talent pool more effectively by paying good people what they are worth internationally, not locally. The differential can be large.

The key problem is to mesh the firm's problems and requirements with whatever the local environments offer. Since we are talking about people problems, the educational and behavioral constraints are important. But legal and economic constraints can also have major effects on personnel policies.

Questions for Discussion

1.   We mentioned in this chapter that it costs an American firm $100,000 per year to keep an American executive or technican overseas. This means that the person has to be worth at least this much to be selected.

Consider yourself now and in the future. When do you feel that you will be worth $100,000 per year to anybody? What will you need to get that you don't have now to be worth this kind of money? Be specific.

2.   A friend of yours who likes to travel is planning to go to Britain this summer. He will vacation a bit and then apply for a job with an American firm in that country. He figures that it will be easy to get a good job at American pay rates. This person majored in History in college and is a pretty good C plus type of student.

Do you think that this is a good strategy to get a job? Why or why not? What kinds of advice, if any, would you give him before he gets on the plane?

3.   Find a foreign student on your campus and ask him or her about culture shock when the person first arrived in the United States. What kinds of things did he or she find here which were very strange as compared to his or her home country? How did he or she adjust to strange customs?

Now suppose that you were going to visit this persons´s home country. What kinds of adjustments, if any, might you have to make? Be specific.

4.   Most European countries have expanded their own universities and technical institutes very rapidly in the past decade, including business education. What likely effect will this have on Americans who might want to get overseas to work? Why?

5.   Many businessmen and educators feel that one of the best preparations for a foreign career for a young American is to study a foreign language and culture. Yet in this chapter we argued that such studies really are not very important.

What good case could you make for language and cultural studies in preparation for a foreign business career? Try interviewing a language professor to get some information.

6.   Most small firms in the United States and other countries feel

that their major bottleneck is shortage of capital. Yet in this chapter we indicated that the typical big bottleneck for MNCs is the shortage of highly trained managers and technicians. Why is this so? What do these MNCs have that smaller firms do not have?

7. The world of MNCs is largely a man's world, since the United States cannot export its own local laws, and almost no other country has an effective law guaranteeing equal employment rights to women.

Do you think that this attitude will change in the foreseeable future in other advanced countries? Why or why not? What pressures may lead to more equality? What pressures may lead to maintenance of present conditions? Consider any single country you choose in presenting your answer.

Supplementary Readings

Bock, Philip K. CULTURE SHOCK: A READER IN MODERN CULTURAL ANTHROPOLOGY. New York: Alfred A. Knopf, 1970.

Desatnich, Robert L. HUMAN RESOURCE MANAGEMENT IN THE MULTINATIONAL COMPANY. Farnsborough, England: Gower Press, 1977.

Frith, Stan W. THE EXPATRIATE DILEMMA: HOW TO RELOCATE AND COMPENSATE U.S. EMPLOYEES ASSIGNED OVERSEAS. Chicago: Nelson-Hall, 1981.

Gabriel, Peter. THE INTERNATIONAL TRANSFER OF CORPORATE SKILLS. Boston: Harvard Business School, 1967.

Gladwin, Thomas N. MULTINATIONALS UNDER FIRE: LESSONS IN THE MANAGEMENT OF CONFLICT. New York: Wiley, 1980.

McNulty, Nancy G. TRAINING MANAGERS: THE INTERNATIONAL GUIDE. New York: Harper and Row, 1969.

Weber, Ross A. CULTURE AND MANAGEMENT: TEXT AND READINGS IN COMPARATIVE MANAGEMENT. Homewood, IL: Richard D. Irwin, 1969.

Weintraub, Leon. INTERNATIONAL MANPOWER DEVELOPMENT. New York: Praeger, 1969.

PART V

A LOOK AT THE FUTURE

Chapter 14

A Look at the Future

For many chapters, we have been looking at what IS in international business. Anyone who made forecasts based on the best information available in 1946 or 1950 would have been wildly wrong in forecasting this part of the future to date. The MNC was an unexpected surprise in the past 40 years. But younger readers now in their twenties have the problem of forecasting the future of international business for the next 30 years or so. In 16 more years, the 21st Century will be on us, yet most of our senior leaders were born and partially educated before World War II even began. It is tempting to sit back and feel that more of the same will happen, yet our adventures since 1945 suggest that this might be the least probable future of all.

For 30 years large American firms have been evolving in a very special manner, one that is just beginning to be understood, and for fifteen years, West European and Japanese firms have been following this same path. Most notable have been trends to multinational operations and conglomerate status; less thought about have been the startling growth of well managed firms in which, if the company doesn't average 15 to 20 percent per year in real sales growth, its management is considered laggard.

As usual, academia lags somewhat behind the trend. Only in the past ten years has a large body of literature studied in some detail what is going on with the MNC giants, although many individual studies date much earlier than that. By the time that academics figure out what they think the MNCs are doing, something else may happen.

It was popular to forecast ten years ago that a handful of giant American MNCs would control over 80 (or even 99) percent of total world business. As the West Europeans and Japanese surged into MNC status after 1975, the forecast is that a handful of MNCs from a few countries will control this much business. All that can be done is to brace for the inevitable takeover of all world business by a small number of privately owned MNCs.

We feel that this sort of simple minded projection into the future may be erroneous. Just as it was not possible to forecast accurately in 1946 what the world would be like today, it is difficult to forecast the future today. Is it possible that we are at a point of discontinuity, where the trends we now see may undergo a major change? Various forces are at work which may change all the current business trends into something quite different from what is anticipated. If this analysis is correct, much of what is now being done in the business world may prove to be wrong. This does not mean that we should abandon forecasting and planning, but we should be aware of possible surprises.

THE PART LESS THAN THE WHOLE

Any large, modern, professionally managed firm can grow at a rate of about 10 percent a year, except perhaps in a few years of major recession, as in 1981-83. Some of the best firms grow at a 20 percent annual rate. At least they have been doing so since about 1945. This follows from the nature of modern management. Although no one admits that management theory or practice is a very precise art, it is true that there now exists a rather good operational management theory, comprised of all sorts of bits and pieces from many disciplines. Moreover, most good managers have well in hand an intuitive dynamic model of the economy and their firm. While these models are crude, they work far better than does the outmoded seat of the pants style of management. The result is that better firms win more than they lose.

So good firms continue to grow rapidly. Moreover, the reward system for managers, both in cash and prestige, is generally structured to reward growth, both in profits and sales. If a new CEO is being sought, it helps to know that Mr. X doubled the size of his firm in four years. No one really cares how he did it, so long as everything was legal. If Mr. Y appears competent, but his firm has stagnated during the same period, consideration of him tends to be dismissed out of hand. Such persons are not considered competent.

The American economy has a long term real growth rate of about three percent per year, although this has dropped to about one percent in the past decade. World figures are much more erratic, but a 6 percent annual GNP growth rate for other countries would be at the high end of the range.

If firms are expanding at 10 to 20 percent per year, while economies are expanding at 3 to 6 percent per year, something has to give. That is, at these disparate compound growth rates, the parts will sooner or later exceed the whole.

Table 1 depicts a situation where a firm with sales of $1 billion in 1970 starts on a 20 percent growth rate, while the world and the American economies grow somewhat less slowly. It doesn't matter what percentages are chosen, so long as the growth rate of the whole is less than that of the firm. The only difference would concern the time required for the part to overtake the whole.

The hypothetical situation depicted in Table 1 is obviously not going to happen. It most decidedly is not going to happen if two hundred or more billion dollar firms start trying to do the same thing. Indeed, events in the past few years in the United States suggest that the turning point may already have been reached, in that the big may not be able to maintain sufficiently rapid growth rates to help them maintain a rate faster than that of the nation.

TABLE 1

Firm and Country Growth Rate

Year	Firm (20%)	United States (4%)	World (6%)
1970	$ 1.0 billion	$900.0 billion	$ 3.0 trillion
1980	6.2 billion	1.3 trillion	5.4 trillion
1990	38.4 billion	2.0 trillion	9.6 trillion
2000	238.0 billion	2.9 trillion	17.3 trillion
2010	1.0 trillion	4.4 trillion	30.9 trillion
2020	6.2 trillion	6.4 trillion	55.2 trillion
2030	38.4 trillion	9.5 trillion	99.0 trillion
2040	238.0 trillion	14.2 trillion	178.2 trillion

STRATEGIES FOR EXPANSION

Firms have grown by following only three basic strategies, or some combination of the three. These are:

1. To become MNCs. As firms find the local market harder to grow in, many have moved to untapped foreign markets. It is easier to start with untapped British, French, or West German markets than to try to gain rapidly in the United States, with perhaps five tough and fast growing competitors to fight, most of them also interested in fast growth. Japanese and West European firms, facing exactly the same local situations, also moved out multinationally.

The big push overseas for U.S. MNCs started in the mid-1950s. Significantly enough, this was just after American firms had had time to get organized and to take advantage of American markets in the postwar growth period. Not surprisingly, this push abroad coincided with a period of subnormal American growth. If the local market is sluggish, new and booming markets must be sought. Western Europe in particular has filled this requirement perfectly. Most other overseas expansion has been mineral related, the firm moving to where the oil, copper, or bauxite is. But such expansion was also related to industrial expansion in Europe.

2. To become a conglomerate. American firms with fast growth rates soon run into the more obvious types of antitrust legislation. As a result, many firms have turned to the conglomerate strategy for growth, often in combination with the MNC strategy, although not always. By buying and merging firms in dissimilar lines, the worst antitrust restrictions can be avoided. Some of the conglomerates have had the fastest growth rates of all until fairly recently.

This is still a good strategy for smaller firms, but it now appears that the game is up for the really big, multi-billion dollar companies. New antitrust suits have been filed against proposed aquisitions, and the larger the merger, the more likely that some parts of each partner are in the same product lines. Disclosure changes may also eliminate some of the more effective internal manipulations of management, so that as the firm grows, the larger firms acquired have also learned to develop some effective anti-takover techniques.

Perhaps the crucially limiting factor is the need to acquire constantly bigger firms in order to maintain growth. A billion dollar conglomerate can buy a ten million dollar company out of petty cash, but this type of acquisition won´t help much with growth. What is needed is a $500 million firm, and these are quite scarce.

3. To create internal expansion: some firms (including most of the earlier giants) have stuck to internal expansion. If the right products and markets can be found, a business can grow at 20 percent or more per year. IBM and Xerox have demonstrated that it can be done, and in recent years the Apple Computer Company went from zero to sales of almost a billion dollars a year in less than seven years.

The trouble is that once the firm reaches the billion dollar range of sales, high start up costs in most cases prevent penetration into existing markets potentially large enough to maintain growth. Moreover, many of these markets are now dominated by other tough, big firms, also interested in fast growth. A further inhibiting factor is that the more recent fast growth firms have had a few great ideas, but really great ideas are very hard to come by, and constant generation of these ideas is difficult.

The best bet is to find some new products and to take off in a new area. Most success stories along these lines result from this (e.g., copiers, computers, electronics, genetics). But there are relatively few new opportunities here, particularly if sales increases of perhaps $200 to $500 million per year are needed to maintain growth that a billion plus dollar firm would require.

IMPLICATONS FOR THE FUTURE

If probable developments over the next thirty years are projected, what are the possibilities? It appears that all these paths to expansion are going to be difficult for the larger firms. Interestingly enough, for non-American MNCs, the United States offers a huge potential market, if they can figure out how to beat out American firms, both MNC and local, on their home ground. The Japanese in particular are moving in this direction in a few key areas, most notably electronics and autos.

For smaller firms everywhere, the end of the road has not yet been reached, and for many competent small firms, the process has barely begun. But rapid expansion of smaller firms merely means that lots of companies will be in the game, not just a handfull of giants. If the PRC, Japan, and India open up more for private foreign investment, even huge firms may yet get another chance to expand rapidly as MNCs.

One possibility is that somehow the growth of the world economy accelerates to the ten percent real annual GNP level. If so, firms can expand at faster rates, together with nations. But in the past decade, since the first oil price increases, world growth rates have trended down, not up, and no one knows how world growth might be accelerated. Countries that have grown very fast are either oil states that struck it rich, or smaller open economies such as Hong Kong and Taiwan that locked into the total world economy. Most countries don´t have the oil, and few are politically ready to become much more open than they now are.

One suspects, incidentally, that if national growth rates were pushed up to ten percent, then the good firms would routinely expect to get their growth rates up to 20 or 25 percent. Beating the average is the name of the game.

None of this will effect smaller firms with under $100 million in sales. They can continue to play in much the same manner as others have done for the past forty years. Some will find fantastic new products, with explosive sales growth possibilities, as Apple did. Others will rediscover the MNC route, since many firms in this size bracket really haven´t begun to penetrate this area of their potential market. And of course still others will go conglomerate, untroubled at the outset by antitrust laws, since they are too small to be bothered by government actions.

But if any of these strategies work, the firm will grow fast, will become a billion dollar enterprise, and the constraints suggested here will become important. Somewhere between the one and two billion dollar sales mark, firms will become severely constrained. Another factor is that a fifty million dollar firm needs only ten million dollars in additional sales per year to get its 20 percent growth, which is relatively easy.

HIGH TECH, LOW TECH, AND SCALE ECONOMIES

One factor helping those smaller, odd MNCs from Korea, Hong Kong, India, and similar places is the fact that so many markets really don´t need huge factories and large production runs to be efficient. In short, there are few economies of scale in intermediate technology. Bigger firms abandon such minor markets, creating opportunities for smaller companies. As we have noted, no major MNC makes bicycle parts or pots and pans in Third World countries, and few MNCs are interested in small Nebraska motels or apartment houses in Bangkok. Smaller firms, capably managed, can do these jobs very well, and it is quite possible that experts from countries where such minor production is important will be better at it than huge, sophisticated Western or Japanese MNCs.

At the other end of the spectrum lurks the new high technology industries. Here we also often find that there are few economies of scale. Indeed, high tech products often create diseconomies of scale. For better or worse, this text is being typeset, edited, and produced in one author´s front room, using about $4,700 worth of modern microcomputer equipment. Ten years ago, it would have taken about a million dollars worth of equipment to do this job, and only a large publishing house could do it. Why should we fight some clumsy bureaucracy in a huge company, when we can do it ourselves? Anyone reading this book who wants to try to write his or her own can do it too, if he or she can figure out how to sell the product!

It is quite common these days to find some brilliant scientist or engineer setting up some small company with a million dollars or so of

venture capital and then growing within a few years to a fifty or
hundred million dollar company. If start up costs are small, then many
can try, and some will succeed. Once again, smaller companies win,
while bigger ones have trouble hiring the truly creative people who have
ideas, both good and bad. These new companies may license their
processes and patents abroad, export the product, or even go
multinational at an early date, since all options are open to a clever
firm with unique and demanded high tech products. And once again we see
a pattern of many smaller firms growing fast, many smaller firms
stagnating, and many failing. But again, the big giants do not take
over the world.

The two major areas that seem likely to dominate the future are
electronics and genetics, and in many cases in these industries there
appear to be few economies of scale. If so, the giants will have many
troubles. In areas where there are real scale economies, as in auto
production, the big firms will continue to dominate, but these areas
appear to be more products of the past than harbingers of the future.
Unless some technology emerges that really requires huge firms and
enormous capital to dominate, we may really be looking at industrial
dinosours in the presently dominant MNCs. Time will tell.

One major surprise in the past forty years has been the relative
failure of publicly owned firms to be better than they were. A state
owned company almost anywhere is a tale of excess costs, sluggish
innovation, slow growth, political rather than economic management, and
general stagnation. In 1946, it was widely felt that these state owned
companies would be the wave of the future. Now, we seem to be
witnessing the bankruptcy of the socialist philosophy.

One major reason why state owned companies did so badly was that
MNCs did so well. State owned firms typically stay home. If they
engage in international activities, they export and import. And as we
have noted, this means that they are trapped with whatever local
constraints exist. If these are rigid or poor, the firm stagnates.

A second, and less noted point, is that state owned firms have real
problems with goals. MNCs and private firms generally try to make
money. If they don´t, they change or fail. State firms try to raise
wages, expand services, serve various political ends, and maybe even try
to make people happy. Since such goals are not only nebulous, but often
inconsistant, a real problem for such firms is that they never really
know what they are doing. Even if they do know what to do, they usually
are constrained from doing it by politics.

One thing state firms rarely do is generate good new technology.
There is a thrust toward stagnation, conservatism, and lack of dynamism
in these companies which was not really appreciated until fairly
recently, and still is not in many countries. Sophisticated observers
can forecast, with near perfect accuracy, that once a firm is
nationalized, it will stagnate and decay, but nationalization is still
tried, and it almost inevitably fails. The very few exceptions to this
rule are really unique.

Thus in the 1980´s, the world looks at a wave of innovation, and the wave comes largely from the United States and Japan, with some support from Western European countries. Socialist and marxist countries generate little, and Third World countries seem to be developing a new kind of MNC that can be most useful in lower level technologies. This is not irrelevant in a world where over two thirds of the population is poor and unskilled. U.S. innovation comes as often as not from start up, venture capital companies, not the big giants, who have their own troubles trying to fend off aggressive Japanese and West European MNCs on their home turf, to say nothing of dealing with declining heavy capital industries in the midst of world recession. Often the big firms think that the most productive thing they can do is take over or merge with other giant firms, but such activities are not often productive.

This new, high tech development may really portend a major revolution, too. Now we worry about feeding an ever increasing world population. Not to worry, say the geneticists. In a few years, we will change wheat and rice and tomatoes genetically, so that they can grow in salt water. If we could irrigate with salt water, our food problems end for a thousand years. And if you have a problem of disease, we will manufacture some genetically new drug or vaccine which will cure cancer, AIDs, or whatever. Just wait. You don´t have to wait...already insulin is genetically manufactured, and more such products are to come.

Over at the computer shop, the boys are working with robots that can do anything a man can, so why have mass production lines in Taiwan? Plug in your robots and produce anything you want, anywhere you want, at a cost unbeatable anywhere. It´s no dream...the robots are already working in many factories, and the only question is how fast they get better. Need a household servant? Try our robot for $3995 f.o.b. Cleveland, or if you want, try our genetically altered chimp to do the same thing, at $3795 f.o.b. Santa Clara. The chimp, incidentally, can also do that assembly line work...

You have enemies anywhere, and you just have to have the best weapons you can beg, borrow, or steal. Some U.S. firm can sell you their new missile that sniffs out enemy tanks in the dark, chases them down, and destroys them before they even know that someone is around. For $62,500 f.o.b. Los Angeles, we´ll deliver all you want...

This particular technology is no dream at all, nor are a host of other nasty advanced weapons that begin to look like the things Flash Gordon used against Ming the Merciless in the comic strips of fifty years ago. Death rays, missiles, you name it, and some one might have it. The things are damned near intelligent enough to be human too, and they will be, when those robots or chimps run them.

That chimp altering genetic firm may now exist as a four million dollar venture capital enterprise somewhere in the U.S. The robot producers exist already in Sweden, Japan (who makes more than anyone, and uses more, too), and the United States. Interestingly enough, few really huge firms are deeply involved in these ventures. Back to creativity and smaller firms again to find where the action is...

There are rumbles in theoretical physics that a general field theory might be in sight. Who cares? Well, it just could mean antigravity, or the control of gravity, and we already have neat spaceships. They're atomic submarines, except that it is hard to get a 50,000 ton sub into space orbit. If it weighed nothing, not to worry. Perhaps the fifth edition of this book will be called INTERGALACTIC BUSINESS...

A real problem with this kind of material is that there is no data, just speculation. Serious scholars do not speculate. Like many huge companies, scholars can rarely innovate. The problem is that something very unique might be about to happen, which will blow all our views about what will occur. We can extrapolate known data into the short run future, but we simply cannot handle antigravity. If it happens, the world changes forever, and what we have been doing for the past five centuries will become a minor footnote to a much larger story, much as what happened on an English manor in 1238 is interesting, but not too relevant to modern conditions. Note that virtually all disaster forecasting, such as mass famine, political collapse, atomic wars, etc. simply extrapolates what is and what can be easily developed into a short term future scenario. We cannot handle what the Soviets might do, or who might not starve if we get antigravity or genetically altered plants. Yet it is quite possible that the next twenty to thirty years could see some developments of the more revolutionary sort.

CREATIVITY AND SIZE

Big firms with slow growth may prove quite different kinds of operations from those with fast growth. One critical thing they will be doing is shedding people, not hiring new ones. The reason is that stagnant, yet productive firms have productivity increases which are higher than their sales increases. When this happens, some one gets fired. All over the world, the slow growth giants are doing this. In the United States, virtually all net new jobs in the past decade have come from smaller firms, while the top thousand or so companies actually have reduced their labor forces.

When this happens, junior managers become actuarial minded, since promotions come only when someone dies or retires. Such a pattern leads to aging and cautious managements. Procedures that a fast growth firm would follow without much argument become relatively important for the slow growth big firm. One does not move abroad to strange and exotic countries, nor does one buy up strange new technology, nor does one venture into turbulent markets with odd new products. One plays it safe and cozy and secure.

This is not exactly the wave of the future, but it is happening. Moreover, such stagnation means that new blood will not be added, and as managers and technicians get older and more conservative, it becomes even less likely that the firm will take risks. In the end, the corporate shell dies, taken over by one of those brash upstarts, or the government, desperate to save jobs, props up the firm with subsidies and import controls. By the time this point is reached, virtually anyone with any imagination or creativity has left to join those high tech firms that get things done. We are seeing a lot of these dying firms in the United States and Western Europe, and we will probably see more, particularly if that new technology moves ahead as fast as it appears to be moving at present.

One dimension of dying or stagnation is foreign disinvestment. We worry about MNCs investing everywhere, but in the past decade, there have been billions of dollars of disinvestment. Thus the Chrysler corporation used to have major investments in Western Europe, but during its difficulties in the early 1980's, it sold off these assets. Many West European firms have sold off American assets, and many oil and mineral assets have been taken over, usually by payment, by Third World states. As most of this book has suggested, it can be very difficult to adjust a firm to a strange environment, and many investments just don't pay off.

Ironically, many of those high tech smaller firms have increasing exports, which gets them back into the traditional international game. Some countries are very willing to import computers or missiles, but unwilling to allow for direct investment. In some cases, the firm isn't interested either.

Governments may also block foreign investment in advanced technology. The U.S. already has very extensive export controls over high tech items, and it could ban foreign investment as well. Other countries that are capable of generating really high tech goods have similar controls. If a lot of future international activity involves high technology items, we may see a return to more traditional patterns of export and import.

GOVERNMENT CHANGES

So far, each national government has tried to control MNCs in its own way. Some have banned direct investments, while others have actively encouraged them. Each local government has acted in a manner which appeared to maximize the local interest. In general, the West European democracies, Canada, The United States, and a few other industrial countries have taken fairly positive attitudes toward MNCs, while CPEs ban them rather completely, and Third World countries take the middle ground. Japan allows joint ventures, but rarely sole direct foreign investment. The most rapidly growing countries of all, those small Asian open economies, generally welcome any and all investments, although even here there are some controls.

In the booming days of the early 1970's, there was much talk of controlling the MNCs more completely, either through individual country actions, the United Nations, or regional groupings of countries. It was widely felt in many circles that the MNCs were too powerful, too dangerous, and too foreign to ever be allowed to expand forever without careful controls. Various countries, even including such previously tolerant ones as Canada, experimented with new investment controls. The United Nations set up study groups to figure out how new controls might be instituted, and how these MNCs might be brought under control by sovereign states.

Come 1973 and the first oil price hikes, and the game changed. Industrial countries have all had growth problems since, as have many

Third World countries and communist ones. Investment stagnation everywhere spread to the MNCs, and countries discovered that with lower investments from abroad, their own growth slowed. Jobs became very hard to get in most countries, and unemployment rates rose. The early 1980's saw the worst recession since the 1930's in most countries, and governments of all persuasions found that obtaining jobs was much more important politically than attacking foreign firms. Investment policies toward MNCs began to change towards a much more favoable posture.

Another fact became increasingly evident, particularly in Third World circles. The countries that welcomed foreign investments and followed open economic policies were the fast growth countries; those that restricted investment stagnated. Oil exporters won; those who tried to do everything themselves lost. It is hard to explain, using conventional economic wisdom, just why it is that Hong Kong, which has a largely Chinese population, and which in 1950 was as poor as the PRC, now has per capita incomes twenty or thirty times as high as those in the PRC. In short, the conventional wisdom was turning out to be wrong.

There is a philosophy about development and growth which is very powerful in the world. It has been around since 1917, and it still is. A country frees itself from its colonial shackles, closes its frontiers, tries to follow an import substitution policy, and becomes socialist or communist. It allies itself with the Soviet Union, which sends many guns, experts, and economic aid. The country goes through its internal revolution, spending more on schools, hospitals, and social welfare, and it leaps ahead. Right now in Nicaragua, this scenario is being played out, and in El Salvador the rebels are trying to carry out a similar policy. Cuba perhaps represents the ultimate flowering of this philosophy. Cuba is IMPORTANT!

But this dream increasingly is becoming dubious. Cuba is important, but it also is poor, just as it was in 1960. Those Soviet guns are nice, but, given high tech developments, Western guns are nicer. And those damn open economies just keep on growing, pulling ahead, gaining prestige. Japan, the ultimate open, export oriented country, is unique, in that it is the only world power in human history that doesn't even have any guns. All the Japanese do is sell you to death, and for conventional marxists, used to guns and troops and military power, it is a crazy place indeed. If you take Japan, you destroy yourself...it could no longer produce those lovely products we all want. And how the hell do you handle Hong Kong? It isn't even a country, for gosh sakes!

And that high tech stuff, coming mainly from the United States, makes everyone nervous. If those Soviet guns are terrific and competitive, then the Cubans and Ethiopias of this world are safe...but how did the Israelis knock off the whole Syrian Soviet made air force in 1982, using U.S./Israeli high tech weapons? If the net result of your having a Soviet built military machine is to have it destroyed on the first day of the war with your enemy, why sell out to get it? Such unsettling thoughts now bother ministers in many countries.

Then the affluent countries look at Canada, which embarked in the 1970's on a highly nationalistic, ban the American investment campaign designed to make Canada more independent. The results were not encouraging. The Canadian dollar steadily sank, economic growth slowed, Canadians invested in the U.S., and unemployment soared. Now Canada is having second thoughts...

The most surprising development in the entire postwar period is the dominance of the world economy by private, profit seeking institutions. The postwar world was supposed to be carefully controlled by governments and international bodies. In Chapter 8 we discussed those postwar organizations and how they function. These organizations, along with the United Nations, are still around, and they still do much useful work.

But the MNCs were unexpected in the postwar period. Also totally unexpected was the rapid development of private international bank lending, the Eurodollar market, the huge private loans to less developed and communist countries, and the dominance of the world economy by private, profit seeking institutions. Capitalism was supposed to be dead, yet the past 30 years have seen international markets more free than they ever have been in world history. At home, governments plan and take over private assets and industries, but no one country can control much in the free wheeling international arena.

Each country can play or not, as it wishes, in this free enterprise world economy. For those who choose not to play, the price can be high. Another surprise in the postwar period has been that countries that did all the wrong things ethically and politically were the big winners, while those countries that did everything right, in the marxist theological sense, were left behind. Burma, North Korea, and Albania may have many virtues, but few outsiders would choose to live in such places. They remain uninteresting backwaters where nothing much happens.

The big winners in the economic race among the poorer contries turned out to be two major groups. One, characterized by the OPEC nations, were those that had valuable raw materials such as oil, and in effect let the MNCs develop this asset as rapidly as possible. If the MNC didn´t actually own the oilfield asset, it held the key exploration and development contract which made exploitation possible. Then the country sold its raw materials or oil to the rapidly advancing Western nations and Japan, earning much foreign exchange in the process, and quite often getting very rich as well. Countries such as Kuwait, the United Arab Emirates, and Saudi Arabia are now among the richer nations per capita in the world. Economically, they have moved from among the poorest to among the richest nations in less than 40 years.

The second group of poor country winners were those states that in effect took a total marketing approach to the world. Seeing that they had few resources beyond a hard working population that would work for little money, they in effect let the MNCs in, allowing them to do what they wished, as long as the country got a piece of the action. Taiwan, Hong Kong, Singapore, and South Korea are members of this group, and Japan, which initially developed this strategy, is now so rich that it cannot logically be called poor any longer. Few remember that in 1946, Japan was totally smashed by World War II, and that the Japanese that year were among the poorest of the poor in the world.

In most cases, direct private foreign investment was not the key motivator. What happened was that local firms produced for export, making whatever foreigners wanted. This strategy only could work if other countries, most notably the U.S., were willing to import from them, and here the genius of the Bretton Woods agreements paid off. The U.S. in effect announced in 1944 that in the future it would lower its trade barriers and let foreigners compete in the huge domestic market, if they could. Japan could not sell many cars or video recorders in the U.S. if prewar tariffs were still in effect. Hong Kong could not sell toys and textiles and consumer electronic products into a totally protected U.S. market.

Both winning groups have one major thing in common. They stuck with the world economy for better or worse, and indeed, along with steadily growing trade among the richer countries, they are a major reason why the world is so much more interdependent and internationalized than it ever was in the past. But there is one fundamental problem with such a strategy. A country now is at the mercy of the world economy. It no longer controls its own destiny. And this, in the intellectual world dominated by marxist thought, is intolerable.

What the world should be, the theorists reason, is a group of self-contained nation states, each controlling its own economy, and each dealing with the others on an arms length basis. Each country should be proud and independent, and each should have its own customs, behavioral characteristics, mores, and folkways. Each, in the view of the theoretical marxists, should also be a marxist state, with all productive assets owned by the government, with these assets used for the common good. When some disturbing factor, such as a crop failure or new technological development occurs, then the state should formulate plans and figure out how to salvage the situation for the good of all. International trade should be conducted by state agencies with other state agencies, in a sedate and well planned manner.

So much for theory. What we expected in 1950 was about what the above paragraph suggested. What we got was a bunch of uncontrolled MNCs running around all over the world, seeking vulgar profits, taking full advantage of their bargaining power over weak governments, utilizing the new forms of international credits granted not by governments, but by private banks. We got wildly fluctuating exchange rates, interrelated economies that grow or collapse together without much control, and a world financial and business community that seems quite beyond any single government´s control. Curiously enough, in most countries we also got domestically a steady trend toward more planning, more government ownership, more state intervention in the economy, and more controls. But when we go beyond our national frontiers, we move quickly back to free enterprise, profits, and all the rest. We have no choice. And this freewheeling external world may well make it just that much more difficult to run the controlled internal worlds within nations we seem to want.

The result of all this is a paradoxical situation. If we want more income and wealth, we play the open ended multinational game. Since most people prefer more income to less, most countries reluctantly join the parade. But intellectually, we yearn for total local control, freedom from the dangers of allowing wild foreigners to dominate our lives, and a well planned, carefully controlled economy. No one yet has figured out how to have it both ways, so the typical intellectual attitude toward the new international economic order is to criticize bitterly the groups and institutions that generate the wealth, yet to accept them simply because there is no viable alternative.

Hence we find vicious attacks on MNCs all over the world, and not only from marxist countries. The MNCs, it is said, are rapacious monopolies. They exploit local labor, buy local governments, play one country off against another, and generally are totally immoral in their behavior. Besides, they are owned and controlled by rich people from Europe, Japan, and the United States, who are getting richer by taking the life blood of our citizens in ------ (Fill in any country you want here, including the United States. The critique is the same everywhere).

Books are written pointing out how MNCs bribe officials. Others are written noting (correctly) that MNCs pay their employees in poor countries less than they do at home. Other books trace the webs of conspiracies in copper, oil, autos, or whatever other industry seems important at the moment. All is rotten, corrupt, vicious, obscene, terrible, and just not nice.

So readers in any country study those books, these articles, nod their agreement, and say there ought to be a law. But somehow the MNCs keep right on expanding, and the banks keep right on lending. When times get tough, as they did after 1981, countries fight to get more MNCs in, not keep them out. Lenders close to default frantically try to figure out how to get just a few more credits to keep the economy running, since defaults could be even worse than taking part in this international world. Poor countries compete to attract MNCS, and states such as Indiana send nice brochures, written in Japanese, to Japan to try to entice just one more Japanese MNC to come to this charming state and invest a little. In the end, there is no choice, since there are no other wealth creating institutions around that could do better.

But there are always those who don´t believe the above. To them, Cuba is a much better model, except that Cuba is still poor, and about all it can offer other countries is a nebulous dream and some troops thoughtfully financed by the Soviets. Iran scorns the world, exiles millions of its own citizens and goes its own way, feeling that it can win this way, or at least live in dignity with its own culture. But even in this proud country, foreign trade steadily increases, even with the United States, as its leaders discover that it cannot do everything. Nicaragua tries to relive the old marxist scenario, and as always, millions elsewhere cheer their efforts and hope for the best. Given world experience with such efforts in the past forty years, it is unlikely that they will win, or even do as well as Taiwan or South Korea, but they try.

We live in a world which in theory is rotten to the core, but in practice works pretty well. Indeed, in the past 35 years the wealth has been unequally shared, but almost no countries, except perhaps those that have totally isolated themselves, have failed to gain something. The more internationalized and interdependent we get, the richer we get, and the less we like it. It is an uncomfortable world, to sit here in Indiana and worry that a decision made in Tokyo by an unknown group of executives can cut one's income in half, or perhaps double it. We don't like that kind of uncertainty. But that is what we have rather inadvertantly developed, for better or worse. Few really feel comfortable in the modern world, but no one can come up with a better one. The MNCs and all those exporters from everywhere rule supreme for the moment, and no one can figure out how to stop them.

As we peer into the murky future, it probably gets worse. Those high tech visions of milk and honey and really effective guns loom large, and they come from the capitalist side, not the preferred marxist one. Until recently, a country could play a Cuba, hoping to get proper support from the Soviets. But just suppose that all the high tech stuff your neighbors buy comes from the West? Just suppose that those Soviet guns aren't quite good enough? Just suppose that the goods you get from the Soviets are very poor compared to Japanese ones? A country can live (with difficulty) without Sony tape recorders, but it can't live without sidewinder missiles, particularly if one's enemy has them. A country may not even be able to live without genetic manipulations and robots within ten to fifteen years. If you want these things, you may have to learn to live with the ambiguities and uncertainties of the open economic system. And that is an unsettling thought indeed.

THREE SCENARIOS

Governments do hold the key to the future. There really are only three possible futures, as follows:

1. The back to nationalism scenario: Here, governments finally become too frightened of world interdependence to live with it. Hence a significant number of countries would turn isolationist and withdraw from the world economic scene. Withdrawal would involve significant restrictions on MNCs, both one's own and foreign ones; protectionist policies to encourage higher cost local industries; tight restrictions on money flows in and out of the country, and restrictions on tourism and immigration. Countries would go back to the 1930's in their relations with other countries. The detested MNCs would disappear, to be replaced by locally owned companies. This book would become interesting history, but irrelevant, since most of what we have discussed would not be happening.

Economists and business scholars almost unanimously agree that this world would be poorer than the one we now have. It would be very difficult, if not impossible, for smaller countries to do everything themselves, as even continental powers such as Brazil, the United States, the PRC, and the U.S.S.R., do not have enough resources or skilled people to do everything. But this world has one major political virtue, which is why this scenario gets tried from time to time by various countries. It is one in which local politicians have real power. They do, that is, unless they get taken over by someone else. After all, it is from this kind of world that the major world wars of this century evolved, and even now, the various wars going on around the world are between nations that firmly believe that they are right and their enemies are wrong. In this world, you don't trade, you shoot. Japan would be destroyed in such a world, and one supposes that this country might try to do what it did in the period 1900 - 1945, namely try to build an empire by force of arms. Those of us who are old enough to have seen that world are not easily convinced that that brutal world was a great one.

2.   To do nothing scenario: Here, we go on about as we have been going. The present rules stay about the same, with few major changes, and the MNCs and banks keep on running the economic part of the world, while local politicans pretend they actually have some power. We have examined this world throughout this book, so you already know what it might be. It is the one we now have, extrapolated into the future.

The difficulty here has been discussed earlier. This world does not seem to be in harmony with our ideals. Moreover, it may be unstable. We may run out of resources, or big companies may become so dominant that they have to be controlled. Those country bank loans may go sour, pushing major banks into bankruptcy. OPEC may push energy prices up so far as to create world depression, or the system may become so economically unstable as to be intolerable, and we are pushed back to scenario 1. Events since 1980 have led to considerable system instability, and many countries and blocs have tried to move a bit back toward the closed system. Thus the United States applied auto and steel import quotas, as did the EC. More Irans and Nicaraguas could lead back to scenario 1.

3.   The One World scenario: Here the world moves toward even more interdependence than it now has. New customs unions are formed, perhaps including such groups as a U.S./Japan/Australia/Canada union, and this may merge with the EC. More poor countries follow the Taiwanese/Japan/Hong Kong strategy of finding new world markets. Very critically, India and the PRC open up and move to integrate their economies with the rest of the world. Rich countries further relax trade barriers, making it easier for these poorer countries to sell labor intensive goods to earn critical foreign exchange to buy needed capital goods. The communist bloc gradually relaxes its trade barriers and joins the world, seeking new Western markets for its products. And, God help us, maybe even the Soviet Union turns capitalist! GATT, the IMF and the World Bank gain more members and become more significant. More currencies become convertible, and more direct foreign investments are allowed. Slowly but surely the new world order emerges. Given trends to date, the world is likely to work only if it is a nominally capitalistic, profit seeking world, although any country can be as marxist as it pleases internally. But even state owned firms operating externally have to behave like good capitalists. Don't expect this world to come tomorrow, since it will be fiercely resisted by many politicians and others who find it quite repugnant, and have a lot to lose personally if it comes about. No one likes to lose power.

But somehow we seem to be struggling toward this kind of world anyhow. The CPEs are opening up, ever so slightly, with many twists back toward a more closed system. Countries like Hungary, under the watchful eye of the U.S.S.R., try to reinvent capitalism, at least for their internationally oriented activities, while calling it something else. Poor countries, contemplating their real options, find that they have no place to go but stagnation or the Taiwanese route. As the world experiences destabilizing impacts, such as the OPEC oil price rise, the necessary adjustments somehow end up being private and integrating, not public and disintegrating. We are all stuck on this planet together, and while a few fanatics would happily blow up the world to win their point, most of us would prefer to try other approaches.

If the new technologies pay off, then this integrated world is more likely. The MNCs, the lively smaller private Japanese and U.S. firms, and the West in general are leading the way toward some kind of world which we as yet can only dimly grasp. It promises wealth, technological achievements beyond our wildest earlier dreams, and the best guns. If countries want it, they have to deal with the MNCs and the West, which means a more open system, one way or the other. Those countries that choose to stay closed and ignore such things will be left far behind, perhaps happy in their ignorance, but of no threat to anyone. We already have quite a few closed countries, and most of them don´t bother us much. One suspects that their capacity to bother us will be less in the future.

Many people, including many Americans, are not likely to favor this open system development too much, but when decisions have to be made, this internationalist option may be the best of all the dismal choices we have. And, in the end, this choice may not turn out too badly after all. If the net result is avoiding World War III, the gradual improvement in wealth and income of most people, and the gradual disappearance of the worst aspects of nationalism gone mad, such as racism, sexism, and all the rest, it might not be such a bad world to live in. Perhaps Mr. Willkie was right, long, long ago.

CONCLUSION

Forecasting is always a dangerous business, particularly in print. One can read the forecast years later and wonder how it was possible for writers to be so wrong. Here, we see a sort of messy, disorganized world, growing slowly more interdependent, faltering and returning to isolationalist nationalism from time to time in various countries. We also see a world of growing MNCs, but not the same ones as have dominated the business world in the past forty years. We could add that there will be plenty of room in this world for quite small, innovative local firms, both to supply local goods and services, and to provide exports for minor markets all over the world. Such firms will also be around to market imports as well, so they will have a significant role in the developing world order. Even totally local firms, such as restaurants and resorts, will be more internationalized as world tourism grows. State owned railways and electric companies will survive and perhaps even prosper, as they perform their local tasks.

We will have plenty of crises, as we always have had. Key countries will have coups and revolutions, and it is possible that a major war could destroy much of the world. There are no sure things on this turbulent planet. Those high tech developments could create a very strange world indeed before the year 2000 rolls around. But the curious part of the past 30 or 40 years is that very little basic change has taken place in the lifestyles of most affluent world citizens. What has happened is that lots of people have become richer, so they too can have cars and bicycles and TV sets and houses. But those items are what affluent people had 30 years ago. The world is not that different. It is just that more people are in a position to enjoy it, and many more are aware of it and want it. While this broadening of wealth and income is disturbing, it is really not revolutionary. And when newly rich individuals and countries arrive, they too join the existing bandwagon. A significant majority of the world's population seems to want affluence and the good life, as presently defined in the now rich countries. They may even get it, as the world grows richer. And if this happens, the world of 2010 may not look all that different from the world of 1960 or 1984, except that more people will be enjoying it.

This is not exactly a romantic forecast nor a dramatic one, but it seems to be the most likely. We rest our case.

Chapter 15

Conclusion

This book has attempted to answer the question, "What is important in international business?" There is commonly an intuitive feeling among managers that when a firm goes international or mutinational, the number of variables which are relevant to the making of proper decisions are increased enormously. Factors which were constants in the local setting become variables in the international framework, and rational managers must integrate these new variables into their thinking before they can perform efficiently in this new setting.

If nothing else, our study has indicated that international business is indeed complicated. For each of the more than 150 countries of the world there are a series of local constraints which are relevant both for local firms and MNCs. In addition, each country has a set of complex international constraints which mainly affect international firms, and which, in the limit, determine whether or not the company can survive. In every case, the nature of the international constraints, both from the country of origin and the country in which the firm operates, will directly influence the efficiency of managements. As we have indicated in previous chapters, even a seemingly trivial rule directed at international firms can cause major internal shifts, as managers adjust their operations to conform to such rules. A tariff is raised, and prices change somewhat. As prices shift, a whole complex of changes begins within the organization. Things which were cheap are now relatively expensive; other items become relatively less expensive. To follow such a change properly through even a simple firm requires very detailed analysis, not just of a few internal factors, but of the entire business activities of the company. Quite often the results achieved are far from the results expected by those who caused the rule to be changed.

Failure to understand thoroughly this interrelationship between the external local constraints, the international constraints, and the critical elements of the management process can be fatal to any firm. It can at the very least cause inefficient operations, leading to high costs, a less competitive position, and the possibility that more perceptive rival firms will be able to compete more effectively than they otherwise might. As a result, our concentration here has been on these key factors, particularly the international constraints. If these constraints are recognized, and if the managers are able to see what general effects they will have on internal operations, our argument is that the managers will be able to adjust to whatever constraints they might face in the most efficient manner. Adjustments will vary for every firm in every country, and this has not been a "how to do it" book in international business. Presumably managers will know their own companies, and they will have far greater competence than academic authors in making whatever changes are necessary for their operations. But practitioners may need some conceptual guidelines to identify their problems, and this book is an effort to supply such assistance.

A major problem in attempting to teach international business is that it is tempting to swamp both students and business people with the enormous quantity of institutional and historic material available in the field. Close study of any country will yield more data, facts, history, cultural factors, and economic insights than any managers could assimilate in 100 years. Many studies of economies or firms within these economies suffer from this problem. In this book, relatively little was said about what might be valid in any country. Except for desriptive examples, almost no institutional or historic material can be found. What was done was to attempt to categorize and classify the various types of material which appears to be relevant for mangers entering a new country. Thus we discuss problems of balance of payments for countries, but not what specific balance of payments problems any given country may have. We have noted that investment laws are important, but we give no handbooks of existing laws. The purpose here is to indicate that in a given situation, here are the variables which are relevant to the managers of a foreign firm, in the sense that these must be analyzed, evaluated, and acted upon if the firm is to produce its goods and services in the most efficient manner.

If our basic hypothesis is correct, firms will find that failure to consider the variables noted in preceeding chapters will result in costly errors. Clearly not every firm has to consider every possible factor, but it is quite useful to decide positively that constraint x is not important, rather than never thinking of it at all. If the manager observes that for his or her firm in a given country a certain legal constaint will be irrelevant, he or she is in effect saying that this is not a relevant variable for this company. But if the manager never ponders how this variable might operate, and proceeds without considering it at all, he or she may find later that it was important, and a critical error was made in ignoring it.

It is true that many firms stumble into international business without this sort of detailed analysis being done in advance. Both authors have talked to many international managers whose firms initially began to operate in several countries, not because of careful analysis or detailed study of the relevant variables, but rather because the president or owner liked the country in question, or because a casual, back of the envelope calculation indicated that there should be a market in the country for the firm's products. The usual results of this kind of decision making have been much confusion, higher than necessary costs as mistakes were corrected, and general failure to take full advantage of the tremendous possibilities in international business.

But however the firms got abroad, they are now there, and many are extremely competent. Any executive who talks off the record can point to dozens or hundreds of blunders, errors, and just plain stupidities which his own company engaged in not too long ago, or even now. Yet compared to the local firms with which such firms compete, they may do very well. The big MNCs may be sloppy or inefficient, but you should see the competition!

As the MNCs go abroad, we see that there really are two critical questions to be faced. One is that the firms are taking the global view and optimizing in this way, while the countries necesarily take the provincial view and try to optimize for the country. This means that the part is likely to be larger than the whole in many cases. Governments everywhere are wrestling with this problem, and they are trying to figure how to control their mNCs, but without great success to date. What is needed is some sort of global control system, or world government, which can control global firms. We seem to be nowhere in sight of such an organization at this point.

The second key point is that the MNCs really play a positive sum game. That is, they do create bigger incomes and wealth. And because they are major wealth generators, they can play the positive sum game, offering all players a piece of the action. Governments, unions, workers, educators, tax collectors, and many others can win at the same time the MNC is winning. Even when the pipers are paid, there is plenty left over for a healthy cash flow and profit to take home. Citizens and governments, used to negative and zero sum games, often do not realize that this particular game can be one where everyone wins. It is clear that our post-1945 experience is much nicer and richer because of the evolution of MNCs than it would have been if such organizations had never evolved. Perhaps the distribution of gains is debatable, but few question the huge gains. They are now so large that even communist countries are beginning to figure out how to get into the game.

And finally, this period we have just been through is likely to evolve into something quite different before too long. IBM or General Motors or Toyota is not likely to own the world, so the simple minded projections of past trends into the future are not very good forecasts. But exactly what will be a good forecast? We have seen that no one knew what the postwar world was going to be like, and we are baffled if we try to figure out what the next thirty years will be like. Different for sure, but there are too many variables, to many discontinuities, for anyone to be very confident in his forecasts.

And so we end with a whimper, not a bang. We don´t know either. But perhaps this book will suggest to others what this new order will be like, along with suggesting to them how the privately owned MNCs might prosper in whatever the new environment might be.

Index